A Handbook for Kṛṣṇa Consciousness

A Handbook for Kṛṣṇa Consciousness

Satsvarūpa Dāsa Goswami

GN Press, Inc.

Persons interested in the subject matter of this book are invited to correspond with our secretary:

GN Press, Inc.
R.D. 1, Box 837-K
Port Royal, PA, U.S.A. 17082

First Printing, 1979 5000 Copies
Second Printing, 1982 5000 Copies
Third Printing, 1985 5000 Copies
Fourth Printing, 1996 2000 Copies

ISBN 0-89647-008-3

GN Press gratefully acknowledges the BBT for the use of verses and purports from Śrīla Prabhupāda's books.

Library of Congress Cataloging-in-Publication Data

Gosvāmī, Satsvarūpa Dāsa

A HANDBOOK FOR KṚṢṆA CONSCIOUSNESS

1. Spiritual life (Hinduism) —Addresses, essays, lectures. 2. Krishna—Addresses, essays, lectures. I. Title.
BL 1228.G67 294.5'4 79-97

ISBN0-89647-008-3

Reprinted with the kind assistance of Nitai-Gaurasundara dasa and Thakur Haridasa dasa

Printed at Rekha Printers Private Limited, New Delhi-110 020

Dedication
To His Divine Grace
A.C. Bhaktivedanta Swami Prabhupāda,
my beloved spiritual master,
the Founder-*Ācārya* of the
International Society for Krishna Consciousness.

Editor's Note

In several places in the text different spellings are used. This reflects how the essays actually appeared in Back to Godhead *magazine when they were published. In the first few years of ISKCON publications, the phonetic spelling was used and diacritic marks were not used; for example, "Krishna". Later the more scholarly "Kṛṣṇa" was used. In some of the early essays, the name of our spiritual master is given as "His Divine Grace A.C. Bhaktivedanta Swami". After 1968, with his permission, we added the term "Prabhupāda" to the end of his name, indicating that he is a master even among masters.*

There are two reasons why we have kept the two different styles. First, it would have taken considerably more time and expense to bring the different styles to one consistency, and we were eager to publish as soon as possible. Second, keeping the form of the articles exactly as they first appeared starting in 1966 adds a historical flavor, giving us a sense of the pioneering days in ISKCON.

Contents

III. Yoga, Karma and Reincarnation

IV. The Guru-Disciple Relationship

V. The Process of Spiritual Education

VI. Topics in the News

VII. Autobiographical Essays

VIII. Letters of Inquiry   356

IX. Poems 1966-1968   371

X. Index   379

XI. About the Author   411

Foreword

This volume is a survey of spiritual knowledge, a basic introductory handbook containing all the essential information needed to proceed further on the genuine spiritual path. What makes these essays at once potent and persuasive is their unalloyed adherence to the truth of the Vedic literatures in which the original accounts and philosophy are found. In this connection one may reasonably ask, "If the real point is to be true to the original, then why not simply translate and be satisfied with that?" The answer is given in the Vedic literature itself, most notably in the First Canto of the ***Śrīmad-Bhāgavatam,*** wherein it is described how the mature fruit of all the Vedic literatures of India was spoken by the great *guru* Śukadeva Goswāmī, who had heard it from his father, Vyāsadeva, the compiler of the *Vedas.* In Sanskrit, the parrot is called *śuka.* When a ripened fruit is cut by the red beaks of such birds, the flavor of the fruit is enhanced. Śrila Śukadeva Goswāmī is therefore compared to such a parrot, not for his ability to recite *verbatim* what he had heard from his father, but for his ability to present the work in a manner appealing to everyone. Similarly, this present volume is written in a way just suitable to the time and circumstances so that it may be easily appreciated by the modern reader. Thus this most ancient spiritual knowledge is further enhanced and glorified. Indeed, spiritual knowledge is *alive.* It is carried, preserved, increased and expanded by enlightened, pure devotees, who are qualified by their surrender and empowered by spiritual authorities concerned with the spiritual upliftment of all living entities.

The reader should try to enter into the pages of these essays with an adventurous spirit and full attention. The reward will be the unfettered soul's glimpse into the transcendental pastimes and philosophy of the Supreme Personality of Godhead, Śrī Kṛṣṇa, and His unalloyed devotees—all beyond the ordinary limitations of material space and time.

Rupanuga das

Introduction

Five thousand years ago, Śrīla Vyāsadeva introduced the eternal Vedic knowledge in written form. Vyāsadeva was the literary incarnation of Lord Kṛṣṇa, the Supreme Personality of Godhead. His presentations are the Absolute Truth, spoken directly by the Supreme Lord and passed down in disciplic succession to Brahmā and Nārada. Vyāsa wrote millions of verses in the form of the *Vedas, Upaniṣads* and *Purāṇas,* and all Vedic writing since that time has been based on his original presentation. Down through the centuries many great followers of Vyāsadeva have made literary contributions expecially suitable for their particular age. For example, following the misleading impersonalistic dissertations of Śankarācārya, Rāmānuja in the 10th century presented authentic commentaries based on the *Vedas* just to reassert the original conclusion of Vyāsadeva. Madhvāchārya in the 12th century made a similar, distinct presentation correcting Śaṅkara in favor of Vyāsadeva. The most notable literary contribution of Vedic literature in recent ages was that made by the followers of Lord Caitanya in the 16th century. Lord Caitanya introduced a great movement reviving spontaneous love of Kṛṣṇa (*bhakti*) by chanting the holy names of God, *Hare Kṛṣṇa, Hare Rāma.* Although Lord Caitanya was widely reknowned as a scholar in his youth, he left only eight verses called the *Śikṣāṣṭaka.* However, he instructed His disciples to write books on the science of Kṛṣṇa. Jīva Goswāmī, Sanātan Goswāmī, Rūpa Goswāmī, Kṛṣṇadās Kavirāj and many others substantiated Lord Caitanya's devotional cult through writings which made innumerable references to the *Vedas, Upaniṣads* and *Purāṇas.* The Goswāmīs demonstrated very clearly that the actual purpose of the *Vedas* is to realize love of God and that Śrī Kṛṣṇa is the original Supreme Personality of Godhead. The same thing is declared by Lord Kṛṣṇa Himself in the *Bhagavad-gītā: vedaiś ca sarvair aham eva vedyo.* "By all the *Vedas* am I to be known. Indeed I am the compiler of *Vedānta,* and I am the knower of the *Vedas.*"

Contemporary followers of Lord Caitanya have continued to present *bhakti-yoga* as the supreme message of the *Vedas* and the supreme goal of human life. Faced with the spreading of atheistic doctrines in the present age of Kali (quarrel and hypocrisy), great spiritual masters such as Bhaktisiddhānta Saraswatī Goswāmī and Bhaktivinode Ṭhākur in the late 19th and early 20th centuries presented many books based on the *Vedas.* They wrote in English as well as Bengali, suitable for the intellectual classes of those days. Then in the 1960s, gathering the accumulated knowledge of the entire Vedic tradition, His Divine Grace A.C. Bhaktivedanta Swami Prabhupāda made a contribution which he envisioned to last thousands of years as the foundation for a world order of

Kṛṣṇa consciousness. Thus he presented *Bhagavad-gītā, Caitanya-caritāmṛta* and the writings of Rūpa Goswāmī, all in English translations with commentary.

Most notable of all is his 29-volume presentation of the *Śrīmad-Bhāgavatam,* the ripened fruit of all Vedic literature. In his Bhaktivedanta purports Śrīla Prabhupāda has given a unique combination of the highest Vedic scholarship along with personal realization, presented in a way understandable even for the common man. These books, as published by the Bhaktivedanta Book Trust, have literally swept over the entire world, bringing a genuine revolution of consciousness in an otherwise hopelessly materialistic age. In addition to writing these books, Śrīla Prabhupāda has personally inspired faith in disciples who are dedicating their lives to the distribution of these books. To date they have distributed some 60 million pieces of Bhaktivedanta Book Trust literature.

Space does not permit us in this introduction to discuss the great debt humanity owes to His Divine Grace A.C. Bhaktivedanta Swami Prabhupāda for his presentation of Vedic literature. We can note, however, that in this age 99.9% of the human population has no real knowledge of self-realization or liberation. People generally do not even know what the self or liberation is but nonetheless choose to lead their lives blindly following different "isms." As Vyāsadeva originally stated, it is only the light of the *Vedas* which can save the people of the age of Kali, and that light is being presently upheld in the books distributed by the followers of Śrīla Prabhupāda.

What is the need for further presentations of Vedic literatures while the light of Śrīla Prabhupāda shines so brightly in our midst? I myself often pondered this question while Śrīla Prabhupāda was still in his physical presence on this earth. In 1971 I was surprised when Śrīla Prabhupāda wrote to an 8 year old boy at our Gurukula, urging him to learn English so that he could write Kṛṣṇa conscious books. I wrote a letter to Śrīla Prabhupāda and inquired from him what would be the need of books written by his followers since he had presented everything so completely himself. Śrīla Prabhupāda replied to me:

> "You ask one question about the nature of books I want you to write as my disciples; on this point Kṛṣṇa consciousness is not limited. Persons like all of the *Goswāmīs* wrote so many books. Viśvanātha Cakravartī and all the *ācāryas* wrote books, and still I am writing books. Similarly also my disciples will write. So any self-realized soul can write unlimited books without deviating from the original ideas."

Having a keen propensity to write Kṛṣṇa conscious literature, I repeated the same question in a letter some years later–whether it was proper for me as disciple to write, since my spiritual master was writing. Śrīla Prabhupāda wrote back that it was not only proper, but that it was my duty as a *sannyāsī* to "help the crippled humanity" by writing Kṛṣṇa conscious literature. He has written similarly in his Bhaktivedanta purports: "The first duty of a person in the renounced order of life is to contribute some literary work for the benefit of the human being in order to give him realized direction toward self-realization." (*S.B.* 2.2.5)

There are many similar statements by previous *ācāryas* and certainly by Śrīla Prabhupāda which clearly establishes the fact that present day *ācāryas* in disciplic succession from Śrīla Prabhupāda should also present Kṛṣṇa conscious literature. As stated in his Bhaktivedanta purports: "Thus it is the duty of the *ācārya* to publish books that will help future candidates take up the method of service and become eligible to return home, back to Godhead by the mercy of the Lord. In our Kṛṣṇa consciousness movement this same path is being prescribed and followed." (*S.B.* 10.2.31)

There are billions of pieces of nonsense literature being distributed all over the world, and almost all of them are bereft of knowledge concerning self realization and love of God. Therefore it is obvious we need many, many books asserting the real principle of truth as given to mankind originally by Vyāsadeva. Even among literatures with a theistic bent there is no path as direct, obtainable and authoritative as that given by the Vedic presentation. For the few persons who have received this knowledge in disciplic succession, surely there is an obligation to present it to the world, not withstanding the unsurpassable contribution of Śrīla Prabhupāda. Śrīla Prabhupāda's literature cannot be outdated, and its distribution will go on full force. But at the same time the tradition must continue, and new writings must come forth, just as new disciples are entering the disciplic succession.

For myself it is specifically because I have been ordered by Śrīla Prabhupāda to take disciples in the Kṛṣṇa consciousness movement and perform the duties of *ācārya* that I have felt the need to publish writings. By the order of the transcendental system, disciples are now approaching me. For their own spiritual development, therefore, it is necessary that they hear from their spiritual master. It is especially for the needs of my own disciples that I am presenting this book entitled *A Handbook for Kṛṣṇa Consciousness.* It is my request that my disciples thoroughly understand the Bhaktivedanta purports. At the same time it is my hope that I may present them with more books of my own which will be composed strictly in accordance with the disciplic succession.

This "handbook" is made up of articles which were published in *Back to Godhead* magazine over the past 12 years. (Because we have covered many phases of *bhakti-yoga,* and because *bhakti-yoga* is itself the complete science of God-realization, therefore the book's title is appropriate.) The essays are clearly the writings of a disciple of His Divine Grace A.C. Bhaktivedanta Swami Prabhupāda. Everything I have written I have learned from him, and thus I have presented the various subjects with reference to the Vedic literatures. I have not manufactured anything out of my own brain; rather I am presenting essays which came to me as so much *mahā-mahā-prasādam* from the merciful hand of my spiritual master, Śrīla Prabhupāda. Although my impetus is to write for my disciples, these writings are not merely an internal affair. When I first wrote them, each essay was intended for the readers of *Back to Godhead* magazine, which is now published with a circulation of 400,000 monthly. Any intelligent person, therefore, will find simple explanations of the science of Kṛṣṇa consciousness in these pages and will be able to derive the highest benefit. Although His Divine Grace Śrīla Prabhupāda has repeatedly assured me "go ahead and write books," I still beg for the blessings of his senior followers.

—Satsvarūpa dāsa Goswami

I. The Incarnations of Godhead

The Reality of Kṛṣṇa's Appearance

May/June, 1974

One should not mistakenly think that Kṛṣṇa's appearance and pastimes are mythical or allegorical. Rather, we should accept Lord Kṛṣṇa as the Absolute Truth, the cause of all causes, who actually appeared in a humanlike form and walked the earth. *Bhagavad-gītā* states that the proper transcendental understanding of His appearance is so important that if one realizes only this one subject, at the time of death he does not have to return to the material world, but goes to join Kṛṣṇa in the eternal spiritual world called Vaikuṇṭha.

One should hear the pastimes of Kṛṣṇa from a pure devotee of Kṛṣṇa who has understood Kṛṣṇa through his own spiritual master in a disciplic succession from Kṛṣṇa Himself. Kṛṣṇa states in *Bhagavad-gītā* that those who thus perfectly understand Him worship Him in His personal form. He declares, "There is no truth superior to Me. Everything depends on Me, as pearls are strung on a thread." Materialistic scientists and philosophers who accept as truth only what they can perceive with their imperfect senses, as well as so-called transcendentalists who speculate that God is impersonal, cannot understand Kṛṣṇa's pastimes, nor can they achieve the perfection of life, love of God. Working outside of Kṛṣṇa consciousness, therefore, they exist in illusion, for whatever they achieve independently from Kṛṣṇa is vanquished at the time of death, and then they must take on new bodies in the various species of material life.

The most elevated transcendentalists, however, understand Kṛṣṇa's *lilas,* or pastimes, and relish them without cessation. *Śrīmad-Bhāgavatam* declares: "The highest perfectional gain of humanity is to discuss the activities and glories of the pious actor [Kṛṣṇa]." The great sages who compiled the Vedic literature, and the great spiritual masters who in turn recited it, such as Vyāsadeva, Śukadeva, Nārada and others, were completely free from all the vices of material attachment because they were aware of spirit's permanence and matter's temporality. Consequently their being fully absorbed in the activities of the Supreme Lord, Kṛṣṇa, is solid evidence that the accounts of His activities are not whimsical tales. Had these pastimes been merely tall stories, such perfect sages would not have relished them. These sages were concerned with the highest good for humanity, beyond the illusion of temporary material welfare work, and therefore we should take seriously their recommendation that we hear the pastimes of Kṛṣṇa. There are many examples of devotees who have attained perfection simply by hearing these pastimes.

THE ETERNAL ROAD SHOW

Yearly we celebrate Janmāṣṭamī to commemorate the day Kṛṣṇa appeared on earth some 5,000 years ago. But that same occurrence, Kṛṣṇa's birth on a planet in one of the material universes, is not a one-time event. It is always going on somewhere, even now as you read this article!

Instructing His great disciple Sanātana Gosvāmī regarding the spiritual technology of the Supreme Lord's descent (*avatāra*), Lord Caitanya explained that just as the sun perpetually seems to rise and set somewhere on earth, so Lord Kṛṣṇa eternally appears and disappears in His transcendental pastimes. The time is always six a.m. somewhere on earth. An hour after six a.m. in New York City, six a.m. arrives in Detroit. An hour later it moves further west, and an hour later it is elsewhere. Similarly, Janmāṣṭamī and all the pastimes Kṛṣṇa displayed on earth continuously move and appear sequentially on planets in various universes. Lord Caitanya told Sanātana, "His pastimes are like the waves of the Ganges River; as there is no limit to the flowing waves of the Ganges, there is no cessation to the different features and incarnations Lord Kṛṣṇa reveals in different universes."

Kṛṣṇa appears in our universe for only 125 years, but in each and every universe He exhibits all the pastimes He performs here, including His apparent birth, His boyhood pastimes and His pastimes as a youth. Since the universes are numberless, His *līlās* are going on at every moment, at every second, without limit. They are therefore called eternal.

To our vision, Kṛṣṇa is born as the son of Devakī and Vasudeva, and after 125 years He disappears or dies. But the fact is that He exists eternally; He simply leaves this world for another. We may again cite the example of the sun, which first rises every day on the eastern horizon but still is not a product of that horizon. Although when we first behold the sun we associate it with the east because of our angle of vision, the sun always shines independently in the sky, regardless of how it appears and disappears to us locally. The sun does not die or set in the evening; it only seems to as it leaves our vision. Kṛṣṇa's coming and going is something like that. He associates with a mother and father and takes birth in a certain family and land, but He exists eternally and travels from universe to universe to enjoy blissful exchanges with His devotees.

Kṛṣṇa's pastimes go on as a kind of road show, visiting one planet after another. Not only does Kṛṣṇa travel; He brings with Him His mother, His father,

His cowherd friends, the *gopīs,* the cows and the land of Vṛndāvana. Thus Kṛṣṇa is never considered alone, without His eternal associates and abode. When He descends, He descends with His entourage and paraphernalia, and when He travels they all travel with Him.

Kṛṣṇa's road show is separate from and yet identical with His supreme original activities on the spiritual planet Goloka in the eternal *brahmajyoti,* the effulgent spiritual sky far beyond all the material universes. It is said that the Lord is so captured by the association of the liberated devotees in Goloka that He never leaves–but He expands Himself to come to the material universes, enact the same pastimes, and thus attract the fallen souls, who are His parts and parcels, to come back home, back to Godhead.

Kṛṣṇa appears in our universe, according to an eternal schedule, once every 4,320,000 *x* 1,000 *x* 2 years. In the *Bhāgavatam,* concerned devotees ask, "Now that Kṛṣṇa has left, where can we find the religious principles?" The answer is that by reciting the pastimes of Kṛṣṇa as related in the *Bhāgavatam* and *Gītā,* one can associate with Kṛṣṇa as directly as one could by being face to face with Him. That is called *līlā-smaraṇa,* association by remembrance. Because Kṛṣṇa's *līlās* in Vṛndāvana are absolute, remembering those pastimes is the same as being with Him.

The perfection of human life, therefore, is to practice *bhakti-yoga* under the direction of a spiritual master and thus attain pure love for Kṛṣṇa, free from all material sense gratification. By hearing Kṛṣṇa's pastimes from the spiritual master, one becomes attracted to the activities of the spiritual world, which are always performed for Kṛṣṇa's pleasure, and thus one is cured of the desire to lord it over the material world. Under the spiritual master's direction, one can take part in Kṛṣṇa's pastimes simply by remembering them. Thus one can eventually join Kṛṣṇa in His eternal traveling road show and ultimately transfer oneself to Kṛṣṇa's Goloka planet in the spiritual sky.

Temple Worship

November, 1970

There have been many newspaper and magazine articles written about visits to the temples of the International Society for Krishna Consciousness. Often, a mundane newswriter reports entering a room filled with sweet aromatic incense and seeing colorful brass and wooden Deities on an altar surrounded by flowers, paintings and other paraphernalia. The newspaper reporters usually misunderstand that they are experiencing an oriental ritual in worship of Eastern gods. They do not attribute great significance to the chanting of the holy names Hare Kṛṣṇa, Hare Kṛṣṇa, Kṛṣṇa Kṛṣṇa, Hare Hare/Hare Rāma, Hare Rāma, Rāma Rāma, Hare Hare; they report only that it is repetitious or loud. They cannot convey the real transcendental meaning of the temple in terms of the devotees, the Supreme Lord and devotional service. What, then, according to transcendental authorities, is the purpose of the temple? What are the Deities? What is the meaning of *kīrtana*, the dancing, singing and playing on musical instruments? What is the purpose of the activities going on in the temple?

The temples of Kṛṣṇa in India are like kings' palaces, and the Supreme Lord who is staying there in the Deity form is considered to be the proprietor. Although the Supreme Lord does not need an opulent temple, the devotees take pleasure in keeping the temple clean and in worshiping the Lord in an opulent manner, and the Lord appreciates this service. Once a devotee asked His Divine Grace A.C. Bhaktivedanta Prabhupāda about the dressing of the Jagannātha Deities, and he replied in a letter: "Clothing is already painted on the Jagannāthas even if there is no cloth supplied, but even if Kṛṣṇa is naked, that does not make any difference. But when we dress Him, our service is appreciated. On Kṛṣṇa's side, naked or dressed, He is Kṛṣṇa. And from our side, if we nicely dress Kṛṣṇa and we nicely feed Him, He appreciates our service, and we are certainly benefitted. Kṛṣṇa is the same. He does not need us to dress Him or to feed Him, but the more we serve by dressing and feeding and caring for Him, the more He appreciates the service, and the more we become Kṛṣṇa conscious."

The Supreme Lord is not in need of big temples, and similarly the pure devotees do not need an opulent setting in which to worship. Pure devotees are prepared to live on a footpath or sleep under a tree if Kṛṣṇa desires. Therefore, the temple is meant not for the Lord or the devotees but for the people in general, and especially for householders. In the Second Canto, Third Chapter, of the *Śrīmad-Bhāgavatam,* which our spiritual master has published as a book entitled *Pure Devotional Service: The Change in Heart,* it is stated in the purport to the twenty-second verse: "Attention engaged in the service of the Lord, especially in dressing and decorating the temple, accompanied by musical *kīrtana* and spiritual instructions from the scriptures, can alone save the common man from the hellish cinema attractions and the rubbish sex-songs broadcast everywhere by radios. If one is unable to maintain a temple at home, he should go to another's temple where the performances are regularly executed. Visiting the temple and looking at the profusely decorated forms of the Lord, well-dressed and in a well-decorated sanctified temple, naturally infuses the mundane mind with spiritual inspiration. People should visit holy places like Vrndāvana where such temples and worship of the Deities are specifically maintained. Formerly all rich men like kings and rich merchants constructed such temples under the directions of expert devotees of the Lord, like the six Gosvāmīs, and it is the duty of the common man to take advantage of these temples and festivals observed in the holy pilgrimages by following in the footsteps of great devotees. One should not visit all these temples with sightseeing in mind, but one must go to them guided by the proper men who know the science."

The Deities are not idols. They are incarnations of Kṛṣṇa appearing in material elements. This is explained in Śrīla Prabhupāda's purport to Mantra Five of *Srī Īśopaniṣad:* "Because He is full of inconceivable potencies, God can accept our service through any sort of medium, and He can convert His different potencies according to His own will. The unbelievers argue that the Lord cannot incarnate Himself or that He descends in a form of material energy. This argument is nullified if we accept His inconceivable potencies as realities. Even if He appears before us in the form of material energy, it is quite possible for him to convert the material energy into spiritual. The source of the energies being one and the same, Kṛṣṇa, the energies can be utilized simply according to the will of that energetic source. For example, the Lord appears in the form of *arcā,* or Deities supposedly made of earth or stone. These forms, engraved from wood or stone or any other matter, are not idols, however, as is held by the iconoclasts." The proper understanding, then, is that because we cannot see the spiritual form of the Supreme Lord with our present senses, He may choose to appear in this material world in a form made of the material elements. But since He is the controller of both the material and spiritual energies, when He appears in such a form, it is no longer considered material. After all, since He is the supreme controller, who can restrict Him from coming in whatever form He chooses? The Lord is so pliable that He has agreed to appear before the neophyte devotees in the Deity form so that they may worship Him, feed Him and dress Him, and in this form the Lord will accept what they offer.

The form of the Deity is not fashioned in terms of the whim of the worshiper. It is eternal with all its paraphernalia, and this can actually be felt by a sincere devotee, but not by an atheist. For His devotee the Supreme Lord is always within reach in the Deity incarnation, whereas for the unsurrendered soul He is far away and cannot be approached. The eternal identity of the Deity is confirmed by the authority of spiritual masters who are able to see past the material energy to the spiritual form of the Lord in His incarnation as Jagannātha or Rādhā-Kṛṣṇa. Therefore, one who is sincerely looking for spiritual union with the Supreme Lord will not refuse to worship His authorized forms in the temple.

Deity worship is especially recommended for householders, those entangled in the material complications of family life. This is stated in *Pure Devotional Service: The Change in Heart:* "Engagement in the worship of the Deity, under the direction of the bona fide spiritual master, will greatly help the householders to purify their existence and make rapid progress in spiritual knowledge. Simple theoretical book knowledge is not sufficient for the neophyte devotee. Book knowledge is theoretical, whereas the *arcanā* process is practical. Spiritual knowledge must be developed by a combination of theoretical and practical knowledge, and that is the guaranteed way for the attainment of spiritual perfection. The training of a neophyte in devotional service completely depends on the expert spiritual master who knows how to lead his disciple to make gradual progress back home, back to Godhead."

The temple itself is not located in the mundane world. Our spiritual master has declared, "This temple is not in Boston, and that temple is not in New York. They are in Vaikuṇṭha, the spiritual planets." The nondevotees argue that there is nothing special about the temple because God is everywhere. But the devotees of the Lord like to gather in the temple, which, because everything there is done in a manner conducive to Kṛṣṇa consciousness, is an entirely transcendental place. It is said in the *śāstras* that although he who lives in the forest is in the mode of goodness, he who lives in the city is in the mode of passion, and he who lives in the liquor shop is in the mode of ignorance, a temple is transcendental. Who, then, can object to going to the temple to see the beautiful form of the Lord surrounded by decorations and flowers? The Deities are honored in special ceremonies such as Jhulana-yātra, at which time They are swung on a swing, the Jagannātha Cart Festival, when the Deities are taken outside and wheeled on carts to the sea, and special festivals when the Rādhā-Kṛṣṇa Deities are taken on processions in beautifully decorated carts. Since the essence of religion is to glorify God, then who can object to these transcendental ceremonies, which spread spiritual emotions to all who take part, even by offering a small flower to the Deities? Our spiritual master has stated that if one simply comes to the temple, even not understanding the spiritual nature of the form of God in the

Deity, but merely appreciating the beautiful setting of the altar, and if one comes again another time and remarks, "Yes, this is very pretty; this is beautiful," then, due to his appreciation of Kṛṣṇa, he will become a devotee. In fact, *Śrīmad-Bhāgavatam,* Second Canto, Chapter Three, verse 22, states: "The eyes which do not look at the symbolical representations of the Personality of Godhead Viṣṇu are like the eyes printed on the plumes of a peacock, and the legs which do not move to the holy places where the Lord is remembered are considered to be like tree trunks."

The Deities are regularly worshiped by a performance called *ārātrika,* which is an offering of foodstuffs, incense, flowers, a waving handkerchief, a fan and a lamp. In the ISKCON temples the Deities are worshiped with *ārātrika* early in the morning, at 4 a.m. Then at 8 a.m. the altar is decorated and breakfast offered. At 11:30 there is again an offering of foodstuffs. At 5 p.m. the temple is opened after the Deities have rested from one to four. Then there is another *ārātrika* ceremony. In the morning fruit and milk are offered to the Deities, and at noon *dahl* and *chapatis* and many other varieties of foodstuffs are offered. At dusk there is *ārātrika* and again at 9 p.m. an offering of *puris,* vegetables, milk and sweetmeats, and after this final *ārātrika* the Deities finally rest.

Śrīla Bhaktivinode Thakur has written a song of prayer for the *ārātrika* ceremony in honor of the Supreme Lord Śrī Caitanya Mahāprabhu, who is Kṛṣṇa in the appearance of a devotee. His song is as follows: "Everyone come see all the glories of the beautiful *ārātrika* ceremony of Lord Caitanya. This *ārātrika* ceremony on the bank of the Ganges to receive Lord Caitanya is so beautiful that it will attract the minds of all the people of the world. Come see how Lord Caitanya is seated on the jeweled throne. To offer *ārātrika* to Lord Caitanya, all the demigods have come, headed by Lord Brahmā. See Nityānanda Prabhu on the right side of Lord Caitanya, and on the left side Śrī Gadādhara. Nearby is Advaita Prabhu, as well as Śrī Śrīvāsa, who is bearing the umbrella above Lord Caitanya's head. Listen to the sounding of the conchshells, the ringing bells and the *kāratals.* All these sounds, along with that of the sweet *mṛdaṅga,* are very relishable to hear."

This worship of Lord Caitanya can be performed with a painting of the *Pañcatattva.* His Divine Grace has said that in this age all that one needs to achieve spiritual perfection is to sit before this picture and chant before the lotus feet of Lord Caitanya. Śrīla Prabhupāda has authorized this form of temple worship, and anyone who takes part will feel natural bliss. All activities and paraphernalia in temple life become meaningful by the grace of the spiritual master. Without the mercy of a spiritual master, one cannot receive devotional service in one's heart. The progress of a neophyte devotee completely depends on the spiritual master who knows how to lead his disciple back to Godhead.

The spiritual master teaches the neophyte devotee all the rules of Deity worship, and it is his duty to help his disciple fix his mind on Kṛṣṇa. It is said in the third verse of Śrīla Viśvanatha Cakravartī's *Śrī Gurv-āṣṭakam:* "The spiritual master is always engaged along with his disciples in the temple worship of Śrī Śrī Rādha and Kṛṣṇa. I offer my respectful obeisances unto the lotus feet of such a spiritual master."

As far as the chanting of Hare Kṛṣṇa is concerned, it is the prime benediction of the Kṛṣṇa consciousness movement, and therefore the temples vibrate with the transcendental sound of the holy names. The chanting is purely spiritual; it is the cry of the individual soul for the Supreme Personality of Godhead, Śrī Kṛṣṇa, like the cry of a child for its mother. Chanting the *mahāmantra* is the prescribed method of worship for this age. "In this age the sacrifice of holding congregational chanting of the holy name of the Lord is the prescribed method." (Bhaktivedanta purport to *Śrīmad-Bhāgavatam,* 1.1.14).

The chanting of the Hare Kṛṣṇa *mantra* is eternal, beyond history, but it was first delivered to this planet by the great sage Nārada Muni, and Lord Caitanya Mahāprabhu, who is accepted by the Brahma-sampradāya (the disciplic succession of Kṛṣṇa conscious spiritual masters) as Kṛṣṇa Himself, gave special impetus to this movement. Lord Caitanya gave evidence from the *Bṛhan-Nāradīya Purāṇa* concerning chanting in this present age: *harer nāma harer nāma harer nāmaiva kevalam kalau nāsty eva nāsty eva nāsty eva gatir anyathā:* "Chant the holy name, chant the holy name, chant the holy name! There is no other means of success in God realization for this age of Kali." In the age of Kali, the age of quarrel and hypocrisy, it is not possible to perform difficult penances or austerities in order to obtain spiritual life. "In this iron age of quarrel, men almost always have short lives. O learned one, not only that, but they are also very lazy, misguided, unlucky, and above all, always disturbed." (Bhāg. 1.1.10). "[But] living beings who are entangled in the meshes of birth and death can be freed immediately by even unconsciously chanting the holy name of Kṛṣṇa, which is feared even by fear personified." (Bhāg. 1.1.14). We cannot overestimate the benefit made available to the average man in the age of Kali by the congregational chanting and Deity worship afforded by the ISKCON temples.

The chanting is glorification of God. There is a difference between American food and Indian food, yet the purpose of both is the same: to satisfy our hunger. Similarly, there are different rituals in churches and temples, but the goal is the same: to achieve love of God. If the goal is otherwise, then that is not real religion. The chanting of Hare Kṛṣṇa is the essence of religion–to glorify God. Who can object? And what is the harm in chanting? The chanting is a prayer to the Supreme Lord to please take the chanter out of the inferior energy, into the spiritual. It is a plea for transcendental loving service unto God. Once, when asked what a man should pray for, His Divine Grace A.C. Bhaktivedanta Swami Prabhupāda answered, "We should pray, 'Dear God, please let me love you.' " And so the musical instruments, *mṛdaṅga* drums and hand cymbals are used in glorification of God, and the dancing is a beginning stage of ecstasy. Anyone may take part in the chanting, even a child. It is so nice.

The temple is also used for lectures and classes in the transcendental science of Kṛṣṇa consciousness. Due to the unbreakable system of disciplic succession, the scriptural elaborations and expositions on the philosophy of Kṛṣṇa consciousness (as found in *Vedānta-sūtra, Bhagavad-gītā,* the *Upaniṣads, Śrīmad-Bhāgavatam,* etc.) are the most voluminous, exacting and consistent of any religious culture in the world. As stated in *Bhagavad-gītā,* the science of Kṛṣṇa consciousness, devotional service unto God, is the king of knowledge. This science teaches one that the material body is merely temporary, whereas one's real identity is as an eternal, blissful spirit soul who is a part and parcel of God. It teaches us our eternal relationship with the Supreme Personality of Godhead as His eternal servants. In daily classes on the Vedic literatures, perfect knowledge is received by submissive aural reception. As stated in *Śrīmad-Bhāgavatam,* 1.2.18: "If a candidate for devotional service regularly attends classes in the *Śrīmad-Bhāgavatam* or renders service unto pure devotees, all that is inauspicious in his heart becomes destroyed almost to nil, and thus loving service unto the Personality of Godhead . . . comes to be an irrevocable fact."

The disciples of His Divine Grace A.C. Bhaktivedanta Swami Prabhupāda are so fortunate that they can partake in the transcendental activities in the temple, and we all acknowledge that the pure devotee has given us all means to reach Kṛṣṇa. As disciples, we invite everyone to come to the Kṛṣṇa consciousness temples and take part in the feasts, classes and other programs.

Lord Jagannath Is Krishna Himself

Fall, 1969

The nature of God is that He has unlimited qualities. It is not that He is without qualities. In the Bhagavad Gita, the Supreme Person describes Himself: "Of all that is material and all that is spiritual in this world, know for certain that I am both its origin and dissolution." In the Sanskrit of the Vedic scriptures His qualities are described as "nirguna," that is, they are beyond estimation. We can at least know that everything which we are seeing now is His quality, His energy. Therefore earth, stone and wood are His energy, and all colors are His energy. They are described as belonging to the Lord's external or inferior, material energy. But when this energy of the material world is combined according to authoritative direction, and a shape of the Supreme Lord is carved or shaped from it, then it is no longer material, it is spiritual. That is the version of all Vedic literatures. In this way, by the Mercy of the Absolute, a firm, easily worshipable link can be set up between the spiritual kingdom and those spirit souls who have temporarily fallen into the ignorance of material suffering.

In the Twelfth Chapter of Bhagavad Gita, Krishna the Supreme Personality of Godhead is asked by His disciple Arjuna, "Which form of worship is more perfect, devotional service unto Your Personal Form, or deliberation on Your impersonal unmanifested effulgence?" The Lord clearly declares, "He whose mind is fixed on My Personal Form, always engaged in worshiping Me with great and transcendental faith, is considered by Me to be most perfect." He further states, "For those whose minds are attached to the non-manifested, impersonal Feature of the Supreme, advancement is very troublesome. To make progress in that–unmanifested discipline is always difficult for those who are embodied." A.C. Bhaktivedanta Swami elaborates on this point as follows: "It is very difficult for the embodied individual to simply theoretically understand that he is not the body. Therefore the Bhaktiyogi accepts the Deity of Krishna as worshipable because there is some bodily conception fixed in the mind of everyone, which can be applied. Of course, worship of the Supreme Lord in His Form within the temple is not idol worship. The Form of the Lord even in the material qualities, such as when made of stone, wood, or oil paint, is not actually material. That is the Absolute Nature of the Supreme Lord.

"A crude example may be given here: We may find some mailboxes on the street, and if we post our letters in these boxes, they will naturally go to their destination without any difficulty. But any old box, or an imitation, which we may find somewhere, which is not authorized by the post office, will not do the work. Similarly, God has an authorized representation in the Deity Form, which is called 'Archa Vigraha.' This 'Archa Vigraha' is an incarnation of the Supreme Lord. God will accept service through that Form. The Lord is omnipotent and all-powerful; therefore, by His incarnation as 'Archa Vigraha', He can accept the service of the devotee, just to make it convenient for the man in conditioned life."

So the transformation of matter into spirit in the Deity Form of the Lord is an act done out of His kindness. In His Universal Form, as described in Chapter Eleven of the Gita, Lord Krishna manifests Himself as the entire cosmic manifestation, including all life and planetary systems. He is the greatest of the great and He is also the smallest of the small. For the ease of His parts and parcels who are estranged from Krishna Consciousness and trapped in the material world, He descends as incarnation in the Form of the most merciful Deity, such as Lord Jagannath. The Absolute Truth is inconceivable, beyond the reach of the philosophers' speculation, but the devotee who is willing to go back to Godhead can have easy access to Him. He can offer Him foodstuffs and eat the sanctified remnants, he can dress Him and glorify Him on the Rathayatra car journey. None of this is done whimsically or with any material sentiment, but strictly according to the rules chalked out by the great spiritual masters, who have themselves never disdained the presence of the Lord in the Deity Form. In a recent Deity installation ceremony at the Los Angeles temple, A.C. Bhaktivedanta Swami said, "The difference between idol worship and Deity worship is life. If there is no life, then it is idol worship, heathenism. And when there is life, feeling, then it is Krishna. We must think, 'Here is Krishna. I have to serve Him, I must do it very nicely.' If you think Jagannath is a wooden idol then He will remain a wooden idol to you forever. But if you elevate yourself to the higher platform of Krishna Consciousness, this Krishna will talk with you. At the time just after Lord Chaitanya, the Deity of Madan Mohan used to talk to the great devotee Sanatan Goswami. Sanatan had no temple. He was hanging his Deity on a tree. Madan Mohan was talking with him: 'Sanatan, you are bringing only a dry chapatti to offer Me, this chapatti is stale and if you don't give it a little salt, how can I eat?' Sanatan replied, 'Sir, where shall I go? Whatever I get I offer You. Kindly accept. I cannot move. I am an old man.' So Krishna had to eat whatever was offered. Because the devotee was offering, He could not refuse. Because the real thing is not what you offer, but your feeling: 'Krishna, kindly take. I have no qualification. I am rotten, false. But I have brought this thing for you, please take.' In that way it will be accepted."

Lord Jagannath is especially liberal and accessible to the aspirant devotee of Godhead. As for the history of the Appearance of the merciful Lord Jagannath, our spiritual master, A.C. Bhaktivedanta Swami, has often told the incident: Five thousand years ago, a great devotee and king named Subal requested a sculptor from one of the upper material planets to carve him a Form of Krishna commemorating Krishna's Appearance on His chariot at Kurukshetra when He was joined with His Brother Balaram and Sister Subadra. The sculptor certainly accepted the commission, but stated one positive condition. He said he must work in absolute privacy in his studio. King Subal agreed, and the work began. The king, however, grew impatient after what he thought was too long a time, and finally he could wait no longer but approached the sculptor's place and actually forced open the door. On sight of the king, the demigod sculptor disappeared, leaving behind the Deity Forms of Jagannath, Balaram and Subadra exactly as we know them today from the Rathayatra Festival. The king simply accepted the Forms of the statues as complete: "These will be my worshipable Deities." In other words, the king was in Krishna Consciousness. As in so many of such incidents involving devotees and seeming accidents, the whole thing was an arrangement by the Lord. This is most significantly confirmed in that Lord Chaitanya, the Avatar of Krishna Himself as a Devotee, has solidly taken Lord Jagannath as non-different from the Absolute Truth. In his biography of the life of Lord Chaitanya, A.C. Bhaktivedanta Swami relates that "At Puri when He entered the temple of Jagannath He [Lord Chaitanya] became at once saturated with transcendental ecstasy and fell down on the floor of the temple unconscious." Srila Prabhupada has said that Chaitanya was in such convulsive ecstasy that He could only utter, "Jag, Jaga," but He was thinking, "Oh, Krishna, for so long I have wanted to see You, and now I can see You." Bhaktivinode Thakur, the great householder devotee in the line of disciplic succession from Lord Chaitanya, emphasized in an essay, "The Golden Avatar" (which appeared in issue number 25 of Back to Godhead), that he who can see the incarnation of the Deity within the shape of stone or wood is the perfect theist. And this is accessible not only to the stalwart realized saints, but to any person making a sincere offering with devotion.

On another occasion Bhaktivinode Thakur conclusively affirmed the Jagannath Deity as nondifferent from the Form of Absolute Truth. Some hundred years ago, the devotee Bhaktivinode was the magistrate of the city of Puri in India. At that time a yogi was going around the city proclaiming that he was himself God, Sri Vishnu, and he was getting some less intelligent people to accept him as the Supreme Lord. The yogi had developed the useless talent of breathing fire from his mouth and he was getting a lot of attention. As magistrate, Bhaktivinode called the man before him. "You say you are Lord Vishnu?" "Yes I am," the man insisted. Bhaktivinode also held the position of caretaker of the large Jagannath temple at Puri and he therefore invited the yogi, "If you are Vishnu, then why don't you go live with Lord Jagannath at the temple?" "What?" The yogi was disdainful of the suggestion. "Go live with some wooden idols?" At this gross mistake in transcendental reasoning, Bhaktivinode was convinced the man before him was not God but an imposter; and he had him imprisoned for false teachings. It is further told that, immediately after imprisoning this false "Vishnu," Bhaktivinode's family members became seriously ill. This continued for one or two days, and the townspeople began to speculate that maybe the fire-breathing yogi was actually God and that Bhaktivinode had committed a great blasphemy. But the Thakur was unflinching in his faith and assured his family that all would be well. After a few days their illness passed and the yogi finally confessed from prison that he had been indeed an imposter.

Let us finally stop petty arguments and accept that the unlimited Supreme Lord can, if and when He likes, enter any Form and any place, and He is not prohibited from entrance simply by the desire of the atheists. So many people facilely declare that "God is everything" and "God is everywhere." Why then do they not admit that He is also present in the temple and in the sculptured or painted Form of Lord Jagannath? For this is the actual case, according to the foremost transcendental authorities, the scriptures and the spiritual masters of Vaishnavism.

By and large, the people of this age are unfit to enter into spiritual affairs with the Lord; they cannot see anything beyond matter. In the Srimad Bhagwatam, A.C. Bhaktivedanta Swami writes of Krishna's solution to the predicament: "Because such fallen souls cannot see anything beyond matter, the Lord condescends to enter into each and every one of the innumerable universes as Garbhodakshayee Vishnu. The Lord grows a lotus stem from the lotus-like depression in the center of His transcendental abdomen and thus the first living being in the universe is born, by the name of Brahma. Therefore the Lord is known as 'Pankajanavi.' The Pankajanavi Lord accepts the Archa Vigraha—His transcendental Form—in different elements, such as a form within the mind, a form made of wood, a form made of earth, a form made of metal or jewel or painting or sand. All such forms of the Lord are always decorated with garlands of flowers in a soothing atmosphere in the temple of worship, in order to attract the attention of the non-devotees who are always engaged in material wranglings. All the great Acharyas have established such temples of worship in all places just to favor the non-devotees, and one should not pose himself as having transcended the stage of temple worship, while actually being in the lower grades of society."

We have it from the authoritative source of Srimad Bhagwatam that even the great impersonalist philosophers and yogis, who have already cut free from all bodily conception of self and fixed themselves in the Brahman conception of the Absolute Self, can become devotees of the Personal Form of Krishna simply by visiting the Archa Vigraha in the temple. This was the case with Sukadeva Goswami, who was fixed in the impersonal conception and later, as the narrator of Srimad Bhagwatam, became the number one speaker on the Pastimes of Lord Krishna. Also, the four Kumaras, who were accomplished yogis, traveled by mystic powers to the gates of the Spiritual Abode of Narayan, Lord Vishnu, in the Spiritual Sky; and although not qualified at first to enter into His Pastimes there, just by smelling the flavor of the dust of His Lotus Feet, their minds became changed and they became Personalist devotees of Godhead. This is the power of the merciful Lord and His Archa Vigraha incarnation. He is always ready to take the souls out of their endless attempts to speculate about Him and to instead fix them up as joyful eternal servitors in the perfection of spiritual consciousness.

The Glories of Rama Chandra

January, 1969

Millions of years ago, according to Vedic sources, the Supreme Lord appeared on this planet as the Warrior Rama Chandra, in order to execute His Will and display the Pastimes of the Personality of Godhead. As is stated in The Bhagavad Gita, "From time to time I come, in order to vanquish the demons and rescue the devotees."

The Pastimes of Lord Rama are revealed in the famous Vedic Scripture called The Ramayana, written by Sri Valmiki. Before being empowered to write The Ramayana, Valmiki had been a plunderer; but, by the grace of the great saint Narada, he became a Vaishnava–that is, a worshipper of the Personality of Godhead. Narada had first asked Valmiki to please chant the Name of the Lord, but Valmiki had replied that he would not. He was a murderer, and so what had he to do with chanting God's Name? Narada then asked him to meditate on his murders, by saying the name of "Mara," which means Death. Valmiki agreed to this, and meditated on "Mara." By rapid repetition of the word–Mara, Mara, Mara–he found himself saying Rama, Rama, Rama, and by the power of reciting the Holy Name of God his heart became purified.

The Ramayana is written down as a historical epic, but it contains all the information of the original Vedas. Vedic literature such as The Ramayana and The Mahabharata (of which the famed Bhagavad Gita is a chapter), are especially recommended for this age, even more so than the highly intricate Vedas, or the philosophical theses of The Vedanta Sutra–all of which are prone to misinterpretation by the fallen mentality of this Age of Quarrel.

So diminished is the capacity for receiving God consciousness in this age that The Bhagavad Gita, which was set down 5000 years ago and was especially intended for the less intelligent, is today not understood by the greatest so-called scholars. These men generally attempt interpretations of The Gita leaving out the importance of the Personality of Godhead, Krishna, Who is the Essence, Speaker, and Goal of The Gita.

Lord Rama Chandra appeared on this Earth as a man. This means that he actually walked the Earth. What is written in The Ramayana, we should note here, is best understood as it is. When the Pastimes of the Supreme Personality of Godhead are narrated, there can be no question of allusion to a higher principle. Allegory means that there is a truth higher than the literal sense of a given text. But the highest realization of spiritual perfection is that the Absolute Truth is a Person—which precludes any possibility of going beyond Him. God means the Highest Reality. He is the One from Whom everything emanates. Although He appeared as a man out of kindness to His devotees, Rama Chandra is the Supreme Lord. His history is, therefore, very marvelous and filled with wondrous feats, as we'll see.

Rama Chandra was the son of King Dasarath, in the line of King Ikshaku, the first ruler of Earth, and an early recipient of the Bhakti Yoga system of The Bhagavad Gita. Lord Rama was the darling of His father and mother, Queen Kausalya, as well as the hero and darling of all Ayodha, the capital of what was then the single world kingdom.

Rama had all the admirable qualities of leadership, even from earliest youth. Rama Chandra possessed all physical strength, all beauty, religious wisdom in submission to Truth, fame for prowess with weapons, royal wealth, and complete renunciation. He played the part of a human, and yet His stature as a human was praised by all His contemporaries as being worthy of the gods.

Inseparable from Rama was Lakshman, His younger brother. Lakshman was born of Sumitra, one of the 350 queens of King Dasarath. His position is like that of Rama's Own Self, and nothing is dearer to Rama than Lakshman. Together, the two Brothers appeared on Earth to vanquish the almost invincible atheist King Ravana and his numberless host of Rakshasa (man-eating) warriors.

Rama Chandra is described as being of greenish hue, His bodily lustre like fresh green grass. And Lakshman is golden-hued. Lakshman is as attractive and as formidable a warrior as Rama Himself. During the course of one of the blood-drenched battles against Ravana's army, Lakshman was rendered unconscious by Rakshasa magic, and at that time Rama gave vent to a spontaneous expression of love for Lakshman: "If I lose the kingdom that I can bear, but I could not bear the loss of Lakshman! I cannot go on if Lakshman is lost to Me!" Lakshman was likewise dedicated to the service of his Brother and had no other pleasure than to do the bidding of Rama Chandra.

RAMA'S FIRST CAMPAIGN

While Rama was still a Boy of 16, the famous yogi, Viswamitra, approached King Dasarath and asked that the Boy be allowed to travel on a military campaign against two Rakshasas who were attacking the hermitages of saintly persons, interrupting the performance of sacrifice. Why did the sage Viswamitra ask for the Boy Rama? Because no one was equal to Him, even though He was as yet untrained in the use of the principal wea; onry, bow and arrow. After some hesitance by Dasarath, who was loathe to have his Son part for a dangerous mission, Rama Chandra went forth.

If we take military history as an evolution of progressively more deadly weapons, we may slight the figure of Rama, possessing no more than a bow and arrow. But the enemies of Rama were allowed no such miscalculation as to His ability to destroy. He stood before them like a hill of nuclear missiles. He discharged His feathered arrows in sheets which blotted out the blue of the sky and which entered the hearts of the enemy in unlimited numbers at incredible velocity. So we shouldn't think of Rama the Archer as quaint or dated. His bow, a gift from the demigod Indra, was a supreme Army and Air Force in itself. His arsenal included many varieties of deadly arrows, charmed by the Science of Mantra, or sound vibration. Once released, those arrows could not be turned back, no matter where the adversary fled for shelter.

In the final battle against Ravana, Lord Rama Chandra resorted to a nuclear weapon, the Brahmastra fire weapon, whose released heat is said to frighten the denizens of the uppermost planets of the material universe. And this Brahmastra, too, was a winged arrow affixed to a bowstring. "Among the weapon wielders, I am Rama," Lord Krishna says in The Gita. God is the greatest Warrior, and He possesses the means to release the ultimate weapon.

On this boyhood military campaign against "the Rovers of the Night," Rama discharged two wind weapons, killing one Rakshasa and landing the other a few thousand miles away in the ocean.

Viswamitra, being pleased with young Rama and Lakshman, narrated many wonderful things to them, about the Appearance of the Lord as the Dwarf Vamana, about the origin of the sacred River Ganges–and about a worshipable bow kept by King Janaka, the father of Sita. This Janaka is mentioned in The Bhagavad Gita as having attained perfection by carrying out his occupational duties as a Kshatriya King. Once, for his part in ameliorating the anger of Lord Shiva the Destroyer, Janaka was presented with a most formidable bow. The bow was so mighty, in fact, that no one could even bend it in order to string it. Janaka made offerings of flowers and prayers before the bow given him by Lord Shiva, acknowledging that the personality who could string the sacred bow must be an extraordinary power. In view of which, King Janaka offered the hand of his daughter Sita to the man who would come and bend the bow.

Sita, of course, had many suitors, and all failed to win her. Her dowry was valor. Of all chaste and beautiful young women, she was the topmost jewel and was very dear to Janaka. Viswamitra brought Rama and Lakshman to Janaka's palace just to show them the bow given by Shiva. A large assembly of people was gathered to see the weapon, as Rama Chandra took it up in His hand, and asked Janaka, "What would you have Me do with it? Shall I string it now?"

"Yes," Janaka assented.

At once, Rama easily bent the bow until it cracked in two pieces, making a thundering explosion which rendered all present unconscious, except for Viswamitra, Rama and Lakshman! At that time the gods showered flowers from the sky upon Rama Chandra, and there was cheering in the heavens. King Janaka then agreed, with great pleasure, that his daughter should be married to the mighty Rama Chandra.

SITA AND RAMA

Sita, the wife of Rama, is not considered an ordinary being. It is understood that, as Lord Rama Chandra was Vishnu, the Supreme Lord Himself, so Sita was actually Lakshmi, the Goddess of Fortune, who serves eternally at the Feet of Vishnu in the spiritual sky. Being the daughter of the royal saint Janaka, she is also sometimes called Janaki. Actually, Janaka found Sita when she was a baby. He had been plowing a field, and he upturned her in a clod of earth. It is stated in The Ramayana that Sita came to Earth for the destruction of Ravana, who was a villifier of married women. As Rama Chandra was the greatest Warrior and Expounder of religion and morality, so Sita was the greatest beauty among women, and the most chaste.

How can the Infinite Lord be sufficiently praised? And who can completely describe the loveliness, in every feature, of His chaste wife, the Goddess of Fortune?

We shouldn't think that, as we desire a woman, so Rama Chandra desired a woman, and thus married one with the desires of an ordinary husband. Sita is Lakshmi, the Goddess of Fortune, and Rama is Lord Vishnu, the Personality of Godhead; and we cannot understand His transcendental position by judging Him on the plane of inebriated sex desire. Sex desire, lust, is the characteristic condition of the ordinary mortal who is at the mercy of the laws of Nature. He is put under these stringent laws out of his wish to enjoy as a lord rather than render service to the Supreme Enjoyer.

The Supreme Personality of Godhead, however, is transcendental to the material laws. What we have here in the material world as sex desire is indeed a reflection of the Lord's desire to enjoy loving affairs. But His loving affairs have no taint of contamination, no limitations of cheating, of old age, or of death. Here, sex pleasure is false in that it is merely a counteraction to the usual condition of misery, and it is temporary. But when the Lord enjoys loving affairs it is in a state of continual bliss in mutual service; and this expands unendingly into greater and greater bliss, each party exhibiting selfless devotion to the other. It is understood that by the process of purification in devotional service, we too can reciprocate transcendental love with God; and that is the perfection of human life.

The impersonalist philosphers whose propaganda is so rampant in this age cannot appreciate the Divine Couple or the Lord's loving affairs. These are displayed in the Persons of Radha and Ḳrishna, Lakshmi and Narayana, and in Sita and Rama. The position of the impersonalist is necessarily loveless. Love means persons. No one can love the Void or a non-person. Therefore, impersonal philosophy is merely the negative side of reality, the denial of material inebriety. The impersonalists accept neither sex as being absolute, but the Vaishnava or Personalist has two sexes, Radha and Krishna, or Sita and Rama. Without understanding the real situation of the Supreme Person and His Transcendental Nature, His Activities and His devotees, such an impersonalist yogi or philosopher is forced to come down from his temporary suspension in the impersonal Void; and again he may enter into entanglement with the material inebrieties which he only theoretically declares to be false.

Valmiki compares the sight of Rama and Sita together to the moon and the brightest star. The Rama Chandra worshipper, therefore, never makes the mistake of thinking Sita an ordinary wife. Throughout The Ramayana, the poetry again and again turns to images of the various moods of natural beauty in the jungle, in the sky, and in the night with its wonderful galaxies for comparisons to the loveliness of Sita. And always the worshipper addresses first Sita, and then Rama–Sita-Rama.

Growing old, King Dasarath decided to confer the kingdom on his eldest son, Rama. On the release of this news, the Kingdom of Ayodha turned to joyous preparation for the coronation of the beloved prince. The Ramayana (Ayodha Kandam) states:

> The streets were crowded with men. People were going in mobs and there were constant shouts of joy, like the roar of the sea. All the places were filled to their utmost capacities. All the highways were swept and watered, garlands hung on every gate, and flags streamed from every house. The whole city was anxiously waiting for the morning of the coronation ceremony.

The night before, Janaki and Rama Chandra were initiated into the observance of a fast, and were given mantras to recite. They worshipped Narayana, and lay down on a bed of grass within Vishnu's shrine.

THE BANISHMENT OF RAMA

The Ramayana goes on to relate fateful events:"Queen Kaikeyi had brought up an orphan girl named Manthara, who served Kaikeyi as a maidservant." Kaikeyi was one of King Dasarath's wives, and Manthara was her hunch-backed maidservant. It was she who sowed the evil seed of the great personal ordeals related in The Ramayana. Amidst universal joy, Manthara had heard the news of Rama's coronation with a feeling of rage. With malicious intent she entered the room of Queen Kaikeyi and proposed to her that the coronation of Rama Chandra was a calamity to the Queen. Kaikeyi was the mother of Dasarath's next oldest son, noble Bharat. Manthara cunningly outlined how Dasarath had recently sent Bharat away on a visit to his uncle, in order to install Rama Chandra. And, after installation, Rama Chandra would surely see that Bharat was killed. With crooked logic, Manthara predicted all the grief ahead for Kaikeyi, and in this way implanted evil wrath into the Queen's heart.

Queen Kaikeyi was now convinced that Rama Chandra must be eliminated. She was very dear to Dasarath, and she was able to strike tellingly by binding him to a promise. Once Dasarath had fallen badly wounded on a battlefield, in a clash between Indra and some Asuras (demons), and Queen Kaikeyi had nursed him as he lay unconscious. At that time he had promised her two boons, but she had said she would ask for them at a later time. By that service rendered by her, and by the oath of Dasarath, Kaikeyi wrought long and bitter grief upon Ayodha.

Lying down in a room in her palace, called "the chamber of wrath," Kaikeyi awaited Dasarath, and when he came and found her there, she infected the coronation day, like a snake biting a calf, by demanding the following two boons: 1. Let Rama Chandra be banished to the forest for 14 years, and 2. Let Bharat be installed as king. Dasarath fell unconscious at her words. He soon regained his senses, understood what she was saying, and again fainted away.

Awakening a second time, he cried out in torment: "Oh how sad! How painful! I suffer from your words, being oath-bound to you! I suffer now as a man does for misdeeds committed in a previous birth!"

We may think, what is this "truth," what is this "promise," if it wreaks such evil? Why didn't Dasarath simply say, "No! Never! I will not banish Rama. Rama is dearer than truth!" But he did not. He had made a promise, and as a Kshatriya (warrior) he must stand by it. His religion was truth. Because he had promised Kaikeyi a boon at a time when she had saved his life, therefore he must now grant her promise, whatever it might be, in this case a fate worse than death.

There are other examples in the Vedic literature of extreme sacrifices to truth, and Kaikeyi mercilessly cited them for Dasarath: A King named Saivya once promised a pigeon who had flown into his arms that he would protect him from a pursuing hawk. The hawk, who was actually a demigod in the form of the predator, demanded flesh from the king's body as substitute for the pigeon, and King Saivya agreed, cutting the flesh from his own body.

But was that the same as banishing Rama Chandra? How could Dasarath banish the rightful heir to the throne? For what offense? Rama was the absolute darling of every living entity in Ayodha. He was the outright Destroyer of the demons. He and His wife were comparable to the moon and the brightest star! When the people came to say, "Where is Rama Chandra?"–what then? In short, Dasarath was ruined, and the Kingdom of Ayodha with him. Dasarath lamented bitterly, and prepared himself to be condemned by his peers and by the future. Still, he was bound to the truth of his promise.

Rama Chandra was called to court by Dasarath. Rama was about 26 years old, and it was His Coronation Day. He rode in His chariot to answer His father's call. The Ramayana states that Rama Chandra came out from His palace surrounded with an effulgence of glory, just as the moon emerges from behind the dark blue clouds. Lakshman stood by Him with a chowri fan. Elephants and horses followed His chariot; and music, shouts and cheers were continually heard. As He passed the windows of beautiful women, they rained flowers on His Head. Some of them praised Kausalya, the mother of Rama Chandra, and others said that Sita was the gem of all women, and must have practiced great penances in former births or she would not have had such a husband as this king-to-be.

But on entering His father's presence, Rama found the old King looking miserable and sad, seated on a sofa with His Queen Kaikeyi. She personally delivered the cruel message to Rama Chandra. Dasarath fainted away in grief at hearing again the wish of Kaikeyi, but he could not deny it.

Magnanimous Rama Chandra, however, was not a bit pained to hear her shameful words. He only replied: "Very well. I shall go from here and proceed to the Dananka Forest for 14 years with an unwavering mind."

Rama Chandra proceeded to inform all those gaily preparing for His Coronation that He was at once leaving for a mendicant's life in the forest. His natural cheerfulness did not leave Him, but He was troubled to have to tell His mother, and He thought both parents might die at His separation from them.

The fateful news soon spread. It spread to the women in Rama's palace, and they began to cry bitterly. The queens and other royal ladies wailed, for He Who used to serve them and Who looked on them as His mothers, and Who never grew angry with them but had sweet words for all, that Rama was going to the forest!

"No! Dasarath should never have forsaken Him!"

When He approached His mother Kausalya, she was still informed only of the Coronation, and she fell at His Feet and offered Him a seat and some refreshment.

Rama Chandra, with clasped hands, said to her, "Mother, you don't know what a great calamity is descending upon you and Janaki and Lakshman. I don't require a seat anymore, for I am now bound for the forest, and shall live there for 14 years on fruits and herbs. Father has ordered My exile, and Bharat's installation."

Kausalya fainted on the ground like a tree felled by an axe. Valmiki describes how, with difficulty, she told Rama that He must fight to win the crown. But Rama Chandra told His mother that it was beyond His power to disobey His father's orders. He could not follow any desire which went beyond righteousness. Similarly, Lord Jesus Christ once taught: "If you gain the whole world, but lose your immortal soul, what have you gained?"

Rama Chandra said to Kausalya: "Father is our preceptor. Who, having any regard for righteousness, will disobey his orders, even though they may be given from anger, joy, or lust? I cannot act against My father's vows. This life is not everlasting, and so I would not wish to acquire even the world by an unjust means."

Lakshman was not consoled. He was brooding and overwhelmed with grief at this turn of events. Lakshman argued that Rama Chandra must not submit; he suspected, in fact, that the whole story of promised boons was just a plea by the King in order to install Bharat, and thus satisfy the lust of his Queen Kaikeyi. Lakshman was prepared to hack to pieces with his sword the King and his whole army. He was ready to bring the whole world under the sway of Rama Chandra. Rama replied that he thought the best course for Himself was to obey His father's orders. Rama's mother gradually, with great sorrow, offered her blessings and prayed that she would someday see Him coming back.

Rama Chandra then took leave of His mother and went to Janaki's quarters. She also knew nothing of Rama Chandra's exile. She was in a state of joyfulness over His installation as King. She was worshipping the deities when He entered with His head hanging down in shame. On telling Sita of His exile, Rama Chandra said that she must stay behind and live under the rule of Bharat. Janaki, who was always sweet in speech, replied to Him with an offended air. How could He say such infamous, unworthy things, especially as He was a hero versed in Vedic science?

"If You repair to the forest, I shall go in front of You and make smooth the path by crushing the thorns under my feet. I shall not leave Your company, nor will You be able to dissuade me. I shall feel no sorrow in passing a long time with You."

But Rama Chandra, thinking of the factual hardships of forest life, told her about the reality of the situation. Prowling animals, sharks, crocodiles in muddy rivers, sometimes no drinking water, no bed, hunger appeased by fruits fallen on the ground, matted locks, bark for clothes, observance of the rules of asceticism, three baths daily, flowers offered on the sacred altar by picking them with your own hand, blasts of wind, reptiles roaming free, great pythons, scorpions, mosquitos, penance, the necessity for bold action–this is the business of forest life.

Rama Chandra said it was too dangerous, but Sita entreated Him that, as a devoted wife, she was happy in His happiness, and sorry only in His sorrow. With Rama, she assured Him, she would find the hardships heavenly. Rama Chandra finally relented and admitted that He was by no means unable to protect her in the forest. And, formerly, many royal saints had repaired to the forest with their wives. So He would follow their example. He advised her to at once give away her beautiful clothes and valuables, and to be ready to leave.

Lakshman, who had been there while Rama Chandra spoke with Sita, caught hold of his Brother's Feet, as it was unbearable for him to be separated from Rama. Rama tried to dissuade him from joining Him. He asked him to stay in the kingdom and keep an eye on the court. But nothing could turn Lakshman. He replied that Bharat would maintain the kingdom, but he must be given leave to join Rama Chandra. He would go before Sita and Rama Chandra as Their guide, and would procure Their foods; and They could enjoy while he would do everything else required, whether Rama was asleep or awake. Rama was pleased, and ordered Lakshman to prepare for departure at once.

Unfortunately, the whole kingdom could not join Rama Chandra in exile, and the people were sorely distressed. Indeed, they proposed to join Him by the thousands, but Kaikeyi would not allow it: If everyone went with Him, it would be no exile at all. No, Rama Chandra must go with only Sita and Lakshman. But the people lamented that the city would become deserted without Him, all religious institutions would be destroyed and dirt and filth would cover the yards, and rats would roam free. Rama Chandra, hearing them carry on, was not moved.

Shortly after Rama Chandra's departure, his father died of grief. He could not live with Rama in exile, and with his last breath he cried the Names of Rama, Lakshman and Sita. Young Bharat was at once called back from his uncle's house by special messengers, who told him no more than to come at once. Bharat arrived before his mother, Queen Kaikeyi, and learned first that his father was dead, and then that his Brother was exiled on the wish of his mother. Bharat was shaken with remorse, and called Kaikeyi a murderess. To Bharat there was no question of assuming the throne without Rama Chandra and Lakshman.

After performing the funeral rites for his father, he set out without delay, with an army behind him, to bring Rama back and himself take the place of the Exile in the forest. Only in that way could he hope to remove the stain of his mother's action.

SITA AND RAMA IN THE JUNGLE

Forest life for a royal prince was supposed to be an abominable insult, but Rama Chandra managed to cheer Sita by pointing out to her the beauty of the natural setting. A jungle is generally supposed to be a place in the mode of goodness, just suitable for the cultivation of spiritual life.

The Shastras, or Scriptures, describe life in the liquor shop as being in the mode of ignorance; residence in the city is said to be in the mode of passion; and residence in the forest is in goodness. But even the so-called mode of goodness is not transcendental to material consciousness. Only a temple of God is specifically helpful for the purpose of transcendental consciousness, or linking with the Personality of Godhead. The forest is actually suitable for material habitation, and for the exploitation of raw resources such as trees and plants. Of course, when the Personality of Godhead was in the forest, it was the most perfect temple and shrine. Picking a leaf, or roaming with Janaki, Rama is in perfection, as He is the Supreme Lord, even though acting as a human.

We are cautioned not to think that if we repair to the jungle we will be like Rama Chandra, or that we will become renounced and saintly by such an act. The forest, in other words, is in itself not conducive to thoughts of the transcendental Lord. It is a place of monkeys and trees and good areas for making material habitation. Spiritual life, however, does not mean to become neatly situated in natural surroundings which may or may not be more pleasant than the shops and streets of the city. Spiritual life means to serve and please the will of the Supreme Lord. To be thinking of the activities of the Supreme Lord, and to hear authorized information like The Ramayana and The Bhagavad Gita, about His inconceivable greatness and His loving intentions toward the living entities–is not attained by automatically putting on rough clothing and plying through the jungles with difficult steps.

Even to sit alone in a yogic posture in the jungle, with forced concentration on the spirit soul, may not be successful if the heart is still impure and the mind roaming to objects of the senses. Lord Krishna has said that He is not to be found in the jungle or in the hearts of the yogis in meditation, but there where His devotees are chanting His Name: Hare Krishna, Hare Rama. "I am there."

So-called holy men who go to the forests to become sannyasis, renouncers, and do not actually follow the authoritative paths for becoming God conscious are therefore called "monkey sannyasis." Simply living like a monkey in a tree is not holiness.

Rama Chandra was actually the Supreme Personality of Godhead. Anything He did was perfect, because He is the Person Who is the Source of all perfection. We simply have to offer a submissive hearing of His activities, and we will ourselves be situated in transcendental meditation. He is the Lord, as Rama Chandra, the Ideal King, and His life is an example of the rigid morality by which we can find the way back to home, back to our original loving relationship with God. Rama Chandra is Himself full spirit, portraying activities on Earth for the vanquishment of Ravana, and we have only to fully comprehend any Pastime of His in order to contact the honey of God consciousness.

Once Sita and Rama were resting on a rocky ledge after straying through the hills, and a bold crow came at Sita and threatened to strike her with its claws. She chased him but he came again and again, tearing at her until, Valmiki describes, "her cheeks were glowing with rage and her lips quivering in anger. Frowns darkened her lovely brow." Rama Chandra tried chasing the bird but it paid no heed and flew at Sita even more. Then He fixed an arrow with mantras, and aimed it at the crow. The bird sprang up and flew, but the arrow followed wherever the bird went. The crow then flew back to Rama and pleaded for its life. Rama Chandra was always prepared to protect the surrendered entity, but since He had already released his fatal weapon, the crow was asked to give up some part of its life so that the weapon would not go in vain. The crow gave up an eye and the arrow struck at once.

After some time, Bharat and his army arrived in the vicinity. One soldier climbed a tree and saw smoke issuing from a cottage. Bharat and a few others then went forward on foot, and Bharat beheld Rama's cottage. Valmiki describes it:

> He found there the formidable bow plated with gold. The quiver was full of sharp arrows flaming like the sun. There were swords in golden sheathes, and gloves spangled with gold. There stood a spacious altar, and fire was burning at its northeast. Bharat found there Lotus-eyed, Fire-like, Effulgent Rama, seated on a hide with bark and a black deerskin, and with matted locks on His head.

The brothers embraced. Bharat told of Dasarath's death and pleaded for Rama Chandra to return and take the kingdom. Rama Chandra replied to His younger brother that none of us have an independent existence, just to do as we please. We are subject to death, all of us. Rama told him to note how people are pleased to see the seasons change, though they do not realize it means their life duration is shortening. And on any walk a person takes, and when he returns, death is with him, and walks with him and rests with him. So in all circumstances, intelligent people subdue grief. He told Bharat to return and take charge, because that was the wish of their father.

Rama Chandra said, "Let me pursue My duties here."

Bharat pleaded that he was only a boy, and Rama must rule over him. But Rama was firm in keeping His father's pledge. He cited to His brother a Vedic proverb: He who saves his father from the hell named "Put," and he who saves his father from all sorts of difficulties, is "Putra," or the true son. Bharat relented, but took back with him Rama Chandra's sandals, promising to dedicate the kingdom to the sandals of Rama, and to wait in ascetic observance for the expiration of the 14-year exile.

THE WAR WITH RAVANA

The first clash with Ravana took place through his sister, Surpanakha. She was a hideous monster who wandered across the cottage of Rama, and was struck with lust on seeing the Lord. She delivered some low insults to Sita, and for that Lakshman cut off her ears and nose. Running back to the camp of Ravana, she howled for revenge, and the death-struggle thus commenced.

Ravana had almost everything. Through long performance of austere penances he had gained great power; he had received specific boons from Lord Brahma, the topmost demigod, so that he would never be vanquished by any race of demigods, or any power or personality except man. But, of course, no mere man could stand against his onslaught. For the sake of war-mongering he had conquered the demigods Kuvera and Indra. He reigned in a vast island kingdom called Lanka, and possessed all material opulence. He and his "Rovers of the Night" roamed about killing and eating the flesh of solitary hermits engaged in spiritual practices in the forest.

Ravana made a career of violating beautiful women wherever he found them, and had a large harem of hundreds who had surrendered to his material effulgence of wealth and strength.

Ravana believed himself unvanquishable. He did not care for God. Perfect materialist that he was, he challenged even the existence of God. He had a plan where he wanted to deport men to the heavenly planets by means of a staircase structure reaching to Indra's Paradise, so that people could go there without qualifying themselves by performing pious works. He challenged anything and everything good, and listened to no cautious counsel about the bad reaction which follows sinful activities. Valmiki says that Ravana's mentality was such that he was living for death. In challenging Rama by the abduction of His wife Sita, Ravana surely chose death, and raced headlong towards his inevitable meeting with it. Therefore, there was no fear of sin in Ravana; until such time as he was actually cut down by a superior power, he would violate the authority of the Lord as far as possible.

We can understand, therefore, that for all his highly developed intelligence, Ravana was ignorant of the soul. By such ignorance one thinks that this one lifetime is all, and that death is the finish of everything. And so one may beg, borrow, or steal if one wishes. And if someone tells him that there will be a reaction in the next life, based on his present behavior, he will disregard that. This is the ignorance by which the conditioned living entity is covered over, and by which he cannot realize his original situation of Sat-chit-ananda—transcendental eternal bliss, and full knowledge in the loving service of the Lord.

As soon as anyone, from the tiny ant up to the conqueror Ravana, takes the attitude that he is the lord and the center, then the material Nature awards him this bodily covering, by which he can go on acting in illusion, ignorant of his real dependence on the Soul of souls, God. Under the illusion that he is independent, he then engages in a futile struggle to conquer the material Nature. Ravana's case is extraordinary because, in defiance of the Supreme Personality of Godhead, he actually did conquer a significant part of the universe. But, as we shall see, his victory, like that of all the worldly conquerors of history, was fleeting, and his every step was actually a step on the path towards his ultimate destruction.

From Ravana's kingdom, 14,000 Rakshasa warriors poured forth to slay Rama and Lakshman. En route, Ravana's troops experienced a downpour of evil omens from Nature. Blood showered upon them with dreadful noise. The beautiful horses pulling their chariots suddenly tumbled. Vultures attacked their royal flags. Birds, beasts and jackals howled.

The demigods situated in the sky prayed amongst themselves: "May victory attend the cows, Brahmins and those who are held in high regard by Him. Let Rama conquer just like Vishnu with His disc."

Valmiki writes that, "As the planets move towards the sun and the moon, so the fierce Rakshasa army rushed towards Rama and Lakshman, in lust of battle." Rama was informed of their coming. While doom was presaged to the Rakshasas by dark clouds and raining blood, the shafts of Rama Chandra were flaming in war-delight, and His gold-plated bow throbbed with ruthless energy.

The 14,000 warriors were demolished by Rama Chandra, alone and on foot. His arrows, resembling fire with smoke, covered the whole sky, and He discharged them and fired more with a speed that the enemy could not follow. One man-eater survived, and ran back to Ravana with the news that Rama Chandra had devoured them with shafts like a five-mouthed serpent. He said that, wherever they had fled, they had found Rama Chandra stationed before them.

Ravana was outraged and reminded the lone survivor of 14,000 that Vishnu Himself couldn't be safe by doing injury to Ravana. But the survivor who had been through the hell of slaughter pleaded that his Lord Ravana just listen to him with attention regarding Rama Chandra's valor as he had experienced it. He humbly submitted to his chief that Rama Chandra could bring down the stars and planets and raise the submerged Earth by His arrows, and could destroy all creatures and create them anew. Rama Chandra was simply unslayable.

The survivor also offered to Ravana that he had seen the beautiful wife of Rama, called Sita. He said that no woman could be equal to her in beauty. She was in the bloom of youth, and most graceful. Her beauty struck one with such deep wonder, the Rakshasa concluded, that if Ravana could somehow enchant Rama into the forest and take her away, it would be the one way to vanquish Him, for He surely could not survive separation from His wife.

THE KIDNAPPING OF SITA

To implement the abduction of Sita, Ravana called on his warlord, Maricha. This Maricha was the same Rakshasa who had been carried 1000 miles through the air and thrown into the ocean by the wind arrow of the inexperienced 16-year-old Rama on His first military expedition. Ravana asked Maricha to take the form of a golden deer, to frisk in front of Sita. When Sita should wish to have the deer for her own, Rama and Lakshman could be induced to follow it and, at that time, Sita might be carried off.

Maricha was filled with alarm on hearing such talk from Lord Ravana. He reported to his chief that the proposal was impossible. For one thing, "as Indra is the king of the gods, so Rama Chandra is King of all." Nobody should dare to take Sita away, as she was protected by chastity and devotion. Maricha knew that Rama Chandra was death-like, and he advised Ravana to desist from his thoughts of crossing the Lord. The King of the Rakshasas, irritated that his subordinate had even attempted to dissuade him, told Maricha that he must perform this service or be killed.

Then Maricha, in the form of a wonderful deer with silver spots and the sheen of jewels, appeared before Sita in the forest. His hoofs were made of blue stones, and he had a little tail that shone like the rainbow. He walked this way and that, browsing on creepers and sometimes galloping. In so many ways, he drew the mind of Sita, who asked Rama Chandra to catch him for her. Rama Chandra was, of course, cognizant that this might be the Rakshasa magic of Maricha, but

He decided to go after the deer, and if it was actually Maricha, He would kill him. Rama firmly ordered Lakshman to stay behind with Sita. Then He pursued the deer. It became elusive, and even invisible. Rama resolved to kill it. He shot one deadly shaft which entered Maricha's heart like a flaming snake.

His counterfeit guise gone, Maricha in the hideous form of a huge Rakshasa bathed in blood now rolled upon the ground. But with his last breath, he remembered the advice of Ravana, and cried out loudly, "Alas Sita! Alas Lakshman!"

Waiting with Lakshman in their cottage, Sita heard the cries and believed it was Rama, and that He was in some danger. She told Lakshman to go at once and help Him. Lakshman dismissed the idea that Rama Chandra could be in danger. Besides, he knew his duty was to remain and protect Sita. But Sita, in great anxiety over Rama, began to speak very strangely. She told Lakshman that she knew he was not going to help Rama out of lust for her, and that in fact he had long been waiting to be separated from Rama so that he could fulfill his own desire for enjoying Sita. Lakshman could not bear to hear such unfair words, and he took his leave of Sita to seek out Rama Chandra. In that way, Ravana was able to find Sita alone, and he carried her off by force.

It may be asked, how could two invincible heroes be tricked by the magic of illusion into leaving Sita alone? How could Sita, with the purity of her chaste insight, accuse Lakshman of being lustful? And, as Rama Chandra is God Himself, how could it come to pass that Ravana carried off Sita by force in his chariot, and was able to cause bitter lamentation for Sita and Rama? These are not very easy questions, it would seem. The aggregate is: how can someone under the direct protection of the Supreme Lord come under any illusion, or fare badly?

If we take it from The Bhagavad Gita, we can know that the pure devotee is never under the power of illusion. The Lord promises that one who surrenders to Him is straightway delivered from illusion. Maya, the illusory energy, cannot act upon one who is surrendered to the Person of the Absolute Truth. This Maya is the external energy of the Lord, intended as a reformatory measure for those souls still desirous of lording it. As its source is divine, this Maya cannot be overcome by any amount of scholarship, technology, or material intelligence. But, as stated in the Seventh Chapter of The Gita, he alone who surrenders to the Lord is released.

A pure devotee is attached to service of the Supreme Person, and is therefore no longer falsely identifying his perishable body as his self, or claiming material possessions as his own. The devotee is under the internal, spiritual energy of the Lord, called Yogamaya. This means that he is being personally cared for by the Supreme Personality of Godhead, due to his constant association by word, thought and deed with the Yogamaya energy. This is just like sunshine. The sunshine is there for everyone, but it cannot benefit one who stays hidden indoors. One who partakes of the sunshine experiences no darkness, because darkness cannot exist where the sun is.

So, if the devotee is freed from all contamination and darkness, why was Rama Chandra banished from His kingdom? Why was Sita, who is Lakshmi the Goddess of Fortune, kidnapped by Ravana? Why was Lord Jesus Christ crucified? Why was the pure saint Thakur Haridas beaten? Why was Lord Krishna shot in the foot by a hunter? And why did Krishna's devotees, the Pandavas, have to undergo so many ordeals? These things, the devotee understands, are working according to some plan of the Lord's Will, to facilitate His mission in this world.

This example was given by Rama Chandra when He responded with even mind to His banishment: "I must obey My father in this. Who are We to try to get control for self-interest over what is being sent to Us by the law of God? We must accept what is sent by God."

Surrender means that the Lord can do with us as He likes. The surrendered soul is waiting for the Lord's Will. He will go back to Godhead at the time when the Lord is pleased to take him. He knows that there must be some plan of the Lord behind what is happening and, as far as he's concerned, the devotee will never be removed from his position of unconditional loving service unto the Personality of Godhead. In this case of Rama's banishment and Sita's abduction, we can understand that these activities had to be carried out in order to fulfill the mission of Lord Rama in coming to Earth–the slaying of the demon Ravana for the relief of the faithful demigods.

Similar occurrences of a devotee in a position of mundane frustration are explained by A.C. Bhaktivedanta Swami as the basis for the presentation of great transcendental literatures like Srimad Bhagwatam and the Bhagavad Gita. In the case of Srimad Bhagwatam, the Emperor Parikshit, who was usually a man of irreproachable behavior, delivered an insult to a brahmin, and was sentenced to death within 7 days. This death curse brought about his revival of God consciousness, and made possible his meeting with the sage Sukadeva Goswami, who narrated the entire Srimad Bhagwatam to him, filled as it is with the Pastimes of Lord Krishna. In this way all humanity was benefitted.

Again, A.C. Bhaktivedanta Swami writes, "By placing Arjuna and the Pandavas in a position of frustration through the intrigues of their cousins, the Battle of Kurukshetra was engineered by the Lord in order to incarnate the sound representative of the Lord, The Bhagavad Gita."

In short, we should understand that these unusual circumstances of the apparent distress of Rama and Sita are ordained and serve the Lord's purposes.

On a chariot pulled by asses, Ravana of ten heads and twenty arms flew through the sky with his arm around Sita. Sita was protected from gross sexual violation by her power of chastity. Also, Ravana had at one time in his career received a fell curse from the yogi father of a girl he had violated: if Ravana ever attempted to again enjoy a woman by physical force, his head would split into pieces.

By this act of abduction Ravana completely sealed his doom beyond a doubt. Not only would he die for capturing another's wife, but he would not even be able to enjoy her in the meantime, not for a moment. A.C. Bhaktivedanta Swami nicely explains the relationship between Sita and Ravana: "The Goddess of Fortune is called Chanchala. Chanchala means that she is not steady. Ravana took away Lakshmi, Sitaji, to his place and instead of being happy by the grace of Lakshmi, his family and his kingdom were vanquished. So Lakshmi in the house of Ravana is Chanchala, or not steady. The Ravana class of men want Lakshmi only, without her husband, Narayana [or Rama Chandra]. Therefore they become unsteady by Lakshmiji. And so materialistic persons find fault on the part of Fortune. Of course, in the spiritual sky Lakshmi is fixed in the service of the Lord, and in spite of her being the Goddess of Fortune, she cannot be happy without the grace of the Lord." From this we can also understand that Sita's essential beauty is that she is associated with the Personality of Godhead.

Unable to forcibly have his lust satisfied, Ravana gave Sita a tour of opulent Lanka. He showed her the swans and ponds, and his harem. He showed her how thousands of mighty Rakshasas awaited his word. And he described Rama Chandra as a weak outcaste who would never be able to come to Lanka. He asked Sita to rule over Lanka, and he would become her slave. Though she was weighted down with sorrow and deeply absorbed in anxious thoughts, Sita seared Ravana by telling him that for this reckless outrage he would be destroyed by Rama and Lakshman.

In the face of his lion-like ferocity, she told him, "How can the consort of a swan, one who sports with her mate amidst lotuses, favor with her glance a water crow, who is straying amongst weeds and bushes? This body is now useless to me. You may chain it or destroy it. I shall not preserve it any more, nor will I ever bear the stigma of unchastity. I am the devoted wife of Rama, and you will never be able to touch me."

Ravana could only threaten Sita that if after twelve months she did not favorably turn to him, he would cut her into pieces and have his cooks serve her to him for a feast.

ALLIANCE WITH THE MONKEYS

In the absence of Sita, Rama Chandra was plunged into unalloyed grief. He was crazed, and His understanding appeared clouded. He was going through the forest asking the flowers and trees if they had seen His love. He feared she had been eaten by the Rakshasas. He and Lakshman searched everywhere. Rama questioned the sun: "Where has My darling gone?" He asked the wind if she were dead or alive or stolen, or had he seen her on any path?

Lakshman attempted to draw off Rama Chandra's despair by sensible words, but he was paid no attention. Finally the brothers found signs of Sita, pieces of clothing torn while resisting Ravana, and ornaments which had fallen from her as she rose up in his chariot. They also found the bloodied dying body of Jatayu, the ancient King of Birds, who had made a valiant attempt to stop Ravana's flight. Frothing in his last blood, Jatayu informed Rama Chandra that it was Ravana, the King of the Rakshasas, who had taken Sita. The brothers got further information that they could obtain the help needed to find Ravana's kingdom by making alliance with Sugriva, the King of the Vanaras, a monkey race who lived in the Pampas region of rivers and lakes.

This chief of the monkeys, Sugriva, beholding Rama Chandra and Lakshman within his province, was at once fearful. The Vanaras were taking refuge from their enemy Vali, who was the chief's brother, and Sugriva thought that Rama and Lakshman had come to do some harm, as they appeared so formidable with their weapons. The monkeys ranged from peak to peak, and joined their leader for a conference on what to do about the two mighty young men who were walking amongst the trees and lakes. The chief counsellor to the King, named Hanuman, assured Sugriva that their enemy Vali had no access to the Pampa region. Therefore, why should they fear these two godlike warriors?

Hanuman approached Rama and Lakshman on behalf of the king, and with eloquent words invited them to meet with the monkey chieftain. Rama was at once delighted with the eloquent speech and appearance of Hanuman, and a meeting was arranged. Seated on giant Sala leaves, Rama, Hanuman, Lakshman and Sugriva spoke out their hearts and concluded a pact of honorable friendship.

Sugriva narrated how he had become confined to this region of the Pampas in fear of his life, having been deprived of his kingdom by his brother Vali. Rama Chandra acknowledged that the expression of friendship is good service, and He agreed to kill Vali, who had also abducted the wife of Sugriva. Rama accepted the hand of Sugriva in embrace, and the monkey chief promised to aid Rama in His search for Sita by employing his vast, worldwide army of Vanaras.

Sugriva, however, had some doubts that Rama could actually subdue Vali. In order to assure him, Rama Chandra shot one arrow which traversed through seven palm trees, a rock, through the innermost region of the Earth and in a minute returned to Rama Chandra's quiver! He then set out, and soon met Vali, and slew him.

After some delay, while Sugriva tasted the sensual pleasures of his regained kingdom, he mobilized his forces and sent them out to all quarters in search of

Lanka, where Sita was imprisoned. But after months of futile searching, the armies began to lose hope. Some returned, and some dispersed in foreign lands. It was Hanuman alone who received information that the Kingdom of Lanka was an island far across the Indian ocean.

Hanuman is eulogized by all sages and scholars of the Vedic Science of God, for Hanuman is the ideal servitor. He simply wanted to carry out the order of Rama Chandra effectively. His career in finding Sita and battling the Rakshasas on behalf of Rama Chandra sets the highest spiritual standard, surpassing all mechanical yogic practitioners and speculative philosophers and scholars in search of the Absolute Truth.

It is clearly stated in the Teachings of Lord Chaitanya, by A.C. Bhaktivedanta Swami, that at the last stage the highest spiritual perfection is favorable service unto the Personality of Godhead. The exact example of Hanuman is not to be imitated, but his service attitude is to be followed. That is, each of us has some capacity. Hanuman had the capacity of enormous physical strength and agility. He used every ounce of that strength, not in pursuit of sense gratification or for conquering some land or women, but in humble devotional service to the Lord of the Senses, Whom he worshipped exclusively as Lord Rama Chandra. We should do likewise.

There cannot be any exaggeration in praising the stature and exploits of this formidable monkey warrior. He is not great because he was wonderfully powerful, but because he used all his strength–even his anger–in discharging service unto the Personality of Godhead in the matter of vanquishing Ravana.

Hanuman resolved to travel through the air in search of Janaki. He was the son of the wind god, Vayu, and thus had the facility for flight. Passage across the ocean is arduous, even for one who can fly like the wind, but Hanuman made it in one leap. His monkey brothers had gathered to watch him off. With a great contraction of strength, Hanuman stood at the edge of the sea and grasped a mountain in his arms. He held his breath and tightened all his limbs. He then spoke these words to his brothers: "I shall reach Lanka with the velocity of the wind, just like an arrow shot by Rama, and if I do not find Janaki there I shall at the same speed go to the region of the gods. And if I do not meet with success even there, then I shall uproot Lanka itself and bring Ravana here in bondage."

With these words he sprang up with ease. Like Garuda, the Eagle of Vishnu, Hanuman flew over the water, raising great waves by his speed, and exposing the aquatics below, who fled in fear. At times Rakshasas rose from the sea for his destruction, but he was not deterred in his mission. Sri Valmiki says that when Hanuman landed in Lanka and went over the city wall, it appeared as if he had planted his left foot on the crown of Ravana.

The perfection of Hanuman in action is open to anyone who will use to the full his own personal capacities in serving the Lord. There is a nice story that occurred at the time Rama Chandra and the monkeys were building a bridge across the ocean to reach Lanka. Hanuman and the other Vanaras were hefting huge boulders and throwing them into the sea. In the course of such tremendous labor, Hanuman spied an insignificant spider, who appeared to be brushing some specks of dust into the water with its back legs. "What are you doing, worthless?" Hanuman asked of the spider. "I am helping Rama Chandra build His bridge," the spider replied.

Hanuman was about to move the spider out of the way of his own serious work, when Rama Chandra interposed, saying, "What are you doing, Hanuman? This spider is worth as much as you are by doing his utmost for Me."

The gist of this is that the topmost position of loving service unto God is made manifest by directly applying whatever you have in the way of words, thoughts and energy. And that will be accepted by the Lord as first class devotion.

HANUMAN IN LANKA

Hanuman was delighted to observe the City of Lanka. For protection, he reduced himself to the size of a cat, and then proceeded to walk into the city, taking careful note of how everything was situated. As a servitor, he was very concerned at every moment, lest he be caught and ruin the project. Hanuman reflected that, "Emissaries proud of their education or intelligence sometimes become the cause of failure." The taking of the city of Lanka and the vanquishing of Ravana appeared to be nearing success, but it could be marred by such an agent as himself.

"If I lose my life," thought Hanuman, while walking down the populated way amidst the nightlife of Lanka, "great obstacles will crop up for the fulfillment of my Master's object."

Still no more than the size of a cat, he walked along the roof of a seven-storied building and saw at a short distance the palace of Ravana, surrounded by a glittering wall. The palace was guarded by armed Rakshasas, whom Valmiki describes as "never shrinking from anything on account of moral principles." Treading past noisy drinking parties and quiet gatherings, past big mansions with spacious halls, Hanuman gained access at last to the inner chamber of Ravana.

The time was past midnight, and the monkey warrior observed a virtual sea of beautiful women, sleeping under the influence of drink. Hanuman was looking for the one woman described to him as Sita, and there was no question of his being moved by a harem full of disheveled beauties. Hanuman's agitation was, rather, that time was passing, and he had not yet found Sita. In the center of the chamber, on a crystal dais, he saw an elaborately decorated bedstead, and upon the bed lay Lord Ravana himself. Ravana was spread out in intoxication, "like an elephant in sleep." Lying like that, his body smeared with red sandal, and wearing bright cloth, he presented the perfect spectacle of a sensualist in royal power.

But where was Sita?

Hanuman paced up and down the city wall. He began to think that his leap across the ocean had been in vain. This is the frustration of the transcendental servant. He does not see all indifferently as One, as the impersonalist philosophers would have it. When engaged in the transcendental service of the Lord, any obstacle unfavorable to the discharge of that service is a source of frustration and even anger, until it is removed. Hanuman was proceeding with the work of Rama Chandra. He was prepared to go to any lengths, and in Hanuman's case the wish of his heart was not mere bravado. He had been blessed with the most intense individual yearning for actual service of the Lord. Actually, there is no impediment in serving the Lord, and once we decide that we belong to God we cannot be stopped from serving Him. We can always chant His Holy Name. God, being omnipotent, is truly in no need of our services, but He is most pleased by the individual who makes an effort on His behalf.

Finally the noble monkey found Sita in the heart of the dense Asoka forest, seated under a tree. Wracked with grief, but still radiantly beautiful, with tears flowing down her face, she is described as "Lakshmi without the Lotus." She was seated on the ground like an ascetic, wane, and sad for the absence of Rama Chandra. She was undergoing a continual, harrowing nightmare of separation from Rama. Hideous Rakshasa monsters of misshapen form danced in a ring around her, telling her rumor s of Rama's weakness and death.

Hanuman's first step was to communicate with Sita and assure her. He was certain this was her because of the information he had received about her appearance. He had to approach her, gain her confidence that he was not another Rakshasa, and convey to her that Rama and the Vanaras would soon be on their way to her rescue, so that she must not give up her life.

Hanuman began to speak to her from his place, concealed within the branches of the tree. Janaki was delighted to hear him. She had some doubt, but Hanuman was very sweet of speech, assuming a large form, reddish and clothed in white. And he recited to her the history of King Dasarath and Rama Chandra and Lakshman and Sita.

Listening to this being who so cheerfully pronounced the Name of Rama, Sita began to shake off her ascetic firmness. She was becoming convinced that she was beholding Rama Chandra's messenger, and that was as good as seeing Rama Himself! She thought for a time that Hanuman might be another mirage, but the monkey told her things too treasured to be Rakshasa deceit. Rama Chandra had given to him the utmost confidence.

With folded palms, Hanuman approached Sita and gave her a ring from Rama. In blissful exchange, Sita offered that Hanuman should ask Rama, "Do you remember the time We were wandering in the Dananka Forest and a crow was disturbing me, and You shot him with an arrow?" Sita then received all of Hanuman's speech like honey. When, however, he related Rama Chandra's grief at her separation, she received it like poison. Assuring her that she would soon be re-united with Lord Rama, Hanuman finally left. In parting, Sita told him that she could only live one more month like this, and then she would give up her life.

Before heading back with his message, Hanuman decided to gauge the enemy's power. He understood that he had been given no direct order to do this, but he reflected in his mind that there is no guilt if the servant, while accomplishing the main objective, does something else in addition. Thereupon, in a miraculous display of prowess, Hanuman broke down all of the trees in the Asoka forest except the one under which Sita was seated.

He then sat upon the main gate of Lanka and, uprooting a bolt, shouted out that he was Hanuman, a Vanara, and the servant of Rama Chandra! Frightened Rakshasas rushed out to see him expanding himself to gigantic size, ranging the sky, determined to fight. Hanuman single-handedly destroyed thousands of Rakshasa warriors and top military personalities, and set fire to every house in the city, declaring again and again: "None of you will survive when you make an enemy of Rama Chandra!" Then he flew back across the ocean, and landed with a great noise upon a mountain peak.

THE SIEGE OF LANKA

Without delay, the Vanaras under Sugriva mobilized, and built the miraculous bridge of stones across the ocean. In this connection, A.C. Bhaktivedanta Swami has written that, as the Supreme Lord floats countless planets in space as though they were no more than little cotton swabs, certainly He can float one bridge of stones upon an ocean.

In millions, with all military equipage, the army marched across the ocean and into Lanka under the very nose of the Lord of the Rakshasas. Even up to the last moment Ravana was oblivious to the warning that he didn't have a chance in his plan to keep Sita and oppose the wish of Rama Chandra.

In hand-to-hand combat, great heroes from both sides fought to the death day after day, with thousands of fatalities among the troops. Finally, one by one, great Rakshasa chieftains, such as Kumbhakarna, Narantaka and Indrajit, the son of Ravana, fell before the unlimited powers of heroes like Hanuman,

Lakshman, Sugriva and Rama Chandra. At the last, Rama Chandra slew Ravana with a Brahmastra released from His bow.

Valmiki tells of the origin of this weapon: It was handed down by Lord Brahma, and passed from sage to sage. The Brahmastra was smeared with fat and blood, and smoked like doomsday fire. It was hard and deep sounding, and when shot by Rama Chandra it cleft Ravana's heart in two, depriving him of life.

THE TRIAL OF SITA

Immediately after the victory, with Lanka under the control of Rama's party, Sita was brought before Him for a joyful reunion. Before the thousands of people gathered, however, Rama Chandra said that He could not take her back because she had lived with Ravana in his house, and had been touched by him. Janaki was mortally ashamed of her own existence, hearing Lord Rama make such an accusation before the multitude. Speaking in defense of her chastity, Sita asked Lakshman to prepare a funeral pyre. As the flames leaped up to a great height, she approached the pyre and bowed down, praying to the fire god, Agni, that if she was actually devoted to Rama the fire might protect her. Then she leaped into the blaze.

At once, Lord Brahma himself, foremost of all the demigods, descended from the sky and demanded of Rama, "Why have You done this to Sita?" And Brahma addressed Rama Chandra as Vishnu Himself, the Omnipresent and Omniscient, Who had descended for the destruction of Ravana.

Agni then appeared from the fire carrying Sita, who was completely unharmed, even her garland and dress being unburnt due to her purity. And thus all those present could be satisfied that Sita had retained her sanctity even though long in subjection to Ravana.

Years later, however, after the happy end of the ordeal, when Rama Chandra was ruling over a joyous Ayodha, He chose to banish His wife again. His subjects had begun speaking against Sita, of the time she had spent with Ravana. And so Rama sent her away in order to prove Himself an ideal king, Who wanted to make His subjects always happy.

Lord Rama Chandra's whole program was based on the concept of the ideal king, and it is in that light that we can best understand Him. As the perfect ruler, Rama Chandra followed the principles of morality and ethics just as they should be followed by the perfect human king or ruler. Rama Chandra submitted Himself to those principles, though He was actually the Supreme Personality of Godhead, and not subject to any moral code. And in this instance He showed that a good leader must think only of the welfare of his people, setting aside his entire life for that purpose, with no private pleasures withheld.

A.C. Bhaktivedanta Swami explains the mood of the Lord in His Appearance as Rama Chandra thusly: "The comparative studies on the life of Krishna and Rama Chandra are very intricate, but the basic principle is that Rama Chandra appeared as an ideal king, and Krishna appeared as the Supreme Personality of Godhead, although there is actually no difference between the Two. A similar example is that of Lord Chaitanya. He appeared as a devotee and not as the Supreme Personality of Godhead, although He is Krishna Himself. So we should accept the Lord's mood in His particular Appearance, and we should worship Him in that mood. Our service should be compatible with the attitude of the Lord. Therefore, in the Shastras, there are specific injunctions, such as: To worship Lord Chaitanya, the method is chanting Hare Krishna."

Sri Valmiki declares that he who always listens to this epic becomes absolved from sins. He who listens with due respect meets with no obstacles in life. He will live happily with his near and dear ones, and get his desired boons from Rama Chandra, the eternal Vishnu, the Personality of Godhead.

Adventures of the Boar Incarnation

November/December, 1969

I: INTRODUCTION

There is a story in the Vedic scriptures of a time when the great sage Narada went to visit the Supreme Lord Narayan (Krishna) in the Spiritual Kingdom of Vaikuntha. Narada was travelling on the earth at the time for the purpose of spreading the Hare Krishna Mantra, and before leaving, he met a brahmin on the road. The brahmin learned that Narada was going to see Lord Narayan, so he requested that Narada find out his spiritual status: how long, how many more births would he have to undergo before he would be liberated from material existence? Narada agreed to inquire about the brahmin's position. Further on he was hailed by a cobbler who was tending his craft while sitting under a large tree by the roadside. The cobbler paid his respects to Narada and asked the great sage to please find out how many births more he would have to spend in the miseries of repeated birth and death before he would attain final liberation. In the Vaikuntha planet, in the presence of the Supreme Lord, Narada reported his missionary activities to Narayan and received all the necessary information for carrying on his loving devotional service. He then inquired about the two conditioned souls he had met on the earth planet. When the Lord was asked about the brahmin He said, "Oh he will have to spend many, many more lifetimes before his liberation." Narada noted the reply, and then asked about the cobbler. On hearing mention of that cobbler, the Lord smiled, "Please tell him that he will be liberated in this very lifetime!" Then Narayan added, "And when you tell them, if they ask what I was doing, please tell them I was threading an elephant through the eye of a needle."

When Narada approached the brahmin on the earth planet the brahmin inquired what the Lord had said. Narada told him, and the brahmin became morosely silent. This brahmin was a rigid practitioner of the scriptural regulations; he took three baths a day and never failed to perform the proper rituals, so he was surprised to hear that he had a long way before being liberated. He then asked what the Lord was doing. When Narada told him that Lord Narayan was threading an elephant through the eye of a needle, the brahmin became outraged with disbelief: "What? Go away! You haven't been to see Narayan. This is just some nonsense you are concocting!" And the brahmin turned away from Narada. Narada next approached the cobbler. On seeing Narada Muni, the man jumped up from his place under the tree and ran to the devotee-sage: "You have just seen the Lord. So tell me when I am to be liberated." Narada was pleased to tell the cobbler that he would be liberated in this very lifetime. The cobbler turned ecstatic and began jumping for joy. Very soon he would be with the Lord! He then asked Narada what Lord Narayan was doing. Narada replied, "The Lord was threading an elephant through the eye of a needle." The cobbler became still more ecstatic. "Ah, how great my Lord is!" he exclaimed. Narada asked him further, "How is it you have such faith that you can believe the Lord was doing such an impossible thing?" The cobbler answered unflinchingly, "Impossible? Just see this large, spacious tree we are sitting under. Do you know that such a big spreading tree came out of a seed no bigger than a pin? So if the Lord can put such a big tree into a tiny seed, why can't He thread one elephant through a needle's eye?"

The purport is clear. The cobbler had more than a blind faith in God. He had understanding that God means Param Brahman, the Greatest, and the Greatest means that He can do anything. So many impersonalists will admit that God means the unlimited, the infinite, but as soon as they hear that the Lord descends as Avatara and acts in a way indicative of His unlimited potency, they take it differently. They say it is a myth or allegory, or they criticize. The mental speculator tries to put God within the restrictions of the understanding of the tiny human brain. This is his error. Rather, the Vedic process for understanding the Absolute Truth is to receive it as it is. The Personality of Godhead, the Absolute Truth, is inconceivable, therefore we cannot measure Him. But we can hear from authorized sources of His Activities. Everyone should be interested in this transcendental hearing, because everyone is intimately connected as part of the One Supreme Lord. By listening, our heart can become cleansed and we can have revealed to us the practical, loving intent of the Lord in His multi-incarnations. If we can understand His Pastimes, all our problems will be solved. By understanding Krishna's Appearance in the world, we reach the perfection of life by leaving this temporary world of ignorance and misery and going back to Home, back to Godhead. That is the version of the Bhagavad Gita.

It is in this spirit that the great sages and transcendental scholars of the Vedic literature request we listen to the Activities of the incarnation of the Lord as Boar, or the Baraha Avatara.

II: THE HOLY BOAR RESCUES PLANET EARTH

At a time far remote from present history, in the Swetabaraha millennium, just at the dawn of the creation of the material world, Lord Brahma was approached by the presiding Manu. The Manu asked Brahma to do something about the earth planet, which had fallen to the bottom of the Garbhodak ocean which fills half of the universe. Lord Brahma, being the chief administrator of the affairs of the material universe, is the direct representative of Krishna. Brahma was presented by Manu with this calamity: the earth had fallen to a filthy place and had to be rescued. Lord Brahma gave it his full attention and meditated as follows: "While I was engaged in the matter of creation, the earth was inundated by deluge and went down into the depths of the ocean. What can we, who are engaged in this creation, do? Better let the Almighty Lord direct us." The chief entity, Brahma, was perplexed, but not discouraged. With full faith in Krishna, his thinking suddenly bore the solution of his duty, by the Grace of the Supreme Personality of Godhead. This is all narrated in the spotless Vedic literature, the Srimad Bhagavatam, Third Canto: "All of a sudden, while Brahma was engaged in thinking, a small form of a Boar came out of his nostril, and the measurement of the creature was not more than the upper portion of the thumb. While Brahma was observing Him, the Boar-like form became situated in the sky in a wonderful manifestation, grown suddenly into a gigantic form like a great elephant. Brahma, along with great brahmins like Marichi, began to argue as to what it was. Brahma exclaimed: "Is this some extraordinary entity come in the pretense of a boar? It is very wonderful." As he was the supermost person in the universe, Lord Brahma could guess that the wonderful Appearance of the Boar was an Avatar of Vishnu, the Supreme Personality of Godhead. Such a form was never before experienced. The symptoms of the incarnation of Godhead are so uncommon that even Brahma became perturbed. While these sages and demigods were deliberating, the Lord as Boar resounded a tremendous sound which echoed in all directions.

It is said that the sound of the Voice of Baraha was gorgeous to the devotees of the upper planets, but to the demoniac, who also heard it, it was the most dangerous sound, the sound of doom to their rebellion. Lord Vishnu is declared by all the Vedic literature as transcendental. The Lord as Boar is also the Supreme Lord, or the Vedas incarnate. Those elevated, pious intellectual beings on upper material planets (such as Siddha Loka and Brahma Loka) replied to the Lord's Voice by praying to Him with Vedic hymns. The earth planet was submerged in the mire on the bottom of the ocean, but on hearing the sound of the Lord as Baraha, the devotees knew that He was present for the earth's deliverance. They understood that Vishnu was appearing as a Boar because a boar can get something out of a filthy place. The Bhagavatam describes the Voice of the Boar and the chanting of the devotees as enacted on a cosmic scale. They reciprocated vibrations of love back and forth through the regions of all outer space. And it is stated that of all the Vedic hymns vibrated in that concert between the Supreme and His loving servants, the most important was the Brihanaradiya Purana verse, Hare Krishna Hare Krishna Krishna Krishna Hare Hare Hare Rama Hare Rama Rama Rama Hare Hare.

Srimad Bhagavatam relates: "He resounded again in reply to the Vedic prayers by the great devotees. The Lord is the Object of the Vedic prayers, and thus He understood that the devotees' prayers were meant for Him." As the mantras were being properly recited, the Lord was pleased. Before entering the water to rescue the earthly planet, the Lord Boar flew down from the sky, slashing with His Tail and quivering His hard Hairs. His very Glance was luminous, and He swatted the clouds in the sky with His Hoofs and His glittering white Tusks. Although the body of a boar is material and contaminated, that is not the case with the Boar Form of the Lord. Nor is it possible, of course, for an earthly boar to assume a gigantic form and perform so many wondrous activities. Baraha is the One Lord Who is without a second Who comes for Pastime functions. As stated in the Fourth Chapter of Bhagavad Gita, the Lord is One, and yet He is appearing in multi-incarnations. The example is given that He is like the Vaidurya stone which changes colors but is one. These things are understood by submissive hearing and inquiry and by devotional service to the One Lord. Bhagavad Gita clearly states that whoever understands how the Lord appears and disappears on the material scene is at once liberated. This is the proper application of the Sanskrit expression, "Tatvamasi," "You are that too." In his purports to the Gita, A.C. Bhaktivedanta Swami writes: "Anyone who understands Lord Krishna to be the Supreme or who says unto the Lord, 'You are the same Supreme Brahman, the Personality of Godhead,' is certainly liberated instantly, and consequently his entrance into the transcendental association of the Lord is guaranteed." When we speak of Krishna, it is to be understood that Krishna includes all the Avataras. Baraha is mentioned in the list of incarnations in the Srimad Bhagavatam: "The Supreme Enjoyer of all sacrifices accepted the Boar Incarnation for the welfare of the earth. He lifted it from the nether regions of the universe." (S.B., 1/3/7)

In any of His eternal Forms, Krishna is God. This is to be understood. When He is playing as Child Krishna on the lap of His mother, Yasoda, He is God; when He appears as the half-lion half-man Form of Nrishinghadeva He is God; and as Baraha, in the Form of a Boar, He is the same transcendental Supreme

Lord. Just as wood is wood, fire is fire, so by the law of designation God is God. He is always God in any Form He takes; and these Forms are all described in the authoritative Vedic scriptures. The materialistic mentality not only thinks that the form of a boar cannot be spiritual or transcendental, but he thinks that the human form is always material. According to the Bhagavad Gita, this inability to accept Krishna as He presents Himself, or is presented by a pure representative, is a disease. A.C. Bhaktivedanta Swami cites this in his purport of the 10th verse of the Fourth Chapter of Bhagavad Gita: "It is very difficult for a person who is too materially affected to understand the Personal nature of the Supreme Absolute Truth. Generally, people who are attached to the bodily concept of life are so absorbed in materialism that it is almost impossible for them to understand how the Supreme can be a Person. Such materialists cannot imagine that there is a transcendental Body which is non-perishable, full of knowledge and eternally blissful. In the materialistic concept, the body is perishable, full of ignorance and completely miserable. Therefore people in general keep this same bodily idea in mind when they are informed of the Personal Form of the Lord. For such materialists, the Form of the gigantic material manifestation is supreme; therefore they imagine that the Supreme is impersonal." Since we are now hearing or reading of Lord Baraha, let us spend the time for the highest benefit and thus take shelter of Srila Vyasadeva, the author of the Vedic Shastra; in this way we can best receive the Activities of the incarnation of Boar, as they are told.

"Lord Boar penetrated the water with His Hoof, which was sharp like arrows, and found out the limitation of the ocean, although it was unlimited. He saw the earth lying as it was in the beginning of creation, as the resting place for all living beings, and He Personally lifted it."

Thereupon Lord Boar killed the demon within the water, just as a lion kills an elephant.

According to the Vedic philosopher-devotee, Jiva Goswami, the topics told of Baraha in the Third Canto of Bhagavatam are of different millenniums. The topics of Baraha's rescue of the earth from the mire is of the Swetabaraha millennium, and the topics of His killing the demon Hiranakya are of the later Caksus millennium in His second Appearance as Boar. In one incarnation His bodily hue is described as whitish, and in the other it is reddish. In either case, just by His glancing over His devotees, all of them felt transcendental happiness. The Body of the Lord is always transcendental in all cases. His assumption of the Form of Boar is only His Pastime. Just as when Krishna played the part of a human being, He was the perfect human being, so He assumed the Form of a Boar and found the earth by smelling, like a perfect boar, and he rescued it by lifting it up on His tusks. Yet His Body is the Vedas Personified.

III: THE FIGHT WITH HIRANAKYA

As the Boar was coming out of the water, He was attacked by the powerful demon, Hiranakya, who had been traveling through all the three worlds and planetary systems, conquering whomever he met, out of bellicose madness. Hiranakya was the twin-brother of the demon Hiranya Kashipu. The pair were born into this world specifically to take up the role of personal combatants or enemies of the Supreme Lord in His respective incarnations of Lord Baraha and Lord Nrishingha, the half-lion half-man Avatara of the Satya Yuga. As the Reservoir of all desires, the Lord also has a fighting spirit, from which comes all fighting spirit as found in the material world. For instance, the natural fighting spirit sometimes displayed by young boys wrestling is but a perverted reflection of this original desire of the Lord. The fighting of the Supreme Lord, however, doesn't result in the destruction of the enemy, but works for his liberation. Sometimes people are suspicious because Lord Krishna taught His transcendental philosophy on the battlefield of Kurukshetra. But, as stated by the devotee Bhismadeva, all those who took part in the Battle of Kurukshetra and were killed while seeing the Form of the Personality of Godhead, Krishna, gained their eternal liberation. Even being kicked by Krishna is eternally auspicious.

When the demon brothers appeared, born from the womb of Diti, the very pores of the earth and the sky and the animals and plant kingdoms virtually cried out with omens of evil portent.

When the Supreme Lord fights, He does not fight with an ordinary mortal or nondevotee. Rather, He exchanges this rasa only with His devotees. By the Grace of the complete revelation of Vyasdeva, the compiler of the Bhagavatam, we are able to understand that Lord Baraha picked His own servant, a doorman of the palace in the spiritual planet, Vaikuntha; and this servant descended in the form of Hiranakya and took on the demoniac life for the purpose of battling with the Lord in hand to hand combat.

Hiranakya was broad and strong, golden-haired and covered with ornaments. He is described as being so tall and big that he blocked the view of the sky. And his prowess was not that of an ordinary man because in fighting he appeared almost on an equal level with the Lord. But his mentality was all demoniac: he travelled for the purpose of fighting with all peace-loving creatures. Wherever he could find anyone with a fighting reputation he would challenge him to fight. He thus made the demigod Indra flee before him, and he challenged Varuna the god of the water. Varuna advised Hiranakya that if he were really so desirous of battle he ought to fight with Lord Vishnu, and he told the demon that at the present moment the Lord had taken the Form of a Boar, and he told him where he could go to meet Him.

The demon came upon the all-powerful Personality of Godhead in His incarnation as Boar, as the Lord was bearing the earth upwards on the end of His tusk. The Bhagavatam says that "the reddish Eyes and Hoofs of the amphibious beast robbed the demon of his splendor."

"Your power is only mystic!" the infatuated demon roared to the Supreme Lord. "Today I shall enliven my kinsmen by killing you, oh fool." This is the demoniac mentality. The Lord is invisible to the eyes of the common man, but His energies are everywhere, acting in various ways. The demons think that God is actually hiding Himself and working by mystic power, and if he can find Him out then he can kill Him. The demoniac are anxiously trying to kill God by words and "philosophy." The idea underlying this is that if one is materially powerful enough, he can kill God by weapons. Actually, the demoniac cannot understand at all how God is working. They can neither kill Him nor touch Him. He can be present everywhere and still remain at His eternal Abode.

The demon continued hurling insults, but the Lord Boar patiently bore them while He carried the earth to safety on His tusks. "When You are smashed by my mace," the demon challenged," then the sages and devotees who offer You devotional service will cease to exist." It is well-known by everyone that the demons do not like the fact that the devotees worship the Lord in the prescribed ways recommended in the scriptures.

The Lord Boar was pained by the abusive words of the demon, but He carefully placed the earth on the water of the universe and enabled it to float by its own power. Then He turned to the business of fighting the demon who was delivering furious insults. The Lord is no myth, but is actually present in multi-incarnations. As He is the Source of all sentiency and feeling, He has feeling Himself, and He is therefore never pleased by insults. According to A.C. Bhaktivedanta Swami. "God is as sentient as we are, and He is satisfied by our prayer and dissatisfied with our harsh words against Him." In order to give protection to His devotee, He is always ready to tolerate all kinds of insults by the atheists. Therefore He patiently placed the earth in a safe place and prepared to dispatch the demon. The Lord said to Hiranakya: "We are creatures of the jungle, and we are searching after dogs like you. One who is freed from the entanglement of death does not fear the insults of the kind in which you are indulging because you are bound by the laws of death." Baraha knew that Hiranakya's position was a false one. The demon doesn't believe in God; he thinks that he can defy the material laws and be freed of birth and death. No one, however, has ever been able to achieve freedom from death, not by any advancement of science nor by mental speculation, Yogic power or sheer brawn, as possessed by Hiranakya. "Give up your nonsensical talking," Lord Baraha went on. "You are supposed to be the commander of many soldiers, so now you can take prompt steps to overthrow us." Hiranakya became so angry and agitated that he began to tremble "like a challenged cobra." The Lord had asked him to fulfill his loud promises to kill Him.

Hiranakya then sprang upon Baraha and dealt Him a blow with his powerful mace. The Lord dodged that blow by moving aside a little. The Personality of Godhead then exhibited His anger and rushed to meet the demon who was hissing and shaking with rage and holding his mace to deliver another blow. The Lord then struck at Hiranakya, but the expert demon protected himself with a maneuver of his mace. In this way, they began to strike at each other with their huge maces, each seeking his own victory.

Lord Brahma, accompanied by his followers and other demigods, came to see the terrible fight for the sake of the world. The Lord is described by the demigods as "Yajna," or "the Body full of worshipful offerings." As learned devotees, the demigods never consider the Lord to have the body of an ordinary boar. He can assume any Form, and He has all such Forms eternally. All forms actually emanate from the Original Form of Krishna, as declared in the Srimad Bhagavatam. So this Boar Form is always Vishnu, transcendental. Lord Brahma addressed Him thus: "This demon has proved to be a constant pinprick to demigods, brahmins, cows and innocent persons. He has attained a boon from me and has turned to be a demon and is always wandering over the earth looking for a fight. My dear Lord, there is no need of playing with this serpentine demon who is very skilled in cunning tricks and arrogant and most wicked. Kindly kill him. The dark evening is fast approaching." It is said that upon hearing the words of Brahma the creator, words which were free from all sinful purposes and were as sweet as nectar, the Lord heartily laughed and "accepted his prayer with a glance ladened with love." The prayer of Brahma was pure, whereas Hiranakya had prayed and performed austerities in order to derive power in the form of a boon from Brahma. It is said in the Bhagavad Gita that those who undergo severe penances and austerities not mentioned in the scriptures, out of pride, ego, lust and attachment, do such things impelled by passion.

The Lord then aimed His mace at the chin of His enemy who was stalking in front of Him. But He was instead struck by the demon's mace, and His mace slipped from His Hand. It is described that the demigods became alarmed at this. Hiranakya, however, respecting the law of combat, did not strike an unarmed foe. The Lord's anger was kindled by this, and He invoked His Sudarshan discus, which is the personal ultimate weapon used by the Personality of Godhead. As the discus revolved in His Hand, the demon sprang into the air, saying, "You are slain!" and threw His mace. The Lord knocked it down with His left Foot. The demon picked up his mace and aimed it again. The Lord stood firm and caught the flying mace and offered it back to the demon to try again. This humiliated the demon, and he took a trident and hurled it furiously. The Lord, however, tore it to pieces with His Sudarshan, which has a sharp-edged rim. Hiranakya then struck the Lord with his hard fists on His Chest. The Bhagavatam says that this was felt by the Lord as an elephant feels the striking of a wreath of flowers. In other words, the Lord desired the fighting in order to enjoy transcendental bliss. The demon then began to conjure tricks on a full scale, as was in his power. The skies were filled with winds and stones were discharged from caves. Puss, hair and blood rained from the skies. At this, Lord Baraha at last discharged His Sudarshan. At the moment the weapon left His Hand, a shudder ran through the heart of Diti, mother of Hiranakya, and her breast ran with blood. When the demon saw that his whole magic show was dispersed by the Presence of the Personality of Godhead, he tried to embrace Him with his arms in order to crush Him. But to his amazement he found that the Lord had again eluded him. Finally, the Lord slapped him at the base of the ear, and though struck indifferently, Hiranakya's eyeballs bulged out of their sockets, his body wheeled, and he fell down like a gigantic tree uprooted by the wind, his arms, limbs and head broken and scattered.

It is described that when the demigods approached the battle area, they saw the so-called corpse of the demon Hiranakya was still rosey-hued, as if full of life. Then it was noticed that the demon's body was still touching Lord Baraha's Body, and therefore the Soul of souls was giving him life. Lord Brahma remarked, "Oh what blessed death is here!" The Supreme Personality of Godhead, Who grants liberation in any incarnation, is so inconceivably great that His kick brings the greatest benefit to the "victim." Because He is inconceivably great, we are warned against thinking that we understand what it is to be a devotee of the Lord, or how it feels to be a friend of Krishna, or to act as His parent when He is partaking of His Childhood Pastimes. And certainly, no one should pretend to grasp the understanding of what it is to exchange loving affairs with the Lord. Most persons actually have no concept of God, or at most they may have heard that "God is great." Yet the mystery of the Pastimes of the Chief of all persons is open to everyone who will hear His Pastimes as presented in the Srimad Bhagavatam and related intact by His pure representatives.

The Lifter of Govardhana Hill

May/June, 1973

There are many religious scriptures teaching man about his eternal relationship with God, but the oldest among them are the Vedic literatures, which were compiled 5,000 years ago in Sanskrit. The special standard of the Vedic literatures is that while they contain all that is contained in other scriptures, the reader will also find in them information that is not to be found elsewhere. In the cream of these literatures, called the *Śrīmad-Bhāgavatam* (which has been presented in English by His Divine Grace A.C. Bhaktivedanta Swami Prabhupāda as *Kṛṣṇa, the Supreme Personality of Godhead*), we find the incident of Kṛṣṇa's lifting the Govardhana Hill.

Kṛṣṇa, the Supreme Lord, descended to earth 5,000 years ago and displayed childhood pastimes as the son of Nanda Mahārāja and mother Yaśodā in the cowherd village of Vṛndāvana, India. When He was only six years old He one day came upon His father and other elders of the community who were preparing a religious sacrifice in honor of the demigod Indra. Kṛṣṇa's whole purpose in descending to this material world was to teach everyone to worship the Personality of Godhead exclusively and thus be saved from all dangers and the reactions to all past sinful activities. Kṛṣṇa, therefore, intending to stop the sacrifice to the demigod, approached His father very politely and meekly said, "My dear father, what is this arrangement going on for a great sacrifice? What is the result, and for whom is it meant? Do you know what results to expect from this sacrifice?"

At first Nanda Mahārāja did not answer his son, thinking that He could not understand the intricacies of sacrifice; but when Kṛṣṇa persisted in His plea, Nanda replied that they were performing the sacrifice because it was traditional. This shows that Nanda Māhāraja was not a whimsical person, for any genuine spiritual practice must have the sanction of previous authorities who have passed down spiritual knowledge. In the case of the Indra sacrifice, however, the object of worship was a demigod, and therefore Kṛṣṇa suggested that the sacrifice be stopped. He had two reasons for doing so. One was that He wanted to discourage demigod worship because its object is material benefit, which is always temporary. Only a less intelligent person engages himself in religion for material benefit. The other reason is that even if one wants material things, he should approach the Supreme Personality of Godhead directly. Kṛṣṇa Himself is the Supreme Personality of Godhead, and He asks for surrender and devotional service unto Him. According to all learned spiritual masters, our rightful position is to serve Him.

Nanda Māhāraja offered objections to Kṛṣṇa's request, and there then followed a logical debate between Kṛṣṇa and His pure devotee Nanda Māhāraja. Our ISKCON artist has depicted Nanda Māhāraja gesturing in this debate while his transcendental son listens and prepares to put forward His own argument. These two principal figures are surrounded by cowherd men, boys and cows, and in the background is Govardhana Hill.

Child Kṛṣṇa had still another intention in stopping the Indra sacrifice, and that was to punish the demigod Indra, whom Kṛṣṇa knew was very puffed up with excessive pride. One may superficially think that a discussion about whether to worship a demigod is not relevant to modern times because no one worships or believes in demigods any longer. But this is not a fact. A demigod is a person who has power and influence far greater than that of an ordinary human. Generally, "demigod" refers to one of the inhabitants of higher material planets who have been entrusted by the Supreme Lord to manage the administrative affairs of the universe. For example, Indra is the demigod in charge of rain, Vivasvān is the demigod of the sun, etc. However, in a broader sense, any influential personality may be called a demigod, and the appeasement of such "big guns" to get favors from them is a process that is still going on. One approaches a movie star, a politician or a big industrialist in hopes that he will get his particular desires fulfilled if he pleases such an important personality. During World War II, for instance, there was a man in India who was profiting greatly from sales on the black market, and considering that his success was due to the engineer of the war, Adolf Hitler, he arranged for worship of Hitler in his home. Such worship is in the modes of ignorance and passion. One never makes spiritual progress by approaching a big personality to get material benefits.

The great sage Śukadeva Gosvāmī, the original speaker to relate the incident of Kṛṣṇa and Govardhana Hill, cautioned those interested in spiritual life not to approach rich householders to beg for material necessities which can easily be gotten from nature. Śukadeva questions, "Why do you need a pillow if you have your soft arm? And if you need lodging, are the caves in the mountains stopped up? And as for food, are not the charitable trees still giving fruits?" The point is that one need depend only on the Supreme Lord, who is factually supplying all our needs, material and spiritual.

Lord Kṛṣṇa is the supreme religious teacher. Although His purpose was to teach worship of the Supreme Personality of Godhead, He at first spoke to His father as if He were an atheist. Kṛṣṇa's first point in their logical debate was that for prosperity the cowherd men did not have to worship the demigod Indra, but they had only to work diligently in their occupational duty of cow protection in their village of Vṛndāvana. Nanda Māhāraja argued back that simply to work was not enough to guarantee the result desired. For example, in spite of having the best care of a physician, sometimes a patient dies, or in spite of all the care and protection which parents give their child, the child dies or goes bad. In other words, material causes are not independent in themselves to bring about the results of activities; there has to be the sanction of the higher authority of Providence. Ultimately everything operates under the will of Kṛṣṇa, the Supreme Lord. A drowning man may be sent a rescue boat or thrown a rope, but if it is the desire of the Lord that this man die, no boat or rope can save him. The saying is, "Whomever Kṛṣṇa kills, no one can save. Whomever Kṛṣṇa saves, no one can kill."

Kṛṣṇa nullified Nanda's point in debate, however, by describing Indra to be like the head of a water department of a city government. One does not have to worship such an official privately in order to derive the benefit of water from him, for the head of the water department is duty-bound to give water to every good citizen. Therefore one simply has to tend to his own business occupation to get the facilities he needs; one need not personally worship a demigod. Kṛṣṇa argued that since the demigods cannot give good benefits to persons who have not executed their duties, the demigods are dependent on the execution of these duties.

Kṛṣṇa urged His father and the cowherd men to concentrate on the activities in their own local world of Vṛndāvana, where their duty was primarily to protect the cows. Indra, He said, was simply bound to deliver water; he even pours rain on the ocean, where no one worships him. Kṛṣṇa therefore requested His father to understand that his real relationship was with Govardhana Hill and Vṛndāvana Forest and nothing more. "My dear father," Kṛṣṇa said, "begin a sacrifice which will satisfy the local *brāhmaṇas* [the priestly order] and Govardhana Hill, and let us have nothing to do with Indra."

Influenced by Kṛṣṇa's words, Nanda Māhāraja offered a compromise. He would agree to do what Kṛṣṇa asked, but since all the paraphernalia had already been gathered for the worship of Indra, he suggested that they first perform that sacrifice and then afterward the Govardhana worship that Kṛṣṇa had suggested.

To this Kṛṣṇa replied, "My dear father, don't delay." Kṛṣṇa does not like wishy-washy compromises which fall short of exclusive devotion unto Him. Readers of the world-famous *Bhagavad-gītā* will recall that Arjuna, Kṛṣṇa's disciple on the Battlefield of Kuruksetra, also did not want to follow Kṛṣṇa's will in the beginning, and he offered compromises and delays, but Kṛṣṇa would not accept Arjuna's arguments. If we understand Kṛṣṇa rightly as the Supreme Personality of Godhead, what is the point of delaying our surrender to Him?

Nanda Mahārāja had already prepared to make an offering to the demigod for material benefit, but Kṛṣṇa said, "That doesn't matter. Take what you have, although it was intended for material gain, and use it in service to Me." This is also the philosophy of Kṛṣṇa consciousness as taught by Śrīla Bhaktisiddhānta Sarasvatī Ṭhākura, the spiritual master of Śrīla Prabhupāda. Whatever talents or capacities one possesses should simply be turned over and engaged in the service of Kṛṣṇa. Everything can be transferred to His account. This is sound philosophy. Because Kṛṣṇa is the supreme proprietor of all that be, we should rightfully engage everything in His loving service. That process will free us from bondage to suffering in this material world.

In the *Kṛṣṇa Book* it is described that all the residents of Vṛndāvana were absorbed in love of Kṛṣṇa and simply wanted to please Him. Nanda Mahārāja therefore yielded to his son's request and turned over command of the worship to Kṛṣṇa, who then began to dictate how He wanted the Govardhana sacrifice performed. This is one's rightful position; one should let Kṛṣṇa tell him exactly what to do. Lord Kṛṣṇa said, "Prepare very nice foodstuffs of all descriptions from the grains and butter collected for the sacrifice. Prepare rice, dāhl, then halavah, pakora, puri and all kinds of milk preparations like sweet rice and sweetballs and invite all the learned *brāhmaṇas* who can chant the Vedic hymns. Give nice grass to the cows. The sacrifice known as Govardhana Pūjā may immediately begin. This sacrifice will very much satisfy Me."

Because He is the Supreme Personality of Godhead, Kṛṣṇa is the only one who can rightfully speak in the imperative tone. If we think that we are God, we become offended to hear Kṛṣṇa ask for what is rightfully His. But since He is actually the Supreme, He should ask for nothing less than complete surrender and tell us, "Now do this. Now do that." This is also the position of the spiritual master, who is the servant of Kṛṣṇa. If one obeys the orders of the spiritual master, he will become free of the false ego which keeps us bound to the cycle of birth and death in the material world.

Kṛṣṇa is sometimes called Kārtamīsa, which means "the boss of the cowherd village." It is said that in the morning in such villages the Kārtamīsa is asked what he would like to eat, and whatever menu he describes becomes the fare for the whole village. That is the relationship which we should have with the Supreme Kārtamīsa, Kṛṣṇa. Whatever He desires should be our desire. If we can satisfy Him, that will make us actually happy. Everyone should do what Kṛṣṇa wants. If we will accept Kṛṣṇa's desire as supreme, we will get far more than we could ever imagine by struggling on our own in the illusion that we are apart from Kṛṣṇa. We should all work as instruments for His satisfaction.

As far as Indra was concerned, he was suffering from a delusion which is common to such powerful personalities: he thought that he was the supreme controller, forgetting that even the greatest demigod is only part and parcel of the Supreme Personality of Godhead from whom everything emanates. The Supreme Personality of Godhead, therefore, with the purpose of chastising Indra, advised the cowherd men to stop the Indra sacrifice and begin the Govardhana worship. The honest and simple cowherd men headed by Nanda Mahārāja accepted Kṛṣṇa's proposal and executed in detail everything He advised. They performed Govardhana worship and circumambulation of the hill, Lord Kṛṣṇa then declared that Govardhana worship is just as good as worship of Him. In this way He identified with the land in which He displayed His pastimes. Therefore, ever since the inauguration of Govardhana worship, people in Vṛndāvana still dress nicely and assemble near Govardhana Hill to offer worship and walk around the hill, leading their cows. In all the temples of Vṛndāvana and outside of Vṛndāvana, huge quantities of food are prepared and sumptuously distributed to the general population.

When Indra understood that the sacrifice to be offered by the cowherd men was stopped by Kṛṣṇa, he became angry, and to express his anger against the inhabitants of Vṛndāvana he ordered his most terrible cloud, which is usually saved only for the time of annihilation, to go to Vṛndāvana and inundate the whole area with extensive floods. Indra was deluded, thinking that he was the all-powerful supreme personality, for when demons become very powerful, they defy the supreme controller, Lord Śrī Kṛṣṇa. Indra, although not a demon, was puffed up by his material position and wanted to challenge the Supreme Lord. At least for the time being, he thought himself as powerful as Kṛṣṇa. Indra said, "Just see the impudence of the inhabitants of Vṛndāvana! They are simply inhabitants of the forest, but being infatuated with their friend Kṛṣṇa, who is nothing but an ordinary human being, they have dared to defy the demigods."

Ordered by King Indra, all the dangerous clouds appeared above Vṛndāvana and began to pour water incessantly with all their strength and power. There was constant lightning and thunder, blowing of severe wind, and incessant rain, which seemed to fall like piercing sharp arrows. Pouring water as thick as pillars, without cessation, the clouds finally filled all the lands of Vṛndāvana with water, and there was no visible distinction between higher and lower land. The situation was very dangerous, especially for the animals. Unable to find any other source of deliverance, they all approached Govinda, Kṛṣṇa, to take shelter at His lotus feet. They all began to pray to Lord Kṛṣṇa, "Dear Kṛṣṇa, You are all-powerful, and You are very affectionate to Your devotees. Now please protect us who have been much harassed by angry Indra."

Kṛṣṇa understood the deliberate exhibition of anger by Indra. "This demigod who thinks himself supreme has shown his great power," He thought, "but I shall answer him according to My position, and I shall thus take away his false prestige." Thinking in this way, Kṛṣṇa immediately picked up Govardhana Hill with one hand, exactly as a child picks up a mushroom from the ground. Thus

He exhibited His transcendental pastime of lifting Govardhana Hill. He then addressed the devotees, "My dear brothers, My dear father, My dear inhabitants of Vṛndāvana, you can now safely enter under the umbrella of Govardhana Hill, which I have just lifted. Do not be afraid of the hill and think that it will fall from My hand. You have been too much afflicted from the heavy rain and strong wind; therefore I have lifted this hill, which will protect you exactly like a huge umbrella." Seeing this mystic power of Kṛṣṇa, Indra was dumbstruck and baffled. He immediately called back the clouds and asked them to stop.

When the sky was completely cleared of all clouds, there was sunrise again, and the strong winds stopped. Kṛṣṇa, who was now known as the lifter of Govardhana Hill, said, "My dear cowherd men, now you can leave and take your wives, children, cows and valuables, because everything is ended. The flood has gone down, along with the swelling of the river." Kṛṣṇa held up Govardhana Hill for seven days. When the flood was over and all the residents and animals had left the shelter of the hill, Kṛṣṇa placed Govardhana Hill back in its position exactly as it was before. There was a great celebration in the heavens at this pastime of Kṛṣṇa's, and many demigods poured showers of flowers from the sky and sounded conchshells. All the people of Vṛndāvana, who were very affectionate to Kṛṣṇa, embraced Him and offered Him incessant blessings.

There is a class of unscrupulous men who declare themselves to be the Supreme Personality of Godhead. Even when they hear the Vedic descriptions of Kṛṣṇa, they attempt to imitate His pastimes such as His dealings of love with the *gopīs* or cowherd girls of Vṛndāvana. Such foolish pretenders sometimes gain followers who are even more foolish because they actually believe that any upstart can become the Supreme Personality of Godhead simply by declaring himself to be so. Such so-called *yogīs* and *svāmīs* who falsely pose as incarnations are challenged by this pastime of Govardhana Hill. A common man may try to imitate the loving pastimes of Kṛṣṇa and claim to be Kṛṣṇa Himself, but we can ask such false incarnations to perform something as wonderful as Kṛṣṇa's lifting a mountain with the pinky of His left hand. Of course they cannot do this. We should understand that Kṛṣṇa comes to this earth to impart to us instructions about how to become God conscious. His teachings are meant to be followed, but His activities as the Supreme Personality of Godhead are wonderful pastimes which can never be imitated by a common man. Anyone who declares himself to be God but is unable to enact wonderful pastimes such as lifting Govardhana Hill is the worst of rascals and most preposterous of fools.

Indra, the King of heaven, was conscious of his offense before Kṛṣṇa. Therefore he stealthily appeared before Him from a secluded place. Conscious of his subordinate position, he appeared before Kṛṣṇa with folded hands to offer prayers. "My Lord," Indra said, "I was a victim of false prestige. When I saw

You stop the sacrifice, I thought that You were taking my share of the profit, and I forgot my position. There is no question of Your being my rival. You are the Supreme Personality of Godhead, and I am simply Your eternal servant, but due to my false pride I forgot that You are transcendental, beyond the disturbance of the material qualities. Your abode is accessible only for one who is completely freed from the onslaught of material qualities like passion and ignorance."

Indra appreciated Kṛṣṇa's right to chastise him and was grateful that Kṛṣṇa had tactfully removed his false prestige. Although Indra had vented all his power in the flood, Kṛṣṇa showed that this power could be thwarted simply by the pinky of His left hand. Indra saw himself as being grossly ignorant, and he thanked Kṛṣṇa for His kindness and mercy in destroying all his pride. Indra said, "I take shelter of Your lotus feet, my dear Lord. You are not only the supreme controller but the spiritual master of all living entities." After thus offering his humble obeisances, Indra took leave of the Supreme Personality of Godhead and returned to his heavenly kingdom.

Regarding the wonderful lifting of the hill, it can be stated that Kṛṣṇa does not need to lift a hill with His hand. He can vanquish the demons by His material energy and therefore does not need to personally appear on the scene. But He lifted Govardhana Hill just to please His devotees. By seeing Kṛṣṇa perform such a wonderful act, or simply by hearing of such activities, we can appreciate specifically the general truth that "God is great." By faithfully hearing of His transcendental activities one can develop love of Kṛṣṇa, which is the perfection of all existence. The most fortunate of all beings are those eternal associates of Kṛṣṇa such as the cowherd residents of Vṛndāvana who take part with Him in His activities in the eternal spiritual world. Anyone can aspire to join with Kṛṣṇa in His eternal, blissful realm, Kṛṣṇaloka. The only qualification is love of Kṛṣṇa, and such love of Kṛṣṇa is our original, constitutional position. We have now simply forgotten our original spiritual relationship, and therefore we have become entangled in temporary material relationships which are likened to the dreams of a sleeping man. For the purpose of awakening humanity's original love of Kṛṣṇa, His Divine Grace A.C. Bhaktivedanta Swami Prabhupāda is presenting the philosophy and activities of Kṛṣṇa from the Vedic literature. We strongly recommend our readers to turn to *Kṛṣṇa, the Supreme Personality of Godhead* to relish further the pastimes of the all-attractive Lord, the cause of all causes.

Subduing the Serpent Kāliya

June/July, 1973

The narrative of Kṛṣṇa and Kāliya, as described in the *Kṛṣṇa Book* Volume One, by His Divine Grace A.C. Bhaktivedanta Swami Prabhupāda, vividly illustrates that Lord Sri Krsna is the Supreme Personality of Godhead, the complete Absolute Truth. The *Kṛṣṇa Book* is a summary study of the Vedic scripture *Śrīmad-Bhāgavatam,* in which the pastimes of Kṛṣṇa are fully described. Many people disbelieve that these narrations of Kṛṣṇa are revelations of transcendental knowledge. They say that the activities of Kṛṣṇa are stories about a mythical figure or ordinary historical person. A mistaken description of Kṛṣṇa in terms of this idea recently published in *Time* magazine stated that the devotees of Kṛṣṇa worship Him as one of many gods and hope eventually to go beyond Kṛṣṇa, and all other gods, to realize the Absolute Truth as the impersonal Absolute, or Brahman. This mistaken conclusion, however, has nothing to do with the Vedic literatures or the great philosophers and spiritual masters of Kṛṣṇa consciousness. The scripture *Vedānta-sūtra* explains that the Absolute Truth, the Supreme Personality of Godhead, Kṛṣṇa, is *janmādy asya yataḥ,* the source of everything.

In *Bhagavad-gītā* Kṛṣṇa Himself states, "Everything emanates from Me" (Bg. 10.8) and "I am the basis of the impersonal Brahman" (Bg. 14.27). The *Śrīmad-Bhāgavatam* describes that the Supreme Person is the highest aspect of the Absolute Truth and that the impersonal infinite is subordinate to Him, as sunshine is subordinate to the sun. The Supreme Person is greater than the all-pervading, impersonal aspect of spiritual truth. Another authoritative Vedic literature, the *Brahmasaṁhitā,* describes Kṛṣṇa to be the supreme controller whose transcendental body is eternal, full of bliss and knowledge. Everything is sustained by His inconceivable energies. Therefore, the highest truth is the Supreme Person.

But when this inconceivable, all-pervading Absolute Truth, Kṛṣṇa, by His mercy appears in human society to attract the fallen souls, fools deride Him. Kṛṣṇa Himself states in *Bhagavad-gītā,* "Fools deride Me when I appear in the human form. They do not know My transcendental nature and My supreme dominion over all that be." (Bg. 9.11) Sometimes people give lip service to the idea that God is inconceivable and capable of anything and everything, but when He actually appears before them and shows just a small fragment of His infinite energy, they reject His activities and say that it is impossible for God to appear as a person. But we must ask such skeptics why, if God is all-powerful, it is not possible for Him to appear here and engage in transcendental pastimes with His own devotees. What is to prevent Kṛṣṇa from coming? We may disbelieve in Him, but we cannot stop Him.

Spiritual authorities all conclude that God is a person, and because His personality is infinite, for Him anything is possible. He is not void or zero. Even ordinary living entities have personalities and activities, so how can God, who is the source of everthing, be without form or personality? One should understand that His form is not material or limited like ours, and therefore when He appears in human society in His original form of Kṛṣṇa, one should worship Him, not reject Him like the fools who say that Kṛṣṇa is less than the impersonal Brahman. Of course, this is a simple matter of knowing the spiritual facts. Only one who is ignorant of the spiritual science will deride Kṛṣṇa, not understanding that He is the Supreme Person. One should not, therefore, hear about the pastimes of Kṛṣṇa from skeptics but from the lips of a pure devotee of Kṛṣṇa, for in that way one can derive the highest benefit. The *Kṛṣṇa Book* is unique because it is a presentation of the pastimes of Kṛṣṇa by a pure devotee of Kṛṣṇa, His Divine Grace A.C. Bhaktivedanta Swami Prabhupāda.

Here is a sample from the *Kṛṣṇa Book* that shows the actual transcendental atmosphere of Kṛṣṇa's pastimes: "When Kṛṣṇa, Balarāma and Their friends entered the village of Vṛndavāna, They played Their flutes, and the boys praised Their uncommon activities in the forest. Kṛṣṇa's head was decorated with a peacock feather. Both He and Balarama played Their flutes, and the young *gopīs* (cowherd girls) were joyous to see Kṛṣṇa returning home. All the *gopīs* in Vṛndavāna remained very morose on account of Kṛṣṇa's absence. All day they were thinking of Kṛṣṇa in the forest or of Him herding cows in the pasture. When they saw Kṛṣṇa returning, all of their anxieties were immediately relieved, and they began to look at His face the way drones hover over the honey of a lotus flower. When Kṛṣṇa entered the village, the young *gopīs* smiled and laughed."

In this way, Kṛṣṇa, the inconceivable cause of all causes, plays in Vṛndavāna as a cowherd boy for the pleasure of His pure devotees, the cowherd men and *gopīs.* These are the actual activities of the spiritual world, and the perfection of appreciating these pastimes is far beyond that of meditating on a void or impersonal Absolute. When we appreciate Kṛṣṇa in this mood, we will best understand the significance of this narrative of Kṛṣṇa and the Kāliya snake.

Sometimes Kṛṣṇa used to go with His boy friends and His brother, Balarāma, to the bank of the Yamunā to tend the cows. One summer, when all the boys and cows were in the field, they became very thirsty and began to drink the water of the Yamunā. The river, however, had been poisoned by the venom of the great serpent Kāliya, and the boys and cows who drank from it suddenly fell down, apparently dead, on the ground.

Kṛṣṇa, the life of all that lives, simply cast His merciful glance over all the boys and cows, and they at once regained consciousness and began to look at each other with great astonishment. They could understand that by drinking the water of the Yamuna they had died and that the merciful glance of Kṛṣṇa had restored their lives.

It is mentioned in the *Kṛṣṇa Book* that when this incident was originally related by Śukadeva Gosvāmī, his disciple, Mahārāja Parīkṣit, was eager to hear about the pastimes of Kṛṣṇa. A pure devotee knows that nothing is difficult for Kṛṣṇa, including even reviving the dead to life. Kṛṣṇa's inconceivable nature is infinite, beyond our ever understanding it completely. But the symptom of one who is advanced in Kṛṣṇa consciousness is that he becomes more and more absorbed in relishing the Lord's pastimes and always wishes to hear further.

The boys had died because the Yamunā had been thoroughly poisoned by the black serpent Kāliya. The grass near the river bank had all dried up, and the river was so contaminated that it emanated a poisonous vapor twenty-four hours a day. If a bird even passed over the river, it would immediately fall dead into the water.

Kṛṣṇa's mission in this material world is to vanquish all undesirable elements; therefore, He climbed up a tree on the bank of the Yamuna, tightened His belt and jumped into the poisonous river. When Kṛṣṇa jumped into the water, the river overflooded its banks as if something very large had fallen into it. Hearing the great noise made by Kṛṣṇa in the water, the serpent Kāliya understood that someone was attacking his home. Coming before Kṛṣṇa, he saw Him to be delicate and beautiful, His bodily hue resembling a fresh raincloud. Kṛṣṇa was smiling and playing in the river with great strength because He is the source of all strength. But Kāliya felt anger within his heart, and thus he grabbed Kṛṣṇa with his coils.

Seeing Kṛṣṇa in the coils of the serpent, Kṛṣṇa's friends the cowherd boys and the other residents of Vṛndavāna were stunned with fear. Kṛṣṇa was their whole life. When they saw Him apparently overpowered by the coils of the serpent, they lost all composure and fell to the ground. Kṛṣṇa's personal associates and family members are understood to have been the most exalted persons in the universe. Having given up all material desires and gone beyond all speculation or impersonal understanding of the Absolute Truth, they became so qualified by dint of their previous pious activities that they were even allowed to play with Kṛṣṇa. They regarded Him not as the Almighty Godhead but as the dearmost friend in existence. They thought of Kṛṣṇa as their master, friend, son or lover.

Ordinary persons do not even think of God, not to speak of lamenting for the Supreme Personality of Godhead when He appears to be in distress. Mostly we lament over our own bodily or mental distress or some distress that affects our friends and relatives. In other words, our feelings are based not on pure love but on sense gratification. Making the mistake of thinking that the body is the self, we are happy when we are able to please the bodily senses, and we become unhappy when there is some disruption to that sense pleasure. But there is no real satisfaction in sense gratification because it is always hampered by the miseries of birth, old age, disease and death.

The associates of Kṛṣṇa, however, always focused all their emotions on Kṛṣṇa, and therefore they were eternally liberated. There was no question of their ever forgetting Him; rather, they forgot all selfish material desires. And one who always remembers Kṛṣṇa in this way is qualified to transfer at the time of death to the spiritual world in an eternal, blissful form, never to return for another birth in the material world.

In the beginning of his discussion with Lord Kṛṣṇa in *Bhagavad-gītā,* Kṛṣṇa's disciple Arjuna lamented over the impending death of his bodily relatives. This is an example of material lamentation. But Kṛṣṇa said to Arjuna that his lamentation was not worthy of a wise man, for a wise man laments neither for the living nor the dead. A pure devotee's anxiety caused by thinking that Kṛṣṇa is in distress is not, however, like the material lamentation of a man in ignorance. The devotee's emotion is transcendental and purifying because it is in relationship with Kṛṣṇa. There is no question of danger or distress for Kṛṣṇa, the Supreme Godhead. Therefore, Kṛṣṇa's appearing to be in difficulty with Kāliya was a pretense, but His devotees' anxiety for Him was a transcendental emotion.

Not only Kṛṣṇa's friends but also the cows and calves were overwhelmed with grief as they saw Kṛṣṇa gripped tightly in the clutches of the serpent. Unable to help, they could only cry in great anxiety. Meanwhile, nature manifested ill omens. The earth trembled, and meteors fell from the sky. When Kṛṣṇa's mother and father, Yaśodā and Nanda, were informed that Kṛṣṇa had gone to the pasturing grounds without His older brother, Balarāma, they were filled with anxiety because they were unaware of Kṛṣṇa's supreme potency. They ran to the Yamunā, fearful that Kṛṣṇa might be vanquished by Kāliya. In a short time all the residents of Vṛndāvana—children, young men, old men, women, animals and all living entities—had gathered on the bank of the Yamunā. All of the residents of Vṛndāvana were pure devotees of Kṛṣṇa who did not know anything but Him. They knew that He was their only means of sustenance. Seeing Kṛṣṇa caught in the coils of the snake, they felt lost. When mother Yaśodā arrived at the bank of the Yamunā, she immediately tried to plunge into the river, but she was stopped by the residents of Vṛndāvana. Only Kṛṣṇa's brother, Balarāma, who was the master of knowledge, knew what was actually happening. He did not grieve but simply stood there smiling. He knew how powerful His younger brother Kṛṣṇa was; there was no cause for anxiety over Kṛṣṇa's fighting with an ordinary serpent of the material world.

For two hours, Kṛṣṇa remained like an ordinary child gripped in the coils of the serpent. One may ask why Kṛṣṇa allowed His dearest associates to be put into such anxiety for such a long time. This question can only be answered in terms of the intimate transcendental relationship between Kṛṣṇa and His devotees. An atheist cannot expect to poke his nose into the sublime exchanges between Kṛṣṇa and His devotees and understand them. Only a devotee who is simply absorbed in love for Kṛṣṇa and does not seek any reward can fully understand these pastimes. As Lord Kṛṣṇa states in *Bhagavad-gītā,* "Only by devotional service am I to be known." (Bg. 18.55)

Devotees of Kṛṣṇa can appreciate that Kṛṣṇa performed these pastimes with the Kāliya snake to give impetus to intensified feelings of love for Him. Seeing Kṛṣṇa in trouble, the devotees in Vṛndāvana became absorbed in remembering Kṛṣṇa, His smiling face, His loving words and His dealings with the various demons He had vanquished. The devotees on the bank of the Yamunā, therefore, demonstrated the highest stage of Kṛṣṇa consciousness–the ecstasy of love in a feeling of separation. Kṛṣṇa did not want to disturb their mood of concern and anxiety for Him by immediately showing them that there was no need for distress. Therefore He remained wrapped in the serpent's coils.

Lord Kṛṣṇa reciprocates and intensifies the love of His devotees. When Kṛṣṇa first appeared as a small baby, He allowed His father, Vasudeva, to carry Him across the River Yamunā as His protector. Because Vasudeva was absorbed in the mood of protecting Kṛṣṇa, Kṛṣṇa allowed Himself to be in need of protection. Similarly, when Kṛṣṇa was dancing with the cowherd girls, at the height of their loving affairs He disappeared from the *rāsa* dance, causing them to become mad with lamentation. They wandered throughout Vṛndāvana Forest searching for Him, feeling intense love in separation from Kṛṣṇa. And when Kṛṣṇa was sixteen years old, He left Vṛndāvana altogether, and thus all the residents of Vṛndāvana, including the *gopīs,* mother Yasodā and His father Nanda, remained in grief over His absence for the rest of their lives. But by always talking about Kṛṣṇa, chanting His holy name and remembering Kṛṣṇa, they were able to feel the same love as when He was present in Vṛndāvana. Because Kṛṣṇa is absolute, remembrance of Kṛṣṇa is the same as direct association with Him. Therefore Lord Caitanya prayed, "I do not know anyone but Kṛṣṇa as my Lord, and He shall always remain as such, even if He handles me roughly in His embrace or makes me broken-hearted by not being present before me."

When Lord Kṛṣṇa saw that all the inhabitants of Gokula, having no other recourse than Him, were practically dead with grief, He made an immediate move to free Himself. Krsna expanded His body within the coils of the Kāliya snake, and because of the strain, the snake's coils slackened, and he was forced to release Kṛṣṇa. He became very angry, expanding his hoods and exhaling poisonous fumes from his nostrils. Kṛṣṇa pounced upon him, and the two began moving in a circle. The snake tried to bite Kṛṣṇa, but Kṛṣṇa pressed the serpent down and then jumped up on top of his hoods. Then Kṛṣṇa, the original master artist of all fine arts, such as dancing, began to dance upon the hoods of the serpent while the hoods moved to and fro. At that time the Lord's lotus feet became tinged with red from the rays of the jewels on the snake's hoods. As Kṛṣṇa danced on the hoods of the snake, the residents of the upper planets rejoiced and began to celebrate with showers of flowers, beating of drums and singing of songs.

The sublime climax of Kṛṣṇa's fight with the Kāliya snake has been depicted by devotee artists. Completely self-assured and transcendental to all danger, Kṛṣṇa is seen vanquishing the hundred-headed serpent by gracefully dancing upon his hoods in the midst of the turbulent River Yamunā. By smashing the serpent's heads with His lotus feet, Kṛṣṇa at the same time bestowed the highest benediction upon Kāliya, for by touching the snake with His holy lotus feet, the shelter of all the worlds, which are sought after by His pure devotees, Kṛṣṇa released Kāliya from his sins. The snake became gradually reduced in strength and began to throw up poisonous materials. It appeared as if the Supreme Personality of Godhead were being worshiped and the poison emanating from the mouth of the serpent were flower offerings. Then Kāliya, now vomiting blood instead of poison, appearing to be almost dead, finally began to realize that Kṛṣṇa was the Supreme Personality of Godhead.

At that time, the wives of the serpent, known as the Nāgapatnīs, appeared before Kṛṣṇa with folded palms and prayed to the Lord to forgive their husband. Recognizing the actual position of Kṛṣṇa, they addressed Him as the Absolute Truth and expressed the understanding that there is no difference between Kṛṣṇa's mercy and punishment. They could understand that the apparent punishment inflicted upon their husband Kāliya was actually a benediction because his sins were eradicated by the kicks of Kṛṣṇa's dancing feet on his heads. They declared that Kāliya must have performed greatly pious acts in his past life to get the opportunity to be touched by Kṛṣṇa's lotus feet. They were perplexed, for although the Kāliya snake, having the body of a serpent, must have been very sinful, he was so extraordinarily fortunate that the Lord's lotus feet touched his hoods.

They prayed, "O dear Lord, we are simply astonished to see that he is so fortunate as to have the dust of Your lotus feet on his head. This is a fortune sought after by great saintly persons. Even the goddess of fortune underwent great austerities just to have the blessing of the dust of Your lotus feet, so how is it that Kāliya is so easily getting this dust on his head?"

The Nāgapatnīs appeared well-versed in the conclusion of Vedic literature because they understood that Kṛṣṇa is the cause of all causes. "You are the ultimate goal of all philosophical efforts," they declared, "and You are actually described by all philosophies and by different kinds of doctrines. Let us offer our respectful obeisances unto You because You are the origin of all scriptures and the source of all knowledge. You are the Supreme Personality of Godhead. You can bestow upon us the supreme knowledge. You are also the supreme enjoyer."

Fully acquainted with the Vedic literature, the Nāgapatnīs knew that Kṛṣṇa is the ultimate goal in the search for the Absolute Truth. They were also chaste wives who could not live without their husband, and so they prayed unto the Supreme Lord to spare Kāliya. "Our dear Lord," they said, "every living creature is Your offspring, and You maintain everyone. This serpent is also Your offspring, and You can excuse him although he has offended You, undoubtedly without knowing Your potency." They concluded, "Every living entity can be relieved from all kinds of despair if he agrees to abide by Your orders."

Thereafter Kāliya himself, having come to his senses because of the kicks of Kṛṣṇa's lotus feet, also offered prayers. He expressed that it was very difficult for him to give up his envious instincts, for they were natural to his snakelike body. Although the real self is not the body but spirit soul and it has an eternal loving service relationship with God, or Kṛṣṇa, even human beings think that they are American, African, black, white and so on in terms of the bodies that they have obtained. As stated in *Bhagavad-gītā,* the illusion of material nature is strong, and to revive one's memory of one's relationship with Kṛṣṇa is difficult. Kāliya, therefore, begged that Kṛṣṇa excuse him for his inevitable material tendencies. He said to Kṛṣṇa, "Now You can punish me or save me as You desire."

After hearing this, the Supreme Personality of Godhead, who was acting as a small human child, ordered the serpent, "You must immediately leave this place and go to the ocean. Leave without delay. You can take with you all your offspring, wives and everything that you possess. Don't pollute the water of the Yamunā. Let it be drunk by My cows and cowherd boys without hindrance." The Lord then declared that the order given to the snake should be recited and heard by everyone so that no one need fear Kāliya any longer.

Kṛṣṇa was very pleased with Kāliya and His wives. After hearing His order, the wives worshiped the Lord with offerings of garments, garlands, jewels, sandalwood, lotus flowers and palatable foods. Then, obeying the orders of Lord Kṛṣṇa, they all left the waters of the Yamunā. When Kṛṣṇa finally came out of the river, He was seen by all His friends and relatives on the bank of the Yamunā. He was decorated with jewels, and all the inhabitants of Vṛndāvana felt as if they had recovered their lives on seeing Kṛṣṇa again. They each in turn pressed Kṛṣṇa to their chests and felt great relief. They were so happy that they felt they had achieved the ultimate goal of life.

According to the Vedic literature, the anxiety of our life in the material world can be alleviated simply by hearing these pastimes of Lord Kṛṣṇa from the lips of a pure devotee. The effect of hearing about Kṛṣṇa is that one becomes absorbed in the eternal, blissful world and forgets his illusory engagements in this world of death, disease and old age. Many such pastimes of Kṛṣṇa are in the *Kṛṣṇa Book,* which describes the activities of Kṛṣṇa's childhood, boyhood and youth in Vṛndāvana. Later, near the end of His pastimes in this world, Kṛṣṇa, as a prince on the Battlefield of Kurukṣetra, spoke the superb transcendental philosophy of *Bhagavad-gītā.* Lord Caitanya, the ideal preacher of Kṛṣṇa consciousness, has said, *yāre dekha, tāre kaha 'kṛṣṇa' upadeśa:* "Whomever you meet, speak to him about Kṛṣṇa or tell him about the philosphy of Kṛṣṇa." To follow this order is to bestow the highest mercy on others, and at the same time, whoever speaks of such pastimes of Kṛṣṇa will also derive the highest pleasure. Many people in this age are too dull to give a patient hearing to Kṛṣṇa consciousness, but whoever can hear about Kṛṣṇa is pious, and whoever can seriously understand and relish the pastimes of Kṛṣṇa is the most fortunate person on earth. Such a person is eternally liberated from all distresses, and he becomes eligible to enter the kingdom of God.

Kṛṣṇa's Universal Form

September/October, 1974

One of the most famous sections of *Bhagavad-gītā* is that in which Lord Kṛṣṇa's disciple Arjuna sees that Kṛṣṇa's body encompasses the entire universe. A prominent university scholar describes the univeral form as "*the mystery*" of *Bhagavad-gītā*. However, one can easily understand the universal form by studying the *Gītā* through the testimony of Arjuna and the devotees who follow him.

Arjuna asked to see the universal form not for himself but for the benefit of others, who might doubt that Kṛṣṇa is God. Arjuna indeed accepted Kṛṣṇa as the Supreme Personality of Godhead. Earlier in the *Gītā*, Arjuna had already expressed his realization that Kṛṣṇa is the Absolute Truth. The Lord had described that He is all-pervading and that He can be seen in everything great and powerful in the material world. "Of purifiers," the Lord said, "I am the wind. Of flowing rivers I am the Ganges. Of all sciences I am the spiritual science of the self. . . . Know that all beautiful, glorious and mighty creations spring from but a spark of My splendor."

Hearing of Kṛṣṇa's opulences, Arjuna declared, "You are the Supreme Brahman, the Ultimate." Arjuna had testified, moreover, that although some might think that his friendship with Kṛṣṇa had swayed his opinion, such great sages as Nārada, Devala, Asita and Vyāsa–and all the Vedic scriptures–confirm that Kṛṣṇa is indeed the Supreme. Nevertheless, so that his acceptance of Kṛṣṇa as God would not be merely theoretical, Arjuna requested Kṛṣṇa to reveal His *viśva-rūpa*, or universal form. Kṛṣṇa therefore agreed to reveal this form to Arjuna, and He blessed Arjuna with the special vision he needed to see it.

The universal form is the form of the Supreme Lord in which one can see everything in the universe, all at once. In the universal form, one can see past, present and future. One can see all the demigods of the material creation, and all other living beings. *Bhagavad-gītā* graphically describes the revelation of the universal form: "Arjuna saw in that universal form many unlimited mouths and unlimited eyes. It was all wondrous. The form was decorated with divine, dazzling ornaments and arrayed in many garbs. . . . All was magnificent, all-expanding, unlimited. This was seen by Arjuna. If hundreds of thousands of suns were to rise at once in the sky, they might resemble the effulgence of the

Supreme Person in that universal form." (Bg. 11.10-12)

While Kṛṣṇa manifested His cosmic form, He nonetheless continued to exist in His form as a human being, sitting beside Arjuna. Arjuna was Kṛṣṇa's friend, but upon seeing Kṛṣṇa in the universal form, he was filled with awe and wonder. Bewildered and astonished, his hairs standing on end, Arjuna began to pray with folded hands, offering obeisances to the Supreme Lord: "O Lord of the universe, I see in Your universal body many, many forms--bellies, mouths, eyes--expanded without limit. There is no end, there is no beginning, there is no middle to all this. Your form, adorned with various crowns, clubs and discs, is difficult to see because of its glaring effulgence, which is fiery and immeasurable like the sun. You are the supreme primal objective. You are the best in all the universes, You are inexhaustible, and You are the oldest. You are the maintainer of religion, the eternal Personality of Godhead. . . . You are spread throughout the sky and the planets and all space between."

With innumerable faces, arms and legs, terrible teeth, and radiant colors spreading everywhere, the universal form bewildered the great warrior Arjuna. "I cannot keep my balance," Arjuna said. "Seeing Your blazing deathlike faces, I am bewildered! All our soldiers and the soldiers of the enemy are rushing into Your mouths, their heads smashed by Your fearful teeth. As the rivers flow into the sea, all these warriors enter Your blazing mouths and perish. I see all people rushing with full speed into Your mouths as moths dash into a blazing fire. I see You devouring all people." In great fear, Arjuna told the Lord, "I do not know what Your mission is, and I desire to hear of it."

Thereupon, the universal form of the Lord replied: "Time I am, the destroyer of the worlds, and I have come to engage all people. With the exception of you, the Pandava brothers, all the soldiers on both sides will be slain." (Bg. 11.32)

Those who have studied *Bhagavad-gītā* know that it is a dialogue between Kṛṣṇa and Arjuna in which Kṛṣṇa, the Supreme Lord, tries to convince Arjuna, His friend and disciple, to fulfill his duty as a warrior by fighting against a demoniac army. Throughout *Bhagavad-gītā,* Kṛṣṇa gives many arguments why Arjuna should fight, and He especially assures Arjuna that he and all the others in the battle are eternal spiritual souls who cannot actually be killed. In His universal form, however, the Lord tells Arjuna that even if he refused to fight, the material bodies of all the warriors would nevertheless be destroyed, for that was the plan of the Lord. If Arjuna refused to fight, they would die in another way; their death could not be checked. Thus Kṛṣṇa explained to Arjuna the mission of the universal form.

Although Kṛṣṇa is the Supreme Lord of the universe, He enjoys eternal personal relationships with His devotees such as Arjuna. However, when Kṛṣṇa appeared in His universal form. Arjuna, overwhelmed, begged Kṛṣṇa to forgive him for all the personal familiarities of their friendship. Arjuna said, "I have in the past addressed You as my friend, Kṛṣṇa, without knowing Your glories. Please forgive whatever I may have done in madness or in love. I dishonored You many times while we were relaxing, lying on the same bed or eating together, sometimes alone and sometimes among friends. Please excuse me for all my offenses. You are the father of the complete cosmic manifestation, the worshipful chief, the spiritual master. No one is equal to You, nor can anyone be one with You." (Bg. 11.41-43) Thus although Arjuna, seeing his friend in the form of Time, was very much afraid, he could not forget that Kṛṣṇa was his friend in a loving relationship.

According to our spiritual master, the main reason Arjuna asked Kṛṣṇa to show this form was to discredit imposters who might come later and claim to be God. Many rascals boast that they are God or incarnations of God, but they should be challenged to show a form as wonderful as the *viśva-rūpa,* in which all the universes appear within Kṛṣṇa's body. No one but the Supreme Lord Himself can display such a form.

Arjuna's vision of the universal form was real; it was not a dream, for the *Gītā* indicates that many other important personalities also beheld the universal form when the Lord revealed it to Arjuna. Moreover, since five thousand years ago, when *Bhagavad-gītā* was spoken, great philosophers and spiritual masters have confirmed the reality of Lord Kṛṣṇa's universal form.

Sometimes fraudulent gods bluff their followers by asserting that they can indeed show them the universal form. One time a boy came to the Kṛṣṇa consciousness center in New York and announced to the devotees that he was God. When asked to show his universal form, he declared, "Yes, here it is," and then he held up his arms so that everyone could behold his cosmic body. But a display of mere insolence and a form of skin and bones—"Here it is. Can't you see it?"—does not constitute a revelation of the universal form. Nor can word jugglery, LSD, hypnotism or charisma induce a true vision of the universal form. Only the Supreme Godhead can reveal that cosmic form, and as stated in the *Gītā,* only His pure devotees are qualified to see it.

Some professors and scholars try to dismiss the universal form by saying that it is a poetic fantasy. Such an interpretation, however, is contrary to all the understanding of Vedic literature. These professors and their students may take *Bhagavad-gītā* to be fanciful, but the real philosophers, the spiritual masters who come in the disciplic line from Kṛṣṇa and who have guided the course of Vedic philosophy for thousands of years, accept *Bhagavad-gītā* as the Absolute Truth. Mundane scholars do not know whether Kṛṣṇa showed His universal form, but the *ācāryas* (the spiritual masters who teach by the example of their lives) do know. That the tiny minds of atheists cannot accept such a wonderful manifestation as the universal form does not disprove its existence. The message of the *Gītā* was spoken by Kṛṣṇa, who showed the universal form, as clearly stated in the *Gītā* itself. We accept the *Gītā* as it is, on the authority of Kṛṣṇa and the Vedic *ācāryas*. Thus we need not consult foolish speculators for their opinions. Since they try to interpret *Bhagavad-gītā* in their own way, they cannot possibly understand the universal form as it is.

After seeing the form of the universe in the body of Kṛṣṇa, Arjuna could not maintain his equilibrium. Thus he begged Kṛṣṇa not only to forgive him for his familiarity as a friend, but to relieve his mind by again showing him the form in which Arjuna knew Him as the Personality of Godhead. Arjuna prayed: "After seeing this universal form, which I have never seen before, I am gladdened, but at the same time my mind is disturbed with fear. Therefore, please bestow Your grace upon me and reveal again Your form as the Personality of Godhead. O universal Lord, I wish to see You in Your four-armed form, with helmeted head and with club, wheel, conch and lotus flower in Your hands. I long to see You in that form."

According to the Vedic scriptures, the Supreme Lord has innumerable forms and incarnations. Among them, the four-armed form of Viṣṇu is often celebrated as the foremost, for He is the source of many other incarnations and is the ultimate controller of the material world. Despite popular Western misconceptions, Viṣṇu is not one of a hierarchy of Hindu deities like the gods and goddesses of the ancient Greeks. According to the Vedic scriptures, God is one without a second, but He can appear in many different forms, just as a gem appears in different colors when viewed under different kinds of light. Thus the Supreme Lord may appear as Kṛṣṇa, as Viṣṇu or as the universal form, but He is always the same Supreme Personality of Godhead.

Thus Kṛṣṇa answered: "My dear Arjuna, happily have I shown you this universal form within the material world by My internal potency. No one before you has ever seen this unlimited and glaringly effulgent form. . . . But your mind has been perturbed by seeing this horrible feature of Mine. Now let it be finished. My devotee, be free from all disturbance. With a peaceful mind you can now see the form you desire." (Bg. 11.47,49)

Thus at the request of His friend Arjuna, Kṛṣṇa stopped displaying the universal form and showed Arjuna His four-armed form as Viṣṇu. Then at last He showed him His two-armed form. This very much encouraged Arjuna. Arjuna said, "Seeing this humanlike form, so very beautiful, my mind is now pacified, and I am restored to my original senses."

Kṛṣṇa's changing from the universal form to the four-armed form and finally to the two-armed form is most significant, for this demonstrates that all other forms are coming from the original form of Kṛṣṇa. Many interpreters say that the universal form is the most important feature in *Bhagavad-gītā.* Others stress the form of Viṣṇu. Actually, however, Viṣṇu and the universal form are but aspects of Lord Kṛṣṇa as we see Him in His two-armed form when He drives the chariot for Arjuna. As stated in *Śrīmad-Bhāgavatam, kṛṣṇas tu bhagavān svayam:* Kṛṣṇa is the source of all other incarnations of Godhead. In that humanlike form, He has such inconceivable potencies that He can expand into the whole universe. Therefore that original form is His most worshipable and most important. Furthermore, Lord Kṛṣṇa, in His two-armed form, is the reservoir of all loving relationships. The Lord appears in various forms to create the material world and perform various pastimes, but in His original form as Kṛṣṇa, the Lord fully reciprocates transcendental love with His devotees.

To say that the impersonal spirit or universal form is more exalted than Kṛṣṇa, the Personality of Godhead, is a great disservice to the meaning of *Bhagavad-gītā.* Kṛṣṇa's humanlike form is His very Self, and there is no truth higher than Kṛṣṇa. As stated in the *Brahma-saṁhitā, īśvaraḥ paramaḥ kṛṣṇaḥ:* Kṛṣṇa is the Supreme Lord, the supreme controller. *Govindam ādi-puruṣaṁ tam ahaṁ bhajāmi:* He is the original form of Godhead. Therefore devotees desire to see Kṛṣṇa in His two-armed form, which is the most confidential form of Godhead. Śrīla Prabhupāda has commented: "Those who deride Kṛṣṇa, taking Him to be an ordinary person, must be ignorant of His divine nature. Kṛṣṇa has actually shown His universal form and His four-armed form, so how can He be an ordinary human being?" Most editions of *Bhagavad-gītā* unfortunately give interpretations that misguide the reader, but an actual devotee is not confused because the original verses of *Bhagavad-gītā* are as clear as the sun. They do not require a lamplight from foolish commentators.

Although Kṛṣṇa gave Arjuna special vision to see the gigantic *viśva-rūpa,* to see Kṛṣṇa in His original form is even more difficult. In the *Gītā,* Lord Kṛṣṇa, after returning to His original two-armed form, tells Arjuna: "The form you are seeing now is very difficult to behold. Even the demigods are ever seeking the opportunity to see this form, which is so dear."

In His original form, Kṛṣṇa eternally reciprocates with His devotees as their master, friend, child or lover. The *viśva-rūpa,* however, is not an eternal form of Kṛṣṇa, but a temporary manifestation to convince even a common man of the Lord's almighty nature. Śrīla Prabhupāda has said, "Don't try to love the *viśva-rūpa.* It is not possible." In the universal form, the Lord displays His opulence and power, but He does not reciprocate love with His devotees. Śrīla Prabhupāda therefore gives the example that if a boy's father is a policeman, even the boy himself might become afraid and forget his love if his father appeared before him, revolver blazing, in the line of duty. Similarly, Arjuna became fearful when he saw Kṛṣṇa's universal form. When Kṛṣṇa returned to His pleasing two-armed form, however, Arjuna was fully satisfied.

Lord Kṛṣṇa displayed His universal form to inspire all men to fix their minds upon Him and devote themselves to Him alone. The universal form is meant to convince us that although Kṛṣṇa may appear like an ordinary human being, He is indeed the all-powerful Personality of Godhead. Therefore Lord Kṛṣṇa, not the *viśva-rūpa,* should be the object of our meditation and our love. He is the original form of Godhead, the reservoir of all beauty, knowledge, wealth, strength, fame and renunciation. Therefore when we revive our dormant love for Kṛṣṇa, we also, like Arjuna, will find full spiritual satisfaction.

The Killing of Kaṁsa

October/November, 1974

Bhagavad-gītā states that Lord Kṛṣṇa descends to this world to vanquish miscreants and rescue His devotees. Once when the world was overburdened with demoniac forces, the demigods prayed for the appearance of the Lord. Lord Kṛṣṇa accepted the prayer, and He decided to appear as the son of two pure devotees, Vasudeva and his wife, Devakī. Years before Kṛṣṇa's actual advent, on the day Devakī and Vasudeva were married, Kaṁsa, the brother of the bride, was driving the couple to Vasudeva's home. In the middle of the joyous procession, a voice suddenly rang out from the sky. "Kaṁsa," the voice said, "you are such a fool! You are driving the chariot of your sister, but you do not know that the eighth child of your sister will kill you!"

Kaṁsa then at once took hold of Devakī and drew his sword to kill her. This shows the essence of Kaṁsa's demoniac mentality: anyone or anything that threatened his bodily enjoyment must be destroyed. Vasudeva at once intervened and pleaded with Kaṁsa not to kill Devakī. Vasudeva spoke in a very enlightened way. Death, he told Kaṁsa, is inevitable, so why should we be afraid of it? After the end of this body, we get another body to fulfill our desires. Death is only a change of bodies. The real self is eternal, so we should try to find our real life beyond the body.

Unfortunately, Kaṁsa, being an atheist, could not listen to good instruction. Although each of us has but little control over the forces of nature, foolish people try to become lords of all they survey. They live only for the pleasure of the body, taking the body to be the self, and disregarding the soul. In ignorance, they say there is no soul.

This philosophy is now very popular, but it has existed since time immemorial. Thousands of years ago, in Vedic times, it was propounded by a philosopher named Cārvāka, who taught that one should simply enjoy sensual pleasures, like eating, as much as he can. One should not hesitate to commit any irresponsible act to reach his goal, and one should not worry about the next life because at death everything will be finished. When modern so-called leaders take up this philosophy, people in general follow, and society becomes hellish. Not considering the will of the Supreme Personality of Godhead, or His supreme proprietorship, men take to animal slaughter, abortion, intoxication—anything. We are seeing only the beginning of this in current times. When Kṛṣṇa conscious persons like Vasudeva try to give enlightenment, many so-called educated men take them lightly and say that the existence of God and the eternity of the soul are myths. And when governments also fail to meet their responsibility to further God consciousness, social degradation is assured.

To dissuade Kaṁsa from murdering Devakī, Vasudeva promised that he and Devakī would bring Kaṁsa each of their children as they were born so that he could do what he liked with them. Kaṁsa relented, and when Vasudeva brought Kaṁsa their first-born child one year later, he became a little compassionate and spared the baby.

Later, however, Kaṁsa became alarmed when he heard from the sage Nārada that Kṛṣṇa was soon to appear. Nārada told Kaṁsa that in his past life he had been a demon named Kālanemi, who had been killed by Lord Kṛṣṇa, the Personality of Godhead. On hearing this, Kaṁsa foolishly became determined to kill the Lord. "Any child might be Kṛṣṇa," he concluded. He at once ordered the imprisonment of Vasudeva and Devakī and killed their child. Kaṁsa committed many other atrocities, all so that he might live and rule at any cost. He made alliances with many demoniac kings and imprisoned anyone who opposed him, including his own father, Ugrasena. In this way he expanded his kingdom, just as modern politicians do, until he became the strongest emperor of his time. He broke the solidarity of the Yadu dynasty, which included all of Kṛṣṇa's relatives, and forced them to hide in caves. Year after year Devakī gave birth to a child, and Kaṁsa murdered every one, six in all, fearing each to be the child who would kill him.

When Kṛṣṇa Himself became the eighth child, He cheated Kaṁsa. He appeared before Vasudeva and Devakī as the Supreme Lord and then transformed Himself into a normal child. Kṛṣṇa ordered Vasudeva to exchange Him with a female child just born to mother Yaśodā in nearby Gokula. Although Vasudeva was shackled and Kaṁsa's prison well guarded, by Kṛṣṇa's mystic potency Vasudeva was able to escape from the prison, make the exchange, and return unnoticed to his cell.

Kaṁsa heard the cries of the newborn child as his death knell, and he rushed in to kill him. But the baby flew up into the air and assumed the form of the demigoddess Māyā. "You rascal," she said to Kaṁsa. "The child who will kill you has already been born elsewhere. You cannot kill Him."

Threatened in this way, Kaṁsa and his demoniac associates began an all-out purge, ordering the murder of all male children born within the previous ten days. Kaṁsa also harassed all saintly persons and *brāhmaṇas*. He knew that the devotees are the heart and soul of his enemy, Lord Kṛṣṇa, so he tried to attack Him by persecuting His closest servitors and putting a stop to all religious activities.

Lord Kṛṣṇa, however, was not at all fearful. He simply enjoyed His childhood pastimes in Vṛndāvana, giving pleasure to His friends, His mother and father, and the cowherd men and women. Kaṁsa, however, tried repeatedly to disrupt Kṛṣṇa's pastimes. First he sent a witch named Pūtanā, who had already killed many babies by her black arts. She tried to kill Kṛṣṇa when He was only a few months old. She smeared poison on her breast, appeared in Vṛndavanā as a beautiful young woman, and took permission from mother Yaśodā to give Kṛṣṇa her breast to suck. Baby Kṛṣṇa, however, not only sucked her breast milk, but sucked out her life as well.

After Putana, Kaṁsa sent many demons, among them Tṛṇāvarta and Aghāsura. Tṛṇāvarta appeared in the shape of a whirlwind and tried to kidnap Kṛṣṇa and destroy Him high in the sky. Aghāsura, the brother of Pūtanā, came before Kṛṣṇa and His friends as a giant serpent. But Kṛṣṇa nonchalantly killed these ferocious demons one after another. Kṛṣṇa's father, Nanda, and other elders of the village were concerned about the constant attacks upon Kṛṣṇa, so they moved their entire village community to a more suitable place, where they hoped to be free from attack. But more demons came: a giant horse, an enormous bull, a pack of asses, and many others. Child Kṛṣṇa killed them all, assisted by His brother, Balarāma.

When Kṛṣṇa was sixteen years old, Kaṁsa discovered for certain that Kṛṣṇa in Vṛndāvana was Devakī's eighth child. Nārada told Kaṁsa of Kṛṣṇa's true identity and related how He had killed all the demons without difficulty. In desperation, Kaṁsa formed his final plot: he arranged for a big wrestling match at Mathurā and sent Akrūra, Kṛṣṇa's uncle, to Vṛndāvana to invite Kṛṣṇa and all His relatives and neighbors to attend the gala affair.

Akrūra was actually a great devotee of Kṛṣṇa. So when he arrived in Vṛndāvana, he confided to Kṛṣṇa that the wrestling match was an elaborate plan to kill Him and His brother. Kṛṣṇa and Balarāma mildly laughed at this. They invited all the townsmen to go to Mathurā, and They Themselves set out with Akrūra.

Kṛṣṇa's arrival in Mathūra was supposed to be His entrance into an ominous trap, but Kṛṣṇa very blissfully and lightheartedly entered the city. And when the news spread that Kṛṣṇa, the Supreme Personality of Godhead, had come, all the residents of Mathurā spontaneously turned out to see Him. The real festival in Mathurā became the festival of seeing Kṛṣṇa. All the young girls were very eager to see Kṛṣṇa, but out of modesty they went to the roofs of the houses to catch a glimpse of Him. The people had heard about Kṛṣṇa and His activities, but only now did they have the chance to see Him. They became ecstatic and rushed from whatever they were doing to see Kṛṣṇa passing through the streets. People talked back and forth about how beautiful Kṛṣṇa was, and they praised the great fortune of the *gopīs* and other devotees of Vṛndāvana who were able to see Kṛṣṇa every day.

There are two kinds of human beings, devotees and demons, and in Mathurā Kṛṣṇa encountered both. While Krsna and Balārama were walking through the streets of Mathurā, They met a washerman carrying various garments. Kṛṣṇa asked the washerman for some clothing and promised to award him all good fortune. This is the basis of Kṛṣṇa consciousness: the devotee offers whatever he has to the Lord, and the Lord, although not in need, accepts the offering to help awaken the devotee's original relationship of service to Him. Unfortunately, this washerman thought himself a servant not of Kṛṣṇa but of Kaṁsa. Not only did he refuse to give Kṛṣṇa clothing, but he called Him impudent. "Don't ask for things that are the King's property," he said, "or You will be punished." Kṛṣṇa became very angry with this servant of Kaṁsa and killed him, using only His hand as a weapon.

A little later Kṛṣṇa and Balarāma met a florist who was exactly the opposite of the washerman. He was very submissive and simply prayed to be eternally engaged in devotional service to Kṛṣṇa. The florist gave Kṛṣṇa a very beautiful garland at his home, and thus his desire was fulfilled.

Kṛṣṇa and Balarāma also met a young hunchback woman carrying sandalwood paste. Her duty had been to bring sandalwood to King Kaṁsa daily, but when she saw the personal beauty of Kṛṣṇa and Balarāma, she voluntarily offered the sandalwood paste to Them. In return, Kṛṣṇa transformed her from a hunchback into a beautiful young woman by touching her with His hand. One may take these extraordinary encounters to be fictitious or imaginary, but they are the actual historic activities the Personality of Godhead performed while present on earth some 5,000 years ago. The great authorities in Kṛṣṇa consciousness who are passing down the narrations of *Bhagavad-gītā* and *Śrīmad-Bhāgavatam* do not doubt these facts. Mundane scholars and people in general may doubt them, but they cannot understand the science of God as presented in Vedic literature. One who is not rendering service to the Personality of Godhead through a bona fide spiritual master can only whimsically speculate about what God can or cannot do.

As Kṛṣṇa and Balarāma approached the sacrificial arena in Mathurā, They saw a big display where a giant bow was being guarded by state soldiers. Kṛṣṇa walked right past the guards, picked up the bow and broke it. The sound of the bow's cracking reverberated throughout the land and sky and even reached the palace of Kaṁsa. The guards rushed Kṛṣṇa and Balarāma, but the two brothers immediately killed them and left the arena.

Thereafter, Kṛṣṇa continued to visit various places in Mathurā, and the citizens turned out to see Him, astonished at His extraordinary beauty and opulence. In *Kṛṣṇa, the Supreme Personality of Godhead,* Śrīla Prabhupāda writes, "The two brothers strolled carefree in the street, not caring for the law and order of Kaṁsa." In this way They hinted at the severe danger awaiting Kaṁsa.

When Kaṁsa heard the bow break and heard how the guards had been killed, he partially realized the power of the Supreme Lord. He understood that the eighth child of Devakī had come to kill him. That night he could not rest at all, for both awake and dreaming he had inauspicious visions. He looked in the mirror but could not see his head. He saw stars in the sky double. He saw holes in his shadow, heard a buzzing sound in his ears, and had ghastly dreams of ghosts, poison and murder. Thus he understood that his death was sure. But when morning finally came, he busily arranged for the wrestling match. In his last hours, with death so near, rather than pray to the Supreme Lord for mercy, Kaṁsa anxiously planned how to avert what he knew was certain.

All those who shared Kaṁsa's demoniac mentality are like that. They can see that material nature will eventually kill them, just as it has killed everyone else in history. Yet they act as if they will never die. A great devotee once called this the most wonderful phenomenon: people see the hand of death take away all their predecessors, but they think that they themselves will not die. The Kaṁsas of this world are always busy planning how to enjoy this life, even up till the second they are snatched away by death. So many modern cities have been built all over the world, but no one who lives in them has any guarantee that he won't be kicked out today or tomorrow by death. Ignoring the next life only insures that we will have to take another birth to suffer miseries again and again. Kaṁsa was like a man trying to raise his temperature when he already has a high fever; when the fever reaches 107 degrees, a man dies. Kaṁsa could not see that all his plans to survive would be vanquished, nor did he care to hear about the next life. Like a typical politician, on the morning of his death Kaṁsa busied himself making plans for this temporary world.

After bathing and performing other morning duties, Kṛṣṇa and Balarāma heard drums playing at the wrestling arena, and They prepared to go see the fun. But when They arrived at the gateway of the arena, a big elephant with a rider blocked Their path. This was another of Kaṁsa's schemes. Kṛṣṇa told the elephant's caretaker to immediately clear the path, but the man became angry and provoked the elephant to charge Kṛṣṇa. Kṛṣṇa moved around the elephant, dragged it by its tail, tripped it and finally killed both the elephant and its rider.

Kṛṣṇa and Balarāma then proceeded into the arena, where everyone at once became attracted to Them. The audience was completely attentive to Kṛṣṇa and

Balarāma. The residents of Vṛndāvana were all reciting Their pastimes, and others, seeing Them for the first time, began to praise Their qualities.

Suddenly, a musical fanfare announced the start of the wrestling match. The famous champion wrestlers Cañurā and Muṣṭika approached Kṛṣṇa and Balarāma, and Cāṇurā said, "We have heard all about You. The King desires to see You display Your wrestling abilities." Kṛṣṇa replied that although He and Balarāma liked to play and sometimes They wrestled with Their cowherd friends, They were not professional wrestlers. Kṛṣṇa said plainly that a match of professional wrestlers against young boys would not be equal, and this would disturb the audience. But the wrestlers insisted that Kṛṣṇa and Balarāma were not ordinary boys, and so the match began.

Many members of the audience called out their disapproval, for Kṛṣṇa and His brother appeared to be delicate boys of tender age, whereas the wrestlers were mountainous strongmen, trained in the art of crushing opponents. In *Kṛṣṇa, the Supreme Personality of Godhead,* Śrīla Prabhupāda specifically describes what the members of the audience said. "But my dear friends," someone spoke out, "just look at the face of Kṛṣṇa. There are drops of perspiration on His face from chasing His enemy, and His face appears like a lotus flower with drops of water. And do you see how the face of Lord Balarāma has turned especially beautiful? There is a reddish hue on His white face because He is engaged in a strong wrestling match with Muṣṭika." Another spectator exclaimed, "Even in front of the King this wrestling match is going on between incompatible sides." Thus the members of the audience were very attracted to Kṛṣṇa, but at the same time they saw great danger and felt anxiety for Him. Even Kṛṣṇa's very intimate devotees, such as His mother and father, were also very anxious because they too did not know the unlimited strength of Kṛṣṇa and Balarama.

Lord Kṛṣṇa is actually all-powerful, and there is nothing to fear when He is fighting a conditioned living being of the material world. Kṛṣṇa is declared throughout the *Vedas* to be the Absolute Truth, the source from whom everything comes and upon whom everything rests. *Śrīmad-Bhāgavatam* says that He alone existed before creation, He is now the only ultimate reality, and after annihilation only He will remain. But by Kṛṣṇa's internal spiritual energy, called *yoga-māyā,* He acts in different relationships with His servitors according to how they approach Him.

Kṛṣṇa is the reservoir of all personal feelings, so we should not be surprised that He reveals Himself differently in various relationships. To the mass of people at the wrestling arena He appeared as the most beautiful personality, but to the wrestlers He appeared like a thunderbolt. The *kṣatriyas* (warriors) saw Him as the strongest ruler, while the females saw Him as the most attractive male. The cowherd men from Vṛndāvana saw Him as their own kinsman, while the *yogīs* saw Him as the Supersoul in everyone's heart. Kaṁsa also saw Kṛṣṇa uniquely, as Death Personified.

Kaṁsa was always fearful that Kṛṣṇa would someday kill him. Thus he spent his whole life absorbed in thoughts of how to kill Kṛṣṇa. Because he was always thinking of Kṛṣṇa, Kaṁsa was Kṛṣṇa conscious. But because he thought of Kṛṣṇa unfavorably, he is not considered a devotee of the Lord. He was not practicing *bhakti* (devotional service). To be always thinking, like Kaṁsa, of how to avoid submitting to the Lord's supreme will is the principal engagement of a whole class of men, including modern educators, scientists, politicians and philosophers. By hearing about Kaṁsa, we can clearly understand why such a mentality is self-defeating.

Kṛṣṇa and Balarāma engaged the wrestlers in the standard wrestling holds and maneuvers for some time, but when the anxious protests of the audience grew too great, Kṛṣṇa simply spun one wrestler in the air, Balarāma hit the other, and the famous wrestlers were dead. Other wrestlers came forward, but the two brothers killed them immediately, and the remaining wrestlers ran from the arena. Musicians spontaneously beat their drums, and the crowd cheered the victory of Kṛṣṇa and Balarāma.

Kaṁsa was enraged. He announced that Kṛṣṇa and Balarāma should be driven from the city of Mathurā, Their riches plundered, and Kṛṣṇa's father killed. Kṛṣṇa could not tolerate such talk. He jumped over the high wall protecting King Kaṁsa and stood before him face to face. Kaṁsa tried defending himself with a sword, but Kṛṣṇa grabbed him and dragged him down from the throne. After throwing him on the ground, Kṛṣṇa killed Kaṁsa by punching him with His fist. Kṛṣṇa then dragged Kaṁsa around the arena the way a lion drags an elephant after killing it, just to assure His parents, relatives and all pious people that Kaṁsa was actually dead.

One may wonder why this narration contains so much violence and killing, since the Supreme Personality of Godhead is said to be all-merciful. But there is no question of wrongdoing in Kṛṣṇa's actions. Because Kṛṣṇa is absolute, whatever Kṛṣṇa does is absolutely good. Fighting and killing is required for a *kṣatriya* (warrior) when there is a need to punish miscreants who threaten the peaceful citizens of society. When such criminals need to be rebuffed, nonviolence is cowardice, as Kṛṣṇa told Arjuna on the Battlefield of Kurukṣetra. Devotees of Kṛṣṇa are naturally nonviolent toward all living entities, even animals, but if the demoniac make a violent disturbance, the devotees are prepared to counter such violence in the service of the Supreme Lord.

Also, when Kṛṣṇa personally kills someone, He gives that person the benediction of liberation. Astoundingly, Kaṁsa was immediately awarded *sārūpya-mukti* upon being killed by Kṛṣṇa. This means that he went to the spiritual planets, where he was able to live in eternity, bliss and knowledge with a form almost exactly resembling the Supreme Lord's in opulence and beauty. Such liberation is very difficult to achieve, even after hundreds of lifetimes spent searching for the Absolute Truth. *Yogīs* and ascetics achieve release from all material desires only after prolonged, severe austerities. But even they do not reach the Vaikuṇṭha planets; they merge into the impersonal *brahmajyoti,* the effulgence of the Lord. Kaṁsa, however, had a personal relationship with Kṛṣṇa. He thought of Kṛṣṇa day and night: "When will He come? What is He doing now? When will He kill me?" So Kaṁsa was given a place more exalted than all the impersonal mystic *yogīs* of the *haṭha-yoga* school or the philosophers who speculate about the impersonal Absolute Truth. This gives a hint of the great power of *bhakti.* If an avowed enemy of Kṛṣṇa is given such a high place, we can barely even imagine the sweet favor the Lord awards to those who relate to Him in a positive, loving way, always rendering service to Him and chanting His glories.

Finally, one might ask why Kṛṣṇa should personally fight with a demon like Kaṁsa. Kṛṣṇa, being the source of all emanations and qualities, has His own transcendental desires. Therefore He also has a fighting propensity, which He exhibits in His playful wrestling with the cowherd boys of Vṛndāvana. Authorities in the science of Kṛṣṇa consciousness inform us that Kṛṣṇa's choice to fight with Kaṁsa indicates that Kaṁsa is actually a liberated devotee of Kṛṣṇa's who was sent to the material world to provide the Lord a suitable opponent. Kaṁsa could not actually threaten Kṛṣṇa; Kṛṣṇa arranged the fight for His personal pleasure. This understanding brings us to a level of consciousness beyond violence or nonviolence, morality or immorality.

Kṛṣṇa displays His eternal pastimes with His devotees just to attract us to return to His loving service. We are all eternal parts and parcels of Kṛṣṇa, but we are now suffering the miseries of repeated birth and death in the material world, in forgetfulness of Kṛṣṇa. We should not struggle to rival Kṛṣṇa; rather, we should understand that the only business of our life is to serve the Lord. We each have a natural aptitude for the service of Kṛṣṇa, and that should be developed, under the guidance of a bona fide spiritual master. The first engagement is to hear the pastimes of Kṛṣṇa. Our present age is very fallen, full of materialistic and impersonal concepts of reality, but the truth is available in the vast treasurehouse of Vedic literature. The sincere seeker will find that truth very easily, if he begins with a submissive ear.

The Appearance of Lord Caitanya

March, 1975

Lord Caitanya Mahāprabhu, who was also known as Viśvambhara ("Lord of the universe"), appeared in Bengal, India, 489 years ago and taught love of Kṛṣṇa. The Vedic scriptures, such as the *Vedas, Upaniṣads, Vedānta-sūtra* and especially *Bhagavad-gītā* and *Śrīmad-Bhāgavatam,* all reveal Kṛṣṇa to be the Supreme Truth and the dearmost friend of every living being. Lord Kṛṣṇa says in *Bhagavad-gītā,* "Give up all other forms of religion and surrender to Me. I shall then protect you." Lord Caitanya, therefore, urged everyone He met, "Surrender to Kṛṣṇa. His holy name is the only shelter."

Because thousands of years had passed since Kṛṣṇa's appearance on earth and because people had not fully understood Kṛṣṇa from *Bhagavad-gītā,* Lord Caitanya, as Kṛṣṇa's dearmost servant, showed everyone exactly how to render loving service to Kṛṣṇa, just according to Kṛṣṇa's own words as revealed in Vedic literature. These Vedic writings were compiled 5,000 years ago, but when Lord Caitanya came He created a great revival of love for Kṛṣṇa. Most importantly, Lord Caitanya delivered the chanting of Kṛṣṇa's holy names: Hare Kṛṣṇa, Hare Kṛṣṇa, Kṛṣṇa Kṛṣṇa, Hare Hare/Hare Rāma, Hare Rāma, Rāma Rāma, Hare Hare.

Śrī Kṛṣṇa Caitanya, as He was also called, did not invent the chanting of Hare Kṛṣṇa; He took it directly from the Vedic scriptures. The *Bṛhan-nāradīya Purāṇa* says *harer nāma harer nāma harer nāmaiva kevalam/kalau nasty eva nasty eva nasty eva gatir anyatha:*"Chant the holy name, chant the holy name, chant the holy name! In the Kali-yuga [the Age of Quarrel and Hypocrisy] there is no other way, no other way, no other way." The *Kalisantarana Upaniṣad* also says that these sixteen words in thirty-two syllables–Hare Kṛṣṇa, Hare Kṛṣṇa, Kṛṣṇa Kṛṣṇa, Hare Hare/Hare Rāma, Hare Rāma, Rāma Rāma, Hare Hare–are the most effective means for counteracting the contaminating effects of Kali-yuga.

According to the Vedic scriptures, the chanting is the only process perfectly suitable for the age in which Lord Caitanya appeared, Kali-yuga, a spiritually fallen age. Kali-yuga is still going on, and we shall feel its disruptive influence more and more. Therefore Lord Caitanya gave a great impetus to the Kṛṣṇa consciousness movement by inaugurating *saṅkīrtana,* the congregational chanting of the holy names. Indeed, He set in motion, by His own example, a movement that would spread all over the world as the greatest benediction for the people of today. Almost five hundred years ago, He Himself foretold, "The chanting of the names of Kṛṣṇa will be heard in every town and village of the world."

We know a great deal about the life and teachings of Lord Caitanya because His immediate followers wrote many books, all authoritatively based on the Vedic scriptures. His chief literary followers were known as the six Gosvāmīs. Among them, Jīva, Sanātana and Rūpa especially wrote dozens of scholarly spiritual books proving *bhakti,* or love of Kṛṣṇa, to be the ultimate goal of the *Vedas.* Kṛṣṇadāsa Kavirāja and Vṛndāvana dāsa Ṭhākura also wrote authoritative biographies of Śrī Kṛṣṇa Caitanya, and many of their learned followers have contributed elaborations and expositions upon the philosophy of Lord Caitanya, thus establishing the basis for a complete and consistent spiritual movement.

As we observe the 489th anniversary of Lord Caitanya's appearance, let us consider His significance for the people of the world today. Kṛṣṇadāsa Kavirāja Gosvāmī, in his biography *Śrī Caitanya-caritāmṛta,* describes the events leading to Śri Caitanya's appearance. We shall try to relate them here, for they tell us much about His mission.

"To fulfill a particular desire within His mind, Lord Kṛṣṇa, Vrajendra-kumāra, decided to descend on this planet after mature contemplation." Kṛṣṇadāsa Kavirāja plainly declares that Lord Caitanya is Lord Kṛṣṇa, the Supreme Personality of Godhead. Lord Caitanya's advent is also mentioned in the *Śrīmad-Bhāgavatam: kṛṣṇa-varṇaṁ tviṣākṛṣṇam sāṅgopāṅgāstra-pārṣadam yajñaiḥ saṅkīrtana-prāyair yajanti hi sumedhasaḥ* "In this Age of Kali, people endowed with sufficient intelligence will worship the Lord, who is accompanied by His associates, by performing *saṅkīrtana-yajña* [congregational chanting of Hare Kṛṣṇa]." (*Bhāg.* 11.5.32) This verse also describes that in the Age of Kali, Kṛṣṇa will appear, but His complexion will be golden. When Lord Caitanya taught His disciple Sanātana how to detect a genuine incarnation of God, He pointed out that the activities and bodily hues of the incarnations are described in the scriptures. Since the time of Lord Caitanya, many men have posed as Gods or *avatāras,* collected money and attracted followers, but such imposters never fool the experts who know the transcendental science.

The scriptures indicate that the incarnation for Kali-yuga is Śrī Caitanya Mahāprabhu, who is also called Gaurāṅga or Gaurasundara (Gaura means "gold") because of His golden hue. His complexion is golden, and His activities engage everyone in chanting Hare Kṛṣṇa. To enact His mission, He always appears with His associates. Thus Lord Caitanya is most often worshiped in His form of *pañca-tattva,* in which He is accompanied by His immediate expansions Nityānanda, Advaita, Gadādhara and Śrīvāsa.

Caitanya-caritāmṛta describes that before Lord Kṛṣṇa took birth as Lord Caitanya, He requested many of His devotees to precede Him. "Lord Kṛṣṇa first allowed His family of superiors to descend on the earth." (Cc. *Ādi* 13.53) These included Śrī Śacīdevī and Jagannātha Miśra, who were to appear as His mother and father; Mādhavendra Purī, who was to appear as a great spiritual master in the line Śrī Caitanya would follow; and Śrī Advaita, Śrīvasa and Nityānanda, three of the Lord's principal associates who would appear as His elders in His pastimes. He also sent Haridāsa Ṭhākura, who, despite his birth in a Moslem family, would become the *nāmācārya,* or master of the holy name, celebrated for chanting 300,000 names of Kṛṣṇa daily. In an important book called *Gaura-gaṇoddeśa-dipikā,* Kavi-karṇapūra has ascertained that the associates or family members of Lord Kṛṣṇa in Kṛṣṇa's pastimes 5,000 years ago in Vṛndāvana reappeared in different roles in the pastimes of Lord Caitanya. Thus Jagannātha Miśra and Sacīdevi were formerly Nanda and Yaśodā, the mother and father of Kṛṣṇa; Nityānanda was formerly Kṛṣṇa's brother, Balarāma; and Advaita Ācārya was an incarnation of Kṛṣṇa's Viṣṇu expansion from whom all the universes emanate at the time of univeral creation.

Śrī Caitanya-caritāmṛta describes the birthplace of Lord Gaurasundara before the Lord's advent: "Before the appearance of Lord Caitanya Mahāprabhu, all the devotees of Navadvīpa used to gather in the house of Advaita Ācārya. In these meetings of devotees, Advaita Ācārya used to recite *Bhagavad-gītā* and *Śrīmad-Bhāgavatam,* decrying the paths of philosophical speculation and fruitive activity and establishing the superexcellence of devotional service." (Cc. *Ādi-līlā,* 13.63-4)

Kṛṣṇadāsa Kavirāja further mentions that devotional service to Lord Kṛṣṇa is the actual conclusion of the Vedic scriptures. Although different sections of the Vedic literature teach different paths, staunch devotees of Lord Kṛṣṇa reject other processes, such as philosophical speculation, yogic gymnastics and unnecessary austerities and rituals, for these are meant only to raise people gradually to devotional service. Kṛṣṇa says at the end of His teachings in *Bhagavad-gītā,* "Give up all other varieties of religion and just surrender to Me." Devotees, therefore, are the topmost transcendentalists and so need not engage in any other process than devotional service. If one takes to another process but doesn't recognize that love of the Supreme Person is the supreme goal, he cannot be accepted as a genuine transcendentalist, and his practice of *yoga* or meditation is a waste of time.

It is stated that the associates who preceded Lord Caitanya were reading *Bhagavad-gītā* and *Śrīmad-Bhāgavatam* exclusively. One who doesn't know the conclusion may search through many literatures and philosophies inquiring for the ultimate. These two Vedic literatures, however, hold the cream of all the *Vedas.* Śrīdhara Svāmi, a great Vedic *ācārya* (spiritual master), wrote, "The *Gītā,* which issued from the lotus-like lips of Padmānabha Himself [Lord Kṛṣṇa], must be well assimilated; what is the use of a multiplicity of other scriptures?" Lord Caitanya Himself prescribed reading *Śrīmad-Bhāgavatam* and *Bhagavad-gītā* as primary because although the *Vedas* and *Upaniṣads* only hint at the Absolute Truth, that Truth is fully developed in the *Gītā,* which records the spoken words of Kṛṣṇa, and *Śrīmad-Bhāgavatam,* which contains narratives *about* Kṛṣṇa and His pure devotees.

The associates of Lord Caitanya are described as Vaiṣṇavas, which means devotees of the Absolute Truth in His aspect as the Supreme Person. *Caitanya-caritāmṛta* continues: "In the house of Advaita Ācārya, all the Vaiṣṇavas took pleasure in always talking of Kṛṣṇa, always worshiping Kṛṣṇa and always chanting the Hare Kṛṣṇa *mahā-mantra.*" (Cc. *Ādi-līlā* 13.66) From this we can understand that the devotees who gathered at Advaita Ācārya's house were fully absorbed in Kṛṣṇa consciousness, either through talking of Kṛṣṇa on the basis of *Bhagavad-gītā* and *Śrīmad-Bhāgavatam,* worshiping the Lord in His form as the Deity, or chanting in *kīrtana* (singing Hare Kṛṣṇa) with musical instruments. Because such Vaiṣṇavas understand that there is nothing but Kṛṣṇa and His energy, they never forget Kṛṣṇa for a moment, and they always engage their senses in some kind of devotional service to the Supreme Lord.

Caitanya-caritāmṛta goes on to cite the predominant mood of the assembled Vaiṣṇavas: "But Śrī Advaita Ācārya Prabhu felt pained to see all the people without Kṛṣṇa consciousness, simply merging in material sense enjoyment." (Cc. *Ādi-līlā* 13.67) Such is the vision of all pure devotees. Śrīla Bhaktisiddhānta Sarasvatī Ṭhākura (the spiritual master of His Divine Grace A.C. Bhaktivedanta Swami Prabhupāda) used to say, "There is no scarcity of anything within this world. The only item scarce is Kṛṣṇa consciousness." The devotee can see that for want of God consciousness people are suffering terribly. In ignorance, people think they can be happy without cultivating spiritual life, and so they absorb themselves in plans and activities just to satisfy their senses. Yet this only causes suffering, all over the world. Food shortages, fuel shortages, war and poverty are all directly traceable to humanity's forgetfulness of its relationship to Kṛṣṇa.

Material nature runs by strict laws, and Kṛṣṇa consciousness is a science of how to live in harmony with the material and spiritual nature by acting always in loving relation to the Supreme Lord, who is in fact the supreme proprietor. Man acts as if no one were in charge but him, and so the masses of people are misled by capitalism, communism, consumerism, voidism and so many other godless "isms." Man breaks nature's laws and suffers from the crises that result. A devotee onlooker is very much aggrieved to see this.

The same materialistic tendencies plagued Navadvīpa 500 years ago, and so Advaita Ācārya expressed His sorrow for the people. The Vaiṣṇavas at His home were free of all anxiety themselves because of their participation in *kṛṣṇa-kathā* (topics about Kṛṣṇa), but a Vaiṣṇava is unhappy to see others unhappy. Another great Vaiṣṇava, Prahlāda Mahārāja, whose life is described in *Śrīmad-Bhāgavatam*, once prayed: "Saintly persons and ascetics generally travel alone, concerned only with their own salvation, but I am not like them. I do not want to go back to the kingdom of God alone, leaving all these bewildered people who have no other shelter but Your Lordship. Unless they can come with me, I shall not go back to Godhead." A Vaiṣṇava feels free of all difficulty, but he also feels compassion for those who have been duped into accepting a false civilization that will cause them only suffering in this life and the next.

"Vaiṣṇava" is not a sectarian designation. Lord Jesus Christ and Lord Mohammed were also powerful Vaiṣṇava personalities who worked to bring humanity to love of God. Only the presence of such Vaiṣṇavas can save human society. Lord Caitanya was to appear in a community of such Vaiṣṇavas, but with one difference: He Himself was the Supreme Lord, the object of the Vaiṣṇavas' prayers. Thus even though appearing as a devotee, He would be able to deliver love of Kṛṣṇa directly.

How Lord Caitanya descended at the specific request of Advaita Ācārya is described in *Çaitanya-caritāmṛta:* "Seeing the condition of the world, Śrī Advaita Ācārya began to think seriously of how all these people could be delivered from the clutches of *māyā* (material illusion). Śrīla Advaita Prabhu thought: 'If Kṛṣṇa Himself appears to distribute the cult of devotional service, then only will liberation be possible for all people.' " (Cc. *Ādi-līlā* 13.68-69) His Divine Grace A.C. Bhaktivedanta Swami Prabhupāda comments on this prayer: "Just as a condemned person can be relieved by a special favor of the chief executive head, the president or king, so the condemned people of this Kali-yuga can be delivered only by the Supreme Personality of Godhead Himself or a person empowered especially for this purpose. Śrīla Advaita Ācārya Prabhu desired that the Supreme Personality Himself advent to deliver the fallen souls of this age." Advaita Ācārya thus promised to cause Lord Kṛṣṇa to descend, and He began to worship the Supreme Lord with offerings of *tulasī* leaves and water of the Ganges. "By loud cries He invited Kṛṣṇa to appear," writes Kṛṣṇadāsa Kavirāja, "and this repeated invitation attracted Lord Kṛṣṇa to descend."

Just as the prayers of Lord Brahmā caused Lord Kṛṣṇa to descend in Vṛndāvana, so the prayers of Kṛṣṇa's pure devotee, Advaita Ācārya, caused Him to come again as Lord Caitanya. Of course, the Supreme Lord comes at His own will for His own mission, as stated in *Bhagavad-gītā:* "Whenever and wherever there is a decline in religious practices, O Bhārata, and a predominant rise of irreligion—at that time I descend Myself. To deliver the pious and annihilate the miscreants, as well as to establish the principles of religion, I advent Myself millennium after millennium." (Bg. 4.7-8) According to these verses, Lord Kṛṣṇa appears specifically to mitigate the anxieties of pure devotees who are eager to see Him in His pastimes. Lord Kṛṣṇa says that He appears in every millennium. This indicates that He also incarnates in the Age of Kali. Thus Lord Caitanya, as the incarnation of Kṛṣṇa, the Personality of Godhead, is described secretly, indirectly, in the confidential parts of revealed scriptures such as the *Upaniṣads, Mahābhārata* and *Śrīmad-Bhāgavatam.*

The devotees of Lord Kṛṣṇa are greatly attracted by the *saṅkīrtana* movement of Lord Caitanya because instead of killing the miscreants, the Lord, through this movement, delivers them by His causeless mercy. When Rūpa Gosvāmī first met Lord Caitanya, Rūpa Gosvāmī therefore offered this prayer: "I offer You my most humble obeisances, for You are the most munificent *avatāra* of Kṛṣṇa, offering what was never offered before, even by Kṛṣṇa Himself—pure love of Kṛṣṇa." These are some of the special features of Śrī Kṛṣṇa Caitanya.

Lord Caitanya's appearing as the son of Śacīdevī and Jagannātha Miśra cannot be compared to the birth of an ordinary conditioned soul. It is comparable only to Kṛṣṇa's appearance as the son of Devakī and Vasudeva. Before the birth of Lord Caitanya Mahāprabhu, Śacīdevī, the wife of Jagannātha Miśra, gave birth to eight daughters one after another, but just after their birth they died. Unhappy at the death of his children, and desiring a son, Jagannātha Miśra worshiped the lotus feet of Lord Viṣṇu. After this, Śacīdevī gave birth to a highly qualified son, whom they named Viśvarūpa. Greatly pleased with their son, the husband and wife especially began to serve the feet of the Supreme Lord.

Śrī Caitanya-caritāmṛta describes elaborately what happened next: "In the month of January in the year 1407 of the Śaka Era [A.D. 1486], Lord Kṛṣṇa entered the bodies of both Jagannātha Miśra and Śacī. Jagannātha Miśra said to Śacīmātā: "I see wonderful things! Your body is effulgent, and it appears as if the goddess of fortune were now staying personally in my home. Anywhere and everywhere I go, all people offer me respect. Even without my asking, they voluntarily give me riches, clothing and paddy.'

"Śacīmātā told her husband: 'I also see wonderfully brilliant human beings appearing in outer space, as if offering prayers.'

"Jagannātha Miśra then replied: 'In a dream I saw the effulgent abode of the Lord enter my heart. From my heart it entered your heart. I therefore understand that a great personality will soon take birth.' " (Cc. *Ādi-līlā* 13.80-5) Śacīdevī did not become pregnant as an ordinary woman becomes pregnant because of sensual indulgence. But exactly as Kṛṣṇa appeared in the heart of Devakī through the heart of Vasudeva, so Lord Caitanya appeared in the heart of Śacīdevī through the heart of Jagannātha Miśra.

While Śacīdevī was pregnant, Nīlāmbara Cakravartī (the grandfather of Śrī Caitanya Mahāprabhu) astrologically calculated that in that month, at an auspicious moment, the child would be born. At the time of Lord Caitanya's appearance, a wonderful natural phenomenon occurred–a full lunar eclipse. Kṛṣṇadāsa Kavirāja writes, "When the spotless moon of Caitanya Mahāprabhu became visible, what would be the need for a moon full of black spots on its body?"

In India all the followers of the Vedic scriptures customarily bathe in the Ganges or the sea as soon as there is a lunar or solar eclipse. Strict followers of the Vedic religion stand in the water throughout the eclipse and chant the Hare Kṛṣṇa *mahā-mantra.* At the time of Lord Caitanya's birth such a lunar eclipse took place, and naturally the people standing in the water were chanting Hare Kṛṣṇa, Hare Kṛṣṇa, Kṛṣṇa Kṛṣṇa, Hare Hare/Hare Rāma, Hare Rāma, Rāma Rāma, Hare Hare. Kṛṣṇadāsa Kavirāja relates that not only were the followers of the *Vedas* chanting Hare Kṛṣṇa, but the Mohammedans and others joined them, imitating the chanting. Thus Hindus and Moslems joined together in chanting the holy name of the Lord when Śrī Caitanya Mahāprabhu appeared. It was miraculously appropriate that He who throughout His life would induce everyone to chant Hare Kṛṣṇa appeared in the world at a moment when everyone was joyfully chanting because of the lunar eclipse. Certainly it signaled the advent of a great leader of *saṅkīrtana.*

Kṛṣṇadāsa Kavirāja relates that the whole world was induced to blissful chanting of the holy names by the appearance of Śrī Caitanya Mahāprabhu. "All the ten directions became jubilant, as did the waves of the rivers. Moreover, all beings, moving and nonmoving, were overwhelmed with transcendental bliss. . . . At that time Śrī Advaita Ācārya Prabhu, in His own house at Śāntipura, was dancing in a pleasing mood. Taking Haridāsa Ṭhākura with Him, He danced and loudly chanted Hare Kṛṣṇa. But when they were dancing no one could understand. . . . In this way all the devotees, wherever they were situated, in every city and every country, danced, performed *saṅkīrtana,* and gave charity by mental strength on the plea of the lunar eclipse, their minds overwhelmed with joy." (Cc. *Ādi-līlā* 13.97,99,103)

After the Lord's appearance, respectable ladies of the neighborhood came to visit the newly-born child, whose bodily color resembled shining gold. Among them, Sītādevī, who was Advaita Ācārya's wife and a recognized devotee, was astonished when she saw Viśvambhara, for she could appreciate that except for a difference in color, the child was directly Kṛṣṇa Himself.

Caitanya-caritāmṛta states, "Lord Caitanya is very merciful to anyone who hears this narration of His birth, and thus such a person attains the lotus feet of the Lord." (13.122)

Kṛṣṇadāsa Kavirāja writes that the pastimes of Lord Caitanya are unlimited and that he can give only a tiny part of them in his book *Caitanya-caritāmṛta.* Of that tiny part, we have here taken only a brief glimpse, as space would permit. The readers are advised to read *Caitanya-caritāmṛta* further, especially for an elaborate discussion, supported by scriptural references, concerning the identity of Lord Caitanya with Kṛṣṇa Himself. There is also extensive material on the happy results of chanting of the Hare Kṛṣṇa *mantra.*

His Divine Grace A.C. Bhaktivedanta Swami Prabhupāda has recently completed his translation, with purports, of the entire *Caitanya-caritāmṛta* (11,555 verses). As Śrīla Prabhupāda's purports establish, the International Society for Krishna Consciousness is genuinely continuing Lord Caitanya's mission of spreading Kṛṣṇa consciousness all over the world.

We hope that these few lines on the appearance of Lord Caitanya will encourage interest in the potent reality of Lord Caitanya's *saṅkīrtana* movement. Kṛṣṇa consciousness is authentically based on the Vedic literature and intended precisely for this age. Kṛṣṇadāsa Kavirāja emphatically states that if one is at all interested in his self-betterment, he should not miss the chance to take to the teachings of Śrī Caitanya Mahāprabhu: "Anyone who attains a human body but does not take to the cult of Śrī Caitanya Mahāprabhu is baffled in his opportunity. *Amṛtadhunī* is a flowing river of the nectar of devotional service. If after getting a human body one drinks the water in a poison pit of material happiness instead of the water of such a river, it would be better for him not to have lived, but to have died long ago."

II. Sages and Saints of the Past

Lord Shiva
The Pure Devotee

March/April, 1972

Once, at the dawn of the universal creation a great sacrifice was performed by the leaders of mankind,–namely Marichi, Dakha and Dasistha. All great personalities, powerful sages, philosophers and demigods, along with their followers assembled. Lord Brahma and Lord Shiva were also present. When Dakha, the leader of the Prajapatis (the first progenitors of the universe), entered into the assembly his bodily luster was so bright that practically everyone else present seemed insignificant. Influenced by Dakha's luster, they gave up their places and stood in respect. Lord Brahma is considered to be the first living entity of the universe and the creator of all the material planets and entities. Lord Brahma is directly empowered by the Original Supreme Personality of Godhead, Sri Krishna or Vishnu, and so he was logically presiding at the head of the assembly. Although Lord Brahma did not rise to honor Dakha, he adequately welcomed him with words and asked him to take a seat of honor. Lord Shiva alone remained seated without showing any respect to the effulgent Prajapati. Dakha was very offended seeing Lord Shiva sitting there, and instead of taking his seat, Dakha began to speak strongly against him.

So begins the history of a great sacrifice and misunderstanding between Dakha and Lord Shiva, which resulted in widespread destruction. It is fully related in the Fourth Canto of Srimad Bhagwatam, the Vedic scripture which deals exclusively in the narration of the transcendental Pastimes of the Supreme Personality of Godhead, Krishna, and His pure devotees.

Lord Shiva is a pure devotee of Lord Krishna, who is accepted as the Supreme Lord by the purport of all Vedic literature, Upanishads, Puranas and Vedanta Sutra, and by the disciplic succession of spiritual masters. The intelligent human being who worships the Supreme Lord Krishna or His immediate expansion, Vishnu, is called a "Vaishnava." And in the Vaishnava Purana it is stated that Sambhu (Lord Shiva) is the greatest Vaishnava: "Vaishnavanan natan Sambhu." Lord Shiva himself declares, in the Shiva Purana, that one should take to devotional service of the Supreme Lord Vishnu. Being a pure devotee and a confidential deputed agent of Krishna, Lord Shiva is beyond reproach in all his actions.

But Dakha spoke against Lord Shiva: "All sages and brahmins and firegods present here, please hear me with attention as I am speaking about the manners of gentle persons. I am not speaking out of ignorance or envy." Dakha very tactfully presented to the assembly that he was going to make a sensible speech, and not out of enviousness. Although he was speaking like a man in ignorance by intending to attack Lord Shiva's behavior, and although all present were perfectly aware of the exalted position of Lord Shiva, Dakha was so envious that he tried to cover his poisonous statements with a plea for gentleness and nonenviousness. He then launched verbally into Lord Shiva and said that he has ruined the good name of the demigods and that he is unclean. Dakha then stated, "Although Lord Shiva has already accepted a position subordinate to me, by marrying my daughter, yet he is not respectful to his father-in-law." The fact was that Lord Shiva's wife, Sati, was the daughter of Dakha and they had married under the instructions of Lord Shiva's father, Lord Brahma. Since Lord Shiva was actually the son-in-law of Dakha, one might ask, why did he not stand up and pay respects when Dakha arrived, and that might have prevented the total holocaust which, as we shall see, soon followed. The answer is that at the time Dakha entered, Lord Shiva was meditating, as he always is, on the Form of the Supreme Lord who dwells in the hearts of all creatures. As the greatest Vaishnava, he was in trance of ecstasy, meditating on the One God of all Being and Nonbeing who is alone factually worthy of all our reverence. In meditation, he might not have seen Dakha enter the arena of the sacrifice. But Dakha took the opportunity of cursing him because he was holding an envious attitude toward him for a long time.

Actually, those who are self-realized think of everybody as a temple of the Supreme Personality of Godhead, as He resides in everyone's body. The respect paid to the body is not paid to the material body, but to the Presence of the Supreme Lord within the body. By offering obeisances to the Supersoul, Lord Shiva had already offered respects to the Supersoul of Dakha and there was no need of offering respects to Dakha's body. But Dakha, not being a transcendentalist, could not appreciate Lord Shiva's irreproachable behavior. To be always in meditation on the Supreme Lord is not a conjurer's trick or something to be imitated. Nor is it anything like meditating on the impersonal void. Just as we are persons, but limited to our individual bodies, so the Supreme Lord Krishna is an individual Person, but He is at the same time one and different from the creation. He is Single, One without a second, and yet He is all-pervading. By His Mercy He is present in everyone's heart, giving the intelligence and pure memory whereby one can go back to Him for personal association in eternal bliss and all knowledge. Lord Shiva then was fixed in mind on the Absolute and therefore he should not have been reproached. Dakha however was thinking only in bodily, materialistic terms, and considered his body insulted by the behavior of his exalted son-in-law. Before the great assembly he vilified Lord Shiva.

Dakha said: "Shiva remains in the filthiest places like the crematorium, and his companions are ghosts and demons and he remains like a madman. He never bathes regularly and puts a garland made of the skulls of dead bodies around his neck for ornamentation. He is very dear to the crazy beings in the mode of ignorance. On the request of Lord Brahma I handed over my chaste daughter to him although he is devoid of all cleanliness and his heart is filled with nasty things."

The name Shiva is auspicious, and yet those who do not bathe regularly are supposed to be in association with the ghosts and crazy creatures. Lord Shiva appeared like that, but his actual transcendental position is that he is very kind to persons who are in the darkness of the mode of ignorance, the drunkards and the unclean. He is so compassionate on the lowest of the low that he gives such creatures shelter and gradually makes them elevated to spiritual understanding. This is the explanation of Lord Shiva's transcendental position, according to the authoritative literature. It is stated in the Vedas that Lord Shiva is all-auspicious, so by his association even the most fallen souls can be elevated. In the creation of the Supreme Lord there are different kinds of living creatures, some of them are in the quality of goodness, some in the quality of passion and some in ignorance. Lord Vishnu takes charge of the persons who are advanced Vaishnavas or Krishna conscious, Lord Brahma takes charge of the persons who are very much attached to material activities, but Lord Shiva is so kind that he takes charge of persons who are grossly in ignorance and whose behavior is less than the animals.

Dakha cursed Lord Shiva out of envy and called him the lowest of the demigods and not worth being offered oblations or taking part in the sacrifice. One of the great commentators on the Srimad Bhagwatam, Sri Viswanath Chakravarty, says in regard to this curse of Dakha by which Lord Shiva was cut off from participating in the sacrifice, that it was an indirect blessing for Lord Shiva. As the greatest devotee of the Supreme Personality of Godhead it is not worthy that Lord Shiva should eat and sit with materialistic persons like the demigods who might be a distraction to his prosecution of devotional service. So he was saved from the calamity of their non-Krishna conscious association.

Dakha was a very powerful mystic brahmin, but under the deadly influence of anger, he declared he could not bear to carry on in the presence of the unclean Lord Shiva, and so he left the area of sacrifice. All the sages and Lord Brahma requested Dakha, "Please do not leave our company"—but in spite of all requests Dakha left the place under the effect of cruel anger. In the Bhagavad Gita it is advised that anyone interested in spiritual advancement must avoid lust, anger and passion, but Dakha was attacked by all three. Nandikesvar, one of the chief associates of Lord Shiva, also caught the evil influence of anger, and he prepared to curse Dakha as well as all the brahmins present there who merely sat by and tolerated the cursing of Lord Shiva. Goswami A.C. Bhaktivedanta writes of this situation: "There is a longstanding dissension among the neophyte Vaishnavas and Shivites, by which they are always at loggerheads. Some brahmins are not admirers of Lord Shiva and might enjoy his being cursed, but this is due to their ignorance of Lord Shiva's position (as the greatest Vaishnava)." Nandikesvar in his anger did not follow the example of Lord Shiva who was silent and tolerant. Nandikesvar could not tolerate the insult to a Vaishnava and he counter-cursed Dakha and his followers, stating that whoever supported Dakha would be bereft of transcendental knowledge of the soul and devoid of knowledge of the Supreme Personality of Godhead. He called Dakha a pretentious house-holder, with only superficial knowledge of the Vedas; and such a person, he stated, although following the rules and regulations of the Vedas, will be attached to the temporary material sex happiness as the all-in-all, with no knowledge of the spiritual, eternal, blissful life. Lord Shiva's aide further deemed that whoever attacked Lord Shiva would be doomed to continue seeking happiness in the nescience of materialistic education and working for mundane rewards, and would therefore continue perpetually in the cycle of birth and death. Such attacks on the brahmins are applicable to the so-called brahmins of the present Age of Kali who claim brahminical or spiritual status simply on the basis of heredity or birth in a family of brahmins. In the scripture Vedanta Sutra, it is stated that the human form of life is meant for realizing the Supreme Brahman or Absolute Truth and that is the real business of a brahmin. But the so-called brahmins cursed by Nandikesvar were more interested in living for maintaining the perishable material body and elevating their family position. And worst of all they refused to recognize the pure devotee of the Lord, in the personality of Lord Shiva. Ignited by the envy of Dakha, Nandikesvar wrongly cursed all the brahmins present in a nondiscriminate condemnation. The whole issue became so complicated that those who were not strong enough forgot their positions, and cursing and counter-cursing went on in the great assembly.

As a reaction to Nandikesvar's cursing, the brahmin sage, Brighu, delivered a brahminical curse to all followers of Lord Shiva, as follows: "One who takes the vow of satisfying Lord Shiva or who follows those principles certainly becomes an atheist, as he becomes diverted from the scriptural injunction." It is understood that the devotees of Lord Shiva sometimes imitate the characteristics of Lord Shiva rather than follow his example. Lord Shiva once drank an ocean of poison, so the followers of Lord Shiva, without being able to drink even a fragment of poison, imitate him and take intoxicants.

Brighu delivers the curse that if somebody follows such principles of intoxication, he must become an infidel against the principles of Vedic regulation. Lord

Krishna Himself declares in the Bhagavad Gita that He descends and corrects the regulative principles when there is too much general disregard of the prescribed rules for spiritual progress. So anyone seriously interested in prosecuting spiritual life has to follow the footsteps of the Supreme Lord, the scriptures and the teachings of His deputed controllers or Mahajans. We have to follow their example, and we are warned not to imitate Krishna or His controllers. Lord Krishna lifted Govardhan Hill in His Childhood Pastime while on earth, and no human being can possibly imitate Him in this. Lord Shiva is a Mahajan or authority in Krishna Consciousness and his unusual activities on behalf of Krishna may be completely independent of the injunctions of the scriptures. But his followers may not assume his stature. The Srimad Bhagwatam plainly states, "One should not try to drink an ocean of poison, imitating Lord Shiva." Brighu further states that the followers of Lord Shiva will turn against the conclusion of the sciptures. It is confirmed in the Padma Purana that Lord Shiva himself (as Sri Shankaracharya) was ordered by the Supreme Personality of Godhead to preach impersonal philosophy for a certain purpose, just as Lord Buddha preached a philosophy of nirvana for a particular purpose. These purposes are mentioned in the scriptures, in those instances where it is required to preach some philosophical doctrine which is against the Vedic conclusion. In the Shiva Purana, Lord Shiva says to his wife Parvati, "In the Kali Yuga, in the body of a brahmin [Shankara], I will preach the Mayavadi [impersonal] philosophy in order to baffle the atheists." So it is found that the followers of Lord Shiva are mostly Mayavadi impersonalists who believe in becoming one with the Supreme. Lord Shiva himself, however, by virtue of austerity and devotion, is more conversant with the actual constitutional position of the individual soul and the Supreme Soul. As stated in the Chaitanya Charitamrita, Krishna is the Supreme Soul and we are His Parts and Parcels; our position is qualitatively one with God, but eternally subordinate in quantity. The most elevated persons, the pure devotees, engage their lives, minds and intelligence in all varieties of service to the Whole Spirit, Krishna. Lord Shiva, as the greatest Vaishnava, was fully aware of all such intricacies, but Brighu cursed both Shiva and his followers as one in fault. He said, "The vow of worshiping Lord Shiva is so foolish that they imitate and keep bunches of hair on their heads and live the life of wine and flesh indulgence and do not take baths." Brighu's point is that those who live without any spiritual regulation are foolish and become devoid of transcendental knowledge. He curses Nandikesvar and says, "Not due to my cursing shall you become an atheist, but you are already situated as an atheist and therefore condemned."

When the cursing and recursing was going on, Lord Shiva was silent and sober and didn't speak a word. Lord Shiva is described as always tolerant, but he became sorry at the unnecessary anger. In order to stop them, he left the arena of the sacrifice, and his disciples followed

DAKHA'S SECOND SACRIFICE

Thereafter Dakha began another performance of sacrifice, and he deliberately did not invite Lord Shiva. Generally, although such sacrifices were meant for pleasing the Supreme Personality of Godhead, Vishnu, yet all the demigods, and especially Lord Brahma and Lord Shiva, were always invited; otherwise the sacrifice was not complete. But Dakha, being very proud of his position as chief of the Prajapatis, and envious and inimical to Lord Shiva, thought to avoid them. He could understand that the purpose of sacrifice is to please the Supreme Lord. His supposed logic in avoiding Lord Shiva was that if Vishnu is satisfied by his sacrifice, then what was the need of satisfying His followers? But Lord Krishna says, "Worshiping My devotees is better than worshiping the Lord Himself." And in the Shiva Purana it states, "The best mode of worship is to offer oblations to Vishnu, and better than that is to worship the devotees of Krishna." Dakha's Shiva-less sacrifice was therefore inauspicious from the start.

But, many sages and demigods from all parts of the universe, with their wives nicely dressed and decorated, were attending the sacrificial ceremony. When Sati, the daughter of Dakha, saw that from all directions the beautiful wives in fine clothing were going there along with their husbands in airplanes, she too became anxious to go and approached her husband, Lord Shiva. She proposed to him that if he would desire to go to the ceremony, then they could go. Being a woman, Sati had some attachment for dressing up and participating in social functions and meeting her relatives in the assembly. But Lord Shiva was a different personality, and not interested in material enjoyment. Sati pleaded that she was not so transcendentally advanced as her great husband and therefore still had a strong desire for a nice social, family gathering; so she begged that they might dress with ornaments and go there like the others. But on hearing reference to Dakha's sacrifice, Lord Shiva remembered the heart-piercing malicious speeches delivered at the last sacrifice, and he became sorry at heart. There is a question raised here: Why did a liberated personality like Lord Shiva feel so unhappy due to the cruel words of Dakha? The answer is that Lord Shiva is an expansion of Vishnu, assigned as controller of the material quality of ignorance. Although he is completely self-realized and enlightened, yet because he is in charge of the material mode of ignorance, he is sometimes affected by the pleasure and pain of the material world. In the spiritual world one may also feel sorry, but in that absolute existence, either pleasure or so-called pain is full of bliss. When the Supreme Personality of Godhead Krishna appeared on the earth in Vrindaban, He had childhood pastimes in which He was chastised by His foster mother Yasoda, and He sometimes cried. But His shedding tears is not in the mode of ignorance. Also, when Krishna played with the cowherds girls, the gopis, it sometimes appeared that they were distressed, but actually that feeling was full of bliss. The temporary material world is declared by the Vedic knowledge to be a perverted reflection of the eternal Kingdom of God, so every variety of feeling that exists here in the material world also exists originally in the spiritual world. But in the spiritual world all the varieties of apparent pleasure and pain are perceived as eternal bliss, whereas in the material world, there is a dualistic perception of pleasure and pain due to the contamination of the modes of passion and ignorance. Lord Shiva is self-realized but due to his contact while in charge of the material mode of ignorance, he could feel sorrow. His position is therefore unique. He is sometimes called almost-God. He is compared in the Brahma Samhita to yogurt. Lord Vishnu the Supreme Personality of Godhead is compared to milk. Yogurt is also milk, but due to fermentation it has become changed. That is the position of Shiva: he has the full godly qualities but he is changed because of contact with matter. Only Vishnu the Supreme Personality of Godhead is 100 percent transcendental and above the material manifestation. Even when He enters the material atmosphere He enters as the Purifier and spiritualizes all matter in contact with Him. As the greatest worshiper of Vishnu, Lord Shiva willingly accepts the position of serving as controller of the mode of ignorance, and he is called the shelter of the most fallen.

Lord Shiva could foresee that as soon as Sati would reach the house of her father, Dakha, being so puffed up with the mistaken identification of the body as the self, would be angry with her although she was faultless. Therefore he ordered her not to go. As the wife of Lord Shiva, she would certainly be insulted by Dakha and his followers; Shiva told her that no one can bear such family insults and that it would be equal to her death if she went. But Sati made womanly pleas. She addressed her husband as he who has no equal in the material world. She knew that no one can match Lord Shiva in his equality to everyone, so why then wasn't he acting equally toward her by letting her go to the ceremony? It is described that Sati took shelter of a woman's last weapon–weeping–and she began walking back and forth in the rooms, like a swinging pendulum, divided in mind whether to obey her husband or to go to her father's sacrifice. At one point she begged her husband calling him Blue-Throated One. Lord Shiva is known widely by this name for a compassionate feat he once undertook. Once some demons and demigods took a sea journey in order to churn the ocean for the purpose of producing nectar. The first effect at churning, however, produced only poison, but Lord Shiva in anxiety that some less strong persons might drink it, took the ocean of poison himself and held it in his throat–which turned blue. Sati called him Blue-Throated and intimated, "You are so kind to others, why not to me?" Finally Sati forcibly left her husband's protection and started out alone towards Dakha's house.

When Lord Shiva saw Sati bent on going, he sent his men with her, and he also followed seated on his bull and accompanied by thousands of disciples. When Sati reached Dakha's house she was greeted only by her mother and sisters. Dakha, her father, completely ignored her. On account of her association with Lord Shiva, he forgot all his affection for his own daughter. Such is the material-familial conception of love, that even by the slightest provocation all intimate affection is gone and a whole relationship is finished. Sati was grieving over this insult and at the same time, as she looked over the arena of sacrifice, she saw that there was no oblation or sacrificial offering being made to Lord Shiva. At once she became angry and looked as if she were about to burn her father just with her eyes. Whenever one offers oblations in the fire, Lord Shiva is one of the demigods honored by the chanting of the mantra, Namah Shivayah Swaha. But under Dakha's instructions the brahmins deliberately omitted Shiva's offering and were not uttering that mantra. She became doubly insulted. The followers of Lord Shiva, the ghosts, were ready to do harm to Dakha, but Sati stopped them in the name of her husband. She was so angry and sorry, however, that she began to condemn Dakha and his sacrifice, speaking in the presence of the large gathering. Anger is usually abominable and leads to the destruction of intelligence. But Sati's anger was special. Regarding such anger, which is transcendental A.C. Bhaktivedanta Swami writes as follows: "When Vishnu and the Vaishnava are insulted, one should be angry. Lord Chaitanya, who is the preacher of nonviolence, meekness and humility, became angry when the Vaishnava Nityananda was insulted by Jagai and Madhai, and He wanted to kill them. That should be the attitude when Vishnu and the Vaishnava are blasphemed or dishonored. One should not be tolerant when a person is offending Vishnu or a Vaishnava." So Sati spoke personally to Dakha in her devotional anger:

"Lord Shiva is the most beloved personality of all living entities–he is universal. Nobody is his enemy, nobody could envy him–only one who is envious by nature. Only you could find fault in him. If somebody has just a little good quality Lord Shiva magnifies it, but you have found fault with such a great soul." Lord Shiva is so magnanimous that he grants his followers whatever they desire. He is sometimes called Asutos, or one who is satisfied very easily. Once a devotee of Lord Shiva asked the irregular benediction from Lord Shiva that whoever the devotee would touch, that person's head would fall off. Lord Shiva granted him as he desired. Such a benediction was not very good because the devotee tried to touch the head of Lord Shiva as soon as he was given the power. Still, Lord Shiva considered the devotee's good quality, that he had come to him and worshiped him and satisfied him.

Sati continued before her father and all persons gathered: "Lord Shiva is the friend of all living entities. He fulfills all desires of the common man as well as the higher personalities who are seeking after transcendental bliss. You think yourself superior to Lord Shiva as his father-in-law and you call him inauspicious for associating with the demons in the burning crematorium, with the locks of hair thrown all over his body and garlanded with human skulls—but greater personalities than you, such as Lord Brahma, honor Lord Shiva by accepting flowers offered to his feet. So you do not know that he is always transcendental. He must be, otherwise, why would such a person like Brahma worship him?" Offering many arguments based on authoritative Vedic information, Sati as a chaste wife, faithfully defended her husband from the slander of her father, Dakha. She certainly spoke in the spirit of eulogy as it was her duty to elevate Lord Shiva to the highest position; but it was not on sentiment, but by facts. Lord Shiva is not an ordinary entity. Someone may take the narrative of Sati as imaginative and conclude that there is no such person as Lord Shiva, but that is not the conclusion of the pure devotees who accept the authority of scriptures and the living chain of spiritual masters in disciplic succession. Doubt-ridden and cynical persons think that there can be no one as wonderful as Lord Shiva. This is because they themselves are limited in body and mind, and they ascribe their limitations to all personalities. Actually it is not so wonderful that there are powerful controllers of universal affairs such as Lord Shiva and Lord Brahma and other demigods. Even in common affairs the president of the country is the final authority in government, and yet he has agents who assist him in his mission. Similarly, the Supreme Controller, God, or Krishna, expands Himself into qualitative incarnations like Lord Vishnu and Lord Shiva and He also empowers ordinary living entities with unusual powers and long duration of life in accord with His inconceivable will. In common affairs or in the workings of nature, men of a poor fund of knowledge see everything as happening automatically. But mature examination to the end of things reveals that there is also personal control behind the wonderful happenings in government, science and nature. The space ships are not flying independently across the sky without the control by the brains of great scientists on earth; the staggeringly complex electronic computers cannot work without the human touch. Similarly, the gigantic space satellites called planets are controlled by a Great Intelligence or God. If artists study and labor so hard to paint the image of a flower, and never duplicate its original freshness and beauty, then who can seriously think that the thousands of varieties of natural flowers are produced "automatically" without the touch of the superior Artistry? Storms at sea, the movements of the luminaries in the sky as well as the movements of our hands and fingers, can all be traced to a power beyond our limited selves, to a Supreme Controller, the Cause of all causes, The Personality of Godhead. The wisdom of submissive reception of authoritative scripture enables one to understand what is inconceivable to the mundane senses and mental speculations of strictly materialistic scientists or philosophers. Those who hear and live in the spirit of devotional service have it revealed to them through the heart, with complete sane conviction, that there is a Controller. And to them it is understandable that for His Pleasure He can expand into multi-energies and personalities for control of universal affairs.

All the Vedic literatures describe Lord Shiva as the agent of destruction. When annihilation is due in the cyclical course of time, after a fabulously long time span by human standards, it is Lord Shiva who is the personal destroyer of the world systems. And until that time he willingly serves as the master of the mode of ignorance and offers his compassion to the most degraded souls so that they can be gradually elevated and have hopes of going back to Home, back to the Kingdom of God. In ordinary life, the mother is the sole authority for knowing who one's father is. So if we want that information on how the controllers of the universe are acting, where they reside and what they are doing, we have to turn to the authority or mother, Vedic scriptures. It is not a question of imagination, but of knowledge. The impersonalists or atheists who say that the scriptures are merely stories can never gain entrance into the Pastimes of the Supreme Personality of Godhead and His associates like Lord Shiva.

Sati was not merely talking. She was deeply mortified to be so intimately connected to Dakha who had committed offenses at the lotus feet of Lord Shiva. Sati said to Dakha: "I have this body produced by you. And I am therefore connected with you and very much ashamed. I shall not anymore bear this unworthy body which is received from you who have blasphemed Lord Shiva. If someone takes poisonous food, the best thing is to vomit." As the potency of Lord Shiva, his wife Sati could have easily killed Dakha. But to best save her husband from ill fame, as if he had no power to himself fight Dakha, she decided to give up her own body. The Vaishnava feels personally at fault for even hearing blasphemy against Lord Krishna or His pure devotee. The body being the source of her unhappiness, she decided to quit her body at once. Dressed in yellow garments, Sati sat on the ground facing the northern side, closed her eyes and became absorbed in the mystic yoga process. She took the required sitting posture, and then carried the life air upwards towards the navel and gradually raised it to the heart and towards the pulmonary passage, and from there she raised the life force between her eyebrows; meditating on the lotus feet of Lord Shiva, she became cleansed of all taints of sin and then quit her body in blazing fire by meditation on fiery elements. Srimad Bhagwatam states, "When the body of Sati was annihilated by anger, there was a great tumultuous roar heard all over the universe." Most astonishing was that Dakha remained disrespectful and unmoved by his chaste daughter and made no attempt to stop her death. Dakha was supposed to provide for all living entities, and his own daughter deserved the most respectful treatment. While the assembled persons were still talking among themselves about the passing away of Sati, Lord Shiva's attendants made ready to kill Dakha and rushed at him with their weapons. As they were coming forward forcibly, the sage Brighu saw the danger and immediately uttered mantras and hymns by which the destroyers of sacrificial performances can be killed. As soon as Brighu offered oblations in the fire thousands of demigods became manifested in the fire and they began to attack the ghosts and attendants of Lord Shiva, scattering them in all directions.

Lord Shiva was at a distance from the sacrifice, but when he was informed that his wife was dead due to Dakha's insult and that his associate soldiers were driven away he became angry. The Srimad Bhagwatam describes his fury: "Lord Shiva in anger pressed his lips with his teeth and from the bunch of hair on his head he snatched a piece of hair that blazed like fire, and laughing like a madman he dashed the hair to the ground. Then appeared a personality as tall as the sky, equipped with thousands of weapons and arms, of a black color and as bright as three suns." Lord Shiva sent this gigantic demon of personified anger to kill Dakha. In Bhagavad Gita Krishna declares, "Of generals I am Lord Shiva," so he is the most formidable of commanders. Led by the demon of anger his army swept into the sacrificial arena and prepared to plunder everything in sight. Seeing the approaching army, the brahmins and their assembled women were filled with anxiety, all due to the danger created by Dakha. In fact the wife of Dakha foresaw, "This is the same Lord Shiva who at the time of dissolution destroys the worlds." So there was no comparing the tiny power of Dakha to that of Lord Shiva. A.C. Bhaktivedanta Swami writes, "At the time of dissolution, Lord Shiva with his trident in hand dances over the rulers of different planets and his hair is scattered like the clouds over all directions, and he deluges the different planets with torrents of rain."

The followers of Lord Shiva are described as running around the sacrificial arena with bodies like sharkfish. They pulled down the pillars of the altars, entered residential and kitchen departments, broke pots and urinated on the sacrificial ground. Some of them blocked the way of the fleeing sages and shackled the women. Two priests who had shown their teeth during the cursing of Lord Shiva had their teeth extracted by the soldiers of Lord Shiva, and a continuous shower of stones was set up, so that all the members of the sacrifice were in miserable condition and running for fear of their lives. It is described that such horrible fighting was not exactly on an inimical basis; everyone present was very powerful, and they all wanted to show their strength by Vedic mantra or mystic power.

Finally Dakha was beheaded by the giant-like personality created by Lord Shiva. The party of Lord Shiva gave out joyful exclamations and the brahmins in charge of the sacrifice also exclaimed in grief at the death of Dakha in such a manner. Dakha's head was thrown on the sacrificial fire and the whole area was set on fire by the followers of Lord Shiva who then departed for their master's place in Kwelas.

The defeated and injured demigods, priests and all members of the sacrificial assembly then approached Lord Brahma with great fear. They offered their obeisances and spoke in detail to him of all that had happened. Lord Brahma already knew what had happened, and having known beforehand he did not attend the sacrifice. When he had heard everything from the members, he replied: "You cannot have happiness if you blaspheme great personalities like Lord Shiva." Lord Brahma said it was good for Dakha that he had been killed, otherwise, without that punishment, he would have committed more and more offenses and would be entangled in future lives. Knowing Lord Shiva's easy, compassionate nature, Lord Brahma advised: "If you go to him without any reservation of mind and surrender unto him and ask to be excused at his Lotus Feet, he is very easily pleased and it will be nice. He has recently lost his wife and is afflicted by the unkind words of Dakha. So go and beg his pardon, who is so powerful that by his anger all the planets can be destroyed."

After instructing all the demigods, Lord Brahma took them along with him and left for the place known as Kwelas Hill, the abode of Lord Shiva. Srimad Bhagwatam describes Kwelas as having different kinds of mountains, filled with valuable trees and plants and deer. There are different types of waterfalls with transparent water. Peacocks, cuckoos and other birds are always vibrating as if in rhythmic tune. There are many varieties of flowers, animals like the forest cow and buffalo, and plenty of decorated lakes. All the demigods were struck with wonder at the opulence of Kwelas. Under a huge banyan tree where it was silent and with unbroken shade, Lord Shiva sat as grave as time eternal, and the demigods approached him. He was encircled by famous saintly persons like the four Kumaras and Narada. Lord Shiva sat with his left leg on his right thigh and his right hand raised in the position of teaching or Tarkamudra, with the fingers opened and the second finger raised. He was instructing the saint Narada, and it is understood that if Narada was forming the audience, the topic must have been bhakti, or devotional service to Krishna. Brahma very respectfully payed obeisances to Lord Shiva on behalf of the party of the demigods. Lord Brahma requested that the priests whose limbs had been broken by the jaws of Lord Shiva's soliders be restored by Lord Shiva's grace. "Please accept your portion of the sacrifice and let it be properly completed." Lord Shiva was pacified by this, and he spoke as follows: "My dear father, Brahma, I do not mind the offenses created by the demigods because they are childish and less intelligent, and I do not take a serious view of it, but whatever I have done is just to punish them in order to set them right." By this, Sambhu (Lord Shiva) expressed his desire for everyone's welfare and asserted that he had chastised only in the way a father punishes his son, not as an enemy. All the priests' injuries were gradually healed and even Dakha was revived to life by Lord Shiva's placing the head of a goat on his trunk. Although he had a goat's head and a human trunk, Dakha was revived in his previous individual consciousness, because it is not the head or bodily construction that makes individuality but the spirit soul whose symptom is consciousness. When he saw Lord Shiva, just by his presence, Dakha became purified in mind. Tears rolled from his eyes and he was finally sorry and affected by the death of his daughter Sati. He could hardly express himself in prayers, overwhelmed with nonduplicitous love and respect for Lord Shiva. "Although I was punished by you for my ignorance, I understand that you have not withdrawn your mercy. I know both yourself and Lord Vishnu are kind to the friends of brahmins."

After begging forgiveness from Lord Shiva, and with the permission of Lord Brahma, Dakha again began the sacrifice in the regular way with fire and oblations. And first they offered oblations of the Holy Name of the Supreme Personality of Godhead, Vishnu, in order to make the whole situation purified. A.C. Bhaktivedanta Swami writes in this matter: "Performance of sacrifice is a very difficult task. In this present Age of Kali (Age of Quarrel) those who are intelligent know it is neither possible to perform the costly sacrifices nor to invite the demigods to participate. Therefore in this age, the Srimad Bhagwatam recommends Samkirtan Yajna (chanting of the Holy Names) as the means to keep the balance of social peace and prosperity and attain spiritual perfection. Samkirtan Yajna means to chant the Holy Names, Hare Krishna, Hare Krishna, Krishna Krishna, Hare Hare/Hare Rama, Hare Rama, Rama Rama, Hare Hare, and invite people and distribute Prasadam. This sacrifice will please all the demigods, and there will be peace and prosperity. The difficulty of performing Vedic rituals is that if you do not satisfy even one demigod out of many hundreds and thousands, just as Dakha could not satisfy Lord Shiva, then there is disaster. But in this age the performance is simplified by the chanting of Hare Krishna. And by pleasing Krishna all the demigods become satisfied automatically."

The sacrificial arena had been desecrated by the followers of Lord Shiva and the recitation of the Name of Vishnu was required to sanctify the procedure. Of course Lord Shiva was now present, and he is all-auspicious, but because in the past his followers had broken the arena and passed urine and done many obnoxious things, so only by chanting the Name of Vishnu in devotion was purity found again. And as complete benediction to this famous Yajna, Lord Narayan (Vishnu) appeared there, seated on the shoulder of Garuda His birdcarrier, and illuminated the whole arena. Lord Vishnu is described as of a beautiful transcendental blackish hue, dressed in yellow garments and many ornaments and appearing in an eight-armed form bearing conch shell, wheel, club, lotus, arrow, bow, shield and sword and being extraordinarily beautiful. Just His smile was pleasing to the whole world and captivated the audience of Dakha, Brighu and all present.

Lord Shiva, beholding the personified object of his constant meditation, bowed and spoke in ecstacy before the Supreme Controller of the worlds. He said: "My dear Lord, my mind and consciousness are always fixed on Your Lotus Feet, which are the Source of all benedictions and fulfillment of desires. They are worth worshiping. With my mind fixed in meditation on Your Lotus Feet I am no longer disturbed by persons who blaspheme, claiming that my activities are not purified. I do not mind their accusations and I excuse them out of compassion, just as You are compassionate to all living entities." So here is the key to the character of Lord Shiva. By his own declaration the most powerful personality in the material world never forgets his transcendental relationship as servant of the Lord; and he continues always in Krishna Consciousness in order to remain free from material afflictions. Without such personal meditation on the Supreme Lord, no one can be free of contaminating material activities, characterized by the disadvantages of birth, death, disease and old age and the struggle for existence. In the Bhagavad Gita, Lord Krishna assures that the dedicated soul who serves with love will never be vanquished by the material devastations. He says: "You simply surrender unto Me and I will give you protection." The practical example of Lord Shiva's worship is that liberation means, not some negative, temporary abeyance of trouble by meditation on the void, but practical eternal engagement in loving service to the Personality of Godhead. Those who cannot surrender their own personality, by submissive hearing, unto the Supreme Person must return again and again to the round of birth and death for attempted enjoyment and suffering in the material world. That is the verdict of the Bhagavad Gita and Srimad Bhagwatam.

By the grace of Lord Vishnu the sacrifice was completed to His full satisfaction.

Finally, out of so many incidences that make up Lord Shiva's eternal career, and prove him glorious, there is one activity which is offered as his most glorious pastime in association with the Supreme Lord Krishna. This activity is stated in the Third Canto of Srimad Bhagwatam: "The blessed Lord Shiva becomes all the more blessed by bearing on his head the holy waters of the Ganges, which has as its source the water that washed the Lord's Lotus Feet. His Feet are like a thunderbolt hurled to shatter sin stored in the mind of the devotee meditating on him." The gist of this incident is a reference to the entrance into the material world of the sacred river Ganges which flows through many planetary systems. Lord Shiva carried this water down in his hair when it first emanated from the

Causal Ocean which is the outside covering of this universe. By carrying this water, the auspicious Lord Shiva becomes even more auspicious. No one should laugh at or attempt to criticize Lord Shiva's unconventional activities or foolishly attempt to imitate him as a so-called Shivite. Lord Shiva is great for doing humble service unto the Greatest. He is no voidist or impersonalist speculating on the Absolute as we often hear him described. With half-closed eyes and beautiful austere form, seated in meditation, he fixes his mind on the dearmost object, his Lord. And that is why he is called the greatest Vaishnava.

Nārada

February/March, 1970

If you have read or heard even a small sampling of the vast Vedic literature, you have come upon the name of Nārada. He is a great *bhakta* (devotee) of the Supreme Lord Nārāyaṇa, or Kṛṣṇa. Etymologically analyzed, *nāra* means of Nārāyaṇa or the Lord (Kṛṣṇa), and *da* means deliverer. Nārada is the deliverer of the Lord and the Lord's message. Of course there are countless preachers, *gurus,* evangelists, mendicants and religious representatives traveling all throughout this planet, but Nārada Muni is eminently distinguished. His pupils include the greatest devotees. Also, he is not restricted to one planet, but has the facility to travel to any part of the universe without the aid of a spaceship. Most importantly, Nārada teaches the topmost process of God realization–*bhakti,* devotion to God–and he is coming in the unbroken line of disciplic succession originating with the Supreme Lord Himself. These qualifications of the sage Nārada are described in Vedic literatures such as *Śrīmad-Bhāgavatam, Rāmāyaṇa,* etc., where Nārada is called the eternal spaceman.

Long ago, as will be described here, Nārada attained the spiritual perfection of liberation from the round of birth and death in the material world. He is thus eternally unconditioned, existing in his eternal, spiritual body. In this way, he is almost as good as the Supreme Lord Himself. Nārada is the deliverer of the Hare Kṛṣṇa *mantra,* called the *mahāmantra* or Great Chanting for Deliverance. He is described: *Nārada Muni bajaya vīṇā rādhikā rāmaṇa nāme.* "Nārada Muni plays the *vīṇā* chanting Hare Kṛṣṇa." The Hare Kṛṣṇa *mantra*–Hare Kṛṣṇa Hare Kṛṣṇa Kṛṣṇa Kṛṣṇa Hare Hare Hare Rāma Hare Rāma Rāma Rāma Hare Hare–is the potent benediction for the present spiritually deprived age, Kali Yuga, in which other spiritual processes are not possible. The *Śrīmad-Bhāgavatam,* First Canto, Chapter 6, text 34, states: "It is personally experienced by Nārada Muni that for persons who are always full with cares and anxieties on account of desiring contact of the senses with sense objects, constant chanting of the transcendental activities of the Personality of Godhead is just the suitable boat for crossing the ocean of nescience."

Most people in this age are not very serious about spiritual advancement and cannot undertake rigorous, austere disciplines, but anyone can chant Hare Kṛṣṇa or simply hear about Kṛṣṇa. Not only can Nārada travel wherever the Lord desires him to go, carrying the first-class spiritual process, *bhakti* (devotional service), but he is an especially empowered authority who can convince the most fallen. In *Teachings of Lord Caitanya,* Caitanya Mahāprabhu reveals Nārada Muni as an *avatāra* of the *śaktyaveśa* category. Nārada is not considered the Personality of Godhead Himself, but he is directly empowered with an opulence of the Supreme Personality of Godhead in order to carry out the Lord's will. Nārada, then, is technically a *śaktyaveśa avatāra* potent with the opulence of devotion. The basis of his teaching is expressed in *Nārāda-bhakti-sūtras* and *Nārada-pañcarātra.* Nārada explains that nobody can check the thinking, feeling and willing activities of the individual. Therefore, if someone is desirous of getting out of the frustrating, death-bound life of material consciousness, he must change the subject matter of his activities, which is not to say he must renounce them. His Divine Grace A.C. Bhaktivedanta Swami, as spiritual master in disciplic succession from Nārada, writes: "Instead of talking in politics of a dying man, one may discuss the politics administered by the Lord Himself; instead of relishing the movie actors he may turn his attention to the activities of the Lord with His eternal associates, the *gopīs.*" Nārada recommends *bhakti,* or activities of the purified senses, as the process by which one can cross the ocean of birth and death, the source of all miseries, and be promoted to the transcendental position. We are already thinking, feeling and willing; if we simply begin to think, feel and will on behalf of Kṛṣṇa, under the guidance of a spiritual master, then we will at once feel transcendental ecstasy and reject the material platform of life. He assures us from his own experience that devotional service activities will be successful. It is advised that we can experience the same success as Nārada if we begin to follow the path of *bhakti* in the footsteps of this great sage, who is the dearmost devotee of the Lord.

In the First Canto of *Śrīmad-Bhāgavatam,* Nārada Muni relates to his pupil Vyāsadeva the incidences of his previous birth, before he became the immortal sage we all know as Nārada: "O Muni [Vyāsadeva], in my past life, during the last millennium, I was born as the son of a certain maidservant engaged in the service of *brāhmaṇas* who were following the principle of Vedānta. When they were living together during the four months of the rainy season I was engaged in their personal service." In his previous life, then, Nārada was engaged in devotional service at the earliest age. Lord Kṛṣṇa says that to do service for His servants is more valuable than direct service to Himself. Nārada's parentage was insignificant as his mother was just a maidservant. Nārada was automatically given the most rare opportunity of rendering personal service to devotees of the Lord. Because some holy *brāhmaṇas* were used to staying at the place where his mother was a servant, Nārada, at less than five years of age, was in contact with them, and thus his door to liberation was opened. He states that the devotee-

brāhmaṇas blessed him with their causeless mercy. They found this poor boy to be without any attachment to sporting habits; he was not naughty, nor did he speak more than required. Thus, although the devotees are impartial by nature, they were able to shower their full downpour of mercy in the form of transcendental knowledge and devotional service onto this uneducated young boy.

The boy Nārada's association with the pure devotees was consummated the moment he took up remnants of their foodstuff. By so doing, all his sins were at once eliminated. As servant, the boy was cleaning up for the devotees, and noticing some remnants of food on their plates he asked their permission to take, and they of course encouraged him. As pure devotees, these *bhakti-vedāntas* (knowers of *Vedānta* through devotional service) ate only *prasādam,* or foodstuffs which are first offered to the Supreme Lord with prayers. It is understood that *prasādam* is not ordinary food, but once accepted by the Lord it becomes as good as the Lord Himself, by His mercy. So the boy took this mercy of the *bhakti-vedāntas* and became infected with their qualities of purity. Having associated with them, and having once eaten the remnants of their food, Nārada advanced into transcendental life.

He then began to hear from them about the absolute truth. This is the way in which Nārada gained eternal life, unlimited knowledge and unfathomed bliss, with facility to travel anywhere in the material worlds. Simply by hearing attentively authentic information about the Personality of Godhead from a bona fide authority, all his past sins were cleaned off and he was liberated from mundane association. Nārada relates to his pupil Vyāsadeva: "O Vyāsadeva, in that association and by the mercy of the great Vedāntists describing the attractive activities of Lord Kṛṣṇa, I purified my aural reception. Thus hearing attentively, step by step my taste for hearing of the Personality of Godhead became manifest."

Our spiritual master has told us many times that love of God is natural, original with us; however, due to our false attraction to the perishable material world and illusion of the body as our self and material things as our possessions, this consciousness is now dormant. So the wonderful change that occurs by chanting Hare Kṛṣṇa or hearing about Kṛṣṇa's activities is not an artificial imposition on the mind, but is the natural return to our original consciousness. We may not be able to completely realize this at first, but very quickly the consciousness of the sincere chanter changes, and his material anxieties and desires fade away. Nārada described how he developed definite realization of the Personality of Godhead as the absolute reality and how his attention became uninterrupted in hearing about the Lord. By hearing about the absolute, one becomes associated with the supreme light which dissipates all ignorance. The *bhaktivedāntas* were never speaking mundane topics of politics or sensuous affairs before Nārada; nor were they teaching him negative concepts of reality, such as speculations on the concept of void or the impersonal aspect of the absolute truth. They were constantly engaged in chanting about the pastimes of the Personality of Godhead, who possesses inconceivable potencies; and by submissively hearing, the son of the maidservant felt his ignorance being removed.

Our spiritual master, His Divine Grace A.C. Bhaktivedanta Swami, writes: "By ignorance only the conditioned soul wrongly thinks that he is a product of the material nature and that the Personality of Godhead is also a product of matter. But in fact, the Personality of Godhead and the living being are transcendental and have nothing to do with the material nature. When nescience is removed, then it is perfectly realized that there is nothing existing without the Personality of Godhead. As the gross and subtle bodies are emanations from the Personality of Godhead, the revival of transcendental knowledge permits one to engage both of them in the service of the Lord." The gross body can be engaged in rendering service, cleaning the temple, distributing Kṛṣṇa conscious literature and bowing down in the temple, and the subtle mind can hear and think of the transcendental pastimes of the Lord. The realization by which one can change his activities into transcendental activities develops without apprehension in execution of the *bhakti* path. Nārada grasped this at once by his superior attraction for the Supreme Personality of Godhead–through the most effective method of hearing from pure souls. As Nārada tells it, "The flow of my devotional service began." Devotional service is natural to everyone, but it is choked up and suspended due to our being covered by modes of passion and ignorance. In Nārada's case, the pure sound vibration of unadulterated devotees speaking the glories of the Supreme Lord at once removed the material coverings and his devotional service thus began. Or in other words, the eternal being who was residing in the body of the maidservant's son woke up, and the ultimate goal–love of God–became manifest in his heart. Nārada's position before his teachers is a model for the disciple who wishes to attain success even within one lifetime: "I was very much attached to the *bhakti-vedāntas*. I was gentle in behavior, and all my sins became eradicated in my heart. I had strong faith in them; I had subjugated the senses and was strictly following the *bhakti-vedāntas* with body and mind."

Eventually the rainy season and the autumn passed, and the *bhakti-vedāntas* left the place where Nārada and his mother were living. But the confidential part of knowledge, devotional service unto the Supreme Personality of Godhead, had been implanted in Nārada's heart. Knowledge of the absolute truth–permanent and blissful behind all temporary shows--is not a cheap or easily attainable thing. According to the *Bhagavad-gītā*, out of millions of men one may know the absolute truth, the Personality of Godhead.

When the immortal sage Nārada told these things to Vyāsadeva, his disciple became anxious to know how the boy passed the duration of his previous life and how he finally quit his body and attained a spiritual body of *sac-cid-ānanda* (eternal life, bliss and knowledge) as Nārada Muni the eternal spaceman. Nārada related that after his initiation by the *bhakti-vedāntas* there was a tangible change in his life, but as he was only five years old and the only child of his mother, he was bound to her with the tie of affection. Instead of being dependent on the Supreme Lord who is the only independent controller, the boy was dependent on his mother's care, and she looked after him as if she were his maintainer. But Nārada relates: "Once upon a time the poor woman, my mother, while engaged in milking a cow at night, was fatally bitten on the leg by a serpent as influenced by the supreme time." In this way, the sincere soul who was being looked after by his mother had her withdrawn from the world by the supreme will, and he was thus put completely at the mercy of the Lord. "I took it as the special mercy of the Lord, who always desires benediction for His devotees. Thinking in this way, I started for the northern side." This may seem surprising: a five-year-old boy, suddenly left all alone in the world, takes it as an auspicious direction from God. We find that most people when they are put into natural frustration and loss bewail the cruelty of their plight and even presume to be critical of the absolute will. But the devotee sees in every step the special mercy of the Lord. Bewailing our material losses is due to our ignorance of the real purpose of human life.

A.C. Bhaktivedanta Swami has written on this point: "Mundane prosperity is a kind of material fever and by the grace of the Lord, the feverish material temperature of the devotee is gradually diminished and spiritual health is obtained step by step." So the orphaned boy at once took the daring step of making God his only shelter and maintainer. He did not spend time trying to make some economic adjustment for his future comfortable living, but he took to traveling. "I passed through many flourishing metropolises, towns, villages, animal farms, mines, agricultural lands, valleys, gardens and forests. I passed alone through many forests full of pipe, bamboo, sharp grass, weeds and caves difficult to go through alone. I visited the dangerous, fearful forests deep and dark, the play-yards of snakes, owls, jackals."

The boy was not making a whimsical youth's journey by these travels. It is the duty of a mendicant to have experience of all varieties of God's creation. This is called *parivrājakācārya,* to travel alone through all forests, hills, towns, etc., to gain faith in God and strength of mind, as well as to enlighten the inhabitants with the message of God. In the present age this is not possible for the ordinary man, but it was possible for Nārada, who was finishing his last lifetime before his liberation.

"After that, under the shadow of a banyan tree in a forest without any human habitation, I began to meditate upon the supersoul situated within myself, using my intelligence as I learned by hearing from liberated souls. With my mind transformed into transcendental love I began to meditate upon the lotus feet of the Personality of Godhead. Tears rolled down from my eyes, and immediately the Personality of Godhead, Lord Śrī Kṛṣṇa, appeared on the lotus of my heart." It is understood that Nārada was not performing a concocted meditation, but he had received knowledge from authoritative sources on how to meditate on the supersoul who is dwelling within every living being. There are five stages of transcendental development leading to love of God described in the *Nārada-bhakti-sūtra.* The first is called *śraddhā,* or an initial interest in or liking for the Supreme Lord. After that, one practices the prescribed rules and regulations of devotional service, which clear away misgivings and personal deficiencies. Then one develops firmness, or standard faith in the reality of transcendental life; then comes attraction, and then *bhāva,* the stage prior to unalloyed love of God. Nārada Muni in his previous birth was able to attain the highest stage shortly after his departure from home. The tears from his eyes indicate his feelings of separation in transcendental love for the Personality of Godhead, after which he actually was able to perceive the actual presence of the Lord by his developed spiritual senses. A.C. Bhaktivedanta Swami writes of spiritual ecstasy such as that perceived by Nārada: "Spiritual feelings of happiness and intense ecstasy have no mundane comparison. Therefore it is very difficult to give expression to such feelings. We can just have a glimpse of such ecstasy in the words of the pure devotees." "O, Vyāsadeva, at that time, being exceedingly overpowered by feelings of happiness, every part of my body became lucid being absorbed in the ocean of ecstasy."

Nārada describes the form of the absolute truth as he saw Him: "The transcendental form of the Lord, as it is, is perfectly apt to the desire of the mind." Nārada did not experience the Lord as formless, but His form is not like anything in this material world. It is described that all the differently cut and shaped forms that we are seeing all through our life do not banish all our mental disparity and dissatisfaction. But the special feature of the transcendental form of the Lord is that once it is seen, one is satisfied forever, and no material form holds any more attraction for the seer. So the Lord's form is like nothing we see now in matter. Another great devotee, Mahārāj Parīkṣit, was able to see the form of Kṛṣṇa even while he was in his mother's womb. On being born into the world, Parīkṣit (the word means "examiner") was always looking this way and that way, his eyes longing to see again the form of the Lord among all the unsatisfying forms and shapes of the material atmosphere.

Nārada saw the form of God, he was completely satisfied in his being, and then the same form was no longer present to his vision. "Not seeing that form again, I suddenly got up, being perturbed in mind, as it happens when one loses that which is desirable." Desiring more than anything to see again the form of the Lord, Nārada tried to concentrate his mind on his heart, but he could not see Him anymore, and so became grief-stricken. Śrīla Prabhupāda writes: "There is no mechanical process to see the form of the Lord. It completely depends on the causeless mercy of the Lord. Just as the sun rises out of its own accord, the Lord also is pleased to be present out of His causeless mercy. One should simply wait for the opportune moment and go on discharging the prescribed duty in devotional service of the Lord."

Not at Nārada's command, but by that same causeless mercy, the transcendental Supreme Personality of Godhead, seeing Nārada's attempt in a lonely place, spoke unto him, just to mitigate his grief. "O Nārada, I regret very much that during this lifetime, you will no longer be able to see Me. Those who are incomplete in service or still immature in being freed from all material dirt can hardly see Me. O virtuous one, you have only once seen My Person. This is just to increase your hankering for Me, because the more you desire Me, the more you will be freed from material desire. By service of the absolute truth even for a short time, a devotee's intelligence becomes fixed firmly on Me. As a result he goes on to become My associate in the transcendental world after giving up the present deplorable material worlds. Intelligence engaged in My devotion can never be defeated at any time. Even at the time of creation, as well as at the time of annihilation, your remembrance will continue by My mercy." How wonderful is the devotee Nārada, that the Lord, the supreme authority personified by sound, unseen, spoke to him, seeing him so sad for lack of the Lord's presence! Again, this is the special gift of Nārada, and the ordinary devotee, what to speak of the non-devotee, should not claim to have access to the voice of the Supreme Lord. We are so puffed up and presumptuous in matters of the absolute truth, although it is the field of endeavor which, more than any other, requires us to give submissively and humbly aural reception to the bona fide authorities. For this age the authoritative Vedic literature recommends the sound vibration of the Lord's holy name, Hare Kṛṣṇa, which is as good as the personal presence of the Lord. If this were not so—that the Lord is present Himself when His name is uttered—then how could He be considered absolute? Absolute means that He is present in His name, His fame, and His devotee. If we wish to exchange transcendental love with the absolute truth we have to qualify ourselves by the purifying process of chanting His holy name. There is no difficulty on His part in coming to us when He wills. It may be very difficult for an ordinary subject to get an audience with the king; but if the king desires to see any citizen, what is the difficulty in his coming? As Śrīla Bhaktisiddhānta Sarasvatī, spiritual master of His Divine Grace A.C. Bhaktivedanta, said, "Don't ask to see God, rather act in such a way that God can see you." Such an elevated standard, the perfection of human life, is easily attained by constant chanting and associating with devotees and the first result of this process is the loss of misgivings. Misgivings means lamenting over something lost and hankering for something we don't have. These vanish when the superior taste derived from executing spiritual devotional service begins under the authorized spiritual master.

Blessed all along and taking each occurrence as an opportunity to increase his hankering for the Lord, the servant boy who was to become Nārada finished the days of his life in chanting and remembering the pastimes of Śrī Kṛṣṇa and in traveling for distributing the Lord's message of back to Godhead, with no thought of material gain.

In the course of time, while fully absorbed in thinking of Kṛṣṇa, Nārada reached that point, commonly called death, when the change of body suddenly occurs. Nārada told his pupil: "Being freed from all material taints, I met with death just as lightning and illumination occur simultaneously." It is told further that just as the illumination follows the lightning, the devotee changed his material body after death and evolved a spiritual body by the will of the supreme. The material body is a product of *karma,* earned by our accumulation of material desire, action and reaction. It is temporary and subject to miseries, and it is unenlightened. The spiritual body residing dormant within the material body, is eternal, blissful and in full knowledge. It is understood from authorized scriptures that even while in the material body, a pure devotee's body becomes surcharged with spiritual energy by the constant engagement of his senses in the service of the transcendental eternal Lord. It is like an iron rod in contact with fire: after a while the iron rod acts not like iron, but like fire. The material body is afflicted with inebrieties and is taken on by the living entity as a result of his desires to enjoy temporary sense gratification, without understanding his real position—that he is an eternal servant of the Lord and meant to please His senses. Therefore when the devotee's body becomes engaged in devotional service he becomes surcharged with the transcendental qualities. His Divine Grace A.C. Bhaktivedanta Swamı writes on this important matter, so often misunderstood by neophytes: "Change of the body means stoppage of the reaction of the qualitative modes of material nature (goodness, passion and ignorance) upon the person of a pure devotee. There are many instances in the revealed scriptures where Dhruva and Prahlāda and many other devotees were able to see the Personality of Godhead face to face apparently in the same body. This means the quality of a devotee's body changes from material affinity to transcendence. By the mercy of Kṛṣṇa the devotee becomes exempt from the karmic reactions of his work." In order to understand how the body of a devotee becomes spiritualized, we have to understand that consciousness is the sign of life. The sensation you have when you are pinched means you have consciousness. This consciousness, which is spread all over the body, is eternal, though the body of flesh and blood is perishable. Consciousness is a symptom of the presence of the soul, which is located in the heart. This is confirmed in the *Upaniṣads* and *Bhagavad-gita.* If an ordinary conditioned human being meets a pure devotee and his consciousness is changed from the polluted desire to enjoy with the body, and he instead starts to use the body as a vehicle for service in Kṛṣṇa consciousness, then his body becomes spiritualized. Any material object, a telephone, a typewriter, becomes spiritualized if used in the direct service of Kṛṣṇa consciousness for propagating the Lord's transcendental message. His Divine Grace A.C. Bhaktivedanta Swami has written that, in the eye of the Supreme Lord Kṛṣṇa, the body of the converted or reclaimed devotee who has changed his standard of consciousness from material to Kṛṣṇa consciousness is as good as the eternal spiritual body of a *jīva* in the spiritual sky who has never fallen under the conditioned state. The example Śrīla Prabhupāda has given is that of a gold box and a gold-plated box. The gold box is compared to those who have never fallen to the material world. But once a fallen soul takes a bona fide spiritual master and becomes one hundred percent engaged in devotional service, then he too becomes liberated, even while remaining in the present body–and he is thus compared to a gold-plated box. The Lord accepts the gold-plated box as equal to and as good as the gold box.

Nārada describes his position then to Vyāsadeva: "At the end of the millennium, when the Personality of Godhead Lord Nārāyaṇa lay down in the water of devastation, Brahmā began to enter into Him along with all creative elements, and I also entered through His breathing. After expiration of a period of 4,300,000 x 1000 years when Brahmā awoke to create again by the will of the Lord, all the *ṛsis* like Marīci, Aṅgirā, and Atri were created from the transcendental body of the Lord, and I also appeared along with them." Nārada's entrance into the body of the Lord at the time of annihilation and re-entrance into the material cosmos occur in the same transcendental body, which is described as being just like the Lord's, without any difference between body and soul. Therefore when Nārada appears in the universe as the son of Brahmā, born from his heart, it is understood that this is not the forced birth of a conditioned entity, but a transcendental pastime of the devotee. Nārada's appearance and disappearance in the world are in the same category of transcendence as that of the Lord, who appeared on the earth as the son of Vasudeva.

Nārada Muni is *brahmacārī,* living the order of celibacy without the complication of family life. He is the greatest emblem of devotional service, and therefore the most learned. And he is worshipable. Kṛṣṇa says in *Bhagavad-gītā,* "Among sages I am Nārada." His *vīṇā* is charged with transcendental sound and was handed to him by Lord Śrī Kṛṣṇa, as stated in the *Liṅga Purāṇa.* The *vīṇā* is therefore identical with Kṛṣṇa, and the glories of the absolute truth as chanted by Nārada are also nondifferent from the Lord. Therefore the presence of Nārada means Lord Kṛṣṇa is present.

Nārada is called the original spiritual master. His disciples, surrendered souls who first heard Kṛṣṇa consciousness from his lips, include Vyāsadeva, the compiler of all the Vedic scriptures, Vālmikī, the author of the *Rāmāyaṇa,* Druva Mahārāj, Prahlāda Mahārāj, and many others.

"Thus I travel, constantly singing the glories of the Lord." Nārada is traveling, vibrating his instrument, the *vīṇā*, by his own free will. He is not being forced. His devotional service is free; he offers it out of his free will and he is free to travel when he likes. By his surrender unto the Lord he has attained complete freedom of life. The illusion of persons in the material world is that they are free, whereas actually they are bound up by the stringent laws of nature. We can only try to imagine, at this point, the unlimited freedom of Nārada, whose freedom is as good as the Lord's.

Let us all help Nārada Muni with his welfare work of the spirit. Encourage everyone you meet to chant Hare Kṛṣṇa Hare Kṛṣṇa Kṛṣṇa Kṛṣṇa Hare Hare Hare Rāma Hare Rāma Rāma Rāma Hare Hare. The *mahāmantra* will enliven the planet, will bring us all a life of transcendental bliss, and help us to have a taste of the full nectar for which we have been anxious from time immemorial.

The Prayers of Akrūra

April/May, 1970

Akrūra, a devotee of Kṛṣṇa, the Supreme Personality of Godhead, achieved perfection by his notable prayers. In his book *Easy Journey to Other Planets,* His Divine Grace A.C. Bhaktivedanta Swami Prabhupāda describes nine processes of realizing God. It is said that perfection of human life and entrance into the spiritual kingdom are guaranteed by execution of any or all of the nine items of devotional activity, and it is recommended that we execute these processes, following in the footsteps of great devotees. A partial list of the nine great devotees who achieved success simply by perfecting one process reads as follows: Mahārāja Parīkṣit achieved perfection by ***hearing*** the *Śrīmad-Bhāgavatam* from Śukadeva Gosvāmī. Śukadeva Gosvāmī achieved perfection by *reciting* the *Śrīmad-Bhāgavatam* to Mahārāja Parīkṣit. Akrūra, the charioteer of Kṛṣṇa, achieved perfection by ***praying*** to the Lord." The Tenth Canto of *Śrīmad-Bhāgavatam,* the transcendental literature containing the most full descriptions of the pastimes of Śrī Kṛṣṇa, includes Akrūra's long prayer, composed spontaneously in the presence of the Supreme Personality of Godhead when Akrūra was carrying Kṛṣṇa and Balarāma by chariot from Vṛndāvana to Mathurā. The circumstances under which he prayed are very wonderful because they involve the pastimes of Lord Kṛṣṇa.

Lord Kṛṣṇa was raised incognito as a cowherd boy in Vṛndāvana in order to prevent His being killed by His uncle, Kaṁsa, who had heard an omen that the child had come into the world to kill him. When Kṛṣṇa was sixteen, the sage Nārada went before Kaṁsa and revealed to him Kṛṣṇa's real identity and whereabouts. In fear of his life, the demon Kaṁsa then arranged for the killing of Kṛṣṇa and His elder brother Balarāma. Kaṁsa was the ruler of Mathurā Province, and he at once arranged for a gala wrestling match and ritualistic sacrifice to be performed in the heart of the city. Kaṁsa called for Akrūra and asked him to go to Vṛndāvana to invite Kṛṣṇa and His father, Nanda Mahārāja, and the cowherd men to join in the festivities at Mathurā. Kaṁsa was the ruler of all the citizens of Mathurā, and he considered Akrūra to be his trustworthy agent. On the instructions of Kaṁsa, Akrūra set out for Vṛndāvana in his chariot, thinking that although he was on a mission for Kṛṣṇa's enemy Kaṁsa, Kṛṣṇa, as Supersoul present in everyone's heart, would know his real feeling. Akrūra was a devotee of Lord Kṛṣṇa, and as he traveled all day in his chariot he remained wrapped in thought, anticipating the sight of the beloved Supreme Lord. He was certain that simply seeing the Lord would cleanse him of all sinful reactions and make his life perfect.

Just outside of Vṛndāvana he observed the footprints of Kṛṣṇa, which are decorated by special markings—a lotus flower, a rod, a flag and an umbrella. Akrūra lost all mental equilibrium at the sight of the actual footprints of Śrī Kṛṣṇa, and he jumped out of his chariot and fell onto the ground, shedding tears and crying, "How wonderful it is! How wonderful it is!"—touching his head onto the footprints of the Supreme Lord.

When they learned that Akrūra had come to take Kṛṣṇa away to Mathurā, Kṛṣṇa's most intimate devotees, the *gopīs,* cowherd girls of Vṛndāvana, were put into madness of grief at the idea of separation from their beloved. They cried out against the cruelty of providence and also expressed displeasure with Akrūra: "You are cruel, although your name is not cruel." (*Akrūra* means "not cruel.") Kṛṣṇa and His brother Balarāma, as well as His father and mother, Nanda and Yaśodā, and many of the cowherd men, accepted the invitation to attend the wrestling match in Mathurā, and thus they prepared to go, bringing offerings of butter and milk products. Akrūra took Kṛṣṇa and Balarāma in his chariot and, despite the *gopīs'* blocking his way in a desperate attempt to keep Kṛṣṇa from leaving, set out on the journey to Mathurā bearing his two glorious passengers.

It is described that Kṛṣṇa and Balarāma asked Akrūra to stop the chariot after some time so that They might bathe in the River Yamunā. When They had finished Their bathing, Akrūra requested that he might bathe also. While Balarāma and Kṛṣṇa waited on the chariot, Akrūra entered the water of the river. To his surprise, however, he saw the two brothers, Kṛṣṇa and Balarāma, within the water of the Yamunā. He was certainly confused, since he had just left Them sitting in the chariot. Akrūra at once emerged, returned to the chariot and, indeed, saw the two brothers seated as before. He was then doubtful as to what he had seen in the water, and he returned to the river. This time he saw Kṛṣṇa in the water in His expansion-form of Garbhodakaśāyī Viṣṇu, the source of the universe, and he saw Balarāma as the white Ananta, or snake incarnation, which is always present with Viṣṇu, serving as His hood or couch while the Lord is resting on the causal water. It is described that Akrūra saw "the four-handed Supreme Personality of Godhead, smiling very beautifully with His beautiful face. He was very pleasing to all and was looking toward everyone. Surrounding His Lordship were His intimate associates like the four Kumāras, demigods like Śiva and Brahmā, and devotees like Nārada and Prahlāda—all offering prayers to the Lord." Seeing the situation of the Personality of Godhead, Akrūra was overwhelmed with great devotion, and he experienced transcendental shivering in his body. Maintaining his pure consciousness, however, he bowed his head before the Lord and, with folded hands and faltering voice, began to compose his prayers: "My dear Lord, I pay my respectful obeisances unto You because You are the supreme cause of all causes and the original inexhaustible personality, Nārāyaṇa."

Akrura first acknowledged Kṛṣṇa to be the source of all sources. Certainly this must be a quality of God. Scrutinize any object in the material or spiritual worlds and trace out its origin or source—ultimately all things go back to one absolute source, or God. As the controller, He controls all other sources; all sources emanate from Him, and He Himself needs no source other than Himself. This is not offered as a research proposition, but is to be accepted as the Vedic conclusion. That the Supreme Personality of Godhead is the source of all sources, although inconceivable, can be accepted on the strength of higher authorities. Just as if one wants to know who one's father is, the only authority for that information is his mother, the authority for transcendental knowledge is the *Veda*, scripture. Transcendental knowledge originates from the Personality of the Absolute Truth and descends through His pure devotees.

As the source of all sources, God is also the source of knowledge about Himself. Man cannot know the source of all sources by his speculative mental power. It is not a matter for research. It is said in the *Brahma-saṁhitā* that if one rides on the airplane which runs at the speed of mind (it can take you to India in a second), and if one travels at that speed for millions of years, he will find the spiritual sky to be unlimited. It is not possible even to approach it. If we attempt to reach this knowledge of the cause of all causes by inductive reasoning, we cannot reach the goal. We will go on experimenting, thinking, "There may be some cause existing somewhere which I have not traced back to God." In Sanskrit this is called *āroha*, or the ascending process, and it cannot work for reaching transcendental knowledge. But it is said in the *Brahma-saṁhitā*, "Kṛṣṇa, who is known as Govinda, is the Supreme Godhead. He has an eternal, blissful, spiritual body. He is the origin of all. He has no other origin, and He is the prime cause of all causes." *Brahma-saṁhitā* is an authoritative scripture and is accepted by the disciplic line of spiritual masters. Although Kṛṣṇa is very difficult to understand, one can very easily learn about Kṛṣṇa from the authentic *śāstras* and from the devotee of Kṛṣṇa. As the cause of all causes, God is also the cause of bringing the Vedic literature into the world, and He is the cause of the pure devotees who move among fallen souls distributing love of Kṛṣṇa. And because He Himself is beyond any cause, the Lord bestows causeless mercy upon the living entity. Causeless mercy does not depend on the qualification of he who is receiving it. Kṛṣṇa's mercy is called causeless because it is not given for any return benefit, but only out of love, whereas in the material world there is always motive or cause. Kṛṣṇa and Kṛṣṇa's devotees are causeless in their mercy. So Akrūra's prayers, although moved by the deepest needs of the heart, are based on the version of the Supreme Lord, as He is, as revealed by scripture and by His pure devotees from time immemorial.

Akrūra prays, "You are the original inexhaustible personality." God is a person; one cannot pray to imperson, and void cannot respond to one's prayers. Because they are under the influence of the stringent laws of the material energy, the impersonalists find this sublime faith in the Supreme Person to be very distasteful. The impersonalist philosophers think in a material way about the Personality of Godhead, Nārāyaṇa or Kṛṣṇa, and they conclude that He cannot be the Absolute Truth. They understand the last word in the Absolute Truth to be the impersonal eternal spirit, Brahman. They understand the Absolute Truth to be distributed everywhere as impersonal. To them, personal identity means materialism, falseness and illusion. They wish to merge with the Brahman. But according to the *Bhagavad-gītā,* that Brahman is but the effulgence of the Supreme Person: " . . . and I [Kṛṣṇa] am the basis of the impersonal Brahman, which is immortal and imperishable, eternal, the constitutional position of ultimate happiness." (*Bhagavad-gītā* 14.27) That the Absolute Truth is a person is affirmed throughout the Vedic literature: "Never was there a time when I did not exist, nor you, nor all these kings; nor in the future shall any of us cease to be." (*Bhagavad-gītā* 14.27) "O my Lord, O primeval philosopher, maintainer of the universe, O regulating principle, destination of the pure devotees, well-wisher of the progenitors of mankind, please remove the effulgence of Your transcendental rays so that I can see Your form of bliss. You are the eternal Supreme Personality of Godhead, like unto the sun, as am I." (*Śrī Īśopaniṣad,* Mantra 16)

He is the chief person, infallible, and His body is nondifferent from His soul. He is a person unlike ourselves, who are but parts and parcels of the whole. Because the Absolute Truth has to be inexhaustible, the impersonalists with their material way of thinking cannot accept that He can be a person. But although every person in the material world is mortal and subject to the defects of illusion, cheating, and limited knowledge, Kṛṣṇa is a perfect person, possessed of inexhaustible potencies. That is the verdict of all Vedic literatures and the direction of all scriptures. He did not exhaust Himself by creation of the material cosmos. Although He has distributed Himself everywhere, His personality has not become lost. That distribution of Himself is not a very difficult job for God. Even the sun, a material object, has been distributing unlimited energy for countless years, and it has not become diminished in heat or bereft of its individuality. If we take a piece of paper and rip it into tiny pieces, we may say that the identity of the whole paper is lost, but in the realm of the Absolute,

Kṛṣṇa is distributed and yet remains aloof from that distribution. Although nondifferent from the creation which is His energy, He is whole and separate from it. This is stated in the *Bhagavad-gītā,* "In My transcendental form I pervade all this creation. All things are resting in Me, but I am not in them. Again, everything that is created does not rest on Me. Behold My mystic opulence: Although I am the maintainer of all living entities, and although I am everywhere, still My Self is the very source of creation." (*Bhagavad-gītā* 9.4-5) Although all creation, spiritual and material, is Kṛṣṇa's energy and His energy is non-different from Himself, He is aloof from everything and is the eternally enjoying Original Personality. This is the sublime doctrine of simultaneous oneness and difference expounded by Caitanya Mahāprabhu. Similarly, the living entity, part and parcel of Kṛṣṇa, is also one of the energies of Kṛṣṇa and is qualitatively non-different from Him. But at no time can any of the qualitatively equal parts become quantitatively equal to or greater than the whole.

Akrūra's prayers continue thus: "You are the cause of all causes. The elements of this cosmic manifestation–earth, fire, air, sky, egoism and the total material energy, as well as nature, the marginal energy, the living entities, mind, senses, sense objects, and the demigods who control the affairs of this cosmic manifestation–all are produced from Your body. You are the Supersoul of everything, but no one knows Your transcendental form. Everyone who is in this material world is influenced by the modes of material nature. Demigods like Lord Brahmā who are covered by the influence of material nature do not exactly know Your transcendental existence, which is beyond the cosmic manifestation and the three modes of material nature."

Akrūra's prayers of personal expression concur with the version of the standard Vedic literatures. Knowledge of the spiritual sky or of the Supreme Personality of Godhead cannot be concocted or self-made. It is stated that for such knowledge we have to take assistance from the *Vedas.* That Kṛṣṇa is the Supreme Personality of Godhead, as accepted by Akrūra, is confirmed by the highest authority, the *Vedas.* All classes of transcendentalists who accept the authority of the *Vedas,* even the impersonalists generally known as *Vedāntists* who are led by Śaṅkarācārya, accept Kṛṣṇa as the highest authority. Although Śaṅkarācārya is supposed to be an impersonalist, in his commentary to the *Bhagavad-gītā* he reveals himself to be a covered personalist. He writes as follows: "Kṛṣṇa, Nārāyana, the Supreme Personality of Godhead, is beyond this cosmic manifestation." This is what Akrūra also prays as he beholds the transcendental form of Śrī Viṣṇu reclining on the snake-couch of Śeṣa Ananta on the Causal Ocean.

Beholding Viṣṇu, Akrūra beholds the spiritual form of the Absolute Truth. Very beautiful in bodily feature and surrounded by hosts of devotees and demigods, Kṛṣṇa, or God, is the chief person, the source of all persons, and yet

He is not like one of the *jīva* souls who are under the influence of the limiting material energy. He is not covered up; His spirit is not encaged in a body of matter which grows old and is subject to disease and death. There is no difference between His inside and His outside.

Viṣṇu is the controller of this material world, and unlike the countless living entities who pervade all the material planets in the bodies of germs and in gigantic bodies, He is not controlled by time, and He is not subject to transmigration in different deteriorating bodies. As stated in the *Bhagavad-gītā,* "Although I am unborn and My transcendental body never deteriorates, and although I am the Lord of all sentient beings, I still appear in every millenium in My original transcendental form." (Bg. 4.6) Kṛṣṇa does everything at His own will, and by that will He sometimes appears in the material world. Nevertheless, He remains unaffected by its material laws, just as a king visiting a prison is not affected by the laws of the prison.

"Except for You," Akrūra prays, "everyone is being carried away by the waves of material nature." The material nature is so powerful that even the demigods like Brahmā are in illusion and do not have knowledge of the spiritual sky and of the nature of the spiritual Personality of Godhead. But by the mercy of the Supreme, if anyone in any species of life surrenders to Him sincerely, he is freed from the deluding energy (*māyā*) and from the stringent laws of nature, and he can be brought up to the spiritual level. This was the special benediction of Lord Caitanya for the especially fallen souls of the present age. Simply by chanting Hare Kṛṣṇa, Hare Kṛṣṇa, Kṛṣṇa Kṛṣṇa, Hare Hare/Hare Rāma, Hare Rāma, Rāma Rāma, Hare Hare, the unfortunate souls of Kali-yuga can cross over millions of births of wandering and attain a spiritual status beyond the material modes. This is achieved simply by switching their dependence from dependence on matter and the energy of illusion to dependence on Krsna and the spiritual energy. And this is done by the guidance of the expert pure devotee or spiritual master. Following the spiritual master and transferring from dependence on illusion to dependence on Kṛṣṇa is the practical experience of Kṛṣṇa consciousness.

Akrūra prays that the Lord is the universal form. "My dear Lord, the fire is Your mouth, the earth is Your feet, the sun is Your eye, the sky is Your navel, the directions are Your ears, space is Your head, the demigods are Your arms, the oceans and seas are Your abdomen, and the winds and air are Your strength and vitality. All the plants and herbs are the hair on Your body, the clouds are the hair on Your head, the mountains are Your bones and nails, and the days and nights are the twinkling of Your eyelids."

Akrūra pays his obeisances to all the different incarnations, such as the fish incarnation, Lord Rāma, Lord Nṛsiṁhadeva, Lord Vāmanadeva, Lord Buddha and Lord Kalki.

Finally Akrūra admits that he himself is helplessly in illusion regarding spiritual knowledge: "My dear Lord, I am also no different from these conditioned souls. I am falsely thinking myself happy by possessing my home, wife, children, property and effects; in this way I am acting as if in a dreamland because none of these are permanent. I am a fool to be always absorbed in such thoughts, accepting them as permanent and true. My dear Lord, on account of my false identification, I have accepted this nonpermanent material body, which is a source of all kinds of miserable conditions. Being bewildered by such a false concept of life, I am always absorbed in thoughts of duality, and I have forgotten You, who are the reservoir of all transcendental pleasure. I am bereft of Your transcendental association, just like a foolish creature who leaves a lush oasis to search for water in the desert. The conditioned souls want to quench their thirst, but they do not know where to find water. They give up a spot where there is actually a reservoir of water and run into the desert, where there is no water. My dear Lord, I am completely incapable of controlling my mind, which is now driven by unbridled senses, attracted by fruitive activities and their results. My dear Lord, Your lotus feet cannot be appreciated by any person in the conditional stage of material existence, but somehow or other I have come near Your lotus feet, and I consider this to be Your causeless mercy upon me. You can act in any way You please because You are the supreme controller. I can thus understand that it is only by Your causeless mercy that when a person becomes eligible to be delivered from the path of repetition of birth and death he becomes attached to Your causeless devotional service."

The *Śrīmad-Bhāgavatam* describes that while Akrūra was offering his nice prayers to the Supreme Lord, the Lord disappeared from the vision, just as a dramatic actor changes his dress and assumes his original feature. After the disappearance of the Viṣṇu form, Akrūra came out of the water and walked back to the chariot where Kṛṣṇa and Balarāma were sitting. Upon seeing Them, Akrūra was struck with wonder. Kṛṣṇa then asked him whether he had seen something wonderful in the water or in space, and Akrūra said, "My dear Lord, all wonderful things that are happening within this world, either in the sky or in the water or on the land, are factually appearing in Your universal form. When I have seen You, what wonderful things remain to be seen? There cannot be anything more wonderful than Your transcendental form." Kṛṣṇa had seen that Akrūra, approaching from the water, was dumbstruck, and therefore He had asked him, "Have you seen anything wonderful?" But Akrūra's expression indicated that there was nothing more wonderful to be seen than the original form of Kṛṣṇa.

Akrura had seen Kṛṣṇa's universal form, and yet upon seeing the original form of Kṛṣṇa seated on the chariot as a cowherd boy with two arms holding a flute, Kṛṣṇa in a bluish hue, wearing beautiful garments and a peacock feather, His hair decorated with flowers, a flower garland around His neck, and accompanied by His brother Balarāma, who wore blue clothing and whose complexion was whitish, Akrūra felt that this was the greatest thing and that what he had just seen in the water could not compare to it. The devotee Arjuna expressed the same feeling after Kṛṣṇa revealed the universal form to him on the Battlefield of Kurukṣetra. After seeing this manifestation, which contained the entire material cosmos, consisting of time and space and innumerable forms, Arjuna requested that he again be allowed to see the original form of Kṛṣṇa. It is stated in the *Bhagavad-gītā* that Kṛṣṇa, having frightened Arjuna with His universal form, displayed His real four-handed form and at last showed Him His two-handed feature, thus encouraging the fearful Arjuna. When Arjuna thus saw Kṛṣṇa in His original aspect he said, "Seeing this humanlike form so very beautiful, I am now settled in mind and am restored to my original nature."

The statement of the Vedic literature is that one who knows Kṛṣṇa knows everything, and once one has seen Kṛṣṇa he has seen everything wonderful. The appreciation of Kṛṣṇa in His original form is the highest perfection of spiritual life, beyond awe of His multipotencies, the cosmic manifestation or universal form, the impersonal Brahman, and even the Viṣṇu form.

Akrūra could see this original form, but others cannot. The ability to see Kṛṣṇa is proportionate to the service offered to the Lord; in that proportion He reciprocates. For example, even in our material world everyone is serving something. The materialists are serving *māyā*, the illusory energy, and therefore they see only *māyā*, not Kṛṣṇa. The impersonalists are serving that concept of Kṛṣṇa which is imperceivable, and therefore they cannot perceive Him. The most recognized transcendentalist, however, is the *Bhāgavata*, or devotee, who is serving the personal form of Kṛṣṇa. Therefore knowledge of how to discriminate between matter and spirit is not sufficient; one must *serve* the Supreme Spirit, Kṛṣṇa.

Akrūra's prayers began with philosophical glorification of the Supreme Lord as the total origin and cause of everything and the energetic source of all energy, and the prayers end with the fervent, personal plea that the Lord allow the individual devotee to become attached to His lotus feet in an attitude of loving service. It is very significant that an elevated devotee of Godhead like Akrūra does not pray that the Lord grant him material benefits such as daily sustenance, a wife, wealth and good health. (These are already granted by the Lord in accordance with the form of species of body in which one is appearing in this material world.) Nor does the pure devotee pray to God for improvement of the material welfare of the people in terms of temporary prosperity or advancement of the national cause, nor does he pray for temporary cessation of a particular war while neglecting to pray for the solution to all war–the world-wide development of God consciousness. It is stated by the Vedic scriptures that the highest benefit will be derived by all living entities when they submissively hear about and glorify the Supreme Personality of Godhead. When one praises the naturally praiseworthy glories of God according to authoritative understanding of His transcendental qualities, and when others give their submissive aural reception to these prayers or chants or glorification, then it is guaranteed that all involved will move very quickly toward the perfection of life, love of Godhead, and then follows an eternal life of bliss and knowledge in the association of Krsna.

Instructions by Vidura

June/July, 1970

A transcendentalist is generally not interested in mundane topics such as history and politics, but when the Supreme Personality of Godhead Śrī Kṛṣṇa appeared in human society 5,000 years ago, the history and politics in which He took part became spiritualized. The transcendental devotees of the Lord take great pleasure in hearing such narratives. The *Mahābhārata,* an important Vedic literature, is such a spiritualized history, and it is accepted by the disciplic succession of spiritual masters as the actual history of Bhāratavarṣa, the ancient land which is now called India. The *Mahābhārata* deals chiefly with the struggles of the Pāṇḍava brothers, great warriors and pious rulers to whom Kṛṣṇa was related as a cousin. Kṛṣṇa's devotees are inseparably one in interest with the Lord, and therefore their activities are also taken to be as good as those of the Lord Himself. There is a famous palace intrigue related in the *Mahābhārata* in which Kṛṣṇa sent one of his pure devotees, Vidura, a brilliant political moralist, to stop an impending war between the Kurus and the Pāṇḍavas. For the purification of all readers, we here present a short transcendental history of Kṛṣṇa and His associates, as related in *Mahābhārata* and the *Śrīmad-Bhāgavatam.*

King Dhṛtarāṣṭra, blind from birth, was ruling the kingdom of the world. He is described as being blind both in material and spiritual vision. Lord Kṛṣṇa, the Personality of Godhead, appeared in the King's court and pleaded for the return of some land which was the rightful property of His powerful but exiled relatives, the Pāṇḍava brothers. Every word Kṛṣṇa speaks, as recorded in scriptures like *Śrīmad-Bhāgavatam* and *Bhagavad-gītā* is relished like nectar by those who are not so entangled in matter that they cannot appreciate the transcendental vibration. But when Kṛṣṇa addressed the assembly of King Dhṛtarāṣṭra and pleaded for a peaceful settlement, the message was not taken very seriously by the King and his one hundred sons, led by Duryodhana. These rulers were thinking themselves independent of the Personality of Godhead and His laws, and they were intent on their own course of destroying the Pāṇḍavas. Due to losing their kingdom in a gambling match, the Pāṇḍavas, the rightful hereditary heirs to the throne, were exiled for a term of thirteen years. When the period of exile was over, they returned to the kingdom which was rightfully theirs, but were refused even so much as the rule of a single village. In fact, Duryodhana, the leader of the sons of Dhṛtarāṣṭra, said that if the Pāṇḍavas wanted even as much land as can fit under the point of a pin, they would have to fight for it.

IMPENDING WAR

After the rejection of Lord Kṛṣṇa's peace offering, the battle loomed like a large black cloud in the sky. At that late, ominous hour, with the armies already making preparations for battle, King Dhṛtarāṣṭra invited in his elder brother Vidura for consultation. Vidura was an expert minister and politician. His instructions are well known in Vedic literature; just the phrase "instructions by Vidura" indicates policies approved by experts in political and moral principles. Therefore, Dhṛtarāṣṭra expected his words to be exactly to the point.

Vidura came into the presence of King Dhṛtarāṣṭra and his one hundred sons, headed by Duryodhana and Duḥśāsana. The hall was silent, and everyone pressed forward to hear Vidura. Vidura was known by those present to be partial to the Pāṇḍavas, who from the time of their birth had to undergo many attempts on their lives by Dhṛtarāṣṭra. Actually, when the Pāṇḍavas were just babies, Dhṛtarāṣṭra acted as their affectionate and protective uncle, but as soon as they began to grow into strong, competent youths, Dhṛtarāṣṭra realized that these boys, and not his own, would take the throne. He then turned to unfair means in order to dispose of them. According to the Vedic system, after the retirement of the previous king, Dhṛtarāṣṭra, as the eldest son, should have been heir to the throne, but he was disqualified by blindness. Therefore, the next in line was Dhṛtarāṣṭra's brother, Pāṇḍu, who duly reigned. After the early death of King Pāṇḍu, his five sons, the Pāṇḍava brothers, led by Yudhiṣṭhira, the oldest, came in rightful line. But Dhṛtarāṣṭra was determined that his sons, and not the sons of Pāṇḍu, should rule. Due to this illegitimate desire, he had many times tried to kill Yudhiṣṭhira and his brothers, Arjuna, Bhīma, Nakula and Sahadeva. Vidura, however, the younger brother of Dhṛtarāṣṭra, took it upon himself to guard the Pāṇḍavas, just as a bird protects her eggs with her wing.

Vidura was filled with compassion by remembering the continual sufferings caused by Dhṛtarāṣṭra to the Pāṇḍava brothers and their mother, Kuntī. But at the same time, he was a great court philosopher and a true friend to Dhṛtarāṣṭra. There was no doubt of his faithfulness to his brother; even Duryodhana knew this to be so. (Ultimately, after the last miseries of the war, it was shown that Vidura was Dhṛtarāṣṭra's only true friend in the entire royal court.) Called in on the verge of war, Vidura stood in the hall and offered his advice to the blind King. He could not help remembering, however, that this was the same royal hall wherein Yudhiṣṭhira and his brothers had lost their kingdom and their wife in a rigged gambling match. Dhṛtarāṣṭra's sons, led by Duḥśāsana, had at that time tried to insult the Pāṇḍavas' wife, Draupadī, by first loosening her long hair and then trying to strip her naked in the presence of a large gathering. At that time, Kṛṣṇa, the infinite Lord, had answered the helpless cries of Draupadī, his pure devotee and cousin, and had become her infinite sari. The more the brothers unraveled her sari, the more sari was supplied by Kṛṣṇa, and she was never disrobed. Another time, Dhṛtarāṣṭra ordered a house built, and when the building was finished, he invited his brother's family to live there. But Vidura gave a hint in the presence of all of the members of the royal family that even a weapon not made of steel or any other material element can be the most sharp for killing. Thus he hinted that the Pāṇḍavas were being sent to the house to be killed and that they should be alert. Later he came disguised as a *brāhmaṇa* and directly warned the Pāṇḍavas that on a certain night the house was to be set on fire. Thus the Pāṇḍavas were able to make a timely escape through a tunnel under the earth. Vidura could remember many such plots, and in each case he had given protection to the Pāṇḍavas, while at the same time trying to restrain his brother, Dhṛtarāṣṭra.

Vidura, however, was not about to be influenced by attachment to the Pāṇḍavas; he had the good of his brother at heart, and he spoke in direct words which made him famous among expert ministers in Vedic history as the giver of the keenest political and moral instruction. This is recorded in the *Śrīmad-Bhāgavatam.* Vidura said, "You have asked me, brother, to come for consultation at this dangerous hour. I say that you must now return the legitimate property of Yudhiṣṭhira, who has no enemy and who has been forebearing through untold sufferings due to your offenses. He is waiting with his younger brothers, among whom is Bhīma, breathing heavily like a snake. Surely you are afraid of him." Vidura offered good counsel, but at his first words, Duryodhana's face turned with rage. But Vidura spoke on: "Lord Kṛṣṇa, the Personality of Godhead, has accepted the sons of Pṛthā as His kinsmen, and all the kings of the world are with Lord Kṛṣṇa. He is residing at home with His family members, the royal order of the Yadu dynasty, who have conquered unlimited numbers of rulers. He is their Lord." Palatably or unpalatably, Vidura wanted to impress on his elder brother that to fight against the Pāṇḍavas would be ruinous for him because they were supported by Lord Kṛṣṇa. Vidura, being saintly, could recognize that Lord Kṛṣṇa was the Supreme Personality of Godhead Himself, enacting His pastimes upon the earth. The Lord had conquered many powerful demons, even in His childhood, and the Pāṇḍavas themselves, prior to their exile, had won their wives by conquering all the rulers of the world. With Kṛṣṇa as their intimate relative, the Pāṇḍavas had all universal power behind them. Such was Vidura's advice.

According to the law of *karma,* that Dhṛtarāṣṭra and Duryodhana were born in the royal family and had reached a position of wealth and power indicates that in past lives they had performed pious deeds. But because they could not hear Lord Kṛṣṇa Himself when He spoke sensibly to them on important topics in a grave hour, it is to be understood that the benefits of their past piety were completely exhausted. There was no way now but downward if they refused to accept the Personality of Godhead or the words of His bona fide representative. Vidura was on a welfare mission to save them from the wrong choice. But by now, hearing Vidura, Duryodhana was angry, and he was cursing. It is said that good counsel given to a foolish person causes the fool to become angry, just as feeding milk to a snake only increases its venomous poison. But Vidura gave these final instructions in an attempt to deliver Dhṛtarāṣṭra from the clutches of death:

"You are maintaining offense personified, Duryodhana, as your infallible son, but he is envious of Lord Kṛṣṇa. And because you are maintaining a nondevotee of Kṛṣṇa, you are devoid of all auspicious qualities. Free yourself from this inauspicious condition as soon as possible, for the good of your entire family."

Duryodhana could stand it no longer, and he delivered a direct insult, like an arrow to the ears of the famous minister, Vidura: "Who asked him to come here, this son of a kept-mistress? He is so crooked that he spys in the interest of the enemy, against those upon whose support he has grown up. Get him out of here immediately. Take all he has, cane him and leave him with only his breath!"

The actual facts behind this slanderous attack by Duryodhana were as follows. When getting married, the kings in Vedic society would take on several other young girls along with the married princess. By intimate association with the king, these girls, called *dāsīs,* would have sons. Such sons had no royal claim, but they were raised with all the facilities of princes. Vidura was such a son of a *dāsī.* Duryodhana not only attacked his birth, but he called him a spy because he seemed to support the cause of Yudhiṣṭhira, whom Duryodhana took to be his enemy. Duryodhana actually knew well that Vidura was a great soul and was Dhṛtarāṣṭra's well-wisher, but, caught up in political intrigue, Duryodhana had become blind to the actual situation. Therefore he slandered his uncle Vidura and threatened to drive him from the palace. Dhṛtarāṣṭra had always been affectionate to his younger brother, Vidura, but he tolerated the insults by Duryodhana because he and his sons were set on wiping out the pious Pāṇḍavas once and for all.

KṚṢṆA'S ADVICE REJECTED

Duryodhana is understood from the first verses of *Bhagavad-gītā* to be a brilliant administrator and political leader. But the most important thing he didn't know. Absorbed in false ego, Duryodhana thought that he was doing everything by himself. Actually, Duryodhana, like every conditioned soul in the material world, is under the direct control of God. In the Bhaktivedanta Purports to *Śrīmad-Bhāgavatam* it is stated: "The external energy of the Lord, or the material nature, is fully under the control of the Supreme Lord, and the conditioned soul is fully under the grip of the external energy. Therefore, the conditioned soul is fully under the control of the law of the Lord. But, illusioned, he thinks that he is independent in his activities."

Duryodhana refused the instructions of the Supreme Personality of Godhead, Śrī Kṛṣṇa, and plotted his own destiny in terms of removing Vidura and warring against the Pāṇḍavas. We can understand that only the first act, rejecting the personal instructions of God—was factually performed freely, of his own volition. According to the revealed scriptural sources, our minute amount of free will can be exercised in choosing either to follow the dictation of God or to follow the dictation of His material energy, *māyā*. There is no other choice. Once one refuses God, one must follow His material energy. Whatever one's personal philosophy may be, one must grow old, one must be subjected to diseases and material miseries (miseries caused by the body and mind, miseries caused by other living entities, and miseries caused by natural disturbances like earthquakes, droughts, etc.), and eventually one must die. And after death, one must go wherever nature sends one. By the law of *karma,* action is necessarily followed by reaction, and all actions in the world take place under mixed modes of goodness, passion and ignorance. The Vedic understanding is that God is transcendental to the material laws and conditions—He is their master. He is eternal, free and unlimited in knowledge and pleasure, and when we, the infinitesimal individual souls, dovetail our own small amount of free will with His, then we can directly experience those same qualities of bliss, eternity and knowledge. By that dovetailing process, we can be freed from the misgivings of the body, mind and intelligence and can be situated on the transcendental plane. But when, instead, we come to this material world due to forgetfulness of the Supreme Person, then our plight (from which only the pure devotees of Godhead are excluded) is that we suffer a covering of our eternally pleasurable qualitative oneness with the Supreme Spirit.

We think, "I am this body," but actually the real person is still spirit soul; due to contacting a material body, however, the spirit soul finds himself frustrated by an incompatible situation, like a fish on land. The example given by the spiritual masters is that the spirit can be compared to electric force. Electricity is unlimited in the tasks it can perform—it can heat, cool, drive giant machines, etc.—but once the unlimited electricity is put into one limited appliance, it can perform only a limited function. For example, the electricity in a toaster can do nothing else but make toast. The electricity has become limited or conditioned in its expression due to the vehicle in which it is confined. Similarly, thinking that we are this body, we are forced to react in terms of goodness, passion and ignorance within the material world, under the control of the inferior material energy. In material consciousness, we are no more free than a cow tied to the end of a rope: even if the rope is long, the cow is still not free.

When God or His pure devotee speaks, that is direct, superior, spiritual energy; by following His will directly, one can return to one's original, eternal, happy state of consciousness, both immediately, in this body, as well as in the next life, after the demise of the body. The atheist or materialist who misuses his free will and derides the Supreme Personality of Godhead, Kṛṣṇa, must nevertheless come under the strict superintendence of the material energy. Thus, one may think oneself the almighty supreme enjoyer, the benefactor and proprietor of all, but despite these grand illusions, one must be limited by God's material laws. Duryodhana is the typical materialist of the present civilization of Kali-yuga (the age of quarrel). He had just heard Vidura criticize him for being a nondevotee of Kṛṣṇa, and he at once affirmed this status by insulting and threatening bodily harm to Vidura. This is the height of rascaldom, adopted here by Duryodhana; he wants to beat Vidura, whose only offense is that he is speaking the truth, that God is great and we are small. The Kali-yuga materialists in today's godless civilization are also intent on destroying the brahminical culture and denying the advice of the bona fide spiritual teachers. "Why should I listen to God? Who is God? I am God! I shall enjoy as I like." These are materialists' symptomatic responses to brahminical or spiritual guidance. It will be seen in the case of Duryodhana that thinking himself to be God Almighty did not prevent him from being broken to pieces on the battlefield and ruining all his allies.

Under the illusion of material energy, he could not see the best course for his people, and therefore he led them into war. But even the present-day peacemakers who are trying to secure peace without authoritative spiritual guidance are finding no success. They are trying to establish Utopia, the kingdom of God without God, but it cannot be. As the expert politician Vidura said, a path without God is inauspicious for the state, the society, the family, and the individual. We can get no profit by saying that we are God or by trying to conquer the material nature, but we can gain all good fortune in this world if we can be directly led by the superior, spiritual energy of Godhead, which comes in the form of guidance from the pure devotees of the Absolute Truth. In his materialistic folly, thinking he was independent, Duryodhana was the dreamer, off in the clouds. In contrast, Vidura shrewdly offered Dhṛtarāṣṭra the key to success.

But the Battle of Kurukṣetra was not avoided. As for Vidura, he took the opportunity of Duryodhana's insult as a blessing in disguise. He saw that Duryodhana was on the path of ruin. As a devotee, he also saw that the Lord's internal energy was helping him to come back to Godhead. A devotee is always in a temperament of renunciation because the worldly attractions can never satisfy him. Vidura had never been attracted by the royal palace of his brother, and now he had the opportunity, by the grace of Duryodhana, to quit the place and devote himself completely to the transcendental loving service of the Lord. Instead of being sorry, he thanked Duryodhana from within because he had given him the chance to live alone in a holy place and thus be fully engaged in the cultivation of spiritual life. Also, he saw no more hope in defending his brother, so he left the palace without Duryodhona's taking physical steps for his removal.

Śrīmad-Bhāgavatam describes the fate of General Duryodhana on the Battlefield of Kurukṣetra: "Duryodhana lost his good fortune, as well as his life, because of the intricacy of ill advice given by Karṇa, Duḥśāsana, etc. Although he was very powerful, he finally lay on the ground, his thighs broken, and his followers were with him." It is described that Kṛṣṇa is harder than a thunderbolt to the wrongdoers and softer than a rose to the devotees. Duryodhana was misled by bad associates and ill advice, contrary to the established principles of the Lord's order, and so he became subject to punishment.

Of course, ultimately, anyone who can be so fortunate as to associate directly with the Personality of Godhead when He appears in this universe to enact His pastimes is liberated as a final result. In this way, all the soldiers and sons of Dhṛtarāṣṭra who were able to see the Lord at the time of their death and could appreciate the beauty of His face and features were transferred, in their original spiritual forms, to the spiritual sky, beyond the material universes which are limited by death and pain. That is the version of the Vedic texts.

As previously stated, the banished saint Vidura turned out to be the only true friend of King Dhṛtarāṣṭra, After the war, the defeated, blind Dhṛtarāṣṭra. whose sons had all been killed, wanted to remain as King in the palace. As a matter of duty, King Yudhiṣṭhira, the leader of the victorious Pāṇḍavas, maintained Dhṛtarāṣṭra in royal honor. Dhṛtarāṣṭra, therefore, was happily passing away his numbered days in the illusion that he was the royal uncle of King Yudhiṣṭhira. At that time, Vidura returned from traveling to holy places all over the earth and especially from inquiring on transcendental topics from the great sage Maitreya. Vidura had of course been thoroughly involved in court politics, but after being thrown out of the palace by Dhṛtarāṣṭra and his son Duryodhana, he had taken full advantage of existing conditions and had become fully Kṛṣṇa conscious, fixed in loving service to the Supreme Lord, by taking instructions from a great devotee-sage. He was therefore received as a godly person on his return to the palace. The court personalities and his kinsmen like Yudhiṣṭhira and the Pāṇḍavas, Dhṛtarāṣṭra, Kuntī, Draupadī and many others with their wives and children, in a tearful post-war reunion, all rushed to hear and see him. The *Bhāgavatam* says that when the court family saw Vidura again after the long separation, it was as if their lost consciousness was revived. They gathered around him like students sitting before a teacher. They were very eager to hear spiritual instructions from him, and they listened with rapt attention. Vidura spoke for the welfare of all, but he especially directed himself to his oldest brother, Dhṛtarāṣṭra.

Vidura knew the situation of Dhṛtarāṣṭra, and he addressed him as follows: "My dear King, please get out immediately. Do not delay in the least. Just see how fearfulness has overtaken you. You are very old, and there is no remedial measure for your death. My brother, please understand that death is identical with the Supreme Personality of Godhead, and it is approaching for all of us. Your father, sons and well-wishers are all dead, your body is overtaken by invalidity, and here at the last stage you are living in another's home. You have been blind from birth, and recently you have become hard of hearing. Your teeth are loosened, you liver is diseased, and you are coughing with mucus."

Vidura's words cut to pieces the network of illusion in which he found his brother rotting. Vidura addressed him as King because actually he was not the King. Overtaken by foolish ideas, Dhṛtarāṣṭra was living for temporary comforts and was trying to make a permanent settlement for his perishable body. Vidura's sharp but compassionate words were to wake up his brother so that, before it was too late, he could make progress for the welfare of his real self, his eternal soul.

Vidura said: "Alas! So powerful is the living being's hope to continue life indefinitely. You are living just like a household dog and taking scraps of food from the warrior who killed your son Duryodhana!" Vidura did not avoid the naked truth of Dhṛtarāṣṭra's humiliating position. Dhṛtarāṣṭra was living at the house of the Pāṇḍavas because he wanted to continue his comfortable life, even at the cost of being humiliated. Vidura pointed out to him that the whole *raison d'etre* of the human form of life is to get a chance to wake up to self-realization and to go back to Godhead, where life is eternal and from where, once going, no one comes back to this material world. "There is no necessity of living a degraded life," Vidura continued, "subsisting on the charity of those whom you tried to kill. In spite of your desires, your body will certainly dwindle and die, like an old, deteriorated garment."

Wakened in no uncertain terms by his well-wishing brother, Dhṛtarāṣṭra left the palace without saying anything, and under the guidance of Vidura, he sat on the bank of the Ganges and engaged in the beginning of *yoga* practice. He took regular baths, performed special sacrifices and fasted by drinking only water. This helped him to control his mind and senses and to free himself from thoughts of family affection. Due to his offenses at the feet of pure devotees, the Pāṇḍavas, Dhṛtarāṣṭra was not able to become a pure devotee of the Personality of Godhead, but by the grace of Vidura, and to the astonishment of all the court, Dhṛtarāṣṭra was able to cut himself off from all external sense attraction and concentrate on his pure being. The *Bhāgavatam* describes, "He had to amalgamate his pure identity with intelligence and then, with knowledge of being qualitatively one with the supreme eternal living entity, merge into the impersonal aspect of the Supreme Being. Thus he rescued his consciousness from the clutches of the five elements and realized his qualitative identity with the eternal Super-soul who is sitting in everyone's heart." Practicing under the instructions of Vidura, Dhṛtarāṣṭra achieved the impersonal perfection of liberation from his body, and after many such liberated births, he transcended the material sky to become engaged in the transcendental loving service of the Lord. Despite Dhṛtarāṣṭra's many offenses, the Lord's mercy was bestowed on him by his contact with Vidura, and he was able to attain the perfectional stage. He quit his body by turning it into ashes in a self-made fire of mystic power.

LIBERATION

Vidura was sorry that he could not turn his brother into a pure devotee in one lifetime, but he was most liberal in his benediction, and so Dhṛtarāṣṭra's time before reaching the topmost perfection was shortened. Ultimately the result depends on the will of the Supreme Lord, and in one lifetime Dhṛtarāṣṭra attained liberation from the material conception of bodily consciousness. Only after achieving such a liberated state can one attain to devotional service.

The conditioned entities are suffering under the illusion that the body is the self and that the temporary world is permanent. Although they have no information of God or eternal pleasure, they can become engaged in the eternal, blissful activities of devotional service to the Supreme Lord by becoming wholly dependent on the instructions of pure devotees like Vidura. One should not only inquire but should render loving service to pure devotees and surrender to them. Only then is inquiry meaningful and fruitful. In no other way can one gain real knowledge of one's position. That is the secret of spiritual knowledge or knowledge of God or Kṛṣṇa: it is revealed from within the heart after serving a pure devotee and receiving instruction from him.

Mahārāja Parīkṣit and The Age of Kali

September/October, 1970

The followers of Kṛṣṇa consciousness are aware that at present the universe and the earth are in the age of Kali. Vedic culture calculates the long duration of time between the creation and annihilation of the cosmos according to repeated cycles of the following four seasons: Satya-yuga, Tretā-yuga, Dvāpara-yuga and Kali-yuga. Of the four, the last, the Kali-yuga, is noted for being the fallen age, the age of hypocrisy and quarrel. Aside from the evidence of Vedic literature, one can observe the fallen condition of the present civilization in everyday common affairs. In Kali-yuga the basic principles of religion are abandoned by a majority of the people, the government is ruled by the lowest class of men, and society lives on the basis of animal life for the goal of sense gratification. Huge quarrels are predicated on various minor pretexts. Kali-yuga lasts for 432,000 years and is supposed to get increasingly worse, until finally men will be eating their own sons and finding sport in hunting down the devotees of God. Let us therefore examine the history of the influx of Kali-yuga 5,000 years ago and try to understand how its degrading influence can be checked.

This information regarding Kali-yuga is recorded in the *Śrīmad-Bhāgavatam,* the transcendental literature which depicts the pastimes performed by the Personality of Godhead Śrī Kṛṣṇa when He appeared on the earth. *Śrīmad-Bhāgavatam* relates that Kṛṣṇa appeared on this earth for a period of 125 years during the end of the Dvāpara-yuga, and when He disappeared from the earth the age of Kali entered. The personification of Kali, the agent for all irreligion and vice, was kept in check, however, even after the disappearance of Kṛṣṇa, due to the presence of a very strong and pious ruler of the earth, Mahārāja Parīkṣit. His life is described as being wonderful in its birth, wonderful in its duration, and wonderful in its completion. We may at this time examine the life of Mahārāja Parīkṣit as the background to understand the strength of Kṛṣṇa consciousness even in the midst of Kali-yuga.

Mahārāja Parīkṣit's strength was due to his being completely surrendered to the words of Kṛṣṇa. And as we shall see, Kṛṣṇa was pleased to work His will through this surrendered soul. Mahārāja Parīkṣit was the posthumous child of Abhimanyu, who was the son of Arjuna, the famous hero of the Battle of Kurukṣetra. While he was still in the womb, Mahārāja Parīkṣit was struck by a nuclear weapon detonated by an enemy of his family; and yet due to the mercy of the Personality of Godhead, Śrī Kṛṣṇa, who entered the womb of his mother, Uttara, and protected him, Parīksit was not burned. When he grew up and began to rule the kingdom, he was always conscientiously surrendered unto the Personality of Godhead and was never afraid nor overwhelmed, even up to his death.

KALI ENTERS

One day Emperor Parīksit was traveling through his kingdom, and he met the personality of religious principles, Dharma, in the form of a wounded, wandering bull. He also met the personality of the earth, in the form of a cow who had tears on her face and who appeared to be greatly aggrieved, like a mother who had lost her child. The *Śrīmad-Bhāgavatam,* First Canto, Seventeenth Chaper, relates that Mahārāja Parīkṣit observed a lower class laborer, dressed like a king but with a large stick in his hand, beating the bull and the cow as if they were without a protector. The bull was as white as a lotus flower and was terrified of being beaten. It was trembling from fear and was standing on one leg urinating. Cows are beneficial because one can draw out religious principles from them, but this poor cow was being beaten by the lower class laborer and appeared very distressed.

Mahārāja Parīkṣit became furious upon seeing this scene. Seated on his golden chariot and equipped with arrows and bows, he came upon the cow's persecutor. "Who are you?" he demanded. "You appear to be strong enough, and still you dare to kill, within my protection, those who are helpless. By dress you pose as a manly king, but by your deeds it is clear that you are against all fighting principles. You rogue, do you dare to beat an innocent cow simply because Kṛṣṇa and Arjuna are out of sight? Since you are beating the innocent in a secluded place, you stand as a culprit and therefore deserve to be killed." Mahārāja Parīkṣit then turned to the bull and said, "O bull, you are as white as a lotus. Who are you?" The *kṣatriyas* or rulers such as Mahārāja Parīkṣit are meant to protect the innocent, and therefore Parīkṣit Mahārāja was outraged to see this brutality taking place in his kingdom.

RELIGION PERSONIFIED

Before the arrival of Mahārāja Parīksit, the bull, the personification of religion, Dharma, had inquired of the cow, "Why are you lamenting? Are you unhappy because people in general do not follow the rules and regulations for eating, sleeping, drinking, and mating and are inclined to do these things without regard for time and place?" In the age of Kali, because the tendencies of sense gratification are not regulated, illicit sex, intoxication, and so many preliminary vices are being engaged in everywhere. When Parīkṣit arrived he said, "For the first time I see you lamenting with tears in a kingdom which has always been well protected by the arms of the kings. Before this I have never seen anyone shed tears because of royal negligence."

The Emperor could see that the bull was standing on only one leg. Dharma explained that his four legs were austerity, cleanliness, mercy, and truthfulness, and three of these legs had been broken because of the people's rampant irreligion, characterized by pride, affection for women, and intoxicating habits. He was left on only one leg, truthfulness. The Emperor took his sword and prepared to kill the personality of Kali who, posing as a ruler, was beating the bull and thus causing all irreligion and causing the cow of the earth to shed tears. In the dress of a king, this lower class man, Kali, was simply gratifying his senses and thinking that there was no suitable king to curb him down. The *Śrīmad-Bhāgavatam,* in which the narration of Mahārāja Parīkṣit is given, is itself the systematic propaganda for educating people in general how to clean up the atmosphere of corruption. Mahārāja Parīkṣit, the ideal executive, was about to kill Kali, but when Kali saw that the King was willing to kill him, he at once gave up his false kingly attire and with great fear completely surrendered unto him.

According to the Vedic culture of the four orders or qualities of occupation, a real warrior never surrenders in a fight. Therefore, when this lower class laborer or *śūdra* surrendered himself, he disclosed his real identity by not accepting the challenge. When he saw that Mahārāja Parīkṣit was ready to fight and that the king was beyond his power to defeat, Kali bowed down his head as a subordinate and gave up his royal dress. Mahārāja Parīkṣit did not want to kill a surrendered soul such as the fallen Kali because he was always compassionate and kind to the poor. Thus the personality of Kali, who was entering earth for the first time to cause corruption and irreligion, was saved by the will of providence.

Out of chivalry and compassion, Mahārāja Parīkṣit said, "Do not fear. You have no need to fear for your life, but you cannot remain in any land of my kingdom." So Kali was allowed to live, but he was afraid that wherever he went he would see the King with his bows and arrows. Therefore he asked for special places where he could live, and Mahārāja Parīkṣit then gave him permission to reside in four places–places where gambling, drinking, prostitution and the slaughter of animals take place. In this way he intended to confine him. The principle was to restrict Kali to these places so that those addicted to irreligious habits might be regulated and not encouraged by the state. Mahārāja Parīkṣit showed the simple way to categorically stop war and vice. He announced that he would collect all the illicit gold collected by exploiting the propensities of the age of Kali and employ it in *saṅkīrtana* propaganda for the glorification of God. He made sufficient plans so that Kali would have little chance to infiltrate the sound structure of human society. Thus the influence of Kali was checked as long as Mahārāja Parīkṣit himself was present to drive him away and uphold the principles of religion for the spiritual enlightenment of all people.

KṚṢṆA CONSCIOUS POLITICS

In the present day we lament that lower class men are voted in and voted out of high posts of political power, but in Mahārāja Parīkṣit we can see the example of a practical king who could progressively advance society and who was intolerant of all kinds of corruption. Often people ask if the Kṛṣṇa conscious movement is apolitical, but the answer is no. Kṛṣṇa consciousness offers the political principle followed by rulers such as Mahārāja Parīkṣit, and the Kṛṣṇa consciousness society wishes to put such a God conscious man in office.

Further activities of Mahārāja Parīksit show how, because of the King's complete surrender to the Absolute Truth, the Lord used him as an instrument to bring about the narration of the *Śrīmad-Bhāgavatam,* which, after the departure of Kṛṣṇa and after the death of Mahārāja Parīkṣit, was to be the standard of religion for all people in the midst of the age of Kali. *Śrīmad-Bhāgavatam* is declared to be the transcendental literary incarnation of the Personality of Godhead, and it is only because of Mahārāja Parīkṣit's relationship to Kṛṣṇa that this story is narrated. All Kṛṣṇa conscious activities are meant to help us remember Him. The purpose of *Śrīmad-Bhāgavatam* and all spiritual literature is to continually glorify God. To hear these literatures is purifying and sublime. When spoken, especially by pure devotees of the Lord, these narratives carry the full potencies of *bhakti-yoga,* or devotion to Kṛṣṇa.

Śrīmad-Bhāgavatam, First Canto, Chapter 18, text 25, relates: "Once upon a time, Mahārāja Parīkṣit, while engaged in hunting in the forest with his bows and arrows, became extremely fatigued, hungry and thirsty while following some stags. In search of a reservoir of water, he entered the hermitage of the well-known Śamīka Ṛṣī and saw the sage sitting silently with closed eyes." The birth of Mahārāja Parīkṣit is wonderful because Parīkṣit was saved in the womb by the Supersoul when the demon Aśvatthāmā sent a fire weapon to kill him. His career as king was wonderful, for he upheld religious principles and drove out Kali. This present description of Mahārāja Parīkṣit's becoming thirsty begins the story of his death, which proved to be most wonderful because it was engineered directly by the will of the Lord in order to bring about a much greater transcendental event—the narration of *Śrīmad-Bhāgavatam.*

As a man of controlled senses, Mahārāja Parīkṣit would never have been disturbed by thirst or hunger. His hunger and thirst on this occasion were irregular in that he became perturbed by these bodily demands. It is therefore explained that the situation was created by the Lord in order to bring about Parīkṣit's renunciation of worldly activities. As a worldly king, even though a great king, Mahārāja Parīkṣit was necessarily involved in much worldly diplomacy, and the Lord was making it possible for him to be forced into a complete state of renunciation. The awkward situation by which the devotee Parīkṣit was obliged to renounce all worldly affairs is to be taken as the grace of the Lord and not as a matter of unfavorable frustation.

ARRANGED BY KRṢṆA

Parīkṣit Mahārāja entered the *muni's* hermitage and saw that the *muni,* long-haired and covered by the skin of a stag, was in transcendental meditation. The King, however, being thirsty, asked the sage for water. Not having received any formal welcome seat or water or sweet words of address, the King felt neglected, and he became angry. His Divine Grace A.C. Bhaktivedanta Swami Prabhupāda explains that this lack of sense control, his immediate anger at not being properly received by the *yogī,* is the same as Arjuna's becoming bewildered on the Battlefield of Kurukṣetra. Had Arjuna not been overcome by illusory family affection by the will of God, there would have been no chance for the *Bhagavad-gītā* to have been spoken because Arjuna would not have asked Kṛṣṇa his questions of doubt, to be answered for all mankind. Similarly, had Mahārāja Parīkṣit not been fatigued, hungry, thirsty, and then angry, there would have been no chance for *Śrīmad-Bhāgavatam* to have been spoken by Śrīla Śukadeva Gosvāmī, who was the prime authority on Kṛṣṇa. Parīkṣit's improper behavior is actually the prelude to *Śrīmad-Bhāgavatam,* which is itself a counteraction to Kali, as much as the upraised sword of Parīkṣit on Kali's neck.

The insulted King took up a dead snake which he found in the front of the cave. Picking it up on the front part of his bow, he placed it on the shoulder of the sage as an insult and then left. He accused the sage of not actually being in meditation on the Supreme but of putting on a false show of trance just in order to avoid receiving him.

Śrīmad-Bhāgavatam goes on to describe that the sage had a son, who was immature but, because he was a *brāhmaṇa's* son, very powerful. While he was spending his time playing with other inexperienced boys, he heard of the King's insult to his father, and he therefore became furious and cursed Mahārāja Parīkṣit to die. It was through this inexperienced boy that Kali found an opportunity to ruin the entire cultural heritage of the four orders of life and bring about the corruption which now exists in India as the caste system. In the perverted caste system, one order of life tends to lord it over another by birth, and enmity is thus created among the orders. As stated in the *Bhagavad-gītā,* because these orders are created by the Lord, they are naturally existing in every society. There is always an intelligent class, a warrior or administrative class, a mercantile or agricultural class, and a laborer class which serves the other three orders. By corruption, individuals claim to possess the qualities of a particular position simply by birthright, and then there is no cooperation among the natural orders, but rather there is friction. The first victim of brahminical injustice was Mahārāja Parīkṣit, and after the incident of his being cursed, the intelligent class was not protected properly by the warrior class, the mercantile class began outright exploitation of the other classes, and the lower classes became dissatisfied because of not being protected and cared for. Because these events occurred at the dawn of Kali-yuga, they are understood to be most significant in ushering in the corruption and degradation which characterize this fallen age.

The warrior class is supposed to protect and not insult the *brāhmaṇas;* therefore the son of the sage, acting immaturely and rashly, used his brahminical power to curse the King. The *brāhmaṇa* boy, Śṛṅgī, cried, "The warrior class is supposed to act as watchdogs. Since when does a watchdog enter the house of the king, sit in the house of the master, and eat with him on the same plate?" In that way he tried to explain away the incident of the *yogī's* not receiving the King. In those days the brahminical class had powers to curse, but the boy committed a great mistake in using this power. Touching the water of the River Kauśikī, he discharged a thunderbolt of words: "In seven days a snake-bird will bite the wretched King on account of his breaking the law of etiquette and insulting my father." The boy then returned to the hermitage, and seeing his father with the snake draped on his shoulder, he began to cry loudly. His father gradually opened his eyes and found the dead snake on his neck, but he did not take it very seriously. On hearing what his son had done, he very much regretted the whole incident. He said to his son, "What a greatly sinful act you have performed over such an insignificant offense by the King. He then chastised his boy and warned him that the King, as a representative of the Personality of Godhead, is never to be placed on an equal footing with common men. The sage foresaw the downfall of cooperation between the orders, the end of the pious monarchical regime, and the plundering of the people's wealth by rogues and thieves. He told his son, "Without protection there will be great disruption and social anomalies in the future, and there will be killing and stealing of animals and women. And we shall be responsible for the reaction of all these sins. Without protection of a good king, the people will be scattered like lambs." The ṛṣi then prayed to the all-pervading Personality of Godhead to please pardon his boy who with no intelligence had committed the great sin of cursing a person who was completely sinless. Kings were considered subordinate to the intelligent or brahminical class, and therefore they should have been protected and not cursed.

King Parīksit returned home, but he regretted insulting the *brāhmaṇa* for his inauspicious act, and he hoped that whatever reaction there might be would come at once. While the King was thus repenting, he received the news of his imminent death. He accepted this news as good and used it at once to detach himself from his worldly kingdom. According to the Vedic system, a man is expected to detach himself from family affairs in the latter part of his life because old age is the notice of death. A householder should leave home and go to the forest and live there in seclusion in order to obtain knowledge from the sages about the real purpose of life, spiritual progress, and about how to prepare for the next life.

SEVEN DAYS TO LIVE

Rather than lamenting that he was to die within seven days, Mahārāja Parīkṣit took it as auspicious in that he knew that for at least seven days he would live. He utilized this accurate notice of death so that he could perfect the responsibility of life before the day of his death. Turning the reign of the kingdom over to his son Janamejaya, bidding his family good-bye, and giving up all royal paraphernalia, Mahārāja Parīkṣit went toward the bank of the Ganges to observe fasting unto death, and he gave himself up unto the lotus feet of the Personality of Godhead Kṛṣṇa, who alone is able to award liberation. In this way he accepted the curse of the *brāhmaṇa* boy and used it to achieve the ultimate goal of spiritual advancement. At that time, because Mahārāja Parīkṣit was such a great personality, both as a king and as a saint, many greatly learned figures arrived with their disciples on the bank of the river where Mahārāja Parīkṣit was fasting and praying. They were of such an elevated status that the places of pilgrimage they visited became sanctified by their presence.

Thus the scene was set for the recitation of *Śrīmad-Bhāgavatam*. The great sages who were present included Bhṛgu, Vasiṣṭha, Parāśara, and Paraśurāma. The King received them by bowing his head to the ground. Then the ṛṣis took their seats, and the King expressed his decision to fast until death. He then stood before them humbly with folded hands and made his spoken obeisances. He began by saying that he understood that the sages generally did not like to associate with kings and that he therefore felt himself greatly fortunate. Sages usually reject royal personalities and keep them at a distant place like garbage. Parīkṣit said, "O *brāhmaṇas,* just accept me as a completely surrendered soul, and let the mother Ganges accept me because I have taken up in my heart the lotus feet of the Lord. Let the snake or anything magical created by the *brāhmaṇa* bite me at once. All I want is that you sages may go on singing of the deeds of Lord Viṣṇu." Because Mahāraja Parikṣit was actually surrendered to the feet of the Supreme Lord, he was not afraid of death. Conditions were very auspicious for the sages to speak about Kṛṣṇa.

It is seen that Mahārāja Parīkṣit was not striving for ordinary spiritual knowledge or merely practicing *yoga* techniques to gain liberation. He said, "I do not even care if I take my birth in this material world again, as long as I have attachment for Lord Śrī Kṛṣṇa, who has unlimited potencies." Mahārāja Parīkṣit, being a very advanced king and saint, was, at the time of his death, already beyond inquiring about liberation or trying to free himself from return to birth and death. He simply wanted to hear the glorification of God or even to be assured that after his demise the glorification of God, the highest pleasure, the highest satisfaction, and the prime benediction for all humanity, would go on. This example is so wonderful that even the demigods in the higher planetary systems scattered flowers over the earth and beat celestial drums to praise the action of the King. The sages said that they were not astonished to see Mahārāja Parīkṣit give up his throne, which was decorated with the helmets of many other kings, in order to obtain eternal association with the Personality of Godhead. And they declared that they would wait there in the King's presence as long as he did not go back to the supreme planet, which is free from all material contamination.

Mahārāja Parīkṣit congratulated the great sages and again expressed his desire to hear of the activities of Lord Śrī Kṛṣṇa, the Personality of Godhead. Parīkṣit then asked them the following question: "What is the duty of people in general and specifically of those who are about to die immediately?" The sages, however, did not answer unanimously in their decision as to what was to be done. In fact, they offered many different prescriptions. It was at that time that the great sage Śukadeva Gosvāmī, the sixteen-year-old son of Vyasādeva, arrived. Despite his young age, he is described by the *Bhāgavatam* as being most experienced in knowledge. All the ages present stood up and offered him obeisances.

ŚUKADEVA

The great devotee Mahārāja Parīksit went near the sage Śukadeva Gosvāmī, who was sitting perfectly at peace and who was prepared to answer everything.

Bowing down before him, Parīkṣit said, "You are sanctified. This place is a place of pilgrimage due to your presence."

This wonderful meeting of Mahārāja Parīkṣit and Śukadeva Gosvāmī is glorified by a whole disciplic succession of spiritual masters because Śukadeva Gosvāmī was authorized by Kṛṣṇa to speak about the pastimes of the Lord, and Mahārāja Parīkṣit, because of his eagerness to hear, was the perfect audience to receive that message. Mahārāja Parīkṣit had just been expressing to the sages that he wanted to hear about the pastimes of Kṛṣṇa and nothing else, and when he expressed this to Śukadeva Gosvāmī, Śukadeva said, "This is very nice because I just was going to tell you that you should hear the pastimes of Kṛṣṇa." This is the perfect combination for Kṛṣṇa consciousness: a bona fide spiritual master and an eager and qualified student.

The teachings of Śukadeva Gosvāmī to Mahārāja Parīkṣit are the subject of the *Śrīmad-Bhāgavatam,* the most elevated of all Vedic literatures. Simply to hear this most authoritative *Śrīmad-Bhāgavatam* can bring one to the stage of devotional service to the Lord. Mahārāja Parīkṣit's death was great because he was able to achieve the ultimate success of going back to Godhead by being favored by Kṛṣṇa, who sent him His true representative. As soon as a devotee meets a true representative of the Lord, he is guaranteed to go back to Godhead after leaving the present body. This depends on the sincerity of the devotee himself. The Lord is seated in the hearts of all living beings, and he knows well the movements of every individual person. And to that particular soul who is eager to go back to Godhead, He sends a bona fide spiritual master. When Mahārāja Parīkṣit was hearing from Śukadeva Gosvāmī, he was receiving the direct help of the Lord Himself in the form of the instructions of his spiritual master. In the *Śrīmad-Bhāgavatam,* First Canto, it is stated that after Kṛṣṇa left the earth, He remained present in the *Śrīmad-Bhāgavatam,* so hearing the *Śrīmad-Bhāgavatam* can be taken to by all peoples as the panacea for the age of Kali. Hearing about the pastimes of the Lord and chanting His holy names will free everyone from the attack of *māyā,* the illusory energy of the Lord.

All of us should follow in the footsteps of the pure devotee Mahārāja Parīkṣit and glorify the Lord by hearing from the bona fide spiritual master. This was the answer given by Śukadeva to Mahārāja Parīkṣit's question. "What should one do at the time of death?" One should glorify God by hearing of His pastimes, as described in the *Śrīmad-Bhāgavatam.* Surely that is the highest occupation for mankind. If one can simply do that, then there will be peace and prosperity, just as in the days when Mahārāja Parīkṣit ruled the earth. Mahārāja Parīkṣit controlled the corruption of the age of Kali, and there is every reason to believe this can be effected again today. By vigorous distribution of Kṛṣṇa conscious literature, *prasadām,* and *sankīrtana* or chanting the holy names, the age of Kali can be transformed into the golden age.

Kardama Muni, A First-Class Yogī

January/February, 1971

First let me offer my humble obeisances to my spiritual master, His Divine Grace A.C. Bhaktivedanta Swami Prabhupāda, the pure servant of God and thus the knower of the scripture. All transcendental knowledge contained in this essay emanates from his teachings, which are exactly in line with the disciplic succession going back to Lord Śrī Kṛṣṇa, the Personality of Godhead and original source of this narration of Kardama Muni. The disciple of Śrīla Prabhupāda has simply to present the teachings of the spiritual master intact; then there will be good benefit for the reader seeking self-realization and spiritual happiness.

In the Sixth Chapter of *Bhagavad-gītā,* Lord Kṛṣṇa teaches the mystic *yoga* process complete with sitting postures and the method of meditation under strict regulations. At the conclusion of the chapter, in the last verse, the Lord describes the topmost *yogī:* "He who, full of faith, offers everything to Me and worships Me, is the most united with Me in *yoga."* Nowadays the *yoga* system, as taught authoritatively in *Bhagavad-gītā* and the *Pātañjali-yoga-sūtra,* is not being followed. Instead, false teachers are allowing their students to engage in all kinds of material sense gratification while collecting a fee from them and inducing them to think in their meditation that they are one with God. Such students of false teachers cannot actually be making spiritual progress in *yoga.*

ULTIMATE YOGA

The Vedic literature contains histories, however, of many great *yogīs* who were accomplished in full mystic perfection. But even these yogic perfections, such as to be able to influence anyone, to be able to attain whatever one desires from anyplace in the universe, to fly in space, etc., are all material perfections, and they are ultimately exhausted. *Yoga* ultimately means to find Kṛṣṇa, the Supreme Lord, in His localized aspect seated in the heart and to engage in eternal loving union with Him through devotional service. Yogīs who are distracted from this path by material perfections have to return to the earth after death and again take another material birth and engage in devotional service before reaching the perfection of liberation, completely spiritual devotional service.

The following narration is an incident from the life of a great devotee *yogī*, Kardama Muni, who was not only a *yogī* but a perfect *yogī*, a devotee of the Lord. The narration of his activities appears in the Third Canto of *Śrīmad-Bhāgavatam*, the most mature and spotless scripture of the entire Vedic literature. Kardama lived long, long ago, in the Satya-yuga, just after the dawn of the creation of the universe.

HIS MEDITATION ON THE LORD

At that time, Lord Brahmā, the original creator empowered by Kṛṣṇa, was ordering his sons to marry and beget children so that the universe might be populated with worthy offspring. Commanded by Lord Brahmā, Kardama practiced meditative penances on the bank of the Sarasvatī River for a period of 10,000 years. It is understood that the *yoga* system, in order to be rightly practiced, must be performed by persons who possess a very long duration of life; otherwise, there is no possibility of attaining real perfection. There is no point in attempting the preliminary practices of *yoga*, such as the different postures of sitting, unless one is able to practice until perfection. Kardama Muni was not one of the so-called *yogīs* of the present age of Kali (age of quarrel and bluffing) who sit for a paltry fifteen minutes a day in *yoga* postures and claim spiritual advancement. It may be noted here that in the age in which Kardama lived, *yoga* meditation was the process recommended by the Vedic literature, whereas today the Vedic literature clearly states that there is no alternative to the chanting of the holy name: ***harer nāma harer nāma harer nāmaiva kevalam/kalau nāsty eva nāsty eva nāsty eva gatir anyathā (Bṛhan-Nāradīya Purāṇa).***

Why did Kardama practice meditation? It is stated in *Śrīmad-Bhāgavatam:* "During that period of penance the sage Kardama devotedly waited upon the Personality of Godhead." In other words, he practiced mystic *yoga* for 10,000 years just to please the Supreme Personality of Godhead. That is stated in *Śrīmad-Bhāgavatam.* Therefore he is the first-class *yogī*. His Divine Grace A.C. Bhaktivedanta Swami Prabhupāda writes in his commentary to the Third Canto of *Śrīmad-Bhāgavatam:* "One has to surrender unto the lotus feet of the Personality of Godhead, Kṛṣṇa, in order to achieve real success. To attain perfection of the *yoga* practice or meditation, one must act in devotional service, namely hearing, chanting, remembering, etc. Certainly remembering is also meditation, but upon whom must one meditate? The Supreme Personality of Godhead. He must not only be remembered, but one must hear about the activities of the Lord, and chant His glories." After engaging himself in different types of devotional service, Kardama Muni attained the perfection of meditation, which is attained only by those who are surrendered souls. Śrīla Prabhupada writes: "Where there is no mention of the Personality of Godhead, then where is there *yoga* and surrender? And where there is no meditation upon the Personality of Godhead, then where is there any question of *yoga* practice?"

THE ETERNAL FORM OF THE PERSONALITY OF GODHEAD

Perfection means that Kardama actually saw the Personality of Godhead. The form he saw was not imaginary. It is not that one can concentrate his mind on some arbitrary form of the imagination in meditation. It is clearly stated in *Śrīmad-Bhāgavatam:* "The form which the Lord showed to Kardama was consistent with Vedic principles and can be understood through the study of the *Vedas* from authoritative sources." The eternal blissful form of the Lord is described in the *Bhāgavatam:* "Kardama Muni saw the Supreme Personality of Godhead in His eternal form, effulgent like the sun. The Lord was wearing a garland of white lotuses and water lilies. He was clad in spotless yellow silk, His lotus face fringed with slick dark locks of curly hair; adorned with a crown and earrings, He held His characteristic conch and disc and mace in three of His hands and played with a white lily while smiling. His smiling captivates the hearts of all devotees. Having set His lotus feet on the shoulders of Garuda, He stood in the air with a golden streak on His breast and the famous Kaustubha gem suspended from His neck." The descriptions given in *Śrīmad-Bhāgavatam* are not products of the material energy. Kardama did not meditate for 10,000 years simply in order to see an imaginary vision concocted by his own brain. Rather, he attained a level of perfection by which the Lord was pleased with him and revealed His transcendental form, which is never revealed to impersonalists. Perfection of *yoga* does not end with voidness; on the contrary, perfection of *yoga* is attained when one sees the Personality of Godhead as He is in His eternal form.

When Kardama Muni saw the Lord, his transcendental desires were fulfilled, and he fell to the ground with head bowed and offered obeisances. He addressed the Supreme Personality of Godhead as follows: "O supreme worshipable Lord, You are the reservoir of all pleasure, and those who are advanced *yogīs* aspire, through many, many births of performance of deep meditation, to see Your transcendental form." Again it is seen that Kardama reached the ultimate in *yoga* and acknowledged the goal to which *yogīs* aspire after many lives of *yoga* practice. The point is not to see void but to see the spiritual form of the Supreme Personality of Godhead. Clearly, then, Kardama was in the most advanced stage. His next words spoken unto the Lord are therefore difficult at first to understand: "Desirous of marrying a girl of like disposition who may prove a veritable cow of plenty in my married life, I too sought the center of Your lotus feet to satisfy my lustful desire."

It is startling to hear a *yogī,* who is supposed to be freed from all attachment to material life by meditating in solitary celibate penance for many thousands of years and attaining sight of the Personality of Godhead, only asking for a nice wife. But explanation reveals to us that Kardama was even more exalted than we have so far understood. Not only did Kardama Muni not actually seek marriage out of lustful desire, but his desire was the desire of Kṛṣṇa. As stated in the *Bhāgavatam,* "I shall accept this nice chaste girl as my wife until she bears a child born out of the ray of the Supreme Personality of Godhead. Then I shall accept the life of devotional service which is practiced by the most perfect human beings. I know that this is the desire of Lord Viṣṇu and that it is a process free from envy."

It was the practice in former ages that great sages and saintly persons, after making their lives perfect, would beget children in order to serve the Lord in that way, and but for engaging in sex life to produce exceptional progeny, they strictly observed the laws of celibacy. As for Kardama's statement about producing a child who would be a "ray of Viṣṇu," it may be told that Kardama Muni is the father of the incarnation of Godhead Lord Kapila, who is Viṣṇu Himself. Lord Kapila appeared as the son of Kardama Muni and Devahūti for the purpose of preaching the godly Sāṅkhya philosophy, which is a combination of mysticism and devotional service. His Divine Grace A.C. Bhaktivedanta Swami Prabhupāda writes in this connection, "One should beget a child who can perform the duties of Viṣṇu, or else there is no need to produce children. There are two kinds of children born of good fathers. One is the child who is educated in Kṛṣṇa consciousness so that he can be delivered from the clutches of *māyā* in that very life, and the other is the child who brings forth the ray of the Supreme Personality of Godhead and who teaches the highest goal of life. Great householders pray to God to send His representative so that there may be an auspicious movement in human society, or they pray to the Lord for an opportunity to train a child in Kṛṣṇa consciousness so that he won't have to come back again to this miserable world. Parents should see to it that the child born of them must not enter again into the womb of a mother."

INSTRUCTIONS ON MARRIAGE

Kardama prayed to the Lord as if he were under the grip of lust and desired the Lord's mercy in the form of an ordinary marriage. By speaking in this way, Kardama, who was actually a liberated soul, brought out for all the future readers or hearers of *Śrīmad-Bhāgavatam* many significant clarifications of marriage and married life. At his request, the Lord was able to show that a man should pray to the Supreme Personality of Godhead for whatever he wants, whether it be liberation, devotional service or the fulfillment of material desires. Material desires should be satisfied in accordance with the will of the Supreme Lord or the *Vedas* wherein there are prescriptions for a married life of regulated sense gratification. Even if one has lustful desires, if he takes his desires to the Supreme Lord and abides by His will, he will get far more than he could imagine, and he will eventually gain spiritual purification and association with the Supreme Personality of Godhead. Ultimately it is God who awards. Man proposes and God disposes. If one can accept what the Lord offers as his share, then he will find it a richer share than he had ever dreamed of attaining by his own endeavors. But if he strains to exploit under the illusion of winning by his own endeavor, he will lose on all counts. For example, Kardama was an austere penniless *yogī* with no facilities for gaining a beautiful wife, yet since he prayed to the Lord for a wife, he was granted the most beautiful and highborn princess in the world.

Lord Viṣṇu, who shone on the shoulders of Garuḍa, spoke to Kardama with transcendental words in accents as sweet as nectar. His eyebrows moved gracefully as He regarded the sage with a smile full of affection: "Having come to know what was in your mind, I have already arranged for that for which you have worshiped Me through the discipline of the mind and senses. My dear ṛṣi, O leader of the living entities, for anyone who serves Me in devotional service by worshiping Me, especially persons like you who have given up everything unto Me, there is no question of frustration." It is stated here that the Lord gives His devotees all pleasures and that He answers all their desires, although He never awards anything which might be detrimental to their devotional service. Even if the devotees approach the Personality of Godhead with material desires, there is no question of frustration in those desires.

THE LORD DISPOSES

The Lord then outlined His plan of benedicting His devotee Kardama with a perfect wife: "Svāyambhuva Manu is well known for his righteous acts. That celebrated emperor, who is head of religious activities, will come to see you with his wife Śatarūpā the day after tomorrow. His daughter, who is grown up and ready for marriage, has all good qualities; she is also searching for a good husband, and her eyes are black, My dear sir. Her parents will come to see you just to deliver their daughter as your wife." In his purports, His Divine Grace

Śrīla Prabhupāda writes of the proper selection of a husband for a girl: "Girls are never thrown into the public street to search out their husband. When girls are grown up and are searching after a boy, they forget whether the boy they select is actually suitable for them. Out of the urge of sex desire a girl may accept anyone, but if the husband is chosen by the parents, they can consider who is to be selected and who is not to be selected." For example, within the family of the International Society for Krishna Consciousness, a husband or wife is selected by the spiritual master or by his representative, the temple president, and so it is by the proper sanction.

The Lord predicted that nine daughters would come from the union of the marriage and that through the daughters great sages would duly beget future children. Finally the Lord said to His devotee Kardama, "With your heart cleansed by properly carrying out My command and having resigned to Me the fruit of all your acts, you will finally attain to Me." Thus the Lord disclosed to Kardama that if he only acted under the direction of the Lord, then all his acts, even in married life, would be completely sanctioned, and he would finally attain the supreme abode. The Lord finally requested Kardama to be compassionate to all living entities. He asked him to please give assurance to all that the universe is identified in Kṛṣṇa and that Kṛṣṇa is in everyone.

KARDAMA ATTAINED REAL ONENESS

The Lord referred to Kardama's upcoming householder life as well as to the last days of his life, when Kardama would again take up the renounced order. He was not simply to receive the potency of the Lord's mercy and keep it for himself, but he was to distribute the knowledge of devotional service to everyone. By following the order of Viṣṇu, Kardama Muni attained real oneness with God because the Lord wants His devotee to always think of Him and worship Him. It is not that the Lord wants the transcendentalist to try to usurp His position and become God Himself, but to always offer obeisances to Him and offer Him unlimited service. The Lord wishes to reciprocate with His devotees and supply the fulfillment of their desires. The Lord revealed to Kardama that he would be the father of an *avatāra* of the Supreme Personality of Godhead. "Manifesting a part of My divine being through your wife Devahūti, O great sage, I shall instruct her in the philosophy which deals with the ultimate principles or categories." This is the first reference to Kapiladeva, the first propounder of Sāṅkhya philosophy. This Sāṅkhya philosophy is not to be confused with the Sāṅkhya philosophy propagated later by an atheistic godless imposter who was also named Kapila.

Having spoken to His devotee, the Lord left the Bindusarovara Lake, on a pathway leading to Vaikuṇṭha. The sage stood below looking up, and he listened to the hymns which emanated from the flapping of the wings of the Lord's carrier. The sage Kardama then waited for the time spoken of by the Lord, and he prayed.

As predicted, the great worldly leader Svāyambhuva and his wife Śatarūpā journeyed on a chariot all over the globe and reached the hermitage where the sage Kardama was completing his long vows of austerity. *Śrīmad-Bhāgavatam* states that the holy lake Bindusarovara was filled with "the drops of tears fallen from the eyes of the Lord, who was overwhelmed by extreme compassion for the sage who had sought His protection." The lake area is described as resounding with the notes of overjoyed birds who were all pious, as were the fruit-bearing trees and the flowers. Svāyambhuva Manu and Śatarūpā entered the hermitage and found Kardama sitting before a sacred fire into which he was offering oblations. Clad in rags, of high stature, and his eyes as big as the petals of a lotus, he looked like an unpolished gem. In these *Bhāgavatam* descriptions of the *brahmacārī yogī,* it is stated that usually a *yogī* is skinny on account of his austerities and lack of comforts, but Kardama Muni had seen the Supreme Personality of Godhead face to face, and he looked healthy due to having received the nectar-like sound vibration.

THE KING AND THE YOGĪ

"Seeing that the monarch had come to his hermitage and bowing before him, the sage greeted him with benediction and received him with due honor." The *yogī* then addressed the King with words of praise because he understood that unless a pious king is ruling, the wicked elements in society can overthrow the whole aim of the society, which is to help the citizens go back home, back to Godhead. He addressed the King as the protecting energy of Śrī Hari (Kṛṣṇa). After offering obeisances, the *yogī* then asked the King why he had come with a glad heart and how he, the *yogī,* could meet his wishes. The royal order formerly gave all protection to the *brāhmaṇas* so that they could advance the society in terms of spiritual culture, and the *brāhmaṇas* would give their valuable instructions to the royal order so that every citizen could become elevated to spiritual perfection.

Svāyambhuva said that he was most fortunate to be able to touch his head to the dust from the feet of the sage, and he thanked him for his words of instruction. "We are seeking a worthy match for our daughter in terms of age, character and good qualities." The father, Svāyambhuva Manu, confided to Kardama that "the moment she heard from the sage Nārada of your noble character, learning, beautiful appearance, youth and other virtues, she fixed her mind on you." So although Devahūti had not seen Kardama Muni, she had fixed her heart upon him after hearing of him from Nārada, and on the basis of that hearing she had decided to marry him. Svāyambhuva offered his daughter with all reverence as a worthy match for taking charge of household duties. By household duties he did not mean sense gratification but mutual execution of Kṛṣṇa consciousness, which is called, in Sanskrit, *gṛhastha.* There are two words in Sanskrit to describe married life. One, *gṛhamedhī,* means to accept a wife for sense gratification and to make one's apartment a center for executing the same propensities as the animals, whereas the other, *gṛhastha,* means to gain a helper in Kṛṣṇa consciousness. Devahūti was eligible to offer such help, for she was equal in age, character and quality to the sage.

KARDAMA ACCEPTS DEVAHŪTI

Kardama at once agreed. "Certainly I have a desire to marry, and your daughter too has not yet married or given her word to anyone; therefore our marriage according to the Vedic system can take place." Kardama expressed appreciation of Devahūti's beauty. He too had heard of her, for she had attracted even the denizens of the heavenly planets by her personal beauty. Kardama had been ordered by his father Brahmā to produce progency, but actually the goal of his life was Viṣṇu, in whom even Brahmā originates, as do all living entities in all the worlds. Therefore, since it was the desire of the Supreme Personality of Godhead, Kardama would marry and father children in the spirit of devotional service. This story in the *Bhāgavatam* is related by the sage Maitreya to Vidura, and it continues. "The sage Kardama thus spoke very nicely regarding Devahūti. Then he became silent, thinking of his worshipable Lord Viṣṇu, who has a lotus on His navel. When he was silent and smiling, his face attracted Devahūti, and she began to think within herself of the great sage." As soon as Kardama Muni stopped talking and became silent, he at once began to think of Lord Viṣṇu. The devotee may seem to be engaged in things other than Viṣṇu, dealing and talking about other matters, but actually he is always thinking of Kṛṣṇa, and thus his smile is so attractive as to win many admirers and followers.

TRANSCENDENTAL MARRIED LIFE

After their marriage and the departure of her parents, Devahūti began to serve her husband with great love. She pleased him by giving up all sorts of lust, pride, envy, greed, sinful activities and vanity by fidelity and purity of mind. These are some of the qualities of a great husband's great wife. Both were great by spiritual qualification. Devahūti was not proud because of her high birth. As can be seen from this narration, the union of Kardama and Devahūti is filled with pertinent instructions regarding how to live in transcendental married life with the goal of life, the center, being Kṛṣṇa. Householders wishing to benefit from their union may listen with an aim to raising their married life to the transcendental stage. Devotion of the wife to the husband is recommended. Śrīla Prabhupāda writes, "The wife is expected to be of the same category as the husband. She must be prepared to follow the principles of the husband; then there will be happy life. If the husband is a devotee and the wife is materialistic, then there cannot be any peace in the home." In the case of Devahūti, by following the strict vows of a chaste woman she became very skinny, and therefore her husband became compassionate. She had formerly been the daughter of a great king and was now serving him just like an ordinary woman. She had become reduced in health, and her service was so selfless that she did not demand sense gratification even with her husband. She was simply acting to facilitate Kardama Muni's engagement in spiritual life. Śrīla Prabhupāda writes, "It is the duty of a faithful and chaste wife to help her husband in every respect, especially in Kṛṣṇa consciousness."

In the case of Devahūti, her husband rewarded her amply. Kardama told her, "My dear Devahūti, I have achieved the grace of the Lord in my discharging of my own religious life of austerity, meditation and Kṛṣṇa consciousness. I shall offer you all these achievements, which are free from lamentation, because you are engaged in my service, although you have not yet experienced these things. Now I am giving you transcendental vision to see how nice they are." By her husband's grace, Devahūti was able to feel practical realization simply by serving a great personality. Similarly, any sincere disciple of a bona fide spiritual master can achieve spiritual life simply by service.

DEVAHŪTI DESIRED OFFSPRING

Coming from a great royal family, Devahūti had much aristocracy and wealth, but the greatest treasure, love of God, she had been unable to fully appreciate. She therefore expressed her full satisfaction to her great husband, who was under the protection of the spiritual energy. But she reminded him, "One thing you promised may be fulfilled now by our bodily union, because for a chaste woman it is very glorious to have children of the same quality." Kardama Muni had certainly promised to her parents that he would stay with her until they had children. Since both were spiritually enlightened, a child was very desirable as an expansion of their qualities. Devahūti then asked her husband what arrangement should be made and what was required according to the scriptures in terms of conditions, time and place for the most suitable sex life. Sex life is meant for having good children. One must arrange everything so that the husband may be attracted by the beauty of the wife and a favorable mental situation may be created so that at the time of sex life the mental state may be transferred into the womb of the wife and nice children will come out of that marriage. Thus we see that the Vedic scriptures provide not only spiritual instructions but instructions on how to prosecute material existence nicely with the ultimate aim of spiritual perfection. It is mentioned in the *Āyur-veda* that when the passion of a man is greater than that of a woman, then there will be a greater chance of a boy being born. And if the passion of the woman is greater, then there will be more chance of a girl being born. Devahūti wanted her husband to instruct her according to scripture so that his passion might be increased. She also requested a suitable house because the hermitage in which Kardama was living was very simple and completely in the modes of goodness, with little possibility of passion.

THE AERIAL MANSION

Śrīmad-Bhāgavatam then describes the miraculous accomplishments effected by the yogic power of Kardama Muni. Since he was completely perfected in *yoga* practice and sought to please his beloved wife, Kardama exercised his yogic power and instantly produced an aerial mansion which was fully arranged according to his will. It was a huge and wonderful structure filled with opulent pleasurable rooms and decorated with rubies, furniture and all kinds of attractive wealth. It was such a magnificent castle that the *yogī* himself was astonished at what he had created. Devahūti, however, because she was so niggardly in her appearance, with matted locks and a dirty dress, seemed afraid of the marvelous castle in the air. Kardama Muni knew her mind, and with further yogic powers he requested that she simply step into the Bindusarovara Lake, where he had arranged for hundreds of beautiful female maid-servants to attend her and beautify her with ointments, scents, beautiful silks, etc. They offered her foods and drinks to improve her bodily condition, and they held a mirror for her, cleansed her, adorned her with garlands and marks of *tilaka,* and in general made much of her so that she finally emerged from the lake looking very beautiful with a smiling face and nice figure. She could understand that all this was taking place due to the yogic prowess of her husband and that nothing was impossible for such a *yogī.*

Husband and wife then travelled in the aerial mansion to the pleasure valleys of Mount Meru, which is frequented by the demigods. They travelled all over the universe and enjoyed pleasures together. Although *yogīs* are known to display such wonderful powers, Kardama was more than a *yogī*, and his life is more praiseworthy than that of ordinary *yogīs*. Even in his travelling through the universe for pleasure with his wife, his actual motivation was to produce good progeny in the service of Lord Viṣṇu. It is stated in *Bhagavad-gītā* (6.47), "Out of many *yogīs*, he who is a devotee of the Lord is a first-class *yogī*." Kardama Muni is therefore understood to be an already liberated soul, better than the conditioned demigods, who also can travel in space. So although he was enjoying with his wife, he was above material conditional life and transcendental to all material limitations. That is the verdict of the *Bhāgavatam*.

HE RETURNED TO HIS HERMITAGE

After showing his wife the different arrangements throughout the entire extent of the universe, Kardama Muni returned to his own hermitage. Despite having such immense powers to travel all over the universe, Kardama did not claim that he was equal to God or comparable with the inconceivable energy of the Supreme Lord, as do some bogus *yogīs*, who cannot travel in outer space but who simply instruct sitting postures and take fees from students. Kardama Muni remained a devotee of the Lord, and that is the real position of every living entity. Finally by his yogic powers he at once produced nine daughters through the womb of Devahūti. Devahūti, the sage devotee, bore all these children on one day, and all were charming in every limb and breathed the fragrance of red lotus flowers. Having begotten children through his wife, Kardama then prepared to leave household life, home and his beautiful wife to prosecute Kṛṣṇa conscious life, as he had promised. His real business was always spiritual realization, and he did not forget this, even while travelling in the mansion.

It is described that Devahūti, seeing Kardama Muni about to leave, was smiling externally, but she was at heart very afflicted. The stories in the *Bhāgavatam*, such as this narration, are not told for entertainment's sake but are filled with instructions pertinent for spiritual advancement of life, even while one is within household life. In the *Bhagavad-gītā*, Śrīla Prabhupāda writes in a purport (p. 257): "As for detachment from children, wife and house, it is not meant that one should have no feeling for these. They are natural objects of affection. But when they are not favorable to spiritual progress, then we should not be attached to them. The best process for making the home nice is to live in Kṛṣṇa consciousness. If one is in full Kṛṣṇa consciousness, he can make his home very happy because this process of Kṛṣṇa consciousness is very easy. It is just to chant Hare Kṛṣṇa, Hare Kṛṣṇa, Kṛṣṇa Krsna, Hare Hare/Hare Rāma, Hare Rāma, Rāma Rāma, Hare Hare, and to take and accept the remnants of foodstuffs offered to Kṛṣṇa, and have some discussion on books like *Bhagavad-gītā* and *Śrīmad-Bhāgavatam,* and engage oneself in Deity worship. These four things will make one happy, and one should train the members of his family in this way. The family members can sit down morning and evening very nicely and chant together Hare Kṛṣṇa, Hare Kṛṣṇa, Kṛṣṇa Kṛṣṇa, Hare Hare/Hare Rāma, Hare Rāma, Rāma Rāma, Hare Hare. If we can mold our family life in such a nice way for developing Kṛṣṇa consciousness by following these four principles, then there is no need to change from family life to renounced life. But if it is not congenial nor favorable for spiritual advancement, then family life should be abandoned. In all cases, one should be detached from the happiness and distress of family life because this world can never be fully happy or fully miserable. Happiness and distress are concomitant factors of material life." Devahūti asked her husband to wait before going out alone and entering the order of *sannyāsa* or renounced life. "My dear *brāhmaṇa,* as far as your daughters are concerned, they will find suitable husbands and go away to their respective places. But who will give me solace after your departure as a *sannyāsi?"* Devahūti, began to lament that she did not know that her husband was so advanced in spiritual realization, and she had been, as a less intelligent woman, mostly prone to sense enjoyment in his association. She pleaded to him, however, that even though she did not appreciate his glories, because she had taken shelter of him he must therefore deliver her from material entanglement. It is a known fact that association with a great personality is most important, and by that means alone one can make great advancement in spiritual life. Devahūti finally realized with whom she was associating, and she wanted to utilize the advantage.

Devahūti pleaded so feelingly that Kardama recalled the words of Viṣṇu to be compassionate to all, and so he replied, "Do not be disappointed, O princess, and just take heart . You are praiseworthy, and I tell you that the infallible Supreme Personality of Godhead will come out from the womb of your body as your son." Kardama Muni advised his wife to just engage in devotional service. "The Personality of Godhead, being worshiped by you, will disseminate our name and fame. He shall be the vanquisher of the knot of your heart by becoming your son and spreading spiritual knowledge." Having received instruction from her husband, the bona fide spiritual master, Devahūti began to worship the master of the universe, the Supreme Personality of Godhead who is situated in everyone's heart. Concerning the appearance of the Personality of Godhead as the son of a couple of devotees, Śrīla Prabhupada writes: "The Supreme Personality of Godhead is the father of everyone. No one, therefore, is His father, but by His inconceivable energy He accepts some of the devotees as His parents and descendants. The devotee may ask the Lord to appear as his son. The Lord is already sitting within the heart of everyone, and if He comes out from the body of a devotee it does not mean that the particular woman becomes His mother in the material sense. He is always there. But in order to please His devotee He appears as her son. In this way the Supreme Personality of Godhead Madhūsudana, the killer of the demon Madhu, after many, many years of worship by Devahūti, appeared as the son of Kardama Muni, just as fire comes out from wood in sacrifice." At the time of the appearance of the Lord, the demigods who fly freely in the sky dropped showers of flowers out of their good will, and everyone smiled and became very satisfied.

DESCRIPTION OF KAPILADEVA

Lord Brahmā, chief engineer of the universe and the father of Kardama, then appeared to the sage, and after praising his obedience and instructing him about the marriage of his nine daughters to nine great sages, he described the incarnation of God who had been born as the son of Kardama and Devahūti. "Your son, Kapila Muni, will be characterized by His golden hair and His eyes just like lotus petals. Sitting in the yogic *āsana* called *padmamudrā,* His feet resembling lotus flowers, this incarnation of Godhead, by practical application of knowledge from the scriptures, will uproot the deep-rooted desire for work in this material world." Kapiladeva's conclusion, after exhaustive analysis of the material elements, is the same conclusion arrived at in *Bhagavad-gītā:* devotional service. "Just become Kṛṣṇa conscious. Just worship Kṛṣṇa and become a devotee of Kṛṣṇa. That is real knowledge, and anyone who follows that system becomes perfect without doubt."

PRAYER TO KAPILADEVA

Kardama approached the Lord, who was Lord Viṣṇu Himself and had descended into his home, and he offered Him obeisances. Kardama said, "The householders are generally negligent, but in spite of that the Supreme Personality of Godhead has taken His appearance in their home, just to support His devotees." Devotional service to the Lord is so sublime that even a householder can have the Supreme Personality of Godhead as one of the members of his household, as his son, as Kardama experienced. This is due to the fact that the Lord is called *bhakta-vatsala;* He is inclined to His devotees. Kardama paid obeisances to the innumerable forms of the Lord, none of which are material. His prayer to Kapiladeva is here stated: "I surrender unto the Supreme Personality of Godhead who has descended in the form of Kapila and who is independently powerful and transcendental, who is the Supreme Person and the Lord of the sum total of matter and the time element, who is fully cognizant and who is the maintainer of all the universe via the three modes of material nature, and who absorbs the material manifestation after dissolution. Now I am liberated from the debts of my father, and all my desires are fulfilled. Now I wish to accept the order of a mendicant. Renouncing this family life, I shall always think of You, and thus I shall remain free from lamentation."

GOD ENTERED HIS HOME

It is described by His Divine Grace A.C. Bhaktivedanta Swami Prabhupāda that there are two kinds of devotees of the Lord. One is called *goṣṭyānandī,* which means those preachers who have many followers for preaching the glories of the Lord and who live amongst those many followers just to organize missionary activities. The other devotees are *ātmānandī,* or self-satisfied, and do not take the risk of preaching work. In this class was Kardama Muni. He remained alone, free from all anxieties, always moving from door to door to enlighten people about Kṛṣṇa consciousness. The wonderful thing about Kardama Muni is that the Lord Himself, as Kapiladeva, had taken birth in his home as his own son, and yet he was preparing to leave that home to search out self-realization. God was present in his own home, so why should he leave? The answer is that Kardama was living an exemplary life just in accordance with the Vedic authority, which says that one who is a householder must leave home after his fiftieth year. Kardama had very rigidly practiced *yoga* before his marriage; then Lord Brahmā had ordered him to marry and beget children as a householder. Kardama did that also. He begot nine good daughters and one son, Kapila, so his householder duty was performed, and now his duty was to leave. Even though he had the Supreme Personality of Godhead as his son, he had to respect the authority of the *Vedas.* He would travel all over the world as a mendicant and always remember the Supreme Personality of Godhead within his heart and thereby be freed from all anxieties of material existence.

Kardama Muni was anxious about his good wife Devahūti, and so his worthy son promised that not only would Kardama be freed but Devahūti would also be freed by receiving instruction from Him. "My incarnation in this form is especially meant for persons who aspire to get free from the entanglement of this material body, and I mean to explain the philosophy of Sāṅkhya in order to disseminate the knowledge of self-realization to interested people. I shall also instruct this sublime knowledge to My mother so that she also can attain the stage of perfection and self-realization, ending all kinds of reactions of fruitive activities. Thus she also will become free from all fear."

After the departure of Kardama Muni, Kapiladeva extensively explained the principles of Śāṅkhya philosophy to His mother. The *Bhāgavatam* states, "By following the principles instructed by Kapila, Devahūti soon became liberated from material bondage, and she achieved the Supreme Personality of Godhead, as Supersoul, without difficulty." There is a Vaikuṇṭha planet known as Kapila Vaikuṇṭha where Devahūti was promoted to meet Kapila and reside eternally, enjoying the company of her transcendental son.

THE ETERNAL ABODE

The sage Vidura concludes the story of Kardama, Devahūti and Kapila by describing the pastimes of the incarnation of Kapila. "Kapila, the great sage and Personality of Godhead, later went out from His father's hermitage with the permission of His mother and went toward the northern side. Even now Kapila is residing there in trance, and all great teachers of Sāṅkhya philosophy are worshiping Him. He is staying in that position for the deliverance of the conditioned souls of the three worlds." It is stated that these descriptions are the purest of all things, and whoever hears or reads these narrations will become a devotee of the Lord and enter the supreme abode."

The Passing of Grandfather Bhīṣma

November/December, 1971

Grandfather Bhīṣma was lying at the point of death on a bed of arrows which had been shot through his body. Because he was the most famous warrior of his time and an expert *yogī,* all the great men of the universe went to the Battlefield of Kurukṣetra where he lay dying.

King Yudhiṣṭhira, who had ascended to the throne by winning the battle, felt a horrible responsibility for all the killing which had taken place in the war, and in hopes of getting counsel he also went at once when he heard that Grandfather Bhīṣma was about to pass away from this mortal world. Lord Kṛṣṇa, who is the Supreme Personality of Godhead, was appearing at that time within human society and was involved in all the affairs of Kurukṣetra. Therefore, He also came to see Bhīṣma, driving the chariot for His famous disciple, Arjuna. Many sages and demigods had traveled even from other planets, and the greatest scholars and personalities and their disciples had gathered from everywhere just to be present at this auspicious occasion.

This opens a scene from the *Śrīmad-Bhāgavatam,* First Canto. The *Bhāgavatam* is a Vedic literature of historical fact recorded 5,000 years ago and handed down from disciple to disciple by the great scholars and spiritual masters of India. More important, however, than the fact that this story of Bhīṣma and Kṛṣṇa actually took place long, long ago is that it can teach us the philosophy of Kṛṣṇa consciousness, by which we can find eternal happiness, as did Bhīṣma. The fruit of hearing stories told in Kṛṣṇa consciousness is very valuable, beyond comparison to worldly wealth or temporary happiness. Simply by hearing, we can revive our eternal relationship with God. Grandfather Bhīṣma's passing away is unique in history. We hope that the reader will enjoy this ancient battlefield story.

We cannot imagine how great a *yogī* was Bhīṣma, for he was able to keep a sound mind even though his body was pierced by many arrows. He thus welcomed the many sages who had come to see him at his last hour. It is stated that Bhīṣma was such an expert religionist that although the great sages and *yogīs* present had different understandings of philosophy–just as we have so many apparently different religious sects–he was able to speak with such command of the Absolute Truth that he adjusted all their differing opinions and had everyone listening with rapt attention, in agreement with his authoritative conclusions.

The sages, eager to hear his instructions, were listening very quietly—that was their qualification for greatness. Anyone interested in making spiritual progress in his own life in this day and age should similarly try to approach the authoritative or bona fide spiritual master from whom he can learn the Absolute Truth.

It was very wonderful that Bhīṣma was able to welcome such a large aristocratic gathering, even though he was neither at home nor in a normal healthy condition. But we should not think that Bhīṣma was writhing in excruciating pain. He was such a great *yogī* that he was in full control of his senses. Moreover, in passing away he was victorious. He was endowed with the power to leave his body at will, and so his passing was by his own choice. Such power over death is beyond our imaginations at present, and there is no sense in arguing the point. If we can accept this authorized narrative, all questions will be revealed gradually in the course of the story.

Bhīṣma was soon to leave this mortal world to gain eternal liberation in the kingdom of God. By the will of God, Bhīṣma was to give instructions, before leaving, to the guilty Yudhiṣṭhira about his duties, and he was also to make his last prayer to the Supreme Lord, who had kindly come to the gathering.

Seeing the distressed Mahārāja Yudhiṣṭhira and his four brothers, the Pāṇḍavas, sitting nearby with great affection for their dying grandfather, Bhīṣma shed tears of ecstasy. Allow us to briefly relate the background for Bhīṣma's being called "Grandfather" and for his deep emotion at the sight of these Pāṇḍava brothers who had gathered beside him as he prepared to breathe his last. Some time before this scene, the world was ruled by King Pāṇḍu, who died at an early age when his five sons were all young children. These boys, the Paṇḍavas, were brought up by the affectionate elder members of the royal family, especially by Bhīṣmadeva. Later on, when they grew up, they were cheated by a rival in the palace and exiled from the court, although they were the rightful heirs to the throne.

Bhīṣma knew that the Pāṇḍavas were innocent and had been unnecessarily put into trouble, but he could not take their side since he had already promised to support the rival party led by Duryodhana, the Pāṇḍavas' cousin. *Śrīmad-Bhāgavatam* explains why Grandfather Bhīsma opposed the Pāṇḍavas in the civil war: "Bhīṣmadeva was not at all satisfied to fight against the Pāṇḍavas, who were his beloved fatherless grandchildren. But the warrior class is very stern, and therefore he was obliged to take the side of Duryodhana because he was maintained at the expense of Duryodhana."

When the Pāṇḍavas came back from exile and asked to have at least a little land to rule, they were driven away by the rival party of cheaters headed by

Duryodhana. Lord Kṛṣṇa also appeared in the royal court at that time and asked that peace be kept and that the brothers be given some land, but He was ignored. Duryodhana's party told the Pāṇḍavas, "If you want as much land as can fit under a pin, you'll have to fight for it." Thus, Kṛṣṇa and the Pāṇḍavas were forced to fight in the great war of Kurukṣetra, a huge family feud in which many brothers, students, teachers and friends found themselves on opposite sides. It appears that Bhīṣma was forced by political intrigue to fight opposite the Pāṇḍavas and Lord Kṛṣṇa.

The ultimate reason why all these events happened as they did and Yudhiṣṭhira and the others were brought together at Bhīṣma's deathbed of arrows can only be explained as the will of the Lord. It is not difficult to understand that everything is happening under a plan of the Supreme Lord. Pure devotees of the Lord are completely agreeable to the fact that nothing happens except by the will of Kṛṣṇa, and the desire of a devotee is to learn Kṛṣṇa's will and carry it out as His servant in a loving mood. It is said that not a blade of grass moves without the will of the Lord.

In the ordinary events of the material world–such as the operation of the physical laws in the universe by which the planets orbit in space and different births in varieties of species of life according to their work–Kṛṣṇa acts through His representative agent, which is called the material energy. The science of how God works and is present everywhere is dealt with in the scripture *Bhagavad-gītā,* and we shall not go into it here. When it comes to the welfare of Kṛṣṇa's devotees, however, it is stated that Kṛṣṇa personally arranges each situation; He even brings them trial and tribulation at certain times just for their ultimate glorification. In other words, God acts through His deputed agents, His energies, in all matters of the material world pertaining to persons who are interested in worldly gain, but for a devotee He does not employ agents; rather, He personally takes charge of their destiny and sees that they become purified.

The passing of Bhīṣma was personally arranged by God for His pleasure, just to exchange love with His devotees. He wanted King Yudhiṣṭhira to receive instructions from a great authority like Bhīṣma, and He wanted to appear before Bhīsma so that His devotee could see Him in his last hour. That is the explanation of why this scene took place. Lord Kṛṣṇa, the speaker of the *Bhagavad-gītā,* stood peacefully beside His dear devotee, Bhīṣma, while Bhīṣma distinguished himself before all the learned sages by his instructions to the new king.

The first advice Bhīṣma gave to Yudhiṣṭhira was that he should not feel sorry for the death of those who had been killed in that way. "In my opinion," Bhīsma said, "it is all due to inevitable time." As long as one is within the material world, he has to bear the actions and reactions of time, which brings about so many wars and sufferings. Even if one is pious, the conditions of material life are such that suffering and devastation will take place. Truly, the world is a shaky place with danger at every step, and even the greatest personalities suffer many reverses in the course of time.

Bhīṣma explained that this time factor was the wish of the Lord Himself, and so it was not right to think that the deaths were the responsibility of Yudhiṣṭhira. It was not by his will that these things were happening; the actual doer was Kṛṣṇa. In His form of time, He annihilated thousands of soldiers of both parties. "Since it is beyond the control of any human being," Bhīṣma said, "there is nothing you can do. So why should you lament?" Bhīṣma said: "All these demonstrations are within the plan of the Lord. Accepting this inconceivable plan, you must follow it."

Bhīṣma knew that since the Pāṇḍavas' cause was just, virtue had triumphed over vice. Yudhiṣṭhira was not personally to blame for deaths which had taken place by the agency of all-devouring time. His duty now was to take over the administration of the people and protect them so that they could perfect their lives and go back to Godhead–that is the sum and substance of Bhīṣma's instructions fo Yudhiṣṭhira.

When we speak of the will of God or the plan of God, these words indicate that God is not a dead lump or desireless void–He is the Supreme Person. In fact, as a person, Kṛṣṇa appeared amidst this clan of Pāṇḍavas as one of their family members. His position is bewildering to the common people. He is the Almighty God by whose will the movement of a blade of grass or the outcome of a spectacular event like the Kurukṣetra War takes place, yet He was present as a friend at the passing away of Bhīṣma. Devotees accept Him both ways, for anything is possible for God. There is no question of restricting Him only to managing the destiny of the universe by saying, "No, God can't come into the human society personally. He can't stand before His devotee and speak loving words. He can't smile. He can't bless. He can't do this. He can't do that." God can do what He likes, as He likes. God is God. He is independent, and when He comes, He comes in His eternal spiritual form. As cousin, friend, well-wisher and messenger of the Pāṇḍavas, He was still the Supreme Personality of Godhead. Although it is bewildering that God can be present as an ordinary family member, it is certainly possible for Him. He appeared, by His mercy, as the unconquerable and eternal Supreme Person and was accepted by Bhīṣma, His devotee. Therefore, we can also accept Kṛṣṇa as He appears in this narrative by His will.

Lord Kṛṣṇa appeared at the deathbed of Bhīṣma because Bhīṣma was a great unalloyed devotee of the Lord. Bhīṣma took it as a great favor that he could see the Lord. We have seen pictures of Lord Kṛṣṇa, the Supreme Personality of Godhead. His transcendental body of eternal youth is of a bluish hue. He is smiling, and in His four-armed form He holds a disc, conchshell, wheel and lotus.

He wears brilliant yellow garments and is opulently ornamented and helmeted. His eyes are beautiful like a lotus.

Kṛṣṇa was standing before Bhīṣma at the time of his death. No general or philosopher in the history of the rise and fall of mundane empires was ever blessed in this way—to have God appear before him, in a friendly reassuring mood, just to satisfy his vision. Bhīṣma was thinking, in all humility, that he might not see God after his death. Therefore he requested the Lord to stay before him so that he could concentrate on His form before passing away.

This scene is unique and astonishing, but it is an authorized description of dealings between the Supreme Lord and one of His devotees. The scene and the intimate relationship which the Lord had with Bhīṣma are verified by the most perfect process of receiving knowledge—to hear it from the Vedic sources, the spiritual master and the scriptures. Such knowledge is never dogmatic. Just as the mother is the bona fide authority for the confidential knowledge of the identity of one's father, so Vedic scripture is the perfect authority for information about the transcendental world. Hearing such literature is a regular process for receiving perfect knowledge.

Bhīṣma's activities have been accepted by all authorities in this spiritual line of disciplic succession, including Lord Caitanya and our spiritual master, His Divine Grace A.C. Bhaktivedanta Swami Prabhupāda. They all accept the version of the *Bhāgavatam* as the word of God. Modern man believes that spaceships have gone to the moon on the authority of modern science. Whatever the scientist or newspaper says is imperfect, whereas the word of God is perfect. If we attempt to guess or theorize about God's existence and appearance rather than accept the authority of scriptures and the spiritual master, we will never have access to this vital information about our eternal relation with God. It is beyond our guessing. What's more, by rejecting the spiritual master's authority, today's society has been degraded by all manner of vices, illicit sex and intoxication, and thus modern society has become very uncongenial for anyone interested in spiritual progress.

When Bhīṣma speaks about Kṛṣṇa, we can accept what he says, since he knows the principles of transcendental knowledge. He appears in Vedic literature as an outstanding authority on Kṛṣṇa consciousness.

Before the great assembly who had come to see and hear him, Bhīṣma prayed to Kṛṣṇa, "Now I am going to die. So in these last moments, let me remember You in the mood in which we met each other as opponents on the battlefield. That vision of You, out of all, is the most attractive to me. Since I am a warrior, I long to see You in that fighting spirit. You came before me like an attacking lion, carrying a chariot wheel in Your hand, because I was about to kill Your disciple, Arjuna."

Bhīṣma said: "In the battlefield, the wavy hair of Lord Kṛṣṇa turned an ashen color from the dust raised by the hoofs of the horses. His hair was scattered; there was perspiration on His face. All these decorations, intensified by the wounds made by my arrows, were enjoyed by Him. Let my mind rest upon that Kṛṣṇa."

Bhīṣma was a warrior by quality and work, and so he worshiped Kṛṣṇa by shooting arrows at Him. Of all bewildering things about Bhīṣma and the Lord, this is the most bewildering–that a devotee expressed his love for Kṛṣṇa by inflicting wounds upon Him on the battlefield as His enemy. It is stated in the *Bhāgavatam,* "The Lord, being absolute, can accept service from His pure devotee even in the garb of an enemy." Actually, the Lord, the Unconquerable, has no real enemy. The wounds from Bhīṣma's arrows were enjoyed by the Lord as much as the service of devotees who worship by throwing soft roses upon Him or bowing before an altar.

Of course, since the Lord has an eternal spiritual body, there was no question of His actually being bruised or cut. Transcendental bliss is of different varieties and is always completely pure. Therefore, the Lord enjoyed the wounds created by His great devotee Bhīṣma, and because Bhīṣma was a devotee in the chivalrous military mood, he fixed his mind on Kṛṣṇa in that wounded condition.

Bhīṣma prayed: "Let my mind be fixed on the Lord's activities on the Battlefield of Kurukṣetra as He fought as the chariot-driver of Arjuna." Bhīṣma reflected, "Just by seeing Lord Kṛṣṇa on the battlefield, the opposing soldiers gained liberation in their next lives."

While the day grew near its close, as indicated by the sun's rays, the great host of eminent personalities from all over the universe listened eagerly and with full faith to the authorized instructions of Bhīṣma. The speaking of Bhīṣma and the hearing by the sages can only be appreciated on the platform of devotional service or transcendental life. There was no mental speculator or doubter present at that meeting. Such persons do not have entrance into the pastimes between Lord Kṛṣṇa and His devotee because they think that such activities are material or impossible or just stories. Those who are qualified to actually be an audience to such a transcendental narration were thrilled, and they forgot all miseries and circumstances of the material world and listened with full feelings of ecstasy and rapt attention.

It is said that actually a devotee cannot completely understand the Supreme Lord because the nature of God is that He is ultimately inconceivable and not subject to our understanding. But a measure of a devotee's advancement is that he increasingly relishes hearing these stories about the Lord. If we hear this narration without envy, we can be included in that host of eternal liberated listeners of the *Bhāgavatam.*

Bhīṣma recalled the battle. One day, after long fighting, Duryodhana criticized Bhīṣma, hinting that Bhīṣma was not fighting as hard as he could because of his reluctance to kill Arjuna and the other Pāṇḍavas. Duryodhana accused Bhīṣma: "Your grandfatherly feelings have made you soft-hearted." In those days, warriors fought with great sporting spirit, as a friend fights with a friend, and Bhīṣma could not tolerate this criticism from Duryodhana. "I vow," promised Bhīṣma, "that tomorrow I will kill all the Pāṇḍava brothers."

Duryodhana had inspired Bhīṣma to a rage. Bhīṣma said: "Kṛṣṇa is the chariot-driver of Arjuna, and He himself will have to take weapons tomorrow. Otherwise His friend Arjuna will die. Kṛṣṇa has promised to be neutral in this war and not to actually fight. But if He wishes to protect Arjuna, He shall be forced to fight me!"

The next day, Bhīṣma drove his chariot across the field, broke and scattered all opposition before him, and headed straight for Kṛṣṇa and Arjuna. His chariot moved against all resistance. Dust arose in clouds. Soldiers fought, knocking each other from their carts. Fully decorated bodies lay dead on the field along with horses and mangled bodies.

Bhīṣma fought so violently that both Arjuna and Kṛṣṇa were in trouble. Arjuna became separated from Kṛṣṇa and put at a military disadvantage. This stalwart fighter Bhīṣma, who is praised as the greatest of all generals, came upon Arjuna with raised weapons, prepared to kill him in a moment.

Then Kṛṣṇa moved to save His devotee, Arjuna. He picked up a large chariot wheel from the battlefield and rushed toward Bhīṣma in an angry mood, as a lion charges to kill an elephant. He ran in such haste that His covering cloth fell from His shoulder without His knowing where it fell.

Bhīṣma at once gave up his weapons and stood ready to be killed by the Lord. The Lord was the ultimate destination of Bhīṣma's life, and to see the Lord in this mood was the fulfillment of Bhīṣma's chivalrous dealings with the Lord. Although Kṛṣṇa had promised not to lend His fighting strength to either side, He broke that promise on Bhīṣma's insistence, just to save His devotee, Arjuna. This was all an arrangement by the Lord to favor His great devotee, Bhīṣma. Bhīṣma wanted to see the Lord break His promise and save His devotee; therefore, the Lord's running towards Bhīṣma with the wheel in His hand was like a lover's going to a lover without caring for checking hindrances.

This cannot be understood by those who try to restrict God by saying, "He cannot do such and such." Devotional service is dynamic, far beyond the selfish aspirations of *yogīs* and impersonal meditators who seek self-satisfaction by mechanical *yoga* processes. Everyone has a unique, eternal, active relationship with God. We can recover our original mellow relationship with Kṛṣṇa by beginning our practice of devotional service according to regulative principles under the guidance of a spiritual master. Those who know even a little of pure devotional service can penetrate the mystery of this loving exchange between Bhīṣma and Kṛṣṇa as so-called enemies. It is astounding that a devotee can please God by playing the part of an enemy. This can happen only in the case of a completely pure devotee like Bhīṣma, who is not actually an enemy but an eternal servant of Kṛṣṇa. At his last moments, Bhīṣma clearly saw and cherished this vision of Lord Kṛṣṇa on the battlefield.

Thinking of Kṛṣṇa in so many ways as his supreme beloved object, Bhīṣma finally left this world for the next. Because he was thinking of Kṛṣṇa in love and Kṛṣṇa was actually present before him, it was assured that he would enter the spiritual realm which lies beyond these material universes to join the Lord in one of the spiritual Vaikuṇṭha planets and constantly engage in loving service without anxiety or misery.

The perfection achieved by Bhīṣmadeva at the time of death can be attained even if Lord Kṛṣṇa is not personally present. By chanting Hare Kṛṣṇa or by hearing narrations about Kṛṣṇa, one can attain this stage. Every man or animal must ultimately die, but one who dies like Bhīṣmadeva attains perfection, and one who dies forced by the laws of nature dies like a cat or dog. That is the difference between a man and an animal.

Human life is especially meant for dying like Bhīṣmadeva. The atheist thinks that at death he is finished and that everything else is finished and there is no after-life or spiritual world. The only possible way to receive knowledge about what is beyond this material world is from the authorities who speak information from the spiritual world. There is a process of spiritual knowledge. If one wishes to know who his father is, the mother is the authority. In the same way, God Himself, or revealed scriptures, can tell us about this eternal life. The human being who takes up the responsibility of recovering his eternal relationship with Kṛṣṇa fulfills the responsibility of human life. As for the atheist, he denies God up until the time of death, and then he is conquered by time, which is the direct representative of Kṛṣṇa.

We should not consider the story of Bhīṣma to be unimportant. It is not simply the story of an old warrior dying, but it is the narration of a great soul leaving this mortal world for the spiritual world. Bhīṣmadeva was perfect because he never forgot the Lord in His transcendental feature as the chariot-driver of Arjuna on the battlefield and because the Lord was personally present before Bhīṣmadeva while he passed to the transcendental world.

Sūta Gosvāmī, the speaker of this narration, describes the final moments of Bhīṣma: "Bhīṣmadeva, merging himself in the Supersoul, Lord Kṛṣṇa, the Supreme Personality of Godhead, with his mind, speech, sight and activities, became silent and stopped breathing. Thus, knowing that Bhīṣmadeva had merged into the unlimited eternity of the Supreme Absolute, all present there became silent like birds at the end of day. Thereafter, both men and demigods sounded respectful honor by beating on drums. The honest royal order offered honor and respect, and from the sky there was a shower of flowers."

The shower of flowers by the heavenly beings has no comparison in the funeral rites performed for an ordinary common man in our materialistic civilization today. In the case of an ordinary funeral, people glorify and lament over the dead body, but in the case of Bhīṣmadeva the men and demigods present were glorifying the ascension of the spiritual body. They were glorifying the passing of Bhīṣma because he was attaining the spiritual planets.

The passing away of a devotee is, therefore, unique and exalted. The *Bhāgavatam* says that the men of this present age are always disturbed and filled with so many cares that they do not have the time and inclination to hear about spiritual life. We are so surrounded by this disturbed civilization that it is very difficult for us to hear about and understand a great Kṛṣṇa conscious devotee like Bhīṣma. But God Himself says that if we can remember and recite about these devotees, it is even more beneficial than trying to connect directly with the Lord Himself.

If we can try to retain a summary of the narrations of Bhīṣma in our minds, if we try to tell others about this great devotee, who met the Lord in a fighting mood, spoke great instructions on a deathbed of arrows, and, passing away at a moment of his own choosing, attained the spiritual world, if we can just experiment in this way by reciting the activities of a devotee in a submissive rather than skeptical mood, then we will be able to feel spiritual pleasure. We highly recommend discussion of these topics about the transference of our real self at the time of death into the next world, and we urge the reader to direct any questions to the editors of *Back to Godhead* so we can discuss this matter clearly, since it is the most important business of life, to fix our own passage from this world into the spiritual world.

The example of Bhīṣmadeva is one of perfect death. It is not that he died only because he was an old warrior. Even if a young man is twenty-five years old, he has already died twenty-five years. So, for all of us, our immediate concern should be how to prepare for death and what our responsibility is. The Vedic literature is full of many satisfying stories and teachings which answer this all-important question. This material is given to us out of the compassion of the great sages who are directed by Kṛṣṇa Himself.

The final conclusion is that by chanting in a humble state of mind the names of God—Hare Kṛṣṇa, Hare Kṛṇṣa, Kṛṣṇa Kṛṣṇa, Hare Hare/Hare Rāma, Hare Rāma, Rāma Rāma, Hare Hare—we can achieve the stature of this great warrior devotee of the old days, Bhīṣmadeva. Just as He did for Bhīṣmadeva, Kṛṣṇa will come before us in the mood in which we most desire Him, and He will fulfill all our desires.

Lord Kṛṣṇa's Friend Sudāmā

September/October, 1972

The wonderful history of Kṛṣṇa and His friend Sudāmā is told in its entirety in the *Kṛṣṇa Book*, Volume II, by His Divine Grace A. C. Bhaktivedanta Swami Prabhupāda. Śrīla Prabhupāda is kindly presenting to the Western world the pastimes of Lord Kṛṣṇa, which can act as a merciful shower upon the hearts of all of us. It is true that we have forgotten our eternal, blissful and loving relationships as servants of Kṛṣṇa or God. The remedy to forgetfulness or ignorance of God is to hear about Him from the lips of His pure devotee. This is the view of authorized scriptures.

When Kṛṣṇa descends from His eternal abode in the spiritual world and appears to this mundane world, as He did 5,000 years ago, He engages with others just as if He were an ordinary human being. Although He is unborn, He appears to have a mother and father. In the village of Vṛndāvana Kṛṣṇa plays as a cowherd boy. He enacts these pastimes for His own transcendental pleasure and to attract all the suffering living entities back home, back to Godhead. Sudāmā was among those devotees who were childhood friends with Kṛṣṇa, and Sudāmā was also His intimate school friend.

Kṛṣṇa left Vṛndāvana at sixteen, and later He married and went to live as King of Dvārakā. Meanwhile Sudāmā was living as a *brāhmaṇa,* which means one who knows that the real self is spirit and who dedicates his life to being a spiritual guide for the whole society.

One cannot properly be called a *brāhmaṇa* simply because he is born the son of a *brāhmaṇa;* rather, there are qualities which one has to show before he can rightly be considered a *brāhmaṇa.* Such qualities are peacefulness, austerity, piety, knowledge and wisdom.

Sudāmā was also a householder, but he was not busy in accumulating wealth for very comfortable living. Whatever income came to him without difficulty, he accepted. He engaged his time in the service of the Supreme Personality of Godhead and thus showed himself to be perfect in knowledge. Externally Sudāmā appeared very poor because he had no rich attire and could not provide rich clothing for his wife. In fact they were not even eating sufficiently, and they were both very thin.

Often Sudāmā's wife used to address her husband, "My dear lord, I know that Lord Kṛṣṇa, the Supreme Lord of all the universes, is your personal friend. You are also a devotee of the Lord, and He is always ready to help His devotee. Moreover, Lord Kṛṣṇa is always in favor of the *brāhmaṇas.* Kṛṣṇa is your friend, and persons like you have no other shelter but Kṛṣṇa. You are saintly, learned and in control of your senses. Please, therefore, go to Him in Dvārāka. I am sure that He will understand your impoverished condition.

"You are a married man, so for you to be without money means to be in a distressed condition. As soon as Kṛṣṇa sees your impoverished condition He will give you sufficient riches. Kṛṣṇa is known to give even His own Self to one who is His pure devotee, so there would be nothing wonderful in His giving you some material riches. He will not hesitate to award you some material benefit for the bare necessities of life."

Although the *brāhmaṇa's* wife was not speaking out of anxiety for her own personal condition (she was, after all, dedicated to her husband, and she treasured his saintly values far above material riches), she nevertheless felt concerned that her husband, who was so pious, was living below the minimum standards for proper physical maintenance. As a good wife, she did not like to dictate to her husband, yet on repeated occasions she would speak to Sudāmā in this way, suggesting that he go to the capital city, Dvārakā, to see the Supreme Lord there.

Sudāmā, however, thought there to be no need to ask material benefit from Lord Kṛṣṇa. But one time when she made this request, Sudāmā thought, "If I do go there, I shall be able to see the Lord personally. That will be a great opportunity, even if I don't ask any material benefit from Him." So he told his wife that he would go and that she should at once prepare some foodstuff that he could offer as a presentation to his friend.

Sudāmā's wife had nothing in the house, but she went out and collected some chipped rice, which is the lowest grade of rice, from her neighbors, and she tied it up in a handkerchief. Sudāmā took the presentation and started at once toward Dvārakā. As a devotee, he was always thinking of Kṛṣṇa, and now he became absorbed in the thought that he would soon be able to see the Lord.

The Dvārakā palace where Kṛṣṇa lived was not accessible to anyone and everyone, for it was a king's palace and was guarded all around. Saintly persons, however, were allowed to enter, and Sudāmā passed through three military camps and many gates until he finally entered the residential quarters of Kṛṣṇa.

At that time Lord Kṛṣṇa was sitting with His Queen Rukmiṇī, but when He saw His friend Sudāmā coming, the Lord got up and went forward to receive him, and He embraced him feelingly. This behavior of Kṛṣṇa toward His friend shocked the women attendants of the palace.

"But we thought Lord Kṛṣṇa only embraced His Queen Rukmiṇī and His brother Balarāma," they said among themselves. "Who is this poor *brāhmaṇa?*

He is not even clean, and he is so skinny, yet Lord Kṛṣṇa has embraced him in His two arms, and now He is washing the *brāhmaṇa's* feet."

Kṛṣṇa, the source of all life, comes to this mortal world to enact His pastimes as a human being. He is actually the supreme pure, yet He sprinkled the water used to wash the *brāhmaṇa's* feet on His own head, as if for purification. He welcomed the *brāhmaṇa* in many ways, giving him food and drink and saying, "My dear friend, it is great fortune that you have come here."

Seating Sudāmā on His own cushioned bed, Kṛṣṇa said, "My dear friend, you are most intelligent and know very well the principles of religious life. I know that after you finished your education at the house of our spiritual master you went back to your home and accepted a suitable wife. I know very well that from the very beginning you were never attached to the materialistic way of life, nor did you desire to be very opulent materially."

Kṛṣṇa then began to remember their days together when they were both entrusted to the guidance of the same spiritual master. They were school friends living at the same house. Kṛṣṇa very highly praised those days and said, "Whatever knowledge we have received in our lives was accumulated in those days." So important is the instruction received from a bona fide spiritual master that Kṛṣṇa, who is God Himself, and thus everyone's spiritual master, expressed great debt for what He learned in His youth at the house of the *guru*.

Sudāmā was sitting face to face with the Supreme Lord, who is also the self-same Lord who is present in everyone's heart. He thrilled to hear Kṛṣṇa describe a particular adventure in which they shared when they were students.

"My dear friend," Kṛṣṇa said, "I think you may remember our activities during the days when we were living as students. You may remember that once we went to collect fuel from the forest on the order of the *guru's* wife. While we were collecting the dried wood, we by chance entered the dense forest and became lost. There was an unexpected dust storm and then clouds and lightning in the sky and the explosive sound of thunder. Then sunset came, and we were lost in the dark jungle.

"After this, there was severe rainfall; the whole ground was overflooded with water, and we could not trace out the way to return to our *guru's* house. You may remember that heavy rainfall–it was not actually rainfall but a sort of devastation. On account of the dust storm and the heavy rain, we began to feel greatly pained, and in whichever direction we turned we were bewildered. In that distressed condition, we took each other's hand and tried to find our way out.

"We passed the whole night in that way, and early in the morning when our absence became known to our *guru*, he sent his other disciples to search us out. He also came with them, and when they reached us in the jungle they found us to be very distressed.

"With great compassion our *guru* said, "My dear boys, it is very wonderful that you have suffered so much trouble for me. Everyone likes to take care of his body as the first consideration, but you are so good and faithful to your spiritual master that without caring for bodily comfort you have taken so much trouble for me. I am glad to see that bona fide students like you will undergo any kind of trouble for the spiritual master. That is the way for a bona fide disciple to become free from his debt to the spiritual master. It is the duty of the disciple to dedicate his life to the service of the spiritual master.

"'My dear blessed ones, I am greatly pleased by your action, and I bless you: May all your desires and ambitions be fulfilled. May the understanding of the scriptures which you have learned from me always continue to remain within your memory so that at every moment you can remember the teachings and quote their instructions without difficulty. Thus you will never be disappointed in this life or in the next.'"

Kṛṣṇa continued, "My dear friend, you may remember that many such incidents occured while we were in the house of our spiritual master. Both of us can realize that without the blessing of the spiritual master one cannot be happy. By the mercy of the spiritual master and by his blessing one can achieve peace and prosperity and be able to fulfill the mission of human life."

Sudāmā well understood that Kṛṣṇa was the supreme controller of both the material and spiritual worlds, and so he appreciated that Kṛṣṇa had played the role of a student and now was acting as King of Dvārakā simply as part of His pastimes, for His transcendental pleasure. Even the pure devotee does not know everything about the Supreme Lord, but he definitely relishes hearing about His transcendental pastimes–how He creates, maintains and destroys the material world, how in His form or incarnation He personally descends into the material world and enacts pastimes, and how He eternally engages in blissful affairs with His devotees in the spiritual·planets far beyond this material universe. The scientists have no information of the spiritual sky beyond this material universe, but the devotee, by performing devotional service, and hearing from bona fide authority, very soon has knowledge of Kṛṣṇa, and the spiritual kingdom is revealed to him from within his heart.

Lord Kṛṣṇa talked a long time with His friend Sudāmā. Then, just to enjoy His friend's company, He began to smile and asked "My dear friend, what have you brought for Me? Has your wife given you some nice eatables?"

Sudāmā hesitated out of shyness to bring forth the chipped rice. The Lord assured him that He was in need of nothing, but that He would gladly accept any offering given in love.

"How can I offer such an insignificant thing?" thought Sudāmā. But the Lord knew his heart. He knew very well, since He is situated in everyone's heart, that the *brāhmaṇa* had come to see Him on the instigation of his wife to get some material opulence. Moreover, He knew fully well that Sudāmā's love for Him was not tainted by any desire for material benefit. Kṛṣṇa then decided He would very lavishly award Sudama.

"What is this?" Lord Kṛṣṇa snatched the bundle of chipped rice, which was tucked in a corner of Sudāmā's shoulder pack. "Oh My dear friend," Kṛṣṇa went on enthusiastically, "you've brought Me such nice palatable chipped rice. It will please not only Me but the whole creation." It is understood from this statement that Kṛṣṇa, being the original source of everything, is the root of the entire creation. As watering the root of a tree immediately distributes water to every part of the tree, so an offering made to Kṛṣṇa or any action done for Kṛṣṇa is to be considered the highest welfare work for everyone. The benefit of such an offering is distributed throughout the creation.

While speaking in this way, Lord Kṛṣṇa ate a morsel of the rice, but when He attempted to eat a second morsel, Rukmiṇī, the goddess of fortune, checked the Lord by taking hold of His hand.

My dear Lord," she said, "by Your taking this one piece of rice Sudāmā will become wealthy not only in this life but in the next. You are so kind that this one morsel of rice is enough to cause him who offered it to become very opulent in this life and continue as such in the next." Rukmiṇī, the goddess of fortune, was already personally obliged to stay as a guest in the *brāhmaṇa's* house in order to benedict him with great fortune.

Sudāmā did not appear to have received anything from Kṛṣṇa, nor did he ask anything; the whole time he was merged in an ocean of transcendental bliss. After taking rest that night in the palace, the next morning he started for his home. He was completely absorbed in remembering the dealings with the Lord, and he was happy to have seen Him.

On the way home he was filled with ecstatic reminiscences: "Kṛṣṇa so respects the *brāhmaṇas* that He embraced to his chest a poor *brāhmaṇa* like me. How can there be any comparison between me and the Supreme Lord Kṛṣṇa, who is the only shelter of the goddess of fortune? He allowed me to sit on His bedstead, and when I was tired, Rukmiṇī began to fan me. She never considered her exalted position. I was rendered service by the Supreme Personality of Godhead because of His high regard for the *brāhmaṇas,* and by massaging my legs and feeding me with His own hand, He practically worshiped me! Yet the Lord was so kind to me that He did not give me even a penny, knowing very well that I am a poverty-stricken man who, if I got some money, might become puffed up and mad after material opulence and so forget Him."

Thinking in this way, Sudāmā reached his home. But when he looked for his cottage he saw in its place a huge, gorgeous palace made of valuable stones and jewels and glittering like the sun.

"What is this?" he thought. "How am I seeing these changes? Does this palace belong to me or to someone else? Surely this is where I used to live–it is the same place–but how wonderfully it has changed!" Then one dazzling opulence and beauty after another was revealed to Sudāmā Brāhmaṇa. His old neighborhood had become transformed into an area of parks with nice lakes full of lotus flowers and lilies and flocks of multicolored birds. Beautiful men and women were strolling in the parks, and musical chanters who looked like demigods came forward to greet him. On hearing of her husband's arrival, the wife of the *brāhmaṇa* ran out of the palace to greet him. She appeared so beautiful that it seemed as if the goddess of fortune herself had come to meet him. The *brāhmaṇa* was surprised to see his wife so beautiful and so greatly affectionate, and without saying a word he entered the palace with her. His inner chambers were like the residence of the king of heaven. The palace was surrounded by many columns of jewels, rich canopies of velvet and silk hung in various places, and everything was opulent.

He could not determine what had caused the change, but then he began to consider: "I have always been poor–what could be the cause of this? It could only have come from the all-merciful glance of my friend, Lord Kṛṣṇa. Surely these things are the causeless mercy of my friend Kṛṣṇa." Sudāmā could understand that the Lord considered such an insignificant offering as a handful of chipped rice, offered in affection by His devotee, a great thing and that He had given him riches more wonderful than any seen on earth, or even possessed by the demigods in the heavenly planets.

Sudāmā then offered his prayers to Kṛṣṇa, praying that he did not want any opulence. He prayed that all he wanted was that he might not forget to offer eternal service to Kṛṣṇa. Whatever opulence he received from the Lord should not be used for his own extravagance but for the service of the Lord, and so he accepted everything that happened as *prasādam* (God's mercy).

Anything which we receive from the Lord, any facility, wealth, fame, power or education–should thus be used for His service and not for our sense enjoyment. In that way, Sudāmā remained in opulent surroundings without detriment to his spiritual life, and his affection for Kṛṣṇa increased day after day. He was made more aware of his friend at every moment and of the Lord's mercy.

One may ask, "But how did the *brāhmaṇa's* wealthy surroundings make him more conscious of Kṛṣṇa? Why did Kṛṣṇa award him with material things?"

The answer is found clearly in the *Kṛṣṇa Book* narrative: "The *brāhmaṇa* accepted his newly acquired opulence, but he did so in a spirit of renunciation, unattached to sense gratification, and thus he lived very peacefully with his wife, enjoying all the facilities of opulence as *prasādam* (God's mercy). He enjoyed varieties of foodstuffs by offering it to the Lord and then taking it as *prasādam.* Similarly, if by the grace of the Lord we get such opulences as material wealth, fame, power, education and beauty, it is our duty to consider that they are all gifts of the Lord and must be used for His service, not for our sense enjoyment. The learned *brāhmaṇa* remained in that position, and instead of deteriorating due to his great opulence, his love and affection for Lord Kṛṣṇa increased day after day.

Material opulence can be the cause of degradation and also the cause of elevation, according to the purposes for which it is used. If opulence is used for sense gratification it is the cause of degradation, and if it is used for the service of the Lord it is the cause of elevation.

If money or wealth can be used in Kṛṣṇa's service, if it can be used to increase remembrance and revive love of Kṛṣṇa, then it must be used. We cannot mistake Sudāmā's motive. Even at the point of receiving riches he thought, "I do not want any opulence. I only desire not to forget His service. I simply wish to associate with His pure devotees." Sudāmā was just as happy when he was very poor because he always engaged in the devotional service of the Lord.

Similarly, in the modern age, the great *gosvāmī* followers of Lord Caitanya, Rūpa and Sanātana, were very highly placed wealthy government officials, but they gave up everything in order to follow Lord Caitanya's Hare Kṛṣṇa movement, and they lived as mendicants without even a dwelling place. Yet they became richer and richer thinking of Rādhā and Kṛṣṇa and Kṛṣṇa's pure devotees, and they never lamented over having given up their wealth.

Rich or poor, the criterion for eternal happiness is to remember Kṛṣṇa in any condition. The point is made, however, that if one does give something to Kṛṣṇa, no matter how little it be, he will not be the loser! What the devotee actually offers to the Lord is not needed by the Lord, for He is self-sufficient. But if the devotee offers something to the Lord, it acts for his own interest because whatever a devotee offers to the Lord comes back in a quantity a million times greater than what was offered. Sudāmā gave a few grains of chipped rice, and in return he received heavenly opulence. As a pure devotee, Sudāmā was expert in accepting the wealth and using it as more facility for serving Kṛṣṇa.

It is related that by his constant association with the Lord, Sudāmā had wiped away from his heart whatever contamination was remaining, and he was very shortly transferred to the eternal spiritual kingdom, which is the goal of all saintly persons in the perfectional stage of life. It is stated in the *Kṛṣṇa Book* that whoever hears this history will become qualified like Sudāmā and will be transferred to the spiritual kingdom of Lord Kṛṣṇa.

The Glories of Sanātana Gosvāmī

November/December, 1973

In his book *Teachings of Lord Caitanya,* His Divine Grace A. C. Bhaktivedanta Swami Prabhupāda describes how Sanātana Gosvāmī, a learned scholar and expert politician, became an important member of the Kṛṣṇa consciousness movement. Five hundred years ago, Sanātana Gosvāmī was a central figure in the government of Bengal, but by leaving his governmental responsibilities to surrender to Lord Caitanya, he fulfilled a far more important responsibility to both himself and humanity in the service of the Supreme Lord.

Lord Caitanya Mahāprabhu, the father of the Kṛṣṇa consciousness movement, was a householder for the first twenty-four years of His life, and He began the Hare Kṛṣṇa movement before He was twenty. But He gave up His wife and home and entered the renounced order, *sannyāsa,* to facilitate His mission of preaching Kṛṣṇa consciousness.

For the first six years of His life as a *sannyāsī,* Lord Caitanya traveled all over India performing *saṅkīrtana,* the congregational chanting of Hare Kṛṣṇa, singing and dancing with thousands of people and thus overflooding the land with love of God. While thus engaged, He came to a village in Bengal named Rāmakeli, and there He met Sanātana Gosvāmī and his brother Rūpa.

Although the two brothers, then known as Sākara Mallik and Dabhir Khās, appeared exalted in their posts as ministers in the Mohammedan government of Nawab Hussain Shah, they were actually degraded. They had been highly placed Hindu *brāhmaṇas* (intellectuals), but their acceptance of posts in government service had jeopardized both their intellectual and religious standing. Indeed, because of the brothers' association with worldly, sinful people addicted to meat eating, illicit sex, intoxication and worldly power, the other *brāhmaṇas* considered them fallen and ostracized them from the Hindu community.

That the Hindus had rejected the brothers, considering them half-Moslem, did not concern Lord Caitanya, for He was a universal teacher who declared that He was neither Hindu, *brāhmaṇa* nor *sannyāsī,* but was a servant of the servant of the servant of the Supreme Lord. Krsna declares in *Bhagavad-gītā* that He is the father of all living entities, not the God of any one sect or religion, and He asks everyone to surrender to Him. Therefore Lord Caitanya, while distributing the chanting of the Hare Kṛṣṇa *mantra,* taught as a devotee that one should surrender to Kṛṣṇa. When the two brothers Sanātana and Rūpa met Lord Caitanya at Rāmakeli, they decided to resign from their governmental posts and join the Kṛṣṇa consciousness movement. And later, despite his former aristocracy, Sanatāna Gosvāmī admitted that Lord Caitanya had saved him from a hellish life.

Once in office, most politicians, being interested only in gratifying their own senses, scheme to stay in office until they die or their constituents kick them out. But Sanātana wanted to disentangle himself from the service of the State. Nawab Hussain Shah, the ruler of Bengal, liked to hunt and conduct military campaigns, and he usually left the government in Sanātana's hands. Therefore, since Sanātana was practically guiding the entire government, how could he leave his post? His resignation would be comparable to our modern Secretary of State's suddenly resigning to become a renounced monk of the Hare Kṛṣṇa movement.

Nevertheless, after handing over his official responsibilities to his immediate assistants, Sanātana stayed home to study *Śrīmad-Bhāgavatam* intensively with ten or twenty *brāhmaṇas. Śrīmad-Bhāgavatam* is called the spotless scripture because it leaves behind all compromising philosophies and religions, teaching only pure love of God. Lord Caitanya has declared that for spiritual perfection one need study no books other than *Bhagavad-gītā* and *Śrīmad-Bhāgavatam,* and therefore His Divine Grace A. C. Bhaktivedanta Swami Prabhupāda, the spiritual master spearheading the modern resurgence of Kṛṣṇa consciousness, is translating the *Bhāgavatam* into English with elaborate purports to teach knowledge of Kṛṣṇa to the people of the West.

Sanātana absorbed himself in studying the *Bhāgavatam* because simply hearing the *Bhāgavatam* can change one's life. One should not think that Kṛṣṇa consciousness is meant only to give shelter to economic failures, for although he was a wealthy aristocrat, a learned scholar in Sanskṛit, Arabic and Persian, and a successful and influential politician, Sanātana Gosvāmī, considering such opulences insignificant, aspired only to be a humble student of *Śrīmad-Bhāgavatam.*

While preparing himself in this way to join Lord Caitanya, Sanātana submitted reports of sickness to the Nawab, but since the ruler was anxious to get Sanātana's advice on governmental affairs, one day he appeared at Sanātana's home. When he entered the assembly of Sanātana and the *brāhmaṇas,* they all stood up to receive him, but unfortunately the Nawab was not interested in hearing *Srīmad-Bhāgavatam.*

"You have submitted reports of sickness," he said, "but I sent my physician to see you, and he reported that you have no illness. Your behavior greatly perturbs me." When the Nawab demanded to know Sanātana's intentions, Sanātana answered that he was unable to work any more and that it would be kind of the Nawab to appoint someone else to do his work. The Nawab then left in anger, and shortly afterwards he went off to conquer the province of Orissa, ordering the arrest of Sanātana Gosvāmī until he returned.

It is unfortunate that the Nawab did not see the value of *Śrīmad-Bhāgavatam,* for it would have been valuable to his administration. Formerly great leaders consulted the *Bhāgavatam* and its brahminical devotees for practical guidance in organizing a peaceful and prosperous society according to principles of God consciousness. But the Nawab, being a rather low-minded hunter, did not take the *Bhāgavatam* seriously.

Despite Sanātana's apparent misfortune in being imprisoned, one should not think him an ordinary conditioned soul entangled in a snare of material circumstances. As confirmed by revealed scriptures, Lord Caitanya Mahāprabhu is Lord Kṛṣṇa Himself, the Supreme Personality of Godhead. To make the knowledge He formerly taught in *Bhagavad-gītā* easily available to everyone, Lord Kṛṣṇa appeared in India five hundred years ago to propagate love of God by chanting Hare Kṛṣṇa, Hare Kṛṣṇa, Kṛṣṇa Kṛṣṇa, Hare Hare/Hare Rāma, Hare Rāma, Rāma Rāma, Hare Hare. Sanātana Gosvāmī is an eternal servant of Lord Caitanya Mahāprabhu, and he appeared in this world to assist the Lord in His pastimes. He was never under the influence of material contamination, but difficulties beset him only so that he might set an example of how to act in Kṛṣṇa consciousness.

Dedication to Kṛṣṇa consciousness is a declaration of war against material illusion. Freeing oneself from sinful life is sometimes difficult because of one's previous attachments, but if one is sincere, like Sanātana, and depends on the Lord, he will emerge from all difficulties and be able to engage freely in devotional service. Therefore, although Sanātana appeared to fare badly as soon as he took to Kṛṣṇa consciousness, his apparent setback was but another feature of his glory, for he had escaped a hellish life and was on the path to becoming a *gosvāmī,* or master of the senses, who always feels transcendental ecstasy.

Sanātana did not stay long in prison, for his brother Rūpa heard of his plight and came to his aid. Rūpa, who had been able to leave his governmental post and start for Jagannātha Purī to meet Lord Caitanya, arranged to make ten thousand gold coins available for Sanātana's release. On hearing that this money was available, Sanātana offered five thousand coins to the jail keeper as a bribe for letting him go. The jail keeper expressed fear that he would be caught, but when Sanātana raised his offer to ten thousand coins, the jail keeper agreed, and Sanatana then set out to meet Lord Caitanya Mahāprabhu, traveling not by the open roads but through the jungles.

One might ask, "You describe Sanātana Gosvāmī as a saint, yet he did not hesitate to bribe a government official to release himself. What kind of saintliness is that?" To understand Sanātana's purity, however, one must first understand that a devotee's foremost duty is to satisfy the Supreme Lord. A devotee always acts to please Kṛṣṇa, not whimsically but as directed by the scriptures and his spiritual master. Since Kṛṣṇa is the absolute morality and the absolute good, one who strives in this way only to please Kṛṣṇa is the greatest, purest moralist.

Impure and selfish men who do not understand that everything belongs to Kṛṣṇa and should be offered to Him try to enjoy God's property themselves, not properly recognizing the Lord's ownership. Despite their social standing and their reputation as public-spirited citizens, it is such men who are actually cheaters and thieves, whereas devotees like Sanātana, who work not for their own purposes but only to serve Kṛṣṇa, are thereby able to make the greatest contributions to human society.

After escaping from prison, Sanātana, traveling on foot with one servant, reached a place in Behar called Pabda, where he rested at a hotel. But when the hotel keeper's astrologer calculated that Sanātana had eight gold coins with him, the hotel keeper formed a plot to kill Sanātana. Treating him with artificial respect, the hotel keeper said, "My dear sir, just rest here tonight, and in the morning I shall arrange to get you out of this jungle trap."

Sanātana, however, suspecting the man's insincerity, asked his servant, Īśāna, if he had money with him. When Īśāna admitted that he indeed had seven gold coins, Sanātana, angry at him for secretly carrying money, demanded, "Why do you carry this death knell on the road?" He then took the seven coins and offered them to the hotel keeper.

"I understood that you had eight coins with you," the hotel keeper admitted, "and I was thinking of killing you to take them. But I understand you are a good man, and you don't have to offer me the money. I'll help you out of the jungle in any case."

But Sanātana insisted, "If you don't take this money, someone else will kill me for it. Please take it." The hotel keeper agreed, and that very night he helped Sanātana past the hills.

When clear of the jungle, Sanātana sent his servant home. Although he was supposed to have been Sanātana's menial helper, he was secretly carrying eight gold coins, and when his master asked about them he lied, saying he had only seven, so he could keep one coin for himself. It is not that one may not use money in Kṛṣṇa's service—indeed, one may collect and spend millions of dollars to build temples and publish books glorifying the Lord. But a devotee, especially one in the renounced order, should be wary of collecting money for his own sense gratification.

Realizing the contaminating influence of his former wealth and aristocracy, Sanātana wanted to divest himself of his opulence and approach Lord Caitanya in a spirit of purity and humility, not as a dollars-and-cents man. To Sanātana, material acquisitions were burdens that weighed him down. He understood that they lead only to future bondage in birth and death. As stated in *Bhagavad-gītā,* "The wise, engaged in devotional service, take refuge in the Lord and free themselves from the cycle of birth and death. Thus, by renouncing the fruits of actions in this world, they obtain the place beyond all misery."

After the departure of his servant, Sanātana Gosvāmī, feeling completely free, wearing torn clothing and carrying a water pot in his hand, proceeded toward Lord Caitanya Mahāprabhu. While traveling he met his rich brother-in-law, who was surprised to see him traveling alone in the guise of a beggar. Sanātana was no longer eager to associate with worldly men, but his brother-in-law insisted that he take an excellent blanket, and Sanātana accepted it.

Sanātana finally arrived in Benares, and he was glad to hear that Lord Caitanya was indeed in the city. When he approached the house of Candrasekhara Ācārya, where the Lord was staying, the Lord, understanding that Sanātana had arrived, asked His host to go outside and ask the great devotee standing by the door to come in.

Candraśekhara went outside, but when he came back he reported to the Lord, "There is no great devotee out there, but only a wretched man with a beard."

"The man you saw," Lord Caitanya replied, "is actually a pure devotee. Have him come in at once." Thus we can understand that unless one already has genuine spiritual knowledge, one cannot recognize a great devotee simply by seeing him. So many false *svāmīs* and *yogīs* make money by growing long beards, dressing up in saffron robes and pretending to be saints. Therefore one should recognize a great spiritualist not by his appearance but by his words. The best way to recognize a genuine pure devotee is by his teachings.

When Sanātana entered the courtyard of the house, Lord Caitanya ran to receive and embrace him. He touched Sanātana with His hand, but Sanātana, thinking himself a lowly, contaminated man, pleaded, "My dear Lord, please do not touch me."

But the Lord replied, "I am touching you just for My purification because you are a great devotee. By your devotional service, you can deliver the whole universe and enable everyone to go back to Godhead." He then quoted a verse stating that one who fully engages in devotional service is the most valuable person, regardless of his birth or any other consideration.

After Sanātana explained how he had gotten free from custody, the Lord introduced him to Candraśekhara. The Lord asked Candraśekhara to take Sanātana to a barber and make him gentle because he had grown a long beard that Lord Caitanya did not like. Candraśekhara also offered Sanātana new clothes, but Sanātana accepted only used garments. When Candraśekhara invited him to have lunch with him every day, Sanātana replied, "As long as I stay in Benares I shall beg from door to door."

When Lord Caitanya heard about this behavior of Sanātana, He was greatly pleased. But He noticed the blanket given Sanātana by his brother-in-law, and although He said nothing about it, Sanātana understood that the Lord did not approve of his wearing it. Therefore he immediately went to the bank of the Ganges, and when he saw a mendicant there washing an old quilt, he asked him to trade the quilt for his valuable blanket.

The poor mendicant thought Sanātana was joking with him. "You appear to be a nice gentleman," he said. "Why are you mocking me?"

"I am not joking with you," Sanātana informed him. "I am serious. Will you kindly take this blanket for the torn quilt?" Then Sanātana exchanged his blanket for the quilt and came before the Lord.

Lord Caitanya was pleased, and He thanked Sanātana. "Being intelligent," He declared, "you have now left behind all your attraction for material wealth."

Sanātana Gosvāmī then brought forward his inquiries about spiritual life. Falling down at the feet of the Lord with great humility, he asked about his own identity. "I have been born of a low family," he said, "and my associations are all abominable. I am the most fallen and wretched of men. Suffering in the dark well of material enjoyment, I never knew the actual goal of my life. I do not know what is beneficial for me. Although in the mundane sphere I am known as a greatly learned man, I am in fact so much of a fool that I even accept that I am learned. You have accepted me as Your servant and delivered me from the entanglement of material life. Now please tell me my duty in this liberated stage of life."

His Divine Grace A.C. Bhaktivedanta Swami Prabhupāda comments: "We see by this plea of Sanātana's that liberation is not the final word in perfection. There must be activities in liberation. Sanātana clearly asks, 'You have saved me from the entanglement of material existence. Now, after liberation, what is my duty? Kindly explain it to me. Who am I? Why are the threefold miseries always giving me trouble? How can I be relieved from material entanglement?"

Sometimes people think liberation is the end of spiritual life, but here we see that although the Lord considered Sanātana already liberated from all material connections, this did not mean that his business in spiritual life was finished. Now he had to take on the activities of spiritual life because acting in Kṛṣṇa consciousness is the true essence of renunciation.

Thus by placing his sincere and relevant questions before the Lord with all humility, Sanātana Gosvāmī provided Lord Caitanya Mahāprabhu with the opportunity to expound upon the true meaning of liberated life. Sanātana accepted Lord Caitanya Mahāprabhu as his spiritual master, not as a matter of fashion or to dominate the spiritual master as one might a pet, but to surrender unto Him and ask sincerely and seriously for direction.

The teachings of Lord Caitanya to Sanātana Gosvāmī begin where the instructions of *Bhagavad-gītā* leave off. In the *Gītā's* last instruction, Kṛṣṇa, the Supreme Lord, answering the questions of Arjuna, said that one should surrender unto Him and thus realize true happiness. But now Kṛṣṇa Himself in the form of Lord Caitanya, answering the questions of Sanātana Gosvāmī, explained the transcendental activities of a surrendered soul. These instructions give the essence of devotional service to the Lord.

The Lord instructed Sanātana not only in the basic principles of liberated life but also in its scientific details. He explained the symptoms of a wise man; how to approach God, and what the expansions and *avatāras* of Godhead are. Describing Kṛṣṇa as the original source of all other forms of God, He explained the Lord's opulence and the practicalities of rendering service unto Him and attaining the highest stages of attachment and ecstasy. Śrīla Prabhupāda's *Teachings of Lord Caitanya* describes these instructions in detail.

Lord Caitanya requested Sanātana to explain these teachings by writing books about devotional service, but Sanātana prayed, "My dear Lord, You have taught me so many things, and now You are asking me to explain the principles of devotional service in books for devotees in the future. But I belong to the lowest caste. I have no knowledge, nor do I know how I can execute such an important task. But if you kindly give me some hints about the preparation of such books, then I may become qualified to write."

The Lord then blessed him, saying, "By the grace of Kṛṣṇa, whatever you write will come from your heart to be accepted as you have asked. I shall give you some notes to take down. The first and foremost thing is that one should accept a bona fide spiritual master, for that is the beginning of spiritual life."

After receiving elaborate instructions from the Lord, Sanātana Gosvāmī went to Vṛndāvana, where he faithfully carried out the orders of the Lord, thus becoming one of the six Gosvāmīs who propagated the immortal teachings of Lord Caitanya Mahāprabhu.

Lord Caitanya Himself wrote only eight verses, which describe the essence of His teachings, but He entrusted to the six Gōsvamīs the task of explaining the teachings in their fullness. Thus it is the grace of the six Gosvāmıs that they scientifically explained devotional service, establishing it firmly on the basis of the ancient Vedic scriptures.

Not only did Sanātana and the other Gosvāmīs write books, but they also taught the meaning of these books by the examples of their own lives. Commissioned by Lord Caitanya, Sanātana Gosvāmī, as a transcendental archaeologist, uncovered all the places where Kṛṣṇa had engaged in His pastimes 5,000 years ago in Vṛndāvana, such as the Govardhana Hill and the area of the *rāsa* dance. With the other Gosvāmīs, Sanātana helped construct seven important temples in

Vṛndāvana for the worship of Lord Kṛṣṇa in the land where Kṛṣṇa appeared. Sometimes writing, sometimes dancing and chanting by the River Yamunā, always feeling the ecstasy of Kṛṣṇa's love for the *gopīs* and faithfully carrying out the orders of Lord Caitanya, the Gosvāmīs hardly slept at all—perhaps one or two hours a night—and they lived very austerely; but they were always feeling great happiness in executing devotional service to the Lord. Although Sanātana had given up an exalted position, he considered it insignificant, and he felt no remorse, for he had gained the great treasure of love of God.

Thus Sanātana Gosvāmī, formerly an aristocratic minister of a materialistic ruler, became a humble servant of the Supreme Personality of Godhead and a confidential assistant in Lord Caitanya's mission of distributing love of Godhead to the fallen souls of this age. *Teachings of Lord Caitanya* describes him as follows: "Sanātana Gosvāmī was a great devotee of the Lord, and he was directly instructed to spread the cult of *bhakti* by writing many books. His brother, Rūpa Gosvāmī, was also a minister in the government, but both of them gave up their lucrative government service and became mendicants to serve the Supreme Lord. Within their hearts they were full of transcendental loving service, but externally they were just like ordinary mendicants with a great liking for the cowherd boy of Vṛndāvana (Kṛṣṇa). Sanātana Gosvāmī was very dear to all pure devotees of his time."

III. Yoga, Karma and Reincarnation

Experience of Karma-Yoga (I)

Issue No. I, 1966

Karma means "material activities subjected to reaction." *Karma* binds us with each act. *Yoga* means "that which connects, links with the Supreme." *Yoga* is the process of self-liberation. These two words combine in a single process called *karma-yoga* which is the seeking-and-attainment of self-realization (liberation) through action.

Everyone has to act. According to Lord Kṛṣṇa:

> Everyone is forced to act helplessly according to one's acquired qualities of the modes of material nature, and thus nobody can refrain from doing something, not even for a moment.
>
> *(Bg. 3.5)*

Everyone has to do something, but by the grace of Kṛṣṇa we can be freed from that place where every action is followed by bondage. If a man is fixed in God consciousness, he does not engage himself in action that is binding, like excessive food indulgence, drug addiction or sexual promiscuity. For instance, no Kṛṣṇa conscious man would pursue sexual encounters, for once he moves into such activities, misery will claim him, bound as he is to his actions. Without *yoga, karma* is entangling, for action quickly becomes binding, and one suffers the good or bad consequences. The lives of such *karmis* lead either to aimless chaotic activity on the phenomenal level or directly to hell. The real way out of the action-nightmare is *karma-yoga.* In the *Bhagavad-gītā* Kṛṣṇa says:

> . . . .if a sincere person tries to control the sense organs and begins *karma-yoga* in Kṛṣṇa consciousness, without being attached, he is far better.
>
> *(Bg. 3.7)*

He is "far better," he is "sorrowless" because he does not suffer any consequences to his actions.

A simple way to begin *Karma-yoga* is to give all you earn to Kṛṣṇa. That is a start. It releases you at once. If all you earn goes to Kṛṣṇa, you are saved from a whole area of materialism. Let the world know that any money coming into your hand is going to Kṛṣṇa, and you are freed from great danger.

In *karma-yoga,* when you are working for Kṛṣṇa, you can do your office tasks, speak to people about business and do whatever your duty happens to be, for it all becomes part of your single aim: to return to God. The more God conscious you become, the more effectively you can function. Whereas formerly you found yourself trapped, once you take to *karma-yoga* and sacrifice every act for Kṛṣṇa, your main objective is no longer to get out of trouble but to love God. Then no powerful mundane personality will awe or frighten you. You can do your work well and unafraid because you work unattached. And your work goes well.

How can you control your sense organs? In the matter of techniques, sincerity is what is needed. In spiritual effort, when you try hard, you succeed. As you work, chant the name of God: *Hare Kṛṣṇa Hare Kṛṣṇa, Kṛṣṇa Kṛṣṇa, Hare Hare.* This means "Hail God," please accept me, be associated with my humble dealings on Your behalf.

Sitting at your desk, waiting for the elevator, answering the phone–make these moments moments of decision and re-affirm your purpose. Are you a *karma-yogī?* Then don't let your senses wander! Remember: *Why have you come here? Why are you working? Why are you living? Who do you love?* Make all your answers Kṛṣṇa. Control is gained by being thoughtful of your position. This thoughtfulness is the beginning of God consciousness. Wherever you are, God offers this consciousness, and you must not fail to grasp it. Aim your heart to this end. When the crowd goes mad, as so often happens, you will not be swept away–if you remember Kṛṣṇa. Remember, you are in control only because Kṛṣṇa is controlling. Receive His rays. That is real control. Work for Him.

This is not a punishing technique. Punishments are dealt by the material nature. According to the *Bhagavad-gītā* we are in these bodies because we desired to have sensual enjoyment and because we more or less hate God.

> All beings are born to delusion, O Bhārata (Arjuna), overcome by the dualities which arise from wish and hate, O conqueror of the foe (Arjuna).
>
> (*Bg.* 7.27)

The material world is a prison. Factories are producing artificially needed items and offices are producing artificially created services at the great cost of daily brute labor. The *karma-yogī*, forced by his original desire into one of three modes of material nature (goodness, passion, ignorance), receives, by way of his control and sacrifice, a sublime touch unknown to the ordinary fruitive worker. He is a tiny speck of God; he realizes this and takes it seriously. In the presence of the Supreme he asks for the touch of association, and nothing more. The advanced form of *karma-yoga* is called *bhakti-yoga,* namely "devotional service to God." As he serves God with his body, words and intelligence, guided by the principles of the revealed scriptures, the *karma* or *bhakti-yogī* develops a personal, individual relationship with the Supreme. He works not for his own gain, nor for a formless impersonal concept, but for the Supreme revealed Lord, and the actuality of his position is that he feels the touch of the Supreme.

This process leads to Kṛṣṇa. It is a question of realizing the Godhead. If God is realized only through His grace, we should at least try to see that this grace is open to us also. As stated in the *Śrīmad-Bhāgavatam,* we are bewildered by the Lord:

> No one can understand, O Lord, your transcendental pastimes which appear to be human, and is misleading. It is bewildering of course, that you, O Soul of the Universe, have to work although inactive, have to take birth although unborn and are the vital force. Still You Yourself descend amongst the animals, men, sages, and aquatics. They are verily bewildered.

When you work for God, the wages are the chance of understanding Him. Our brains are tiny. To realize the personal God is most difficult. We have His word (scripture), His form (Śrī Kṛṣṇa), His devotees (Lord Caitanya and the disciplic succession), and today, most easily available and life-saving, His holy name for chanting. But we are nonetheless ignorant and covered up by contamination. Without grace, the human brain can conjecture about God for eternity and get nowhere. Nonsense babbling is endless, fools crowd the streets and governments, waves of illusion throw us around like flies. Therefore we must be wary and take shelter of the Supreme Lord. Faced with this material nature, and yet in sight of divine light, the *karma-yogī* says, "Let me work for Him. God is a person, not like me, but yet like me. Let me do His work here. Since I must act, let my actions be for Him. I am nonsense, but He is the true reality of which everything on earth is a perverted reflection."

A *karma-yogī* does not lose heart. He is not staggered or made "punchy" by labor. There is no taste of dread despair in his labor, nor the terror of the abyss, nor the wholesale nausea over having to live, nor the mad fear of Yamarāj, the demigod of Death. At worst, when the path gets very hard, the *karma-yogī* does what he can, and beyond that point the Supreme provides. The Lord, as revealed in the *Bhagavad-gītā,* has promised protection and deliverance to such a devotee:

> Come to Me alone for shelter. Be not grieved, for I shall release thee from all evils. (*Bg.* 18.66)

Karma yoga is the fulfilling of His promise in reciprocal love, through the energy of His work.

Experience of Karma-Yoga (II)

Issue No. 2, 1966

In the few minutes before 9 A.M. the office *karmīs* are rushing to each other for idle talk. Pray that you will have no business with anyone who will divert you from those thoughts that lead like arrows back to home, back to Godhead. The work begins, and hopefully the chant is in everything and everything is in the chant. *Hare Krishna, Hare Krishna, Krishna Krishna, Hare Hare, Hare Rama, Hare Rama, Rama Rama, Hare Hare. Karma-yoga* is not only a matter of the paycheck going to Kṛṣṇa and not for the sense gratification of the worker. It has to be done favorably. (The Lord doesn't need your *karma-yoga* at the office; your joy in the morning doesn't sustain Him, nor do you cause the planets to float in space. But your faith and devotion please Him: "My devotee is dear to Me," (*Bg.* 12.14). You must establish a moment to moment link with the Supreme. Therefore the practice of penances in mind, speech and body is prescribed, and we shall see why.

The *Gītā* declares purity, uprightness, continence and non-violence to be the penance of the body. "The utterance of words which give no offense, which are truthful, pleasant and beneficial" is said to be the penance of speech. Serenity of mind, gentleness, silence, self control and purity of mind is called the penance of the mind. (*Bg.* 17. 14-16) These penances, performed without expecting reward, put one in the nature of goodness. Goodness is the level from which we can most easily progress to transcendence. If you are shackled to the illusion of nonsense talk, or if you are gambling with co-workers on the outcome of sports, and "killing time" whenever possible, then you are not likely to be performing actions acceptable as *yoga* (toward union with God). Be absorbed. The work is the medium. "Hard to understand is the way of works." (*Bg.* 4.17)

When Kṛṣṇa consciousness is no longer mere sentiment or spiritual recreation, and when your love for Kṛṣṇa is no longer merely a good-time, speculative, "fair-weather" friendship–this will occur in the fire of work. To the limited eye, what is going on in the office is simply the action of a fruitive worker engaged in mundane turmoil. The boss is saying he is God, and he is applying the full force of his authority upon the workers and clerks. Of course in some instances, the boss-worker relationship is running smoothly. Whether he is favored or oppressed by his boss does not concern the *karma-yogī;* he is really not concerned one way or the other with the prevailing mundane temperament. It is part of a *karma-yogī's* skill that he is able to perform work expertly. He maintains an even temperament under fire, and by a constant activity of work he avoids all embarrassment. To the *karma-yogī,* this desk, these drawers, these forms and files are the paraphernalia of a sacrifice. He is practicing celibacy, and concentration, and meditation and worship. "He who is trained in the way of works . . . he is not trained by works, though he works." (*Bg.* 5.7)

The true *yoga* of the *Bhagavad-gītā,* in which one takes a firm seat covered with sacred grass, a deerskin and a cloth one over the other, in a solitary place, for the purpose of the purification of the soul, is a way leading to the same realization (love of Kṛṣṇa) for which the *karma-yogī,* in his shirt, pants and neck-tie, is ever intent on. In the Chapter of the True Yoga, the Lord describes him at his task:

> "Serene and fearless, firm in the vow of celibacy, subdued in mind, let him sit, his mind turned to Me and intent on Me alone." (*Bg.* 6.14)

"With the heart undismayed," and disconnected from union with pain, the *karma-yogī* makes his hymn to Kṛṣṇa while fully engaged in the tasks of the office. Because he is using the body, which includes the mind, to perform these tasks, his senses are occupied with the sense objects in sacrifice: by offering each act to God, he "is not touched by sin, even as a lotus leaf (is untouched) by water." *(Bg.* 5.10) Even in the beginning stages, a sincere devotee can practice such work in relaxation and with no uneasy sense of being scrutinized by the world. The devotee is confident that everything belongs to Kṛṣṇa. Fixed in the assured protection of the Supreme Lord, there is no worldly power that can drag him down. The medium of work is a constant purification, a form of penance, and its end-aim is to achieve love through his service. As long as he works, he can't go wrong.

Karma-yoga has been described by His Divine Grace A.C. Bhaktivedanta Swami Prabhupāda as *yoga* for those who are addicted to work and activity; in this sense, it is being practiced by the man who "can't stop" fruitive work itself, but who is enlightened enough to dovetail his labor with the pleasure of the Supreme. This description of *karma-yoga* places it in a transitional stage between material and spiritual life. The direct, *karma*-less service is called *bhakti-yoga,* or devotional service. *Bhakti* is loving service of man to the Supreme Lord; such a devotee in *bhakti* performs only the Lord's work in the world, as a direct, confidential servant, who is compact in love for his influential Master. We can understand that the *karma-yogī* is on the path to *bhakti.* He (the *karma-yogī*) is working behind enemy lines (with the *karmīs*) and waiting for the day when the

Supreme Lord will bring him closer into confidence. Man cannot presume to speed up his approach to God. He can't take Kṛṣṇa by "storming" His abode. A man in *karma-yoga* turns over his work to the Supreme Personality, Kṛṣṇa, Who is realized within his heart–where he perceives that he himself is part of God. And it is also realized personally in that ecstatic inconceivable name of Kṛṣṇa found kindly dancing on the *karma-yogī's* tongue when saying the *maha-mantra: Hare Kṛṣṇa, Hare Kṛṣṇa, Kṛṣṇa Kṛṣṇa, Hare Hare, Hare Rāma, Hare Rāma, Rāma Rāma, Hare Hare.* Average workers who are trapped in the material (non-spiritual) concept of work believe that they themselves are matter, and the work is matter, and so they slug it out–one piece of matter against another–for a fixed rate of pay, for a certain number of hours a day. They will make demands for reduced hours and more pay and better lighting, but they make no demand for *karma-yoga,* the only process which can relieve them from hopeless labor.

As a fellow worker, we humbly invite each and every employee at any job whatsoever to take to this process of dovetailing with God consciousness in action. The principles of *karma-yoga* are sound. The results are definite and immeasurably good. Try it whole-heartedly for one week. Chant the Holy Name all day and sing it at lunch hour, and chant yourself to sleep at night. See for yourself. No one will have to tell you.

The Deliverance of the Fallen

July/August, 1967

Mercy is kindness delivered from the Supreme Power. People are partaking of mercy whether they acknowledge it or not; Krishna's Mercy shines into all the acts of the universe.

Our position as living entities is that we have sensual bodies. According to Vedic wisdom we have these bodies because we wanted them:

> "All beings are born to delusion, Bharata, overcome by the dualities which arise from wish and hate, O conquerer of the foe."
>
> (7/27 Bhagavad Gita)

In delusion, hating God, we thought we could better enjoy ourselves as lords of matter–and so, at our wish, we have been put into these bodies which are bound by the three-fold miseries (those arising from the body and mind, those inflicted by other living entities, and those inflicted by Nature). Chief among these are the miseries of birth, death, old age and disease. And yet this very state of temporal life, beset with unavoidable misery, is revealed, on thoughtful examination, to be the mercy of the Supreme.

In our original constitutional position we are infinitesimal fragments of the Supreme Consciousness:

> "The living entities are eternally fragmental parts of Me. They are dragging on in a bitter struggle for existence in the material Nature, with the six senses including mind."
>
> (15/7 Bhagavad Gita)

We cannot lose this status, even entangled in the delusions that led to our desiring the perishable body, we cannot lose our eternal part and parcel constitution. Being put into material bodies is God's mercy, and being given the chance to return to Him is also His mercy. This constantly radiating mercy of the Lord is without cause. We are His fragmental portions and He is compassionate toward us, even if we make ourselves strangers and enemies to Him.

His mercy is clearly seen in the Sanskrit word *Maya.* Maya means "what is not." It also has a second meaning--"God's grace". It works this way: Maya is the illusory energy, the material world. Maya is what is perishable, what we living entities take as the real and the all-in-all. These 60 to 100 years of life, the family ties, the working hard for a living, the struggle to get on, the struggle to enjoy with mind and body, the attachment to matter as the final substance—these temporal things work as illusion when we think of them as permanent. In other words, when we forget God and look on the world without Him, we are in illusion. When we do not transcend this world, that is Maya.

But Maya is also "God's grace." If we want illusion, it is granted to us. God has the power to smash us into powder for being disobedient sons, but as we go on, forgetful of Him, constructing our Times Squares of the world and living for the 'enjoyment' of our blunt, misery-bound senses, the Supreme Lord gives us—does not deny us—this freedom for mischievous self-damage. He has shown us the approach to Himself—to Him Who is defined as *Sat-Chit-Ananda Vigraha,* eternity, knowledge and bliss in their fullness—and we choose instead to mate and sleep, to defend and eat alone. And for this revolt we are given more mercy; we are given more and more of what we want, even if what we want is the lower animal status, or hell. And so the transmigration of the eternal individual soul progresses.

If we live demoniac lives we are granted more of the same, that is, mercy. The godly rise and reach His abode. The demons refute their eternal portion and come back to this world to enjoy the pangs of duality (i.e. pleasure and pain, life and death, heat and cold, etc.) If you study it, you can see that the world is all-merciful: whoever wants problems, has them. The Lord has granted you the facilities to spend your life as you wish. You have His instruction and can lift yourself or be your own enemy. In the Bhagavad Gita Sri Krishna states:

> "Fixing thy thought on Me, thou shalt, by My grace, cross over all difficulties; but if, from self-conceit, thou wilt not listen, thou shalt perish."
>
> (18/58 Bhagavad Gita)

After many births a person may find himself disillusioned with Maya and the pleasures of the body, or if he is so fortunate he may have gained some devotion toward the transcendental Lord of all life; and such a person may desire to go back to Home, back to Godhead where there is real pleasure in association with Krishna.

> "Those men of virtuous deeds in whom sin has come to an end, freed from the delusion of dualities, worship Me steadfast in their vows."
>
> (7/28 Bhagavad Gita)

To live for the pleasure of the merciful Lord is called devotional service. Everything is God's; the flowers, the grains, the morning, the opportunity contained in a human life, *everything* goes back to Him, just as the streaming sunlight, which penetrates every corner of darkness, can be followed back to it's source in the sun. Life in devotional service is the offering of the consciousness in everything we do, as a gift to Krishna. We are assured in the Bhagavad Gita that He will accept our gesture.

> "Whosoever offers to Me with devotion a leaf, a flower, a fruit, or water, that offering of love, of the pure of heart I accept."
>
> (9/26 Bhagavad Gita)

When we offer our food to the Lord that is called *prasadam*, which in Sanskrit means "mercy". When we offer our speech, our bodily acts and our human consciousness, this is also devotional service, and releases us from the bondage of birth and death and brings inner peace and equipoise to all our hours. This service is the secret of yoga, described as the "plus" to life or the link with Godhead. Once it is attained, one never comes back to the perishable and sorrowful. This is confirmed by scriptures:

> "Achieving that transcendental devotional service a man becomes perfect, immortal and peaceful."
>
> (Narada Bhaktisutra, Code 4)
>
> "Great souls who are engaged in devotional service and attain the Supreme Lord do not again come back to this miserable material conditional life."
>
> (8/15 Bhagavad Gita)

But how does this state come about? If, admittedly, long long ago we chose these bodies for sensual enjoyment, in ignorance—how does enlightenment come about? That too, is Krishna's mercy. We don't grow wise automatically. Whenever anyone takes a step away from dullness or ignorance, that is a manifestation of His mercy. That is why a yogi or a devotee is called a *fortunate* man. Every individual life is an opportunity for one to realize his actual goal and purpose—those who don't miss the opportunity are receiving the mercy of the Lord. Swami Bhaktivedanta writes:

> "Such pure devotional service of the Lord cannot be achieved without the mercy of the pure devotee or the bona fide Spiritual Master, and the Supreme Lord Himself. If somebody is fortunate enough to find a pure devotee for his Spiritual Master, then that Spiritual Master by his causeless

mercy imparts the knowledge of pure devotional service . . . only by the combined mercy of the Supreme Lord and the Spiritual Master."

(from the Purport to Code 8, Narada Bhaktisutra)

The present age is called Kali Yuga, a period of 432,000 years symptomized by quarrel and disorder. Evidence of Kali Yuga is seen in people's turning away from God. In our own country, the USA, and in this city of New York, we can see the proud citadel of Maya in its arrogant, temporal victory. Witness the flags and towers of uptown buildings dedicated completely to the 80-100-year life span of economics, politics and sense pleasure. The insidious illusion and perversion of mass advertising has dulled millions into daily acceptance of a nightmarish war on the integrity of the human mind. Add to this the administrative cheating, the promotion of political wars, the disillusionment of the nonconformists and the bewilderment of the drug-takers—and you have perfect ingredients for Kali Yuga. And it is supposed to get worse.

Simultaneously, we are witnessing the mercy of A.C. Bhaktivedanta Swami's Samkirtan movement. Srila Prabhupada is in the line of disciplic succession from Lord Chaitanya, Who originated the movement of chanting the Lord's Holy Name 500 years ago in India. Chaitanya's movement is the magnanimous light of Supreme mercy shining through the death-fog of Kali Yuga. Lord Chaitanya offers to all Mankind the invitation to sing God's Name, and join with Him in our original association.

Even an intelligent man is pelleted and polluted by the constant force of mass media; and so it grows increasingly difficult for him to see his real obligations in this life. But we do have obligations. We all have the human form of life and our single purpose should be to realize ourselves and to discover the ultimate goal for which we are living. That goal is Krishna.

By chanting God's Name in the age of Kali Yuga, The Lord is conveniently available to everyone—through the Mercy of Lord Chaitanya. A.C. Bhaktivedanta Swami writes:

"Lord Chaitanya is especially merciful to the innocent, unsophisticated person. His name is Patitapavana, or the deliverer of the most fallen conditioned soul."

(from *Teachings of Lord Chaitanya*)

Lord Chaitanya is offering every man, woman and child this gift: simply chant the Lord's Name, and you will see that with this chanting, comes everything else truly desired, the blessing of the full moon of pleasure and peace. Through the magnanimity of Lord Chaitanya what is available is the greatest gift—Love of Godhead, and it is simply handed over. This strong, helping hand of Lord

Chaitanya is so direct that many may miss it; they think their entanglement and the world's entanglement to be so complicated that any direct solution is a hoax. But nothing is too complicated for God. Nor do those who have seriously tried the chant speak of it except in terms of strength and ecstasy and constant revivification, as though they have drunk of a secret, magic water from an eternal source.

The people who have taken to chanting in this age are fortunately released from all desires and impure hankerings even while moving in the midst of materialistic insanity. Those who are constantly chanting the Lord's Name are not troubled by impersonal conceptions of void or atheism, nor do they foolishly think themselves God. It is said that Krishna Himself takes control of such surrendered souls and brings them further to Himself, the All-Attractive. In the Vedic scripture Srimad Bhagawatam, set down 5000 years ago, it is stated:

> "In this age of Kali, people who are endowed with sufficient brain substance worship the Lord, Who is accompanied by His associates, by performance of Samkirtan Yajna (Sacrifice by chanting the Holy Name.)"
>
> (Srimad Bhagawatam 1st canto)

Again, note that the gift is "endowed." Mercy is operating. We begin to chant and the highest reciprocation between the Supreme Lord and His infinitesimal sparks is at once established and grows ever greater, more intimate, and more pure. Instead of spending our time engrossed in the senses and the temporal world, we are singing His Name; and as we sing we realize that He is the giver of all abilities, even the mis-spent. Then, how fortunate to be singing the Name of the Source while at the Feet of the Source itself! The Lord has endowed His Name with His full presence. Hare Krishna, Hare Rama is a sound incarnation. It is not an ordinary thing. It is not a laborious exercise. Nor is the chant a secret guarded by a few priests. In this age of severely limited concentration, Samkirtan is the auspicious way to God. Here indeed is the highest mercy for the living entities.

Liberation at Last

January/February, 1970

Recently I spoke to an acquaintance who is practicing "meditation" and I asked him the goal of his practice. The answer was, "Liberation. To merge with the one." Expressions such as "annihilation of the ego" and "merging with the Supreme" are commonly passed back and forth in this age of the widely attended Yoga and meditation class. Regarding liberation, one significant question is, "What is liberation?" And also, we want to know–what are the chances of a person actually gaining liberation? For answers, we best go to the source of the very concept of liberation and the place where all its techniques are elaborately and carefully taught; that is, the scriptural literature of India, called the *Vedas.* Yoga technique and meditation are given in gist in the *Bhagavad-gītā,* spoken by Lord Kṛṣṇa, the Personality of Godhead, and expounded further in the *Śrīmad-Bhāgavatam* which is considered the postgraduate study of the *Bhagavad-gītā.*

Liberation generally refers to freedom from the bodily concept of life. But unless there is positive, non-bodily activity or spiritual activity, then liberation is a merely theoretical, lip-service liberation. To sit in a posture of meditation and think, "I am moving the moon, I am moving the sun, I am moving the stars," and then 10 minutes later to be dictated to by the tongue–"I must have a cigarette"–is not liberation; nor at the time of death can such a "yogi" be expected to be liberated to the spiritual sky. Without practical devotional service to Śrī Kṛṣṇa, Giver of Liberation, the idea of liberation is just a negative concept of material life. The Vedic literature describes four material categories of civilized life, and liberation is among them. The first is religiousness. This means to perform sacrifice, churchgoing or pious acts with the aim of being rewarded by promotion to a heavenly material planet. The aim behind such acts is personal gratification; by being religious I will be rewarded. It is noted by A.C. Bhaktivedanta Swami in the *Śrīmad-Bhāgavatam* that nowadays the church, mosque or temple is an empty place because the people believe that they can get their desired economic ends without making prayers to God. Therefore, the second material activity of civilized persons is economic development–building, making money, doing business. The third activity is sense gratification culminating in sex life. In fact, sex life is the essential background for the first two material activities. The fourth, *mukti* or liberation, is a little different, although it is a material activity. After being frustrated by all the material activities and seeing that either failure or success are really failure due to the disadvantages of birth, death, disease and old age, a person desires liberation. He desires to become One with the Supreme. He is too bitter with all his experiences to be happy in material life. But in itself this is only a negative concept. By such liberation he thinks he wants to lose the individuality which has caused him so much pain, and instead, to merge with the Oneness of spiritual existence.

The background for understanding liberation starts with gaining true identity of the self. In the beginning stages it expresses itself in the desire to be One with the Spirit. This is called *Brahman* realization. If someone is actually realized in *Brahman* that is a great thing. It is called *Brahma-bhuta* stage, and it is characterized by joyfulness. The joyfulness is due to understanding that, "I am not this body." This is carefully described by Lord Kṛṣṇa in the Second Chapter of the *Bhagavad-gītā.* The living entity is there declared to be spirit-soul, or *Brahman.* In the Third Chapter Lord Kṛṣṇa reveals that for full realization of *Brahman,* you have to work in *Brahman. Bhagavad-gītā* (3/5) says, "Nobody can refrain from doing something, not even for a moment." And in his Purport to that verse, A.C. Bhaktivedanta Swami writes, "This is not a question of embodied life; it is the nature of the soul to be always active. The proof is that without the presence of the spiritual soul there is no movement of the material body. The body is only a dead vehicle to be worked by the spirit soul and therefore it is the nature of the soul itself to be always active, and cannot stop even for a moment. The spirit soul has to be engaged in the good work of Kṛṣṇa consciousness, otherwise it will be engaged in occupations dictated by the illusory energy." When one realizes "I am *Brahman,*" that means he has no death, just like Kṛṣṇa, the Supreme *Brahman.* This is a joyful position, "I am not this perishable body, that is not my self, I am spirit soul." That is all well and good, but then, what do I do? It is not that the liberated state is without activities. This question was asked by Sanātana Gosvāmī, the learned disciple of Lord Caitanya: "You have said that I am already liberated, now what are my duties in the liberated state?" The impersonalists, however, do not like to take up the devotional service path; they are simply desirous of merging into the One, described as the *Brahma-jyoti* effulgence. That destination is explained in the *Gītā. Brahma-jyoti* is not material, it is the spiritual effulgence coming from the Body of Śrī Kṛṣṇa; it is eternal spiritual light. This light illumines the spiritual world and the naturally dark material world is lit by its reflection. And to merge in this light is the goal of the impersonal liberation. A.C. Bhaktivedanta Swami, who is a fully realized devotee of the Personality of Godhead, states the disadvantages of aiming at the *Brahma-jyoti* as the topmost goal: "In the *Brahma-jyoti* the spirit souls on account of their impersonal views are devoid of a body, exactly as here in *māyā* there are ghosts who are devoid of any gross bodies. The ghost, being devoid of a body, suffers terribly because he is unable to satisfy his senses. The spirit souls in the *Brahma-jyoti,* although they have no desire for sense gratification, feel inconvenience like the ghost; and they fall down again in *māyā's* atmosphere and develop a material body. In the *Bhāgavatam* therefore it is said that intelligence of persons who are impersonalists and do not develop the dormant devotional attitude is not pure; because for want of a spiritual body, they come down again to the material world. In the *Bhāgavad-gītā* it is clearly said by the Lord that the only way of not coming back to the material world is to be promoted to the spiritual planets. For the impersonalists there is no such assurance of not falling down in the whole Vedic literature. The conclusion is that without developing the spiritual body and without being situated on one of the spiritual planets, the so-called liberation is also illusion, or it is not complete. A spirit-soul who falls down from the *Brahma-jyoti* to the Kingdom of *māyā* may have a chance of associating with a pure devotee, and then he may be elevated to the spiritual planets of Vaikuṇṭha or to the Goloka Vṛndāvana. From the *Brahma-jyoti* there is no direct promotion to the spiritual planets."

In the *Śrīmad-Bhāgavatam,* many questions regarding liberation are asked by Devahūti the mother of the incarnation of Godhead Kapiladeva. Lord Kapila spoke the Sāṅkhya philosophy whereby the material entanglement is analyzed and found to be not the true identity of the spirit soul. Lord Kapila describes to His mother that liberation from material entanglement can be considered in three different ways. As expounded by philosophers like Lord Buddha it is annihilation or cessation of material existence altogether; and after the cessation of material existence there is void. Then another concept, according to the Śankarite school, is that the material existence is false, and therefore one has to transfer oneself into the spiritual existence and that is not void but spiritual existence without variegatedness. This is the *Brahma-jyoti.* Devahūti, however, asks not only for freedom from matter, not only to be situated in the spiritual existence without variegatedness, but to be always associated with the Supreme Personality of Godhead. As expounded by Kapiladeva this is actually the goal of the Yoga system. Some target at impersonal *Brahman,* some at the *Paramātma* realization and some aim directly at the Supreme Personality of Godhead. By understanding the Supreme Personality of Godhead, all other features including His different energies and manifestations become understood. As A.C. Bhaktivedanta Swami once said, "When you get to the top, everything is included." This *Bhakti-yoga* is explained in *Bhagavad-gītā* where it is said that after many, many births of understanding, when one comes to understand that Vāsudeva the Supreme Personality of Godhead is everything, he is a Mahātmā, a great soul—and that is very rare. It is further explained in *Bhāgavatam* that the Lord is called Hṛṣīkeśa, the Master of the senses. The senses and mind are naturally inclined to work, but when they are materially contaminated they work for some material benefit or for the service of the demigods, but actually they are meant for serving the Supreme Personality of Godhead. A.C. Bhaktivedanta Swami writes to this point in *Bhāgavatam:* "When the senses, without any reason, without any material profit and without any selfish motive, are engaged in the service of the Supreme Personality of Godhead, that is devotional service and that service spirit is far, far better than salvation (*mukti*). *Bhakti*, then, begins after liberation. Without being liberated nobody can engage the senses in the service of the Lord. When the senses are engaged either in material activities or by Vedic injunction, it is for a motive of personal gratification, but when the same senses are engaged in the service of the Lord, there is no motive, and that is the natural, original inclination of the mind. When the mind is not deviated but fully engaged in Kṛṣṇa consciousness for devotional service of the Supreme Person, that is beyond the most aspired after liberation from material encagement."

There is a nice example regarding liberation in the case of a man who is confined to bed with a fever. His fever is compared to material activities. To bring down the high temperature of the fever can be accomplished by *Brahman* realization. Having brought the fever down, the man may be still lying in bed, in convalescence. Of course, full health is not enjoyed until he can get up from the bed and resume his normal activities. Those who are impersonalists or *māyāvādīs,* however, do not desire to get up from the bed of convalescence, but are content simply that their fever has gone down. They are described as afraid that because activities in the feverish state were so bitter, painful, if they take up activities again, it will be painful again. In this way the impersonalists fail to take up transcendental loving service of the Personality of Godhead in individual spiritual form. Refusing to take up full healthy activities, one puts himself in the dangerous position of facing a relapse in health; the patient who doesn't resume his normal activities cannot expect to stay fixed in inactive convalescence, rather he will fall ill again. It is commonly experienced that those *sannyāsīs* or *svāmīs* of the impersonalist path, after declaring "all is false" but failing to take on the activities of real liberation, fall down to the material platform and become engaged sometimes in humanitarianism and material welfare work, opening hospitals, etc. For failing to take on the greatest service, preaching Kṛṣṇa consciousness to those in the clutches of illusory matter, the impersonalist *svāmī* falls back into feverish material activities. The failure is his neglect of the Lotus Feet of the Supreme Personality of Godhead, called *Mukunda,* the Giver of Liberation.

The endeavor to get liberation from the material encagement is automatically served in devotional service. A devotee doesn't have to try separately for liberation. Śrī Bilvamaṅgala explains, "If I have unflinching devotion unto the Lotus Feet of the Supreme Lord, then *mukti* or liberation serves me as my maid servant." Liberation is no problem at all. The impersonalists are after *mukti* and they undergo severe penances and austerities to attain it, but the *bhakta* passes liberation by engaging his senses and especially chanting Hare Kṛṣṇa, Hare Kṛṣṇa, Kṛṣṇa Kṛṣṇa, Hare Hare/Hare Rāma, Hare Rāma, Rāma Rāma, Hare Hare and accepting the remnants of foodstuff offered to the Personality of Godhead. As soon as the senses are controlled in the tongue, the other senses follow automatically and the perfection of the Yoga principle is there. The devotee Prabhānanda says that for a devotee sense control is as easy as anything, the pleasures of gorgeous life and fabulous duration on the upper planets is just phantasmagoria, and the pleasure of merging into the Supreme is seen as hellish. Lord Kapila states before His mother: "A pure devotee who is attached in the activities of devotional service and always engaged in the service of the Lotus Feet of the Lord does not ever desire to become One with Him. Such devotees are unflinchingly engaged and always glorify the Pastimes of the Lord." Liberation becomes of no consequence and is realized as a material desire tainted with selfishness.

There are five kinds of liberation stated in the Vedic scriptures. One is to become one with the Supreme Personality of Godhead or to forsake one's individuality and to merge into the supreme spirit. A devotee never accepts such kind of liberation. The other four kinds of liberation are: to be promoted into the same planet as the Supreme Lord, to achieve the same opulence as the Lord, to associate personally with the Supreme Lord, and to attain the same bodily feature as the Supreme Lord. The pure devotee does not aspire to any of the five kinds of liberation, and especially he rejects the prospect of merging with the impersonal effulgence of the Supreme Personality of Godhead as being hellish. A.C. Bhaktivedanta Swami Prabhupāda writes in the *Bhāgavatam;* "Many so-called devotees say that we may worship the Supreme Personality of Godhead in the conditioned state but ultimately there is no personality, the Absolute Truth is impersonal. One can imagine a personal form of the impersonal for the time being and as soon as one becomes liberated, the worship is stopped—that is the theory. Actually, if the impersonalists merge into the Personal luster of the Supreme Person that is no different from His Personal Body, but that sort of oneness is not accepted by a devotee. The devotees are simply wanting to be fully engaged in reciprocatory loving devotional service."

Aside from its desirability, what are the chances of the meditators really attaining liberation? The answer is stated in the Twelfth Chapter of *Bhagavad-gītā:*

> He whose mind is fixed on My Personal Form, always engaged in worshiping Me with great and transcendental faith, is considered by Me to be most perfect. But those who fully worship the unmanifested, that which is beyond the perception of the senses, the all-pervading, inconceivable, fixed and immovable—the impersonal conception of the truth . . . at last achieve Me. For those whose minds are attached to the nonmanifested, impersonal feature of the Supreme Lord, advancement is very troublesome. To make progress in that unmanifested discipline is always difficult for those who are embodied.
>
> (12/2-5 *Bhagavad-gītā*)

Speaking as the Supreme Personality of Godhead, Lord Kapila, the incarnation of Lord Kṛṣṇa, makes clear that there is no salvation outside of direct reference to Lord Viṣṇu (Kṛṣṇa): "The terrible fear of death and birth can never be forsaken by anyone or by resorting to any other shelter than Myself, because I am the almighty Lord the Supreme Personality of Godhead, the original Source of all creation, and also the Supreme Soul of all souls."

One may try to understand the Absolute Truth by mental speculation or through the mystic Yoga process, but unless he comes to surrender his attempts cannot give him liberation. That is the conclusion of *Bhāgavatam.* Lord Brahmā prayed to the Lord: "They think they are liberated or one with God, but in spite of thinking in such a puffed-up way, their intelligence is not laudable." In spite of austerities, then, if there is no surrender unto the Personality of Godhead, the intelligence is understood to be not clear. The nondevotee transcendentalists can go to the brink of spiritual realization in *Brahman* realization, and they are suspended in the effulgence; but because they have no transcendental activities they fall down.

As for devotional activities, Lord Caitanya prescribed five items as the sum and substance of performing devotional service. These are: 1. to associate with devotees; 2. to read *Śrīmad-Bhāgavatam*; 3. to worship the Deities; 4. to chant the Holy Name; 5. to live in a holy place. As the perfect devotee, Lord Caitanya described His own desires, transcendental to the desire for liberation from the chain of birth and death: "O Almighty Lord, I have no desire for accumulating wealth nor have I any desire to enjoy beautiful women; neither do I want numbers of followers. What I want only is that I may have Your causeless devotional service in my life birth after birth."

Liberation does not mean to grow four heads and four arms, but to change the consciousness, to live in understanding. The bodily encagement means sense gratification, and when that is dissipated in favor of pleasing the transcendental senses of Kṛṣṇa, then liberation is there. Finally, the pure devotee never thinks that he is fit for liberation. He prays, "My dear Lord, I may be born anywhere, that does not matter; but let me be born as an ant in the house of a devotee." A pure devotee does not pray to the Lord for liberation from this material bondage. A.C. Bhaktivedanta Swami describes the mind of the devotee: "He thinks he is fit for being sent into the lowest region of all considering his past life, his mischievous and miscreant activities. Anyone in this material world must have committed so many misdeeds. If I am trying to become a devotee it does not mean I was 100% pious in my past life." Therefore the devotee is always conscious of his real position. He knows that only for the purpose of attaining his full surrender unto Kṛṣṇa, the Lord makes the suffering of the devotee shorter. Ultimately, even his attainment of the topmost spiritual planet, Kṛṣṇa-loka, is not desired by the devotee; he goes there but he does not desire it. His desire is simply to work in a service mood for Kṛṣṇa and Kṛṣṇa's devotees. Liberation then is not the goal of spiritual life, but it is an automatic by-product of devotional service. With that understanding we can achieve success.

How To Get Out of the Clutches of Māyā

August/September, 1970

The Sanskrit word *māyā* means that which is not. In other words, it is illusion. For example, if a servant of a king thinks that he is the king, that is illusion. Generally, it is the illusion of all human beings that they are the lords of all they survey. But the actual fact is that they are under the grip of strict laws. They are trying to exploit the resources of material nature, but are becoming more entangled in nature's complexities. Since this *māyā* is illusion, or unreality, it can be stopped simply by reviving the real, original nature of the human being. This is called Kṛṣṇa consciousness. According to the *Bhagavad-gītā,* the mistaken idea that we have of ourselves and of our environment makes it impossible for us to enjoy our real, eternal nature. Moreover, once into the predicament of being under illusion, it is very difficult to get out of it.

On hearing the description of our entanglement in *māyā's* clutches, one might well ask, "How did we ever get into such a complicated predicament in the first place?" Another fair question is, "Why should God put anyone into the illusion that he is something which he is not?" The third question to be answered is, "How can one actually get out of *māyā?"* We fall into *māyā* because we are forgetful of our real selves. His Divine Grace A.C. Bhaktivedanta Swami Prabhupāda has explained that it is not very important to trace out when this happened. When people hear of the kingdom of God and of the original nature, blissful, eternal and full of life, they ask, "If it were so nice, why would I leave?" The answer to the question of when we fell is there in the Vedic literature. Specifically, in the Seventh Chapter, twenty-seventh verse, of *Bhagavad-gītā,* it is stated that we are born into this material world of delusion when we are overcome by our desire to be God and by our hatred of Him. As for the time when we fell, it is untraceably long ago, so long that it is called a time immemorial. But more important than tracing out just when we fell is finding out how we can be rescued from our present fallen state. In other words, if one is now very poor, it is not important that he was once rich. Or if one says, "Once I had much butter," but now he does not have butter, the important thing is that now he has no butter. Similarly, we can observe that we are now in illusion.

Some may think that these statements are word jugglery. Often a person tells us, "Never mind spiritual consciousness. I am already completely liberated. Do not call this illusion–I am happy here." But let us examine the real nature of the material world, the kingdom of *māyā*.

Māyā means to live in this material world and to think that it is one's permanent place and that one can become happy here. Ask a person living in this *māyā*, "Are you happy?" and he may answer, "Yes, I am happy." But what is this happiness? Ask him further, "Do you like to grow old?"

"No," he'll answer.

Then, "Do you like disease?"

"No."

"Do you like to die?"

"No." Then where is happiness? As long as we have to suffer these very basic defects to life, there can be no happiness.

The way out of *māyā* is the process of self-realization. By understanding who we are and understanding our relationship to God, we can understand that we are in *māyā* and that it is no good. Self-realization and God-realization begin with dissatisfaction. When we are dissatisfied, then we can search out liberation in our original state. By finding out our true nature, we can become free from the miseries of *māyā*. But we must not think that we are happy in *māyā*. To accuse the transcendentalist or spiritualist of being morbid because of his extreme criticism of the material world and its attractions is false. Rather, it is morbid to think that this life, which leads only to death, is everything. It is morbid to think that one is enjoying his body and its sensual pleasures when every day one can see side by side a beautiful young girl and a decrepit old woman and observe how quickly the change takes place. It is morbid to try to squeeze pleasure out of the body, mistaking the body for the real self. To treat the body as the self is as foolish as to try to eat by putting foodstuffs in one's ear rather than one's mouth. We can see from common affairs or learn from the *Gītā* that we constantly change our body, but the real self exists eternally. The craziness of thinking that our eternal self is the temporary body is *māyā*. But because the majority of people are in *māyā* consciousness, this has become the standard of sanity in modern civilization. The proper use of the human form of life is to inquire with dissatisfaction about this state of suffering in *māyā*. Usually when someone is afflicted with a disease, he will say with a feeling of dull resignation, "All right, let me go to the doctor." But one who inquires, "Why do I have to suffer? Who am I? Why must I endure disease and old age?" is intelligent. When such a process of inquiry begins, the sincere, determined searcher finally ends with God.

These are not questions of mental exercise or philosophical speculation. Rather, the inquiries, "Who am I? What am I meant to do? Where do I go after death?" are questions that are dormant and natural in all living entities. These questions are asked by intelligent men, and the real answers to these inquiries satisfy the innermost need of the soul. Of course, one may ask such questions without sincerity, or one may ask them of someone who is not an authorized spiritual master, and so one may go on suffering birth after birth because it is very difficult to free oneself from the stringent laws of material nature. Therefore, among the qualifications of a devotee is gravity. One should listen seriously when questions about suffering in life are discussed, and one should not think that simply because one is young or intoxicated, there are actually no problems. The problems of birth, death, disease and old age cannot be done away with by medicine or technology or poetry or philosophy, nor should one think that one can become God and thus become free from material nature's stringent laws. Actually it is very simple: *māyā* is there because of our false consciousness. And it can be removed as soon as the consciousness is changed to reality. If a servant is trying to act as king, he will be frustrated because his real position is servant. But if he lives as a servant, he can enjoy all the facilities of his real position, without the anxieties of trying to be something he is not. Therefore, everyone should understand that this material life is a diseased state and that because we are diseased, we cannot enjoy. We must first become well. We must first get out of *māyā*. Anyone who is teaching a process whereby people can enjoy without changing from bodily consciousness to real or spiritual consciousness, Kṛṣṇa consciousness, is cheating, just as a doctor cheats if he tells an ailing patient, "Please get up and enjoy." No! The true doctor who has diagnosed an illness, says to the person, "You cannot enjoy now: you must lie in bed, take these medicines, and when you become well, then you can enjoy."

Māyā traps us by offering us allurements in the way of sensual pleasures and by confining us to designations of the ego. By surrender to Kṛṣṇa these attractions vanish before the superior attractions of true spiritual life. Of the sensual pleasures, the chief is sex life. The difficulty with sex life is that it necessitates trying to enjoy on the bodily platform, whereas our real nature is not satisfied by the sexual act, but is left unsatiated, just as a hungry man is left unsatisfied if one buys him expensive clothes or takes him to see a movie. Impetuously, madly, one thinks that he can become happy by sex life, but after repeated attempts, the complete satisfaction is still not attained. The satisfaction is only flickering. The *Śrīmad-Bhāgavatam* states that by engagement in illicit association with women a man loses the qualities of truthfulness, cleanliness, mercifulness, gravity, spiritual intelligence, shyness, austerity, fame, forgiveness, control of the mind and senses, and fortune. Even when a man has sex with his wife and decides to raise a family, he becomes trapped in a desire to maintain economic status and social prestige and to elevate the material standard of his family. In this way *māyā* manipulates a man by his attraction for sex and leads him away from all possibilities of taking to the path of self-realization and real eternal enjoyment. We must understand that although *māyā* is dictating, we are victimized only because of misuse of our own free will.

THE CALL OF KṚṢṆA

Opposed to *māyā's* dictation is the call of Kṛṣṇa, coming through the spiritual master or pure devotee. Kṛṣṇa appears in the form of scriptures and in the form of His instructions carried by pure devotees. The devotees always seek to call back the lost souls from the kingdom of *māyā* to where they can enjoy their real nature. The human being has wandered through many species of life—animal life, plant life, and all other lower forms of life—and in most forms of life one is unable to free himself from the experience of repeated miseries. The human form of life, however, is a special advantage for getting out of this entanglement. Therefore, it is imperative that we hear and take to a practical path before death comes.

The chief symptoms of the disease of *māyā* are desire for sex life and false identification. The ideas that one is an American or a Russian or a black man or a white man are designations that cover one's real self. Our real self is spirit soul, part and parcel of God. These other things are only the outer coverings and are not our ultimate identity. It is stated in the *Śrīmad-Bhāgavatam* that a person who thinks that he is his body, which is made of air and bile, or who thinks that the land of his birth is worshipable, is no better than a cow or an elephant. We will only be Americans or Russians for this one body, and at the time of death we do not know where we will go. To cling to that false identification is also *māyā*, or "that which is not." Rather, we should put our energies into finding our real, eternal nature, which continues from one body to another. Actually I do not even belong to the human race; it is only a temporary designation. I am now wearing a shirt and pants, but I do not think that my shirt and pants are my real self. When the shirt and pants wear out, then I get new ones. But my self will continue. Similarly, I am not my car when I drive in my car.

In forgetfulness of our real Kṛṣṇa consciousness, we are trying to enjoy in a false way in terms of bodily pleasure and false designation, and we do not find real happiness because we are without Kṛṣṇa, who is our true and dearmost friend. To understand that we are not the lords of all we survey, we do not need to inquire into scriptures. Simply by common affairs, anyone can see it. One may think that he is free, just as a cow on the end of a long rope with a ring in his nose may think himself free because he has a long rope, but eventually he sees that he is not free. When one comes to the conclusion that he is under the stringent laws of material nature, that he is in fact bound up by limiting conditions and limiting senses, and that he is not satisfied by any amount of sensual enjoyment, and when he can conclude that his position is temporary although he desires an eternally happy position, then he can seek out something greater, and he can inquire about God, the controller.

MISUSE OF FREE WILL

Let us examine the intents of the controller. Why is He putting the living entities under the stringent laws of material nature? Kṛṣṇa says that all the living entities who are struggling in the material nature are His parts and parcels. Therefore one might ask why He doesn't stop this struggle at once and simply bring the souls out of their illusion. The answer is that although the Supreme Lord is full of compassion for His parts and parcels, they are eternally individuals by His divine will, and thus each individual has a minute amount of free will. His free will is such that he can decide either to be in *māyā* or to be with Kṛṣṇa. Once he decides to be in *māyā*, his free will stops, and *māyā* acts upon him. For example, one can decide whether or not to put his finger in a flame, but once he puts his finger in the flame, the flame will act and burn him. That action of the flame is called the material nature. The individual spirit souls are just like Kṛṣṇa and are originally intended to be with Him in spiritual bliss, yet because they are small, they are prone to come under the jurisdiction of material nature. Kṛṣṇa Himself never comes under the influence of *māyā* because He is the controller of *māyā*. So why has He set up this material nature? Because the living entities desire it. The example is given of a child who sees her mother cooking in the kitchen and becomes envious of the mother's superior position. The child declares to the mother, "No, I will be the cook. I will be the cook." The mother, just out of a desire to quiet the child, may give her a toy kitchen set and let the child think that she is actually cooking. Another example is that when serious men are discussing something and a little child is in the room causing a disturbance, the child is put out of the room. Once the living entity becomes envious of God, then he is removed from His association and put into the material world where he himself can act as God. He must, however, come under the material laws. This is actually the reality under which we are all existing.

Influenced by *māyā*, we forget our real position. A perfect example of the total forgetfulness to which one may come when he is put under the spell of the illusory nature of God was displayed by the demigod Indra when he was cursed by his spiritual master to become a pig on earth due to acting licentiously in the heavenly planets. When Indra was thus degraded to take the body of a pig, he took up his piggish activities and soon lived on a farm with a she-pig and piglets. After some time, the spiritual master returned to retrieve Indra, but Indra as a pig refused to be liberated to his former grand position, thinking in delusion that he had so many responsibilities. He refused his spiritual master: "No. I cannot go to heaven. Why are you saying that I am Indra? I am not Indra. I am a pig. I have so many responsibilities; I cannot leave. I am happy. I have my wife. I have my piglets. I have my stools." This is the influence of *māyā*.

Although it seems to be a punishment, *māyā* also means God's grace. If someone does not want the topmost spiritual life, the opportunity to go back to Godhead, but instead desires to cultivate ignorance, then he is put under the agency of *māyā* so that he can try for happiness in the material world. The basic idea is that anyone who is born into a body has made a foolish choice; being born into the material world certifies one as a fool.

AFTER DISSATISFACTION

The signs of return to sanity are dissatisfaction and inquiry. Dissatisfaction refers to the realization that all is not well. Why must I grow old and diseased? Why must I die? After dissatisfaction comes the desire to inquire, to find a solution. The materialist is also seeking his solution to happiness, but his efforts are all patchwork. He tries to repair his body by going to a hospital, but soon the body will end. The real solution to bodily miseries is liberation from bodily existence. This spiritual knowledge solves things once and for all. When one realizes that this material world is useless to him, then he can come out of *māyā*. Everyone born into a body is in *māyā*, but by dissatisfaction and inquiry one may escape from *māyā's* clutches. The process to do this is God consciousness or self-realization. Therefore, the first step out of *māyā* is to realize that one is in *māyā*. This is not ignorance. This is intelligence. Ignorance is to think that one is living in reality within material life.

Śrīla Prabhupāda refers to the material world as the world of names. To a transcendentalist, buildings, machines, war, peace, politics and family are all just names, like the babble of waves at sea. The way out of *māyā* is not through mental efforts. In the *Bhagavad-gītā* it is stated by Kṛṣṇa, "My divine energy, *māyā*, is very difficult to surmount, but for one who has surrendered, it is very easy."

The way to get out of *māyā* is outlined by the Supreme Lord Himself in His incarnation as Kapiladeva. In the Third Canto of the *Śrīmad-Bhāgavatam*, Devahuti, the mother of Kapila, asks Him questions exactly to this point: "How can there be any freedom for the soul as long as the material nature acts on him and binds him?" The living entity may desire freedom from the contamination of matter, but he is not given release. Once he desires to come into the material world, then he is already conditioned by it, and he has no opportunity to get control of it. *Bhagavad-gītā* says that it is very difficult to get out of the clutches of material nature. Mental speculators, concocting in different ways, try to think that everything is void, that there is no God, and that even if there is a spiritual background of everything, it is impersonal. This speculation may go on, but actually it is very difficult to get out of the clutches of material nature. Devahūti asks, "One may speculate in many ways, but where is the chance of liberation as long as one is under the spell of material nature?" The answer is given in the *Bhagavad-gītā* that only one who has surrendered himself unto the lotus feet of the Supreme Lord can be freed from the clutches of *māyā*. When one gradually comes to the point of surrender, he can ask such an intelligent question: "How can one be liberated, how can one be in a pure state of spiritual existence, as long as he is strongly held by the modes of nature?" This is also an indication to the false meditators who artificially think that they are the Supreme Spirit and that they are controlling the activities of material nature. They may think, "Under my direction the sun is moving; under my direction the moon is rising," and they may think that they can become free by such meditation. But it is seen that three minutes after their meditation, they are immediately captured by the modes of material nature, and they become thirsty: "I want to smoke or drink." So they are under the strong grip of the material nature, although they are thinking that they are separated from the clutches of *māyā*. Such a person sometimes thinks that everything is void and that there are no sinful or pious activities. But actually these are just atheistic inventions. The truth is that unless a living entity surrenders unto the Supreme Personality of Godhead as instructed in the *Bhagavad-gītā*, there is no liberation or freedom from the clutches of matter. That is the transcendental fact.

When one misuses his free will and challenges, "Why shall Kṛṣṇa be the all-in-all? I am as good as Kṛṣṇa," then desire and envy of Kṛṣṇa bring about his material bondage. One may be a philosopher or a salvationist or a voidist and think that he is the Supreme and that he is everything, but as long as he has this desire or thinks that there is no God, the cause of his bondage remains, and there is no question of liberation.

SURRENDER UNTO KṚṢṆA

His Divine Grace A.C. Bhaktivedanta Swami Prabhupāda writes in this regard, "Theoretically one may analyze things and say that by knowledge he has become freed and so on, but actually as long as the cause is there, he is not free. The *Bhagavad-gītā* confirms that after performing speculative activities for many, many births, when one actually comes to his real consciousness and surrenders unto the Supreme Lord, Kṛṣṇa, then his fulfillment of research in knowledge is actually achieved. There is a gulf of difference between theoretical freedom and actual freedom from material bondage." So if one gives up the auspicious path of devotional service and tries to know things by speculation, he is wasting his valuable time. The labor of speculation is ended only by exhaustion, and the result is only labor. It is like husking the skin of an empty paddy; there is no benefit because the rice is already gone. To get out of *māyā*, one has to nullify the cause of entanglement, and then the effect will be different. In the *Śrīmad-Bhāgavatam*, the Supreme Personality of Godhead says, "One can get liberation only by seriously discharging devotional service unto Me. One must hear for a long time about Me or from Me and execute one's prescribed duties without reaction. One will thus become freed from the contamination of matter."

It is not that one has to leave the material world. One can remain in association with matter and still remain unaffected, if he is performing service to Kṛṣṇa. If someone is in connection with the police department, that does not mean that he is a criminal. As long as one does not commit criminal acts, even though there is a police department, he is not punished. Similarly, the liberated soul is not affected, although he is in the material nature. Even the Supreme Personality of Godhead comes into association with matter when He descends, but He is not affected. So we can exist side by side with matter, but by using it for Kṛṣṇa we are unaffected. This is called liberation and is achieved simply by engaging in devotional service.

One must perform his prescribed duties in Kṛṣṇa consciousness. One does not have to change his duties; he just should perform them in Kṛṣṇa consciousness. The criterion for success is whether by one's profession or occupation the Supreme Personality of Godhead is satisfied. Everyone has some duty to perform, and its perfection is achieved if Kṛṣṇa is satisfied by one's acts. For example, Arjuna was a warrior. His prescribed duty was fighting, so the perfection of his fighting was tested by the satisfaction of Kṛṣṇa. Kṛṣṇa wanted him to fight, and as long as Arjuna was not willing to fight, he did not reach perfection. If a man wants to achieve perfection, then he should discharge his prescribed duties for the satisfaction of Kṛṣṇa. All actions should be performed as a sacrifice for Kṛṣṇa. In this age especially, one simply has to chant the names of God to achieve the perfection of sacrifice. By chanting, hearing and associating with devotees, one can bring this about. When one is fixed in serious devotional service and acts in that way, then he has no reaction and is freed from all contamination of the influence of the three modes of material nature. By continuous and regular hearing of the holy names and pastimes of the Personality of Godhead, the effects of contamination, such as lust and greed to enjoy and lord it over the material nature, are diminished, and one becomes situated in the mode of goodness. In that way he becomes fixed on the transcendental platform. To remain on the transcendental platform is to be liberated from material entanglement. That is the way in which to get out of the clutches of *māyā.* The personification of *māyā,* Māyādevī, the superintendent of the material world, performs the thankless duty of punishing all living entities who have the enjoying mentality, but she herself, as a servant of Kṛṣṇa, becomes pleased when someone finally gets out of her clutches, and according to Prabhupāda, she exclaims, "Ah, you have triumphed." So everyone becomes happy when a soul becomes freed from *māyā* and joins the association of Kṛṣṇa in the kingdom of God. That kingdom of God begins as soon as one begins serious devotional service.

IV. The Guru-Disciple Relationship

Initiation Into Kṛṣṇa Consciousness

February, 1975

If a casual onlooker attends an initiation ceremony at a Hare Kṛṣṇa temple, he will find the action colorful and absorbing, but most likely he will be bewildered as to what it all means. For a typical initiation, about one hundred devotees gather in the temple. The men and women to be initiated–perhaps a dozen of them–sit in two rows, facing the devotee designated to be the priest of the ceremony. The priest sits on a pillow before a smooth dirt mound about three feet square, which is decorated with incense and flowers. Later, during the ceremony, a fire will be built on this mound. Beside the mound is a stack of firewood, five bowls of brightly dyed rice flour, and bowls of sesame and barley seeds, clarified butter, fruits and spices. Objects considered auspicious in the Vedic culture, such as large banana leaves, coconuts, flower garlands, and clay pots filled with water, decorate the temple. Throughout the ceremony, except during a lecture by the priest, all the devotees individually chant the *mahā-mantra*–Hare Kṛṣṇa, Hare Kṛṣṇa, Kṛṣṇa Kṛṣṇa, Hare Hare/Hare Rāma, Hare Rāma, Rāma Rāma, Hare Hare. The sound of many voices chanting produces the powerful effect of a droning, humming prayer.

Often these ceremonies are held in the presence of His Divine Grace A.C. Bhaktivedanta Swami Prabhupāda, the founder and spiritual master of the Hare Kṛṣṇa movement. In that case, the most important moment for the initiate comes when Śrīla Prabhupāda calls him forward to be accepted as a disciple. The devotee bows before his spiritual master and then stands before him face to face. "Do you know the four rules?" Śrīla Prabhupāda asks. "Yes," he answers. "How many rounds do you chant daily?" The disciple answers, "At least sixteen rounds." Śrīla Prabhupāda nods: "All right. Try to avoid the ten offenses. Your name is Govinda dāsa." The other devotees then congratulate their new Godbrother.

But what does all this mean? What are these four rules and ten offenses? And why rules? What are these initiates agreeing to? How did apparently ordinary people change to become disciples at a Hare Kṛṣṇa initiation? To understand what is going on at the initiation ceremony and what has led these people to become disciples–and to understand how one goes about becoming a disciple–let us look back from the time of the ceremony to the time when the initiates first heard about Kṛṣṇa consciousness.

The first invitation may come in many different ways. "Someone gave me a book about Kṛṣṇa," recalls one devotee. "The Hare Kṛṣṇa people came to speak at our school," says another. "They held a festival in my town." "I met one on the street, and we talked." Because of the active preaching of the Hare Kṛṣṇa devotees, thousands of people daily hear something about Kṛṣṇa consciousness. But when some people hear they become eager to hear more, whereas others do not.

The hearing that sparks initial attraction to Kṛṣṇa is called, in Sanskrit, *śraddhā*, which means "faithful hearing." Of course, when we speak of "faith" we risk the immediate distaste of atheists and agnostics, and if we say "faith in God," they sour. But such faith is exactly what is required. Sometimes they argue, "Kṛṣṇa consciousness requires faith even in the beginning? We'll never accept something simply on faith." The materialistic investigator says, "We must experiment, prove, give evidence, and even then we never say that something is true. We constantly experiment and revise." Nevertheless, although materialistic scientists and scholars constantly revise their latest versions of the truth, they cannot rightly assert that they have done away with faith. We find, rather, that everyone places his faith in something or someone. One may not have the faith to join a society for God consciousness, but then he has faith instead that if he joins the Bank of America, for example, his money will be safe. Or he has faith, as most people do, in news reports and airline schedules, or in the quality of the food he buys, although he cannot always inspect it. A man even has enough faith in his barber to allow him to shave his throat with a sharp razor. Kṛṣṇa consciousness, however, means to have unflinching trust, not in barbers and news media, but in something sublime.

Yet Kṛṣṇa conscious faith is never blind, for it is based on knowledge. Lord Kṛṣṇa discusses different aspects of faith in Chapter Seventeen of *Bhagavad-gītā*. "The living being is said to be of a particular faith," the Lord explains, "according to the modes he has acquired." Śrīla Prabhupāda comments upon this verse, "Everyone has a particular type of faith, but his faith is considered good, passionate or ignorant according to the nature he has acquired. The real fact is that every living being is originally the fragmental part of the Supreme Lord. But when one forgets his relationship with the Supreme Personality of Godhead and comes into contact with the material nature, the resultant artificial faith is only material." A Kṛṣṇa conscious person, however, has faith in great authorities, such as Lord Kṛṣṇa and the disciplic succession of spiritual masters, whose words are always in accord with the Vedic literature, originally spoken by God. A communist places his trust in Marx or Lenin, but a devotee trusts Lord Kṛṣṇa, the speaker of *Bhagavad-gītā*. Both have faith, but beyond that one must examine whether the leader or authority he trusts is perfect. In the beginning, one may not accept or understand that Kṛṣṇa is the all-perfect Personality of

Godhead, the source of everything spiritual and material, but a faithful person thinks, "These people are speaking something about God consciousness. Let me hear what they have to say." This is *śraddhā,* faithful hearing, the first step in Kṛṣṇa consciousness. One who has *śraddhā* will go further; one who does not will turn away.

According to *Bhagavad-gītā*, the inclination to hear topics about Kṛṣṇa develops progressively from life to life. Thus one who in his past life took to spirituality but could not follow it to perfection takes to it again in the next life automatically, from where he left off. In any case, authorities in Kṛṣṇa consciousness tell us that hearing about Kṛṣṇa in the association of devotees of the Supreme Lord is the perfect religious process for enhancing one's spiritual development. The prospective devotee, therefore, likes to hear about Kṛṣṇa consciousness and to hear the chanting of Hare Kṛṣṇa.

The next step is a natural one: the person who is hearing wants to hear more. Only to spend his spare time reading books like *Bhagavad-gītā* and *Śrīmad-Bhāgavatam* is no longer enough. He wants more association, and not just with the books but with people who understand the books and follow their instructions. The *Vedas* explicitly say, "Unless one associates with devotees, one cannot develop love of God; one cannot achieve it on one's own." In the *Gītā* Lord Kṛṣṇa describes the lives of such devotees: "The thoughts of My pure devotees dwell in Me, their lives are surrendered to Me, and they derive great satisfaction and bliss enlightening one another and conversing about Me."

The beginning candidate starts to find his materialistic association unsatisfying. Usually he tries to introduce Kṛṣṇa conscious ideas to his own family or friends. Sometimes he is successful and his friends also want to hear about Kṛṣṇa, but often they think he has gone crazy. In any case, he decides to seek practical advice from advanced devotees on how to proceed further in Kṛṣṇa consciousness. He visits the temple more frequently, reveals his mind to the devotees, and spends more time chanting and reading.

By now, having progressed by hearing, he desires friendship with the Lord's devotees and even thinks ahead to his relationship with the spiritual master. The Vedic literature repeatedly stresses that saintly association is the most important necessity in spiritual life. *The Nectar of Devotion, the Complete Science of Bhakti-Yoga,* enumerates the most important principles of devotional service. The first three are as follows: (1) accepting the shelter of the lotus feet of a bona fide spiritual master, (2) becoming initiated by the spiritual master and learning from him how to discharge devotional service, and (3) obeying the orders of the spiritual master with faith and devotion. From reading or from hearing lectures, one may also learn this verse from the *Kaṭha Upaniṣad*: "To learn that transcendental science, one must approach a bona fide spiritual master who appears in the disciplic succession and who is fixed in the truth." Or this famous quotation from *Bhagavad-gītā*: "Just try to learn the truth by approaching a spiritual master. Inquire from him submissively . . . ."

Friendship with the devotees is one thing, but approaching the spiritual master means surrendering to him and following his instructions. Is the candidate ready to do it? He becomes thoughtful. According to the Vedic system, one should stay with a spiritual master for a year before deciding whether to accept him as one's *guru*, and the *guru* also should observe the candidate for a year to ascertain whether he is eligible. Whether to surrender to a spiritual master is the most important choice in life, and it should be considered as thoroughly as possible. Having read some of the books and associated with devotees, one may consider his decision in this way: "I have heard from the Vedic literatures that I must take initiation. I must use this human life to go back to Godhead and become free from birth and death in the material world. I have heard it, but now what am I going to do about it?"

If one finds that he does not deeply desire to live in the Absolute Truth, he should not seek initiation from a spiritual master. If he is not serious, why make a superficial commitment to the spiritual path? Unfortunately, however, it has become fashionable to accept a spiritual master as one would accept a pet. Especially from India, many cheaters have come for those who are insincere about spiritual life but who want to be flattered that they are making spiritual advancement. They take to spiritual life as a kind of recreation. Nowadays we commonly hear how so-called *gurus* have taken money and cheated their disciples with bogus teachings. A serious candidate, therefore, may be hesitant about surrendering to a spiritual master, for he wants to be sure that he does not naively accept someone who will cheat him.

To find a real spiritual master is crucial. However, there is a standard way to ascertain who is a genuine *guru*. All the Vedic literature proclaims that the Absolute Truth is the Supreme Personality of Godhead, Lord Kṛṣṇa. As stated in the *Ṛg Veda*, "Viṣṇu is the Supreme, and those who are godly think only of His lotus feet." Lord Viṣṇu, or Kṛṣṇa, is the ultimate object of all paths of meditation and *yoga*. The spiritual master, therefore, is one who preaches the message of Kṛṣṇa without adulteration. We have already quoted from *Bhagavad-gītā*, wherein Lord Kṛṣṇa Himself advises, "Try to learn the truth by approaching a spiritual master." In the verse after that, the Lord says, "And when you have learned the truth from the *guru*, you will know that all beings are but part of Me—and that they are in Me, and are Mine." If a so-called spiritual master does not present Kṛṣṇa as the highest truth, if he changes the message originally spoken by Kṛṣṇa or if he concocts teachings of his own, he cannot be considered a genuine *guru*. To be genuine, the *guru* must follow the instructions of anothe genuine *guru* who comes in the disciplic succession from Kṛṣṇa. If one is sincere, the Lord, who is within everyone's heart, will guide him in taking the right step by approaching the genuine teacher, not a pretender. If one desires real spiritual life, Kṛṣṇa will help him. But if he wants something else, Kṛṣṇa may allow him to be cheated.

If one is convinced that he has indeed found a genuine spiritual master, the next step is to follow his instructions. Śrīla Prabhupāda's most basic request to everyone is that one chant the Hare Kṛṣṇa *mantra*. One need not be initiated to begin chanting. The chanting is recommended for everyone, in all circumstances. In fact, the scriptures recommend chanting the holy names of God as the only suitable means of God realization in our present age of quarrel and hypocrisy (Kali-yuga). The name of Kṛṣṇa is not different from Kṛṣṇa Himself, and therefore chanting brings one into direct contact with Kṛṣṇa. As stated in the scripture *Nārada-pañcaratra*, the syllables of the *mahā-mantra* contain all other *mantras* and the results of all other spiritual processes. The *mahā-mantra* may be sung with other devotees or chanted to oneself on *japa* beads, a string of 108 beads that devotees use for chanting. The process is to say the *mahā-mantra* while fingering each bead; chanting on 108 beads is called "chanting a round." In the beginning one should set himself a quota of a certain number of rounds daily, even if only one or two. Once having set that quota, he should never go below it. Initiated disciples agree to chant a minimum of sixteen rounds daily. In the beginning neophytes find it difficult to chant more than a couple of rounds daily, but in the highest stages pure devotees chant the holy names constantly, day and night, in the profound ecstasy of love of God.

In addition to chanting, Śrīla Prabhupāda asks his initiated students to strictly refrain from four major sinful activities: (1) illicit sex, (2) meat eating, (3) intoxication and (4) gambling. On the basis of knowledge alone, one should see these activities as detrimental to his advancement. To actually give them up, however, one must feel a superior pleasure from transcendental consciousness. Most people indulge extensively in all four of these activities. Wherever we go we see advertisements for liquor and cigarettes, and nearly all advertising depends in some way upon sexual attraction. In today's culture, therefore, giving up these things requires a whole commitment. One has to decide if he really wants spiritual life, for there is no question of cultivating these sinful activities and at the same time advancing spiritually. Consequently one who is insincere will try to find some fault with spiritual advancement and will fall back into material desires, but one who sincerely chants Hare Kṛṣṇa will be freed from all misgivings and will then make rapid progress.

The prerequisites for initiation, therefore, are to chant sixteen rounds daily and follow the four rules.

If one takes to these principles, he usually decides he wants to live with devotees like himself. The International Society for Kṛṣṇa Consciousness has therefore been formed so that devotees may live together, with Kṛṣṇa as the center of their lives. Their living together is not ordinary communal life. In all Kṛṣṇa temples the Deity of the Lord is installed, and by Kṛṣṇa's mercy wherever there is Deity worship Kṛṣṇa is actually present. The Deity worship is not idol worship, for it is authorized by all Vedic scriptures; the Deity is as much Kṛṣṇa as His name or His word. Thus devotees live in the temple as servants of the Lord, who is present in the Deity form. It is stated that to live in a brothel or bar is to live in the mode of ignorance; to live in the city, the mode of passion, and to live in the forest, the mode of goodness. But living in the temple of the Lord is transcendental, beyond all material modes.

Temple life has special potency because everything done in the temple is an act of *bhakti-yoga*, or devotional service to the Lord. All such acts are sanctified and free of *karma*, or material reactions. For example, the devotees eat only food first offered to Kṛṣṇa. Just by eating the remnants of such an offering, which are called *prāsada*, one advances toward the goal of life, love of God. Because the devotees in the temple, directed by a pure devotee of Kṛṣṇa, thus act within the spiritual energy, although they may live in New York or London they are not actually anywhere within the material world; by virtue of their *bhakti* activities and consciousness, they are in the spiritual world. This is not to be known academically, but it is realized by devotees who live in association with the *mahā-mantra*, who eat Kṛṣṇa's *prāsada* and who work for Kṛṣṇa.

One may also live in his own home with his family and regular occupation, but by following the instructions of the spiritual master he can make his home as good as a temple, provided he follows the same procedures. It is imperative for one who wants to be an initiated devotee to rise early in the morning, no later than 4 a.m., and, after bathing, to begin chanting and reading from books like *Bhagavad-gītā* and *Śrīmad-Bhāgavatam*. Early rising and restriction of eating and material pleasure may seem pointless and troublesome for a materialist, but the devotee who wants initiation takes to these austerities with love and enthusiasm, and he feels happy results very quickly. The first result is that one becomes freed from material despondency and becomes jolly and hopeful about going back to Godhead.

One's initiation really takes place when one gains firm determination to dedicate his life to following the instructions of the spiritual master. His initiation ceremony, although very important, follows automatically once he decides to become a devotee and dedicate his life. After he begins sincere, regulative service, the day will surely come when the temple's leaders recommend him for initiation.

During the inititation ceremony, the initiates come forward, one after another, and are personally handed beads upon which Śrīla Prabhupāda has chanted for sanctification. Śrīla Prabhupāda or the priest performing the ceremony asks each candidate if he knows the four rules and is willing to follow the requirements for daily chanting. The first initiation is technically called *hari-nāma* initiation, or initiation into the holy name. There are further initiations in Kṛṣṇa consciousness, such as brahminical initiation, which may be given one year after the first initiation, and initiation into the renounced order, but the *hari-nāma* initiation is sufficient in itself to bring one to the highest perfection of love of God; if the student will faithfully follow the spiritual master, nothing else is needed but *hari-nāma*.

To be effective, however, the chanting must be performed without offenses. *The Nectar of Devotion* lists the following ten offenses to be avoided while chanting: "1) To blaspheme the devotees who have dedicated their lives for propagating the holy name of the Lord. 2) To consider the names of the demigods like Lord Śiva or Lord Brahmā to be equal to, or independent of, the name of Lord Viṣṇu. 3) To disobey the orders of the spiritual master. 4) To blaspheme the Vedic literature or literature in pursuance of the Vedic version. 5) To consider the glories of chanting Hare Kṛṣṇa to be imagination. 6) To give some interpretation of the holy name of the Lord. 7) To commit sinful activities on the strength of the holy name of the Lord. (Because by chanting the holy name of the Lord one can be freed from all kinds of sinful reactions, it should not be taken that one may continue to act sinfully and after that chant Hare Kṛṣṇa to neutralize his sins. Such a dangerous mentality is very offensive and should be avoided.) 8) To consider the chanting of Hare Kṛṣṇa one of the auspicious ritualistic activities offered in the *Vedas* as fruitive activities (*karma-kāṇḍa).9)* To instruct a faithless person about the glories of the holy name. (Anyone can take part in chanting the holy name of the Lord, but in the beginning one should not be instructed about the transcendental glories of the Lord. Those who are too sinful cannot appreciate the transcendental glories of the Lord, and therefore it is better not to instruct them in this matter.) 10) To not have complete faith in the chanting of the holy names and to maintain material attachments, even after understanding so many instructions on this matter." Anyone serious about becoming a devotee of the Hare Kṛṣṇa movement should be careful to avoid these ten offenses.

As for the spiritual name given at the time of initiation, it is usually a name of Kṛṣṇa or one of His devotees. The name is always affixed with the word "*dāsa*" for men, or "*devī dāsī*" for women, both of which mean "servant." One is not given the name "Kṛṣṇa," "Govinda" or "Caitanya," but "Kṛṣṇa dāsa," "Govinda-devi dasi" or "Caitanya dāsa," indicating that the initiate is not God Himself but a humble servant of God. (Bogus spiritual masters make the great mistake of simply giving their disciples names of God, such as Govinda or Nārāyana, without indicating that the disciple is a servant of Govinda or Nārāyana. Thus the unfortunate followers think that by becoming initiated they have somehow become as good as God.) As the *guru* is the real eternal father, so the spiritual name he gives his disciple is an eternal name by which the spiritual master and Godbrothers and Godsisters know the disciple.

After each initiate has been given his beads and spiritual name, he sits down, and the priest, under the guidance of Śrīla Prabhupāda, continues the ceremony. After spreading colored dyes over the dirt mound in decorative crisscrosses and building a small fire, the priest begins chanting *mantras* glorifying the past spiritual masters in the succession from Kṛṣṇa Himself. The priest and devotees chant responsively, and at the end of each verse the priest pronounces the word "*svāhā*," which indicates the offering of oblations. Handfuls of sesame and barley mixed with clarified butter have been handed to the initiates, other devotees and guests, and when the priest says "*svāhā*" and pours a ladle of clarified butter into the fire, everyone throws grains into the fire as well. This simple procedure surcharges everyone present with spiritual happiness, and it is better experienced than described in words. Formerly such sacrifices were held on a grand scale, with tons of grains and clarified butter offered into the sacrificial fire. But this present age, Kali-yuga, finds mankind short in natural resources, and so a token amount of grain and butter is offered. The primary sacrifice for this age, however, is the congregational chanting of the Hare Kṛṣṇa *mantra*, and therefore we need not lament for our lack of huge amounts of grains to offer in sacrifice. If there were no other paraphernalia but the holy name, it would still be complete, and without the holy name the sacrifice would be only a false show.

After all the *mantras* are chanted, the priest anounces, "*kīrtana*!" ("Chanting!"). Immediately *mṛdaṅga* players start striking their drums, *karatāla* players beat their brass hand cymbals, and a lead singer begins melodiously singing the Hare Kṛṣṇa *mantra*. Congregational chanting with the participation of many devotees thus becomes the ultimate perfection of the initiation sacrifice. This chanting process is so auspicious that it is envied by denizens of higher planets, even though they have all the material wealth and knowledge for opulent sacrificial ceremonies. Nevertheless, a Vedic ceremony is considered incomplete without distribution of *prasāda*, food offered to Kṛṣṇa, and so the initiation ceremony is also an occasion for full, sumptuous feasting for all who attend.

In summary, the initiation ceremony, far from being merely a colorful ritual, is a necessity for genuine spiritual life. Although everyone, even if not initiated, is encouraged to chant Hare Kṛṣṇa and will receive spiritual benefit if he does so, unless one is initiated by a genuine spiritual master he will not receive the spiritual strength to remain steady in chanting Hare Kṛṣṇa and following spiritual principles, and after some time he may slide down again to material consciousness. The non-initiate is sometimes compared to a student who is allowed to sit in on a professor's class but who has not officially registered for the course. Although such a student may benefit by auditing the class, he must formally join the class if he wishes to receive college credit. Similarly, only when one is initiated does he become eligible for the full benefits of Kṛṣṇa consciousness, for then his link to Kṛṣṇa is established, through his own spiritual master and all the great spiritual masters of the past. Then, by implicit faith in his own spiritual master and in Lord Kṛṣṇa, all the truths of the Vedic literature are revealed to him. This is the path for the serious candidate on the path of spiritual perfection.

The Man of Wisdom

Issue No. 6, 1967

According to the *Bhagavad-gītā*, those "virtuous ones" who actually come to God, are of four kinds: "the man in distress, the seeker for knowledge, the seeker for wealth, and the man of wisdom." (*Bg.* 7.16) The distressed, who ask sanctuary at the feet of the Lord, are quickly given ease and shelter. This is a fact: the life of devotional service leads one out of the entanglements of the perishable world. Refuge is granted through worship. For those in distress (anyone without Kṛṣṇa consciousness is in some measure of distress) God's mercy grants peace, the easing of their burden. Whatever the frustration, whatever the pain, whatever the loneliness, loss or tragedy, it is balmed with the sincere and faithful hearing of the Vedic message (scripture). People in distress, however, are liable to come and go. With the rise of new opportunities, or after a period of rejuvenation in association with the Lord and His devotees, the distressed may leave the Supreme's service in order to make a fresh attack on the mazes of illusion, thus falling back into the clutches of the temporary, material world.

The second "virtuous one" is the man who is seeking knowledge. He is curious to know God. God is all-famous, and so the curious man becomes interested, and wants to know Him. Curiosity is a good reason—as any reason is—to turn to God, but if such a man applies only his curiosity to the Godhead, his intellectual enquiry will soon show itself to be endless, since the Divine Person cannot be measured by our human potencies. The Ruler of all universes and planets, the Source and Proprietor of Life and Wisdom will be enquired after by the speculative, knowledge-seeking man in birth after birth, until at long last the seeker concludes that "Vāsudeva (Kṛṣṇa) is all." (*Bg.* 7.19) Only then does imperishable wisdom begin.

In a similar way, the seeker for wealth (whose virtue is in turning to God to satisfy his desires), will probably never actually be satisfied, not even by a deluge of gold. Neither will he ever advance closer toward God, until he goes beyond wanting God to be his order-supplier. In the *Gītā* Lord Kṛṣṇa says, "But temporary is the fruit gained by these men of small minds." (*Bg.* 7.23)

That leaves us the man of wisdom. "Of these, the wise one, who is ever in constant union with the Divine, whose devotion is single-minded, is the best. For I am supremely dear to him, and he is dear to Me." (*Bg.* 7.17) Why is the man of wisdom dear to God? Because he wants nothing in return. The man of wisdom puts aside his desires for those things for which others are searching, and seeks Kṛṣṇa's pleasure. He realizes that his true, original life is beyond the color of this temporary world of sense-pleasure, sadness, wealth-hankering and puffed-up knowledge-seeking. The wise man knows that he is transcendental, like Kṛṣṇa. Kṛṣṇa is above and unaffected by the pangs of bondage; and we are Kṛṣṇa's parts and parcels. While of course Kṛṣṇa has the power to bestow gold and to dry up our tears of misery, asking for these things is like praying in hell-fire for a sumptuous meal and a woman, rather than asking for release from the flames. Kṛṣṇa is transcendental, and when we pray to Him it is only for His association. Never mind the list of special requests for our particular situation on earth. Just pray to please Kṛṣṇa. Kṛṣṇa is the fullest Enjoyer, and the wise man has the single desire to become His devotee. We have a chant in praise of Kṛṣṇa: *Hare Kṛṣṇa*, *Hare Rāma.* This chant bestows the very wisdom of which we are speaking. Therefore, the wise man's position is to withdraw from all material attachment, both good and evil, and to chant the holy name of God. This is the wise man's single need and prime duty.

How does the wise man subsist? He subsists on the nectar of transcendental service to the Lord. He feeds and cares for his body as one would care for the upkeep of a functionary pushcart. He eats for Kṛṣṇa, after first offering his food to Him. He works at Kṛṣṇa's business and talks on Kṛṣṇa's behalf. Kṛṣṇa says in the *Gītā*, "Whose devotion is single-minded is best." Single-minded devotion is best because Kṛṣṇa says so, and He is the Single Supreme Person. Devotion to that to which *we are inseparably connected* is, after all, wise. Since we are all parts of the Godhead, our constitutional function is to serve as His parts, just as the hands serve the body, of which they are part. The hands never try to consume food themselves, absorbing it through the fingernails. Nor do they make a request of the body that they be given their "independence." Yet, the hand performs well in its own miraculous sphere, making music, typewriting, grasping weights. Why, therefore, are we clamoring to God for special benediction? We already have the blessings of function: to serve the Eternal eternally. The wise man is aware of his natural, original position and is using both body and soul in the service of his Lord. If we frantically try to consume God's gifts for our own enjoyment, we will very quickly reach a fruitless end on this mortal road and will have to begin again; and, if we are not wise, the next time we will again meet the end of the road.

To do transcendental service is to surrender our will unto His Will. But no, we have to learn it again and again, stubbornly. We have to learn that we actually have no business apart from God. We are wise when we reach the conclusion that God is the Bestower and is truly all. "Vāsudeva is all that is." (*Bg.* 7.19)

> When thou hast known it, thou shalt not fall again into this confusion, O Pāṇḍava, for by this thou shalt see all existences without exception in the Self, then in Me. (*Bg.* 4.35)

Our independence from Him is our illusion. Similarly fantastic is the pursuit of our own gratification, the desire for love apart from Him, or wealth apart from Him, or happiness apart from Him. The wise man leaves the mirage in favor of the Reality. Absolute Reality is to willingly serve the Lord. We are already His servitors; we cannot avoid the work. All miseries stem from *forgetting* this factual situation: there is the Lord, and there are ourselves–and we are *His own.* He is dear to us because we are dear to Him. Love is the key. And the wise man loves God.

Fathers and Sons

Summer/Fall, 1969

It is said that one's body is an inheritance from one's father, that the sins of the father are visited on the son, that in terms of progress we stand upon our fathers' shoulders. So many "truths" have defined the relationship of father to son; but ultimately, all these affairs of father and son are unreal, because they are material. This relationship, which seems so firm and certain, is actually just an illusion, because it is temporary. This is the conclusion of the great sages who have developed and passed down to us our knowledge of spiritual life. The real father is the spiritual master. One who is liberated from identification with temporary existence factually experiences that his "guru" is his spiritual father forever.

His Divine Grace A.C. Bhaktivedanta Swami once explained the transcendental situation of father and son in a letter to one of his disciples: "You have accepted me as father, so I have also accepted you as my dear and real son. This relationship of father and son on the spiritual platform is real and eternal, while on the material platform such a relationship is ephemeral."

In the relationship of the bodily father, the son asks for something and the father gives. That is, something material is exchanged. If one is so fortunate, however, as to receive "second birth" by initiation under a bona fide spiritual master, then he receives the spiritual gift of eternal life through chanting the holy name of God. By chanting the holy name of God and hearing the scriptural teachings, the student can have his eyes opened from the blindness of material life. From the blessings of the *guru*-father, the disciple-son derives all knowledge of reality.

The most crucial thing to be learned, the first important gift of the spiritual master, is that we are eternal spirit soul, part and parcel of God, the Supreme Person. The true situation is not, as the bodily father may tell us, that we were created by him, according to his plans, and that we are thus his private investment or possession.

Actually, all beings live under the plan of Kṛṣṇa, the Supreme Father. Individually—fathers and sons alike—we are coming here on our own, by a choice of free will we wander down the ages, taking various births among the 8,400,000 species of creatures, taking different bodies in life after life, living in different countries, on different planets, being born of countless different fathers—all according to the works we perform. The Vedic scriptures say that if we lead pious lives we will be born into aristocratic, rich or beautiful families. The *Bhagavad-gītā* specifically states that if we take up Kṛṣṇa Consciousness or yoga practice, but fail to execute it perfectly, then at the time of death we will be transferred to the higher or heavenly planets; and when the results of our piety are used up, we are again born on some earthly planet—in the families of *yogīs,* so that we can continue our spiritual progress.

To be born into the family of a *brāhmaṇa* or *yogī* should be very advantageous to spiritual life, but of course we can always spoil such an opportunity, just as a rich man's son can turn to idling and intoxication. This is why the term "born *brāhmaṇa*," and the whole latter-day caste-by-birth system, is a misconception of the spiritual path. The qualities of a *brāhmaṇa* (intellectual or priest) or of a *kṣatriya* (soldier or statesman), etc., do not depend on material birth, and even the most lowly-born person can advance unimpeded to perfection simply by chanting in the association of a pure devotee.

In his letter to a disciple, my own spiritual master explains what the *guru,* the transcendental father, can do for his spiritual son: "Although I cannot give you anything as a father, still I pray to Kṛṣṇa for your more and more advancement in Kṛṣṇa consciousness."

Through the spiritual master we learn the actual relationship that exists between God and the individual living entity. The Supreme Personality of Godhead, who is Father, Mother and Friend of all life, is usually approached by Christians as the Father, and is prayed to more or less as a Supreme Order Supplier. God is the Great Supplier of bread. This is, however, an elementary conception of the Personality of Godhead. Only through the grace of the spiritual master, who has very scientific, realized information about the Absolute, can we advance beyond the idea of God as no more than a material father, a supplier from whom we demand. To learn to love God as a friend and playmate—or even as a lover—comes only through the process of devotional service to the spiritual master. To please the *guru*-father is the perfect way to liberation, happiness and still greater freedom in the service of Kṛṣṇa.

It is also possible, of course, that the man who brought you into this world through the shelter of your mother's body could also impart to you the same spiritual instruction that is coming from the spiritual master. In such a case, he is not exactly a "material" father. When a devotee of Godhead marries, under the guidance of his spiritual master, his marriage is not material but spiritual. Such a marriage is not undertaken for sense gratification, but in the service of Kṛṣṇa. The issue of such a union is not, therefore, comparable to the offspring of cats and dogs—that is to say, productions of accident and lust.

It is said in the scriptures that no one should become a spiritual master, father or husband unless he can deliver his charge from the clutches of death. This means that unless he can free his disciples, his son or his wife from material consciousness, he should not take on the responsibility of master or parent. The mission of the real father is to impart spiritual wisdom. We can say, then, that the father who brings a child into the world for Kṛṣṇa conscious purposes is not material, as he is not operating in temporary, illusory consciousness, which is held to be the standard of material life.

An important example of such a transcendental father is the great saint Ṭhākur Bhaktivinode, who appeared in India during the nineteenth century. A perfect example of productive, spiritual household life, Śrīla Bhaktivinode fathered 12 Kṛṣṇa conscious babies, the most notable among them being Bhaktisiddhānta Saraswatī, founder of the Gaudiya missionary movement. Śrīla Bhaktisiddhānta was the guru of His Divine Grace A.C. Bhaktivedanta Swami, the spiritual master of the present Kṛṣṇa Consciousness Movement. Just as anything–an airplane, money, talent, etc.–can be used in the service of Kṛṣṇa and thus made spiritual, so sex and fatherhood can work this way.

There is a question one may ask at this point. Since Lord Caitanya, the incarnation of God who played the role of the perfect devotee, gave up his wife and only then took spiritual sons–disciples–what is the purpose of procuring only one, or even a dozen souls for the service of Kṛṣṇa via the complicated and laborious method of material childbirth? If the only true sons are spiritual, why not adopt *sannyāsa*, the renounced order, at once and make many disciples? His Divine Grace A.C. Bhaktivedanta Swami has generally encouraged his students, both boys and girls, to marry and raise Kṛṣṇa conscious children. He has said that, although we are canvassing for Kṛṣṇa, we are after quality and not quantity. It is not by votes that one goes back to Godhead. If a spiritual master can find one precious soul and carefully train him in Kṛṣṇa consciousness from the very start of life, then there is a very good chance for him to become a devotee or future spiritual master. In this way, to raise one individual in pure consciousness can benefit many people.

It should also be noted that one does not stop his personal service to Kṛṣṇa by becoming a father or mother. Everyone serves Kṛṣṇa, and every devotee, regardless of whether he is married or unmarried, can be a true *guru* in the style of Lord Caitanya by simply persuading whoever he meets, anywhere in the world, to chant Hare Kṛṣṇa.

It is stated in the *Śrīmad-Bhāgavatam* that in previous, more congenial ages, *yogīs* or devotees would first attain spiritual perfection, and only then find a wife and produce some children. Their purposes for having children were: 1) to bring a fallen, conditioned entity into the world, and then to enlighten him so that he could develop love for God and transfer to the spiritual world at the time of death; or 2) to bring into the world a ray of Viṣṇu Himself—to have a liberated, saintly child, as did Śrīla Bhaktivinode.

The ultimate perfection of such spiritual fatherhood is to be the instrument for the appearance of an incarnation of God. Such was the case of the *yogīs* Kardama Muni and Devahūti, through whom Kapiladeva, the Teacher of the sublime *sāṅkhya* philosophy, entered this world. The mother and father of Kṛṣṇa Himself achieved the ultimate in this perfection of parenthood. One devotee sings in this way to Nanda Mahārāja, the worshipable foster father of the Supreme Lord: "People have taken shelter of the Vedic literature from fear of material life. Let them worship *śruti* or *Mahābhārata*. I am not going to do that. I shall worship Nanda Mahārāja, because he has captivated the Supreme Lord into crawling as a child in his courtyard."

The Cure for All Despondency

May/June, 1971

The original source of knowledge is the *Vedas.* From the *Vedas* emanate all the spiritual or scriptural writings known to this planet, and all material knowledge also has been passed down by exponents of the original *Vedas.* The original *Vedas* were known by the aural tradition, or simply by hearing. The knowledge contained in the *Vedas* actually has no origin in history; the *Vedas* are so ancient as to be untraceable, but we have it from authority that they were set into writing 5000 years ago, when they were compiled by a great sage, Śrīla Kṛṣṇa Dvaipāyana Vyāsadeva. Vyāsadeva put this aural tradition into writing because, as a liberated sage able to see the future, he foresaw that in the coming age, the age of quarrel and hypocrisy, people would be interested only in that which is temporary and would lose their ability to retain the Vedic knowledge by memory. The people of the age of Kali, which is the present age in modern civilization, are characterized by a short duration of life, diminished memory, distraction from the spiritual path, and lack of seriousness in searching out the ultimate goal of life.

It is told in the Vedic literature *Śrīmad-Bhāgavatam* that Vyāsadeva was fully equipped in knowledge and could see by his transcendental vision that all the good qualities of people in the future would gradually deteriorate, up to the point where 99% of the population would be thoroughly atheistic. A sage like Vyāsadeva who is a devotee of the Supreme Lord is factually far more a friend of the people in general than the so-called public leaders who cannot even know what will happen five minutes ahead. Thus 5000 years ago this philanthropist, Vyāsa, foreseeing the need to edit the *Vedas* and put them into writing, divided the *Vedas* and expanded them into histories and narrations so that the less intelligent people, who are interested only in hearing stories, could understand the purport of the scriptures and thus be delivered back to the eternal joyful home, back to Godhead.

When the scriptures are heard from a bona fide spiritual master, their real meaning comes alive. There is no special educational qualification for understanding God. By the mercy of Vyāsadeva the Vedic literature is readily understandable when handed down by a bona fide spiritual master who has realized the truth of the scriptures. Vyāsadeva was therefore a great spiritual master for all people, and he is known to be a literary incarnation of Lord Kṛṣṇa, the Supreme Personality of Godhead. Vyāsadeva and Lord Kṛṣṇa are on the same transcendental platform, and they collaborated in a plan to benedict the fallen souls of this age by presenting scripture in the form of stories and histories, such as the *Mahābhārata* (in which appears the *Bhagavad-gītā*, which is the gist of the entire Vedic philosophical literature).

"I STILL FEEL WANTING"

After having worked so hard for the cause of humanity and after compiling so much transcendental literature, it would be expected that Vyāsadeva would be satisfied by his worthwhile activities. Yet as Vyāsadeva sat down in meditation one morning, he thought to himself that he was not very satisfied in mind or heart. Vyāsadeva considered, "I have certainly worshiped the *Vedas*, the spiritual masters and the altar of sacrificial fire under strict disciplinary guidance and without pretense, and I have also abided by the Vedic rulings, I have shown the import of the disciplic succession through the explanation of the *Mahābhārata*, in which even women, *śūdras* and others can also see the path of religion. Yet although I am already fully equipped with everything needed in the matter of Vedic principles, I still feel wanting. It may be that I did not direct myself enough to the devotional service of the Lord, which is dear both to the perfect beings and to the infallible Lord." From these thoughts we can see that Śrīla Vyāsadeva was able to express to himself a hint of the lack that he felt. Somehow or other, although fully equipped in all the details of Vedic achievements, Vyāsadeva appeared to have lost the clue to his normal transcendental happiness. Therefore he felt dissatisfaction.

The despondency of Vyāsadeva must not be thought of as an isolated case unrelated to our own lives. If every man and woman reading this essay would only examine himself with introspection, he would most likely find something akin to the lack felt at heart by Śrīla Vyāsadeva. Whether one has achieved great success in business, or has amassed great wealth, a nice family, fame, or any amount of worldly or mystical power, that dissatisfaction at the inner core of one's being is liable to occur. This dissatisfaction is manifested in many ways, such as boredom, frustration, loneliness and disillusion, and in general it exists because our innermost desires for happiness and fulfillment are not being satisfied. This is certainly true for those persons who have made gross sensualism their purpose for living. As such a person grows older and increases in his career of sex enjoyment and intoxication, he realizes that it is hellish and that he is not satisfied. Any man who feels great hopes for a fulfilling life in this material world will find that his actual position falls far short of his wished-for happiness. We may have idealistic plans for our own enjoyment or our families' enjoyment or for the improvement of our nation or humanity, but because of the nature of the material laws–such as old age, death, disease and other miseries–our ideals are never fulfilled in the material world. His Divine Grace A.C. Bhaktivedanta Swami Prabhupāda has written in this connection: "Perfection is never attained until one is satisfied at heart, and this satisfaction of the heart has to be searched out *beyond the material world.*"

THE SPIRITUAL MASTER

Just as Vyāsa was trying to locate the defect in himself, Nārada Muni, his spiritual master, reached Vyāsa's cottage on the bank of the River Sarasvatī. On seeing Nārada, Śrīla Vyāsadeva got up in respect and offered his master all worship. Nārada then took a comfortable seat and began to address his disciple. As Nārada spoke, he was smiling because he knew well the cause of Vyāsadeva's disappointment. Nārada inquired, "Are you not satisfied with identifying the body or mind as the object of self-realization?" By his first words Nārada hinted that despite his compilation of sacred and instructive transcendental literature, Vyāsadeva had actually identified the body and mind with the self. But the concept of the body and the mind as the self can never bring happiness because the body is subject to so many miseries and is only temporary, whereas the real self is eternal. How is it that Vyāsadeva, who was such a great sage, could miss the real point of spiritual life and spiritual happiness? Nārada admitted that Vyāsadeva had certainly studied fully and had with deliberation compiled a full explanation of the original knowledge of the *Vedas*. So why should he be disappointed just when he should be feeling satisfied by a full lifetime of great welfare work for all humanity? Vyāsadeva humbly submitted himself before his spiritual master and asked him to please point out the root cause of his despondency.

Śrī Nārada said, "You have not broadcast the sublime and spotless glories of the Personality of Godhead. Anything that does not satisfy the senses of the Lord is considered worthless philosophy." That was Nārada Muni's prompt diagnosis. Śrīla Vyāsadeva was despondent because, despite writing so many books, he had deliberately avoided glorifying the Supreme Lord, but he gave more attention to religiosity, economic development, sense gratification and salvation, which are the material activities of civilization. Vyāsadeva had neglected to give his full attention to devotional service, which starts with hearing and glorifying the name and pastimes of Kṛṣṇa. Therefore Nārada concluded that Vyāsadeva had more or less wasted his time. Nārada was saying, in other words, that all the scriptures that Vyāsadeva had compiled up to this point had dealt mainly with material activities, and this was the reason for his despondency. Vyāsadeva was interested in regulating material activities so that people could gradually come to the spiritual platform. But if people simply perform the regulative material principles and do not come to the spiritual platform, that will not help them. The only point of regulating sense gratificatory activities is to gradually gain the transcendental taste of love of God. Only when one tastes transcendental pleasure can he abandon satisfying his own senses and be intent on satisfying the senses of Kṛṣṇa.

IN THE NAME OF RELIGION

It has been stated that Vyāsadeva had been concerned with religiosity, which involves preparing oneself for being elevated to the spiritual platform. Vyāsadeva had outlined *dhārma*, or religious faith, as meaning to very punctually go to a church or temple, execute all ritualistic ceremonies very rigidly and follow religious rules and regulations. In this way a materialistic man can gradually be purified. But if at the end a person does not develop love for God, then the rituals are simply useless labor and empty formality. The objective of religion is not material happiness. The objective of religion is Kṛṣṇa. When religious rituals are followed for the goal of material happiness, all the prescriptions and regulations are simply a waste of time. Thus Vyāsadeva could be said to have actually encouraged materialistic activities. The sacrifices he described in the scriptures were presented with the understanding that everyone comes into this material world in order to satisfy his senses. So in order for people to enjoy sense gratification while at the same time following the codes of religion, the *Vedas* were prepared. Now Nārada told Vyāsadeva that he had actually encouraged sense gratification in the name of religion. We commonly see that when someone is involved in some basically illicit activity, he may try to find sanction for it within his religion. "My religion says I can do it. I can eat meat. I can smoke. I can have sex. It is sanctioned in my religion." If scriptures are presented in material terms, people who seek authoritative approval for their sinful activities will screw out false meanings from them. And he who compiles such scriptures is to blame. That sort of religiosity in which the object is to achieve material happiness by following regulative principles will not help one, and Nārada condemned this religiosity as abominable. "If you simply stick to this principle, because you are an authority, people will understand that this is religion. People will think that religion is nothing more than this." Even if one becomes very expert in executing religious performances, that does not mean that he can be elevated to the spiritual platform. Such performances may be a little helpful for rising to the spiritual platform, but unless one actually engages in the service of the Lord he cannot achieve perfection. Nārada Muni said, "Therefore, now please write literature that will attract people to Kṛṣṇa, the Supreme Lord. Thus far you have only given an official understanding of Kṛṣṇa. You have indicated that God is great or all-powerful, but people are not attracted because you have distracted their attention to the improvement of their material condition."

THE ANCHOR

In this connection there is a nice story told by our spiritual master, His Divine Grace A.C. Bhaktivedanta Swami Prabhupāda, concerning a wedding party that was traveling to the bride's home. In India the bridegroom and his father and other relatives go to the bride's home, and the marriage ceremony takes place there in the presence of all the relatives. This particular marriage was to take place in a village miles away. In Bengal the land is full of rivers, and the rivers are used as highways. So it was settled that the bridegroom's party would start out on the evening before the marriage day and would arrive the next morning. They could rest the whole day, and that evening before the marriage would take place. The party hired a ferry and got into the boat, and as the boat started, all the members of the bridegroom's party fell asleep. The breeze on the river was strong and very pleasing, but the next morning when the wedding party arose they saw that they were standing in the same place. They were surprised. "How is it," the boatman was asked, "that we are still in the same place? We have not proceeded even a few yards. How is that?" The boatman said, "We were rowing the whole night. We don't know how this has happened." Then one boatman found that the anchor had not been raised. The whole night the men were plying the oars, but the boat was only going around the anchor and did not go forward an inch.

Similarly, our anchor in the material world is our desire for material happiness, for which we may even worship God, go to a temple and offer our respect. But if our goal is only material happiness and if that is accepted as the ultimate goal, then it is useless. We have to go above that position. If one approaches Kṛṣṇa and says, "My dear Lord, I am in distress, please help me," that is good in the sense that somehow or other one has approached God. But his motive is not pure. The motive is material enjoyment. Therefore Nārada told Vyāsadeva, "This kind of instruction in your books will not help people to come to the standard of pure devotional service, which alone can save them from all material bondage."

If this criticism is actually valid for Vyāsadeva, who was at least trying to bring people to the spiritual level, then how severely Nārada's criticism applies to those so-called authorities or teachers who do not even encourage that one follow the regulative principles of religion. Famous writers, poets and philosophers who are taken as authorities and are followed by people in general, but who present only their speculations or sinful motives in writing, may write books which are read by millions, but the effect is disastrous. Śrīla Vyāsadeva, by encouraging material sex life under the regulative principles of marriage but not stressing sufficiently that Kṛṣṇa is the center of married life and of all activities, may have been at fault in that way, but the mundane writer who presents sex life as virtuous and enjoyable, even outside of marriage, has an abominable influence.

PILGRIMAGE FOR CROWS

The *Śrīmad-Bhāgavatam* deals with such literatures. In the First Canto, Chapter Five, it is stated, "Those words which do not describe the glories of the Lord, who alone can sanctify the atmosphere of the whole universe, are considered by saintly persons to be like unto a place of pilgrimage for crows. Since the all-perfect persons are inhabitants of the transcendental abode, they do not derive any pleasure there." In his purport to this verse His Divine Grace A.C. Bhaktivedanta Swami Prabhupāda has written: "Crows and swans are not birds of the same feather because of their different mental attitudes. The fruitive workers or passionate men are compared to the crows, whereas the all-perfect saintly persons are compared to swans. The crows take pleasure in a place where refused remnants of foodstuffs are thrown out, just as the passionate fruitive workers take pleasure in wine, women, and places for gross sense pleasure. The swans do not take pleasure in the places where the crows are assembled for conferences and meetings. They are instead seen in an atmosphere of natural scenic beauty where there are transparent reservoirs of water nicely decorated with stems of lotus flowers in variegated colors of natural beauty. That is the difference between the two classes of birds. Similarly, there are different kinds of literature for different kinds of men. Mostly the market literatures which attract men of the crow's category are literatures containing refused remnants of sensuous topics. They are generally known as mundane talks in relation with the gross body and subtle mind. They are full of subject matter described in decorative language full of mundane similes and metaphorical arrangements. Yet with all that, they are devoid of glorification of the Lord. Such poetry and prose, on any subject matter, is considered decoration of the dead body and the superficial agitated mind. Spiritually advanced men who are compared to the swans do not take pleasure in such dead literatures, which are sources of pleasure for men who are spiritually dead. These literatures in the modes of passion and ignorance are distributed under different labels, but they can hardly help the spiritual urge of the human being, and therefore the swanlike spiritually advanced men have nothing to do with such mundane remnants. Social literary men, scientists, mundane poets, theoretical philosophers and politicians who are completely absorbed in the material advancement of sense pleasure are all dolls of the material energy. They take pleasure in a place where rejected subject matters are thrown. According to Svāmī Śrīdhara, this is the pleasure of the prostitute hunters."

THE BEST LITERATURE

The essence of human activities is to describe the glories of the Lord. Literature which does not engage people in the devotional service of Kṛṣṇa will not be substantially pleasurable. "On the other hand, literature which is full of descriptions of the transcendental glories of the name, fame, form, pastimes, etc., of the unlimited Supreme Lord is a different creation of transcendental words meant for bringing about a revolution in the impious life of a misdirected world civilization. Such transcendental literature, even though imperfectly composed, is accepted by purified men who are throughly honest."

(*Bhāg*. 1.5.11)

It is understood that by broadcasting the holy name and fame of the Supreme Lord, the polluted atmosphere of the world will change, and as a result of propagating transcendental literature, people will become sane in their transactions. Of course at first people are inclined towards literature concerning sensuous topics, and they find this to be more entertaining and attractive than descriptions of the Supreme Lord. This is due to their diseased condition of thinking that the real self is the temporary body. The *Bhagavad-gītā*, however, points out that this body is just like a jacket and that the real self is the eternal soul. Until we realize this, we think that our happiness is in this body, and therefore we like to hear literatures describing the joys and pleasures of this body.

It is stated that reading literature glorifying God acts on the conditioned soul as sugar candy does upon a person affected with jaundice. Although in the beginning one who is suffering from jaundice is reluctant to take sugar candy because of his diseased state, it is well known that sugar candy is the remedy for jaundice. Sugar tastes bitter to a jaundiced person, but the symptom of his cure is that he tastes the sugar candy to be progressively sweeter. Similarly, when people develop a taste for transcendental literature, they will automatically cease to read other literature. When transcendental literature like *Śrīmad-Bhāgavatam* is available for the reading propensity, the material literature, which is catering poison to society, will automatically cease to be popular. "There are thousands and thousands of literary men all over the world, and they have created many, many thousands of literary works for the information of the people in general for thousands and thousands of years. Unfortunately none of them have brought peace and tranquility on earth between men or between nations. This is due to a spiritual vacuum in those literatures; therefore Vedic literatures are specifically recommended for suffering humanity to bring about the desired effect of liberation from the pangs of material civilization, which is eating the vital part of human energy." (Bhaktivedanta purports to *Śrīmad-Bhāgavatam,* 1.5.13)

CONCENTRATE ON KṚṢṆA

Nārada therefore advised his student Vyāsadeva, "Anything which you have described under any vision apart from that of the Lord will react and result in oscillating the mind as the wind rocks a boat which has no resting place." Nārada stressed the effect of the Vedic literature compiled by Vyāsadeva and tried to emphasize to him that he should concentrate on describing everything in relation with the Supreme Lord and no one else. In fact, there is nothing existent but the Lord. The Lord is the root of the complete tree, and He is the stomach of the complete body. Pouring water on the root is the right method of watering a tree, just as feeding the stomach is the means of supplying energy to all parts of the body. Śrīla Vyāsadeva was an authority on the scriptures, and therefore Nārada condemned his compromising spirit and advised him to speak directly on the prime necessity of human life—to realize one's relationship with the Lord and thus surrender unto Him without delay. Nārada said, "The Supreme Lord is unlimited. Only expert personalities understand this knowledge of spiritual values. Therefore those who are not so well situated, due to being attached to material qualities, should be shown the ways of transcendental realization, by yourself, through descriptions of the transcendental qualities of the Supreme Lord." Nārada indicated that because Vyāsa actually knew about the Supreme Lord, he should compile scriptures according to the synopsis which Nārada had given him. Living beings must accept the supremacy of the Lord and agree to render loving service unto Him for whom they have been created. Without this there cannot be peace and tranquility in the world. Śrīla Vyāsadeva was advised by Śrīla Nārada to expand this idea in the *Bhāgavatam*. To surrender fully unto the lotus feet of the Supreme Lord is the only proper engagement of the living being. Therefore, intent on describing the Lord more vividly, Vyāsadeva set about to both wipe out his own despondency and to benefit all humanity by following the orders of his spiritual master.

VYASĀDEVA'S VISION

"On the western bank of the River Sarasvatī, which is very intimately related with transcendental subjects like the *Vedas*, there is a cottage for meditation. In that place Śrīla Vyāsadeva, in his own *āśrama*, which is surrounded by berry trees, sat down to meditate after touching water for purification. Thus he perfectly engaged his mind in the linking process of devotional service without any tinge of material affection, and he saw the Absolute Personality of Godhead along with His external energy, which was under full control." (*Bhāg.* 1.7.2-4) By the instructions of his spiritual master, Vyāsadeva became absorbed in transcendental thought of the Personality of Godhead. He did not take notice of the impersonal effulgence coming from the body of the Lord, but concentrated on the Personality of Godhead who is personally controlling all energies. Upon seeing the all-perfect Personality of Godhead along with His energies, Vyāsadeva observed the unwanted miseries of the conditioned souls bewildered by illusion, and at last he saw the remedial measure for the conditioned souls, namely the linking process of devotional service. Thus, based on the instructions of his spiritual master and his subsequent meditation, Vyāsadeva understood that the process of hearing and chanting of the name, fame, and glory of the Supreme Personality will alone revive one's dormant love of God. The way this works is that when the Lord is satisfied with the efforts of the devotees, He endows them with His loving transcendental service. As soon as one takes up chanting and hearing in an attitude of service, at once his unwanted miseries disappear. There is no other requirement necessary but simply to give aural reception to the glorification of God.

The final result is that Vyāsadeva set to work compiling the mature work of his life, *Śrīmad-Bhāgavatam*, which contains full descriptions of the pastimes of the Supreme Personality of Godhead and His pure devotees. In this work there is no tinge of dry philosophical speculation, study of the impersonal nature, execution of sacrifices to the demigods, or the pursuit of sense gratification under the sanction of religiosity or mechanical *yoga*. Vyāsa compiled the *Śrīmad-Bhāgavatam* in twelve cantos of eighteen thousand verses. *Śrīmad-Bhā-*

gavatam which is the narration of the Lord's activities, is the postgraduate study of *Bhagavad-gītā*, which is spoken by the Lord Himself. Often someone says, "God is great," but how great He is, what He is doing, what His energies are, what He is like, what His pastimes are, what His qualities are (His gentleness, gravity and beauty as well as His specific dealings with His intimate devotees) is all disclosed in *Śrīmad-Bhāgavatam*. This is the crowning glory of Vyāsadeva's compilation of the scriptures. Simply by reading *Śrīmad-Bhāgavatam* and *Bhagavad-gītā*, one can assimilate all knowledge and reach the ultimate end of knowledge—to develop love for Kṛṣṇa.

Kṛṣṇa Consciousness: Secret and Confidential

November/December, 1972

In *Bhagavad-gītā* Lord Kṛṣṇa tells His disciple Arjuna, "I shall give you the most secret wisdom," and our spiritual master, His Divine Grace A.C. Bhaktivedanta Swami Prabhupāda, declares that Kṛṣṇa consciousness is the most confidential knowledge. So what is the secret? And how can it be found out? Like any good secret, Kṛṣṇa consciousness can only be revealed to one who can be trusted.

Śrīla Prabhupāda tells a story from his own life to illustrate what it is to be accepted in confidence. When he was only twenty-two years old, Śrīla Prabhupāda was placed as manager in charge of a department in the chemical concern of a Mr. Bose in India. Śrīla Prabhupāda's father was a very intimate friend of Mr. Bose, and therefore the son was immediately able to take on a responsible post. From the very first day on the job, in fact, he was signing large checks on behalf of the company and was in charge of a number of workers in his department. Some of the older workers, however, were dissatisfied that a young man should suddenly be placed as their superior. Some of them were elderly and had been in the firm for forty years. After expressing their dissatisfaction among themselves, they finally decided to speak to Mr. Bose about the situation. When he was asked why the young man had at once been put in charge, Mr. Bose replied, "Oh, for that position I needed someone I could trust as my own son. I could only entrust the personal handling of my accounts in that department to him. His father and I are very close, and this young man is known to me practically as my son." In short, Śrīla Prabhupāda's qualification was his intimate friendship; he could be trusted confidentially.

Similarly, the secrets of Kṛṣṇa conciousness are revealed only to the confidential devotees of Lord Kṛṣṇa. What are these secrets? Often people watch the Hare Kṛṣṇa dancing and singing parties in the downtown streets of their cities, and they wonder about this mystery: Why is it that these boys and girls of American and European backgrounds have made this chanting of Hare Kṛṣṇa their whole lives? Also, people who visit any of the many temples of the International Society for Krishna Consciousness sometimes wonder why these young persons have changed from the normal ways of modern civilization and taken to a life centered on transcendental consciousness. They wonder what it is that is attracting so many young men and women to Kṛṣṇa consciousness, and sometimes they guess at the answers. But for most people it is a mystery.

Then there are those who have read or studied the sacred scripture *Bhagavad-gītā*, which forms the basis of the Kṛṣṇa consciousness philosophy. *Bhagavad-gītā*—another mystery. Great scholars and professors of religion and philosophy have applied their intelligence to *Bhagavad-gītā*, and they even attempt to teach it—but they cannot penetrate its mystery. They confess that they do not really know what it means. They are mystified. And, actually, *Bhagavad-gītā* deals with a subject that is very mysterious and is therefore generally called "the unknown." What lies beyond death? What is eternity? What is God? Who am I? Why are we suffering? What is the purpose of existence? Where did we come from? The wonderful quality of the *Bhagavad-gītā* is that it clearly answers all these questions. And it reveals even greater mysteries besides—but only to devotees.

This brings up another important characteristic of confidential knowledge. "Confidential means," Śrīla Prabhupāda says, "that not everyone will like it." For example, a young father may want to show us a collection of photographs of his newly born baby, but if we are not friends of his, are we particularly interested in looking at a collection of baby pictures? No. Those pictures are actually confidential, and only those who are interested in the young man and his family want to see them, for they take real pleasure in looking at them. It is the same with knowledge about Kṛṣṇa consciousness.

Kṛṣṇa consciousness is the topmost *yoga* system, and Śrīla Prabhupāda describes why it is that Kṛṣṇa chose Arjuna as His disciple and told him the "most secret wisdom." "Arjuna is a devotee," Śrīla Prabhupāda writes. "He is submissive, and he is in contact with Kṛṣṇa as a friend. Therefore Kṛṣṇa is revealing Himself to him. What is the qualification? Kṛṣṇa says, 'One who has developed the service spirit with love and devotion can understand Me.' Not otherwise can He be reached. The big scholars and mental speculators cannot understand. But a child can understand Kṛṣṇa if he has full faith in Him. So faith and devotion qualify one. Simply by such faith and service you will understand that Kṛṣṇa is the Supreme Personality of Godhead."

In other words, certain persons, due to their devotion and service to Kṛṣṇa, have had the secrets of Kṛṣṇa consciousness revealed to them. Anyone can also become such a confidential devotee, provided he approaches one who is already a pure devotee and tries to learn from him by inquiry and service. The chief quality of such pure devotees of Kṛṣṇa is that, more than anything else, they crave this confidential relationship with Kṛṣṇa. They are mad after performing some service for Kṛṣṇa. They will give up everything just to enter into this confidential association of Kṛṣṇa.

It is only fair that we consider many readers who may be asking at this point, "Who is Kṛṣṇa that just knowing Him solves all these questions, such as what is beyond death and what is God?" Who is Kṛṣṇa? Śrīla Prabhupāda has described in conversation what the devotees are aspiring for and whom they are thinking of when they say "Kṛṣṇa."

"The earth spins and turns around the sun, and the sun spins, and the universe turns, and there are millions of such universes. And this is all running to the exact ten-thousandth of a second in the right way. Think of what a brain devised this plan! That is Kṛṣṇa. And just think: We are trying to associate with such a personality. Think of how great our ambition is. It is no small thing."

Kṛṣṇa is God, the supreme controller. Kṛṣṇa is worshiped in churches, temples and mosques all over the world and the universes, and He is prayed to in thousands of different names, like Allah, Jehovah, etc. He is the one God without a second. Since time immemorial He has been coming Himself to the earth and sending His confidential messengers, incarnations and sages. He has sent His son, Lord Jesus Christ, and the prophet Mohammed. They have all proclaimed the same message: "You are all servants of God; kindly give up the senseless life of selfishness and just love God."

But although the Supreme Lord has broadcast through scriptures and through His pure devotees that the way to end suffering and bring about peace and prosperity is to love God, the world remains in misery and ignorance, and very few actually take up the confidential path of loving service to God. Now, in the current scientific age, there is even much propaganda saying, "God is dead," or, "There is no God." Thus people become confused by so many contradictory doctrines. There is even rampant hypocrisy among so-called representatives of God—cheaters posing as pure, confidential devotees. In this way, since the secret mystery of Kṛṣṇa consciousness has become covered up by man's madness, people think, "Well, there may or may not be God, but it is too confusing—let me simply enjoy life for now. If there is God, He won't mind." Thus they become content to be other than a friend of Kṛṣṇa's. In despair, people turn to other activities, and they do not crave their original confidential association with Kṛṣṇa. They forget that it is even worth their interest or that it is at all pleasurable to associate with God. Actually, it is impossible to even exist without Him, since we are eternally His parts and parcels, and yet we have fallen into forgetfulness of this greatest love, which is the very purpose of life. Rather, people now seek confidential knowledge on how to improve sex desire, how to succeed in business, how to become famous in the world, or how to become God oneself through *yoga* exercise. These materialistic versions of confidential knowledge are available, but they are just illusions, like mirages on the desert, and therefore they cannot satisfy. Each of us is originally and forever a servant of God. To be a servant of God means to live eternally in bliss and knowledge, but in confusion and in lust for enjoying without Him we have thrown away the secret.

Nonetheless, the situation is very hopeful. The devotees of Kṛṣṇa are very hopeful because although people in this age are for the most part not interested in spiritual culture, they can still very easily begin Kṛṣṇa consciousness and enjoy full spiritual bliss. This is the unique contribution and potent mystery of the Kṛṣṇa consciousness movement. The mercy of this movement is that people in the grip of forgetfulness can very easily feel love of Kṛṣṇa, which is itself the most intimate secret, by taking to the simple process of chanting Hare Kṛṣṇa, Hare Kṛṣṇa, Kṛṣṇa Kṛṣṇa, Hare Hare.

Because there was no other hope, because people had completely fallen away from God consciousness, Kṛṣṇa appeared in India 500 years ago as the incarnation called Lord Caitanya with a mission to show how to love Kṛṣṇa. In other words, God Himself arranged to show us how to be devotees of God. It was for that purpose that Lord Caitanya came. His method, specifically, was chanting of the holy names of God, hearing of the glories of God from the lips of pure devotees, and taking *prasādam*, or food offered to Kṛṣṇa. That is the gist of this dynamic movement of spiritual culture which is now sweeping over the present world situation.

The secret is open. The Hare Kṛṣṇa *mantra* (chant) is the secret. Hare Kṛṣṇa, Hare Kṛṣṇa, Kṛṣṇa Kṛṣṇa, Hare Hare/Hare Rāma, Hare Rāma, Rāma Rāma, Hare Hare. Anyone can chant these holy names constantly, and there is no hard and fast rule to chanting. You can have it at no expense, and there is no tax. The benefit is very great. It is revealed—the name of Kṛṣṇa is nondifferent from Kṛṣṇa Himself. The name Kṛṣṇa has all the qualities of the Supreme Person Kṛṣṇa. If you chant Hare Kṛṣṇa, you immediately enter His association. That is the sum and substance of the chanting. There is some initial difficulty only in that people are suspicious, for they are used to being exploited by free offers.

Śrīla Prabhupāda's spiritual master, Bhaktisiddhānta Sarasvatī, anticipating this reluctance, described that preaching Kṛṣṇa consciousness is like going door to door with the best fruit, a nice fresh mango, and trying to give it away. People will be suspicious: "Oh, what is this? Why don't you want any money for it? What is the catch?" So they will be reluctant to take it. But even that difficulty is being overcome due to the overall attraction of devotional service.

The chanting, Hare Kṛṣṇa, Hare Kṛṣṇa, Kṛṣṇa Kṛṣṇa, Hare Hare/Hare Rāma, Hare Rāma, Rāma Rāma, Hare Hare, is the special benediction for this age. What was possible in former ages only by many years of meditation or *yoga* or difficult austerities is now, by the mercy of Lord Caitanya, being distributed freely. That is especially because of the fallen nature of this age. It is frankly stated in the scripture *Śrīmad-Bhāgavatam*: "Men in this iron age of quarrel are very short-lived. O learned men, they are also very lazy, misguided and unlucky, and, above all, they are always disturbed." (*Bhāg.* 1.1.10)

His Divine Grace A.C. Bhaktivedanta Swami Prabhupāda is a pure devotee in the disciplic line from Lord Caitanya, whose teaching is identical to that of Lord Kṛṣṇa. Although Lord Kṛṣṇa is merciful, in His form of Lord Caitanya He is even more merciful. Lord Kṛṣṇa promised, "Do not be afraid, for I will grant you all protection. Just surrender to Me." But in His most merciful, liberal and generous form, His appearance as Caitanya Mahāprabhu, Kṛṣṇa is simply saying, "Be joyful. Chant, dance, sing, take *prasādam*." It should be noted, however, that this movement is not sentimental. It is authorized by all the Vedic scriptures. Into the Hare Kṛṣṇa *mantra* are compressed all the Vedic rituals and all other holy *mantras*. It is the conclusion of all Vedic study. For persons who, in the midst of this age of atheism, are at all interested in love of God, there is no surer way to success.

By their mercy, those who hold the secret have let it out, and they are energetically distributing it. The purpose of the loud congregational chanting of the names and glories of the Lord is to enable not just a few persons but all humanity to benefit. It is very sublime even to try to understand how infinite is God's mercy in the form of the Hare Kṛṣṇa *mantra*. Because no one in this age can perform the difficult procedures of *yoga* and austerity, everyone can be brought to the topmost perfection and revive his confidential relationship with God just by chanting. The same qualifications still apply, however: one must receive this gift from one who is already a trusted confidential associate of the Lord. Such a person is very rare, but he is present. His Divine Grace A.C. Bhaktivedanta Swami Prabhupāda is spreading this teaching everywhere—through literature, lectures, and by his deputed agents, his many spiritual sons and daughters—not for any personal motive but because he was ordered to do so by his spiritual master. You can inquire and verify for yourself that he is actually an intimate associate of Kṛṣṇa.

All that remains is for you, on your part, to take this chanting. It is for this purpose that the Kṛṣṇa consciousness centers are maintained. You can accept freely this matchless gift. Kṛṣṇa consciousness temples dot the map, appearing in virtually every major United States city and many European and Eastern cities, such as London, Hamburg, Bombay, Sydney and Singapore. They are like oases in the material desert. Every Sunday in each center, a feast is held. It is not an ordinary feast. The offering is sumptuous *prasādam*, which means spiritual food offered to Kṛṣṇa, and the menu includes sweet rice, *saṁosa* (a spiced vegetable pastry), and *lāddus*, a milk sweet which is so delicious that it is sought after by Kṛṣṇa Himself, as described in the book, *Kṛṣṇa, the Supreme Personality of Godhead*. These festivities can get you out of hellish existence. Go take part in the chanting and read the literature of Kṛṣṇa consciousness. This is not a bluffing movement. You will feel spiritual strength. Take advantage of this special mercy being distributed in this age. Enter the confidential secrets of Kṛṣṇa consciousness and find your happiness.

Delivering the Message Unchanged

August, 1975

The day on which a disciple celebrates the appearance of his spiritual master is called Vyāsa-pūjā. The word "Vyāsa" indicates Śrīla Vyāsadeva, a powerful incarnation of Kṛṣṇa (God) who compiled all of the Vedic literature, and "*pūjā*" means worship.

Vyāsadeva appeared five thousand years ago, at the dawn of the present Age of Quarrel, just when widespread moral deterioration was about to begin. He could foresee that the people of this age would be short-lived, unfortunate and always disturbed.

Before Vyāsadeva, all the Vedic scriptures were taught and received verbally in disciplic succession. The memories of both the students and the spiritual masters of those ages were so sharp that once they heard a transcendental message from their spiritual master, the message was immediately imprinted into their brains and considered a written language.

To give the unfortunate people of the modern age a chance to partake of the knowledge contained in the *Vedas*, Śrī Vyāsadeva undertook the enormous task of compilation. He composed the millions of Sanskrit verses of the *Mahābhārata*, the *Vedānta-sūtra* and the *Purāṇas*, including *Śrīmad-Bhāgavatam*. No one else in history can compare with him as a poet, philosopher or writer, and he is thus known as Mahāmuni (the great sage). He is the spiritual master of all who follow the teachings of the *Vedas*. His final, mature work, *Śrīmad-Bhāgavatam*, is known as the "ripened fruit of the *Vedas*" and is sufficient in itself for God realization. The precious *Bhāgavatam* has been handed down in disciplic succession, from *guru* to disciple, in an unbroken chain, and today His Divine Grace A.C. Bhaktivedanta Swami Prabhupāda, spiritual master of the International Society for Krishna Consciousness, is delivering it in turn to his disciples.

Out of his causeless mercy, Śrīla Vyāsadeva wrote *Srīmad-Bhāgavatam* for the benefit of the fallen people of Kaliyuga (the modern age), and out of *his* causeless mercy Śrīla Prabhupāda is personally translating and expanding this monumental work—and he is preaching it throughout the Western world as well. At the advanced age of seventy, he traveled under great hardship from

India to America to found the International Society for Krishna Consciousness, and today, nine years later, he tirelessly works eighteen to twenty hours a day, still translating and preaching the eternal message of *Śrīmad-Bhāgavatam*: pure, unalloyed service to Kṛṣṇa (God).

There are many so-called *gurus*, in India and elsewhere, who preach something other than pure devotional service to God. But such "*Gurus*" are condemned by Vyāsadeva at the beginning of *Śrīmad-Bhāgavatam:* "The supreme occupation for all humanity is that by which men can attain to loving devotional service unto the transcendent Lord. Such devotional service must be unmotivated and uninterrupted in order to completely satisfy the self." (*Bhāg.* 1.2.6) And they are condemned by Lord Kṛṣṇa Himself in *Bhagavad-gītā*: "Just give up all other forms of religion and surrender unto Me. I will protect you from all sinful reaction. Do not fear." (*Bg.* 18.66) Those who are followers of the Absolute Truth, the source of all emanations, accept that all knowledge of the Absolute Truth is coming from the Vedic scriptures compiled by Vyāsadeva, which include *Śrīmad-Bhāgavatam* and *Bhagavad-gītā.* The emphatic conclusion of these scriptures, which are the cream of the *Vedas,* is that Lord Kṛṣṇa is the source of all incarnations and manifestations. And this conclusion has been reiterated by all the spiritual masters in disciplic succession, such as Lord Brahmā, Nārada, Vyāsadeva and, in the modern age, Lord Caitanya, who stressed the chanting of the Hare Kṛṣṇa *mantra.*

Therefore one who is an actual spiritual master, who is imparting genuine knowledge of the Absolute Truth, must preach the message of Vyāsadeva without change. So on his appearance day, the disciples of His Divine Grace A.C. Bhaktivedanta Swami Prabhupāda will worship him as a bona fide representative of Vyāsadeva, who is faithfully preaching the pure message of Vyāsadeva throughout the world.

Breaking the Bonds of False Fatherhood

June, 1977

When a young person joins the Kṛṣṇa consciousness movement, his parents often doubt the wisdom of his decision. Admittedly, to join the Hare Kṛṣṇa movement is to commit oneself to values completely contrary to the "normal" way of life in today's Western civilization. A Kṛṣṇa conscious person strictly avoids the four pillars of sinful life—meat eating, illicit sex, intoxication, and gambling—which the average Westerner takes to be life's basic necessities. Yet after observing the fine character their sons and daughters attain through spiritual discipline, most parents of devotees adjust to their acceptance of Kṛṣṇa consciousness. However, a small group of parents, especially in America, consider the Hare Kṛṣṇa movement a great evil and are violently opposed to their adult children's choice of living in Kṛṣṇa consciousness. These parents' attempts to recover their sons and daughters by kidnapping and "deprogramming," as well as their accusations of "brainwashing" directed against Kṛṣṇa conscious preachers, have ignited a major civil rights issue: whether parental control can take precedence over the individual's right to freely choose his own course in life.*

This bitter conflict is not new. We find a similar case in the five-thousand-year-old Vedic history *Śrīmad-Bhāgavatam*. There we read of a very powerful father named Dakṣa, who became outraged when his sons renounced material life to follow the teachings of a Kṛṣṇa-conscious sage, Nārada Muni.** In light of

*In a landmark judicial decision handed down last March 17, 1976, New York State Supreme Court Justice John J. Leahy threw out indictments charging two leaders of ISKCON's New York chapter with attempted extortion and illegal imprisonment of members through "brainwashing." Declared the judge, "The entire and basic issue before this court is whether or not [the Hare Kṛṣṇa devotees] will be allowed to practice the religion of their choice—and this must be answered with a resounding affirmative."

**Nārada Muni is a direct representative of Kṛṣṇa, the Supreme Personality of Godhead. Throughout Vedic history Nārada helps the conditioned souls by teaching the topmost science of *bhakti-yoga*, or love of God. His disciples include many great devotees, like Prahlāda Mahārāja, Dhruva Mahārāja, and Śrīla Vyāsadeva. His mission, the mission of the Supreme Lord, is to deliver humanity from the cycle of birth and death.

the modern controversy, the account of how Nārada preached to the young men to convince them to give up family life, how Dakṣa cursed Nārada, and how Nārada persisted in his Kṛṣṇa conscious mission makes a revealing case history.

Our story begins at the dawn of creation. The Supreme Personality of Godhead has instructed Brahmā, the first living entity in the universe, to increase human population through his married sons, the Prajāpatis (progenitors). One of the chief progenitors was the demigod Dakṣa. *Dakṣa* means "expert," and this particular Dakṣa was expert in producing offspring through sexual intercourse. In union with his wife Pāñcajanī he fathered ten thousand sons, known as the Haryaśvas. Dakṣa intended that they also marry and increase progeny, following their father. Being devoutly religious, Dakṣa wanted to train his sons in the disciplines of Vedic culture to make them responsible, productive householders. So he sent them on pilgrimage to a holy place named Nārāyaṇa-saras, where, in the past, many saints and sages had meditated and performed other religious practices.

In that holy place, the Haryaśvas began regularly touching the lake's waters and bathing in them, gradually becoming very purified. They became inclined toward activities of the *paramahaṁsas* (the most highly advanced renounced saints). Nevertheless, because their father had ordered them to increase the population, they performed severe austerities to fulfill his desires.

One day the great sage Nārada Muni entered Nārāyana-saras. Seeing the boys performing such fine austerities, Nārada approached them. He saw that although Dakṣa's ten thousand sons were preparing for materialistic family life, they were simultaneously becoming eligible to hear of the path of liberation due to their austerities. Nārada thought, "Why should they become entangled in family life, which is so dark that once one enters it, he cannot leave?" (Generally, when one becomes too involved in his material environment, he does not look within the core of his heart to find the situation of the soul and the Supreme Soul.) One may argue that since increasing progeny is also a necessary function of the material creation, why should Nārada disturb these boys in their preparation? Later, Dakṣa put forth this very argument when he confronted Nārada. However, Nārada had no doubt that eternal liberation is of far greater value to a person than good progeny. Therefore, he approached the Haryaśvas to divert their attention towards spiritual life.

Nārada intrigued them by speaking in an allegorical way: "My dear Haryaśvas, you have not seen the extremities of the earth. There is a kingdom where only one man lives and where there is a hole from which, having entered, no one emerges. A woman there who is extremely unchaste adorns herself with various attractive dresses, and the man who lives there is her husband. You have not seen all this, and therefore you are inexperienced boys without advanced knowledge.

Alas, your father is omniscient, but you do not know his actual order. Without knowing the actual purpose of your father, how will you create progeny?"

The Haryaśvas could understand the meaning of Nārada's allegory. When he said that they did not know the earth's extremities, they knew he meant the "earth" of the body, or the field of material activities. Every one of us is an eternal spirit soul, encaged in material bodies life after life. But out of ignorance we take each body to be our real self. The Haryaśvas immediately understood that Nārada wanted them to become enlightened about the self–not to continue in perpetual bondage, taking material bodies birth after birth, but to use this human life for becoming free from this encagement.

Nārada mentioned a kingdom where there is only one king, with no competitor. The Haryaśvas understood him to mean the kingdom of God, which encompasses the complete spiritual world and all material universes, and where there is only one proprietor and enjoyer, the Supreme Personality of Godhead. Although sometimes appearing within the creation by His own sweet will, the Supreme Lord is never forced to take birth like the infinitesimal living entities. He is completely transcendental, and thus He is never destroyed, even with the destruction of the universe. One who misunderstands this transcendental position of Kṛṣṇa is a fool, and his hopes for knowledge, wealth, and liberation are all baffled. The Haryaśvas realized, therefore, that their duty in human life was to understand the Supreme Personality of Godhead.

When the sage Nārada spoke of entering a hole from which one does not return, the Haryaśvas could understand that he was referring to entering eternal, blissful Vaikuṇṭha (the spiritual planet). Kṛṣṇa teaches this same subject to Arjuna in the *Bhagavad-gītā*, where He says: "One who knows the transcendental nature of My appearance and activities does not, upon leaving the body, take his birth again in the material world, but attains my eternal abode, O Arjuna" (*Bg.* 4.9). The Haryaśvas agreed with Nārada's instructions: "Yes, if there is a place from which, having gone, we will not have to return to this miserable material life, what is the use of impermanent fruitive activities?"

Nārada had described a woman who was a professional prostitute. The Haryaśvas understood this woman to be the living entity's unsteady intelligence. As a prostitute changes dress to attract a man's attention for sense enjoyment, so, when one's intelligence is not turned toward Kṛṣṇa consciousness, it is a prostituted intelligence and will force the living being to change bodies, one after another. If one becomes the husband of a prostitute he cannot be happy. Similarly, one who follows the dictates of material intelligence and material consciousness will never be at peace.

Nārada had said that the Haryaśvas did not know the order of their father. They understood that Nārada meant their *spiritual* father, the bona fide spiritual master, who imparts scriptural knowledge to the faithful disciple. Therefore, the spiritual master is the real father. The scriptures instruct that one should end his material way of life. The Haryaśvas expressed their enlightenment: "Yes, if one does not know the purpose of the father's orders, the scriptures, he is ignorant. The words of a material father who endeavors to engage his son in material activities are not the real instructions of the father."

This brings us to the crux of the parent-child issue. In every form of life, one takes birth from a mother and father. (Even cats and dogs have their kittens and puppies.) However, human life is more advanced than other forms, because in the human form one has the chance to escape from the misery of birth and death by accepting a spiritual master and being educated in scriptural knowledge. The material mother and father are important only if they are interested in educating their child to become free from the clutches of death. In the *Śrīmad-Bhāgavatam*, the saintly king and father Ṛṣabhadeva advises his one hundred sons that no one should strive to become a parent if he cannot save his dependent from the imminent danger of death.

Therefore, parents who actually wish their children well will not object to their taking shelter of a bona fide spiritual master and getting the opportunity to achieve the perfection of life. Opposition is raised only by those parents who have no idea that the goal of human life is liberation from material bondage, and who, in ignorance—"good intentions" have no value—want to force their children to remain like themselves, trapped in the dark well of material life.

So, defying the orders of their materialistic father, Dakṣa, the Haryaśvas accepted Nārada Muni as their spiritual master. Dakṣa had instructed them to increase the population, but, after hearing the words of Nārada Muni, they could no longer heed that instruction. Rather, they followed Nārada's advice to give up material life and become devotees of the Lord. (Incidentally, all the world's scriptures advise relief from material life. In the Buddhist scriptures Lord Buddha advises that one achieve *nirvāṇa* by giving up the materialistic way of life. In the Bible one will find the same advice: cease materialistic life and return to the kingdom of God.)

Needless to say, Prajāpati Dakṣa was not very happy to hear that all his sons had defied his order and taken up Kṛṣṇa consciousness. When Dakṣa was lamenting for his lost children, Lord Brahmā pacified him, and thereafter Dakṣa begot one thousand more sons in the womb of his wife Pāñcajanī. This time his sons were known as the Savalāśvas. Here we can see that, whereas Nārada was very expert in delivering all the conditioned souls back to home, back to Godhead, Prajāpati Dakṣa was expert in begetting children. Unfortunately, the material expert did not agree with the spiritual expert. Be that as it may, nothing could deter Nārada from chanting the Hare Kṛṣṇa mantra and imparting spiritual knowledge to his qualified disciples. In this regard His Divine Grace A.C. Bhaktivedanta Swami Prabhupāda has written:

> **The Kṛṣṇa consciousness movement is preaching this higher knowledge of retiring from materialistic life to return to Godhead, but unfortunately many parents are not satisfied with this movement. . . . However, we have no alternative other than to teach our disciples to free themselves from materialistic life. We must instruct them in the opposite of material life to save them from the repetition of birth and death.**

Ordered by Dakṣa to beget children, the Savalāśvas went to Nārāyaṇa-saras, the same holy place where, by the grace of Nārada, their brothers had previously attained perfection. One might wonder why Dakṣa risked sending his second set of sons to the same place where he had lost his first set. The answer is that, despite his materialistic outlook, Dakṣa was a dutiful father who followed the principles of Vedic culture. Therefore, he did not hesitate to let his sons receive spiritual instructions concerning the perfection of life. He allowed them to choose whether to return home, back to Godhead, or to remain in the material world, transmigrating life after life in various species. In all circumstances, the duty of a responsible father is to give a spiritual education to his children and then allow them to freely decide whether to adopt a spiritual or a material way of life.

The Savalāśvas performed the same penances as the Haryaśvas had. They bathed in holy water, and its touch cleansed away all the dirty material desires in their hearts. They also chanted sacred mantras and underwent a severe course of austerities. Soon, Nārada Muni approached the Savalāśvas and spoke enigmatic words to them, just as he had spoken to the Haryaśvas. Then, before departing, Nārada advised them to follow the same spiritual path as their beloved elder brothers. Deeply affected by the words of Nārada, the Savalāśvas also gave up the idea of producing children and took up Kṛṣṇa consciousness.

When Dakṣa heard that the Savalāśvas had also defied him, he became very angry at Nārada and almost fainted in despair. Nārada then approached Dakṣa, thinking that since Dakṣa was lamenting, he would be a suitable candidate to appreciate spiritual instructions. But when Nārada came before Dakṣa, the bereaved Prajāpati confronted him and angrily accused him, "Alas, Nārada Muni, you wear the dress of a saintly person, but you are not actually a saint. By showing my sons the path of renunciation, you have done me an abominable injustice."

Dakṣa finds his counterpart in today's angry parents, who accuse Śrīla Prabhupāda of misleading their inexperienced children. Śrīla Prabhupāda replies,

> We are instructing all the young boys and girls in the Western countries to follow the path of renunciation. We allow married life, but even a *gṛhastha* [a Kṛṣṇa conscious householder] has to give up so many bad habits that his parents think his life has been practically destroyed. We allow no meat eating, no illicit sex, no gambling, and no intoxication, and consequently the parents wonder how, if there are so many *no's*, one's life can be positive. In the Western countries especially, these four prohibited activities practically constitute the life and soul of the modern population. Therefore, parents sometimes dislike our movement, just as Prajāpati Dakṣa disliked the activities of Nārada and accused him of dishonesty. Nevertheless, although parents may be angry at us, we must perform our duty without hesitation, because we are in the disciplic succession from Nārada Muni.

The point is that every human being must prepare himself for his next life. It will not do simply to remain in materialistic household life without regulation or spiritual discipline. One cannot expect to be happy in this life or the next without following the injunctions of the scriptures.

Dakṣa next accused Nārada of obstructing his sons' good fortune by making it impossible for them to repay their debts—especially their debt to Dakṣa. The Vedic culture recognizes that everyone is born a debtor, being obligated to great saints, to the demigods, and to his father. To liquidate one's debt to his father, one must beget children. Similarly, today's parents somtimes appeal to their children in the Kṛṣṇa consciousness movement: "Don't you appreciate all we've done for you? Please return to your family." However, scriptures such as the *Śrīmad-Bhāgavatam* state that although everyone is indebted to his family, if he surrenders to Kṛṣṇa he is freed from all debts. Unfortunately, Dakṣa did not understand the great service rendered by Nārada Muni, so he called him a sinful person. Nārada Muni, however, being in reality a great saint, tolerated the accusations of Dakṣa, performed his duty, and delivered Dakṣa's sons back home, back to Godhead.

Along these same lines, Dakṣa accused Nārada of breaking the natural ties of family affection. We have already pointed out that one may maintain an affectionate relationship with his mother and father—provided they help and not hinder him on the path of spiritual enlightenment. But since Dakṣa's sole motive was to engage his sons in producing progeny, clearly the best course they could have followed for their Kṛṣṇa consciousness was to break their family ties with him. Today we find that many members of the Kṛṣṇa consciousness movement have left family situations beset with fighting, divorce, hypocrisy, and sin. Breaking such family connections cannot be considered bad. Sometimes modern parents also say that taking up Kṛṣṇa consciousness is bad because it destroys a young person's budding career. But, again, if that career is one of materialistic ignorance–if it involves no consideration of spiritual values–it is better to leave such a career and become Kṛṣṇa conscious. This does not mean that one should stop working at an honest occupation, but if the career is an impediment to spiritual advancement, better to leave it.

One may argue that although Nārada was a saint and his advice authoritative, still, this incident took place in a culture entirely different from our own; therefore its lessons cannot be applied to our modern situation. But spiritual culture is not a matter of East or West; it is the eternal, inalienable right of every human being, for it leads to the perfection of life. Certainly our Western culture differs from the Vedic culture. Ours is a culture that permits slaughter of the cow; that neither respects nor protects saintly persons (*brāhmaṇas*), who are much needed to guide society; that allows the murder of children within the womb; that encourages illicit sexual relations outside sanctified marriage; and that has a government which supports sinful activities like intoxication and gambling. So ours is certainly a different kind of culture from the Vedic one, but must we necessarily follow the culture in which we were born and raised, if it is so entirely opposed to the progressive values of life?

Finally, Dakṣa cursed Nārada: "You made me lose my sons once before, and now you have again done the same inauspicious thing. Therefore, you are a rascal who does not know how to behave toward others. You may travel all over the universe, but I curse you to have no fixed residence anywhere." This curse was considered a great punishment by Dakṣa, who, as a householder, wanted to remain in one spot and enjoy family life. However, this "punishment" was a boon for a Kṛṣṇa conscious preacher like Nārada, because a preacher always travels for the benefit of human society. Thus, Nārada replied, "Yes, what you have said is good. I accept this curse." Then Nārada Muni departed, and since that time he has been traveling throughout the spiritual and material worlds, chanting Hare Kṛṣṇa, playing his *vīṇā*, and enlightening everyone in Kṛṣṇa consciousness.

EPILOGUE

We hope this narration from the *Śrīmad-Bhāgavatam* may stimulate the few parents who oppose Kṛṣṇa consciousness to reconsider their condemnation of the Kṛṣṇa consciousness movement for diverting their offspring from the material path. Unlike Dakṣa, many parents of devotees, as well as many important citizens, *do* appreciate the immense value of Kṛṣṇa consciousness to the younger generation and to people in general. Recently, Governor Jerry Brown of California personally called on the Hare Kṛṣṇa movement to help him bring spiritual encouragement to hospital patients in his state. Learned scholars in virtually every major university around the world have written warm appreciations of Śrīla Prabhupāda's books on Kṛṣṇa consciousness. In addition, many devotees' parents have helped form organizations for the protection of their childrens' right to practice the religion of their choice.

The small minority of modern-day Dakṣas who cannot or will not try to understand Kṛṣṇa consciousness may continue their efforts to hinder this movement and its preachers, but we shall not fear them. We shall simply go on humbly performing our duty, trying to follow the orders of the Supreme Personality of Godhead, who has said, "Teach everyone to follow the instructions of Lord Śrī Kṛṣṇa as they are given in the *Bhagavad-gītā* and *Śrīmad-Bhāgavatam*. In this way become a spiritual master and try to liberate everyone in the world."

Compassion Means Spreading Kṛṣṇa Consciousness

September, 1977

India's greatest gift to civilization is her highly advanced spiritual culture, based on the eternal truths of the Vedic literatures. Sometimes, however, we hear the strange idea that this culture is not meant to be shared with others. I have heard more than one Western professor of Indian religion say, "The idea of preaching about God in a missionary spirit is not part of India's religion. That's something the Christians introduced into India a few hundred years ago." And self-styled *yogīs* sometimes say to me, "People should be left alone to realize God in their own way, in their own time. You can't go out and preach about inner life." I have also heard seemingly devout Hindus say, "Why are you teaching of Kṛṣṇa in America? To follow the *Vedas* you have to be born in India." Is Kṛṣṇa's message, then, just for a few?

No. Both the Vedic literatures themselves and the living examples of India's greatest saints disprove that idea. Moreover, such disdain for preaching Vedic truths reveals a sad lack of compassion for fallen humanity.

In fact, the Vedic literatures (the world's most time-honored scriptures) fully support the idea of preaching the gospel of Kṛṣṇa consciousness. In the five-thousand-year-old *Śrīmad-Bhāgavatam*, the self-realized sages who compiled the *Vedas* at the beginning of creation offer their prayers to Lord Kṛṣṇa, the Personality of Godhead: "All glories unto You! O Lord, You can deliver all suffering conditioned souls from the clutches of *māyā* [illusion]. O Lord, we fervently pray that You do so. As the personifications of Vedic knowledge, we always try to help the conditioned souls understand You" (*Bhāg*. 10.87.14).

Unless devotees of God broadcast His message, the ignorant living entities can never know that the ultimate purpose of life is liberation from material bondage. Thus, in mad pursuit of sense gratification, they will commit sinful acts and have to suffer the painful reactions, according to the law of *karma.* They will have to transmigrate from one body to another, repeatedly suffering the miseries of birth, old age, disease, and death. Since surrender to the will of the Lord is the only way to nullify *karma* and stop the process of transmigration, the merciful devotees of the Lord always preach His glories widely. And the Supreme Lord Himself regularly visits the earth to reclaim the fallen souls. As Lord Kṛṣṇa states in the *Bhagavad-gītā*(4.8), "In order to deliver the pious and annihilate the miscreants, as well as to establish the principles of religion, I advent Myself millennium after millennium." And in the *Śrīmad-Bhāgavatam* we find that the sage Vyāsadeva, who compiled the Sanskrit Vedic scriptures, also felt the same compassion for the suffering souls: "The material miseries of the living entity, which are superfluous to him, can be directly mitigated by the linking process of devotional scrvice, but the mass of people do not know this. And therefore the learned Vyāsadeva compiled this Vedic literature, which is in relation to the Supreme Truth" (*Bhāg*. 1.7.6). Thus, thousand of years before Christianity appeared in the world, the Vedic literature stated emphatically that souls suffering in darkness should be helped by the torchlight of Kṛṣṇa consciousness. From the historical perspective, then, the Christians could not have introduced the preaching spirit to India.

Another misconception is that one should cultivate spiritual knowledge only by private meditation and should not "bother" those who are spiritually ignorant. But the great devotee Prahlāda Mahārāja rejects this view in the *Śrīmad-Bhāgavatam* (7.9.44): "My dear Lord, I see that there are many saintly persons indeed, but they are interested only in their own delivcrance. Not caring for the big cities and towns, they go to the Himalayas or the forest to meditate with vows of silence. They are not interested in delivering others. As for me, however, I do not wish to be liberated alone, leaving aside all these poor fools and rascals. I know that without Kṛṣṇa consciousness, without taking shelter of Your lotus feet, one cannot be happy. Therefore, I wish to bring them back to the shelter of Your lotus feet."

Thus, while there undoubtedly is a kind of *yogī* who neglects others' welfare, he is hardly of the highest standard. In the *Bhagavad-gītā* Kṛṣṇa says that the highest *yogī* is His devotee–and that His dearmost devotee is he who takes all risks to approach others and give them the same liberation and bliss he has found in Kṛṣṇa consciousness.

Finally, we must also take issue with the sectarian notion that Vedic knowledge is meant only for people born in India. This idea finds support neither in any scriptural statement nor in the heart of any intelligent and compassionate person. As the *Śrīmad-Bhāgavatam* states, "If someone is ignorant and addicted to the path of *saṁsāra* [birth and death], how can one who is actually learned, merciful, and spiritually advanced engage him in material activity, and thus further entangle him in material existence? If a blind man is walking down the wrong path, how can a gentleman allow him to continue on his way to danger? No wise man can allow this."

The greatest of India's saints–Rāmānuja, Madhva, Bhaktisiddhānta–toured as widely as possible to broadcast Kṛṣṇa's message. (Outside India, spiritual teachers like Jesus Christ and Hajrat Muhammad displayed the same preaching spirit). And the most enthusiastic preacher of all was Lord Caitanya, the incarnation of Kṛṣṇa who appeared in India five hundred years ago to spread Kṛṣṇa consciousness in the form of the chanting of God's holy names: Hare Kṛṣṇa, Hare Kṛṣṇa, Kṛṣṇa Kṛṣṇa, Hare Hare/Hare Rāma, Hare Rāma, Rāma Rāma, Hare Hare. Lord Caitanya taught that chanting the Hare Kṛṣṇa mantra is the best form of God consciousness for the present fallen age, and He predicted, "The names of God shall be chanted in every town and village in the world." Thus, Kṛṣṇa consciousness, the science of God, is universal; it is meant not just for Indians but for every living soul in creation.

His Divine Grace A.C. Bhaktivedanta Swami Prabhupāda, founder-*ācārya* of the Kṛṣṇa consciousness movement, came to America in 1965, impelled by the very same desire that moved Vyāsadeva, Prahlāda, Madhva, Lord Caitanya, and other great saints of the past. Śrīla Prabhupāda wanted to rescue the unfortunate souls who are blindly trying to enjoy material pleasure in this life, oblivious of the suffering they will inevitably experience in their next life. Despite great personal inconvenience, Śrīla Prabhupāda came here at the advanced age of seventy to fulfill the order of his spiritual master. He introduced the same message that Lord Kṛṣṇa taught in the *Bhagavad-gītā* and that Lord Caitanya practically demonstrated through His *saṅkīrtana** movement.

What Śrīla Prabhupāda has taught is the sum and substance of India's spiritual message—to glorify the name, fame, and pastimes of the Supreme Lord, Kṛṣṇa—and Śrīla Prabhupāda had delivered this message without change. Thousands of young Westerners who had never heard of Kṛṣṇa, and who certainly had no plans to give up sinful life, have taken up devotional service to Kṛṣṇa and are now becoming purified.

So we can see that an essential part of the Vedic teachings is that one should first perfect his own life, and then try to teach others how to perfect their lives. In that way one most quickly attains Kṛṣṇa's recognition, and he performs the greatest welfare work for humanity. Teaching people to become devotees of God is far more beneficial than any mundane altruism in the form of food, shelter, hospital care, or materialistic education. Why? Because if a person overcomes the disease of his soul, he attains the Supreme Lord's eternal abode and never has to come back again to this miserable material world.

***_Saṅkīrtana_ is the congregational chanting of the _mahā-mantra_.**

V. The Process of Spiritual Education

Varṇāśrama-Dharma

March/April, 1971

The followers of the supreme will as taught by Lord Kṛṣṇa in the *Bhagavad-gītā* are generally called Hindus. This word Hindu, which has only come from recent times, is a name given by Mohammedans to those followers of the *varṇāśrama-dharma* who used to gather at the Indus River in India. "Indus" became "Hindus" by mispronunciation, so "Hindu" is an empty designation. The religion of the four social orders and four spiritual orders created by the Supreme Personality of Godhead Kṛṣṇa, as revealed in *Bhagavad-gītā* (*Bg.* 4.13), is properly named *varṇāśrama-dharma*. Basically, the four orders of social life called *varṇa* are scientifically arranged for the material progress of society, and the four spiritual orders called *āśrama* are designed for natural progress in self-realization. Both the *varṇa* and *āśrama* systems are interrelated; each is dependent on the other. The purpose of this plan, created by the Lord Himself, is to accelerate the transcendental qualities of the individual so that he may gradually realize his spiritual identification and act in order to get free from the material bondage of conditional life. It is a system by which the civilized human being can successfully perform the human mission, which is to be distinguished from the animal propensities of eating, sleeping, mating and defending.

SPIRITUAL, PEACEFUL LIFE

The *varṇa* system of four castes–*brāhmaṇa, kṣatriya, vaiśya* and *śūdra*–is perfectly organized in material terms in order to allow people to live peacefully and pursue spiritual life while engaged in their regular occupation. In every society there is always a class interested in business and agriculture. According to the Eighteenth Chapter of *Bhagavad-gītā*, the *vaiśyas*' duties are "farming, cattle raising, and business." The *śūdra* class does the labor or serves the other classes. The *kṣatriyas* are the administrators and protectors or policemen. "Heroism, power, determination, resourcefulness, courage in battle, generosity and leadership are the qualities of work for the *kṣatriyas*." (*Bg.* 18.43) The *brāhmaṇas* constitute the intelligent class and offer spiritual knowledge and guidance to the people. Whether or not one accepts the names *brāhmana, kṣatriya, vaiśya* and *śūdra*, there is naturally in every society an intelligent class interested in spiritual understanding and philosophy; a class interested in administration and ruling over others; a class interested in economic development, business and money-making; and another class of men who are not intelligent or martial spirited and have no capacity for economic development but who can simply serve others for their own bread. This system has been extant from time immemorial, and it will continue through time immemorial. There is no power which can stop it.

Due to India's dependency on foreigners and those who are non-*varṇāśrama*, that country is now witnessing the degradation of the caste and order system in the form of the hereditary caste system. Because the *varṇāśrama* system is created by God, it will always exist, either in degraded form or in original; it cannot be extinguished. It is like the sun, a creation of God. Either covered by clouds or in a clear sky, the sun will exist. When the *varṇāśrama* system becomes degraded, it appears as the hereditary caste system. The four natural orders are still there, but there is no actual regulation for cooperation between the communities. According to the original system in the *Bhagavad-gītā*, caste is determined not by birth but by qualities. The Vedic literature is perfectly clear on this point. Lord Kṛṣṇa Himself used the phrase *brahma-bandhu*, meaning "relative of a *brāhmaṇa*," to describe a person who happens to take birth in the family of a *brāhmaṇa* but is not qualified as a *brāhmaṇa*. This was the case with Aśvatthāmā,, as described in the *Śrīmad-Bhāgavatam* (1.7.36). He was a *brāhmaṇa's* son, but he killed the five sleeping sons of Draupadī, and therefore Kṛṣṇa said that he should be called a *brahma-bandhu*. As the judgeship is a post for the qualified man, so also the post of a *brāhmaṇa* is attainable by qualification only. By birth alone one cannot become a high court judge, but a qualified person, regardless of birth, is eligible for the post. Similarly, any man who attains the qualities of a *brāhmaṇa* but is born in a lower caste family must be recognized as a factual *brāhmaṇa*. There is an example in the *Chāndogya Upaniṣad* of a student boy who approached a *guru* for instruction. The *guru* asked the boy his family name. On inquiry from his mother, the boy was told, "I do not know. I was a servant girl in my youth and worked in many places. I do not know who was your father." The boy related this exactly to the sage, and the sage declared: "None but a *brāhmaṇa* could speak as truthfully as this," and the boy was thereby accepted as a *brāhmaṇa* because of his acting like a *brāhmaṇa*. Similarly, in *Hari-bhakti-vilāsa*, which is the standard literature for regulative behavior in devotional service, it is stated: "As bell metal can be transformed into gold by the proper chemical process, similarly by the bona fide process of initiation any human being can be transformed into a twice-born *brāhmaṇa*."

NEED FOR BRĀHMAṆAS

It is the Vedic ideal that everyone is trained according to his particular qualities and inclinations. It is necessary in every society that there especially be guides, qualified men whose work is not to put bricks together or anything else, but to simply guide with real intelligence, while the others do work according to their desires. Where there is such guidance, working becomes happy. Kṛṣṇa is the author of the orders, and thus the existence of a guiding class is eternal and natural–but training is needed. In the democratic society, education makes no provision to train *brāhmaṇas* for the role of guides. Although the need for such *brāhmaṇas* is clear, there is no educational institution to train proper *brāhmaṇas*.

The present Society for Krishna Consciousness is unique in supplying training for spiritually inclined persons. Under a bona fide spiritual master, His Divine Grace A.C. Bhaktivedanta Swamī Prabhupāda, they are being trained in a higher science. Those intellectual persons who have the brahminical qualifications are being restrained as students–they don't eat meat or take part in intoxication, gambling or illicit sex life. In this way they are becoming an intellectual, purified class. It is said that a true *brāhmaṇa* can sanctify all society. In the conception of the four orders as parts situated on the universal form of the Supreme Lord, the *brāhmaṇas* are said to be the head, the *kṣatriyas* the arms, the *vaiśyas* the waist and the *śūdras* the legs. Just as in our own body, for proper maintenance we require all parts; we cannot say that we do not need the head. We need everything. If there is a body without a head, it is a dead body. Similarly, if there is not a *brāhmaṇa* or intellectual, spiritual part in the society, it is a dead society. If someone is working to understand the Supreme Lord, he is a *brāhmaṇa.* Why should he be called for military action? The arm of the body is needed also. The military arrangement should be there–but not the *brāhmaṇa.* Where there is no arrangement for protection of *brāhmaṇas,* that society is headless and brainless–dead. And there is no peace in such a society.

PRESENT DEGRADATION

Due to the lack of training of people in the present age and to their practice of the vices of illicit sex, meat eating and intoxication, Lord Caitanya declared that *kalau śūdra-sambhava*–in the age of Kali everyone is a *śūdra*. The Vedic ceremony called Garbhādhāna–in which the man and wife make vows before having sex and declare that they are coming together to have sex in order to produce a Kṛṣṇa conscious child–is no longer observed. And so widespread are illicit connections that no one can know for certain whether he is born of a *brāhmaṇa* or someone else. With the extinguishing of the original *varṇas* and *āśramas*, the entire world has become deplorable, being governed by unwanted men who have no training in religion, politics or social order. In the institution of *varṇāśrama* there are regular training principles for the different classes of men. Just as now we need engineers and doctors and there are places for properly training them in scientific institutions, so the social orders, the intelligent class, the ruling class, etc., can be properly trained up. This was actually the case in early Vedic times. The duties are described, and the training must be there. Without training, one cannot claim that simply because he is born in a *brāhmaṇa* or *kṣatriya* family, even though he may act as a *śūdra*, he is therefore a *brāhmaṇa* or *kṣatriya*. Such claims have degraded the system and thrown it into chaos, with no peace or prosperity. The result is that there are *śūdras* everywhere; where there should be a *kṣatriya* in the presidential palace and leading the army on the battlefield, there are men who are untrained and unintelligent, who are less than *śūdras*. When there is no provision for training the natural orders, we find that the leadership is ineffective and corrupt. In the Vedic system, because there was proper education, the society was peaceful and so structured that all people were able to develop Kṛṣṇa consciousness. That is real human society, where the entire society is making progress toward spiritual realization. Kṛṣṇa advises in *Bhagavad-gītā* that one stay in his own work:

> It is better to be engaged in one's own occupation, even if imperfectly performed, than to accept another's occupation, even if perfectly done. Prescribed duties, according to one's nature, are never affected by sinful reactions. (*Bg.* 18.47)

Working according to his nature, *for the purpose of serving the Lord*, one can attain perfection by that work, no matter how abominable or pleasant it may appear. One should prosecute his work, even if there is some difficulty in it. Of course, even if a man steadfastly performs his work, but does not serve God by his labor, he is doomed by that very steadfast but godless work. The absolute meaning to all work is that one offers the fruits of his work to Kṛṣṇa. This art of working in devotional service can be learned, and that is why the *brāhmaṇas* are there.

A great devotee of Lord Kṛṣṇa, the boy Prahlāda Mahārāja, told his school fellows: "What is required is that we change our consciousness from what we are now thinking–that I am the supreme enjoyer, lord of all I survey–and instead become the loving servants of the actual enjoyer, the Supreme Personality of Godhead Kṛṣṇa." This transcendental loving service, a change of consciousness, can be perfectly completed under proper guidance while working at one's occupational duty. According to Lord Caitanya, everyone must surrender to Kṛṣṇa. As the *varṇa* orders are natural because they are created by God, so they have meaning only when they are utilized for devotional service unto God.

THE ĀŚRAMA

The spiritual impetus in training is *āśrama*. The *āśrama* system is arranged in four stages of life in order for one to reach spiritual perfection. The first stage is *brahmacarya*. *Brahmacarya* means student life or education with the spiritual master. According to the *āśrama* system, at five years of age a boy goes to live at the *guru-kula*, or the place of the *guru*. There, in order to understand spiritual life, all students serve as menial servants of the *guru*. This way is advised by Kṛṣṇa in the *Bhagavad-gītā* (4.34): "Just try to know the truth by approaching a self-realized spiritual master with all submission and with inquiries and render service unto him. Such a learned spiritual master initiates knowledge unto you because he has seen the truth." By performing this service unto a pure devotee, the *brahmacārī* is making direct service contact with God. Because such pure devotees or spiritual masters have as their only business to spread Kṛṣṇa consciousness and devotional service, to come in contact with them is like an iron rod's coming in contact with fire—the rod eventually acts like fire itself. Lord Caitanya taught that we should become a servant of the servant of the servant 100 times removed—the more faith in the chain of disciplic succession, the better is the service unto Kṛṣṇa Himself. The *brahmacārī* is trained to be celibate and temperate and to follow the scriptural injunctions for purification of consciousness. Many great personalities from the Vedic literatures, such as Śaṅkara, Nārada, the Kumāras, Bhīṣma, and Bhaktisiddhānta Sarasvatī, remained unmarried *brahmacārīs* throughout life and devoted their full time to the cause of Kṛṣṇa. Moreover, one must enter *brahmacārī* training, even if he is to be later married, so that he can learn the principles of restraint. Spiritual life has as its goal the cessation of the round of birth and death in this material world and transferral to the eternal, blissful spiritual world. According to *Bhagavad-gītā*, we are wandering through thousands of species of life, always forgetting Kṛṣṇa, thinking that we are God, the enjoyer, the center, the Lord. So there is no way out of this material condition except hearing from a spiritual master what our actual position is: that we are eternal parts and parcels of God. Then we must act accordingly. This practice of *brahmacarya* inculcates in one the desire for Kṛṣṇa because it restrains the sensual propensities which are the cause of our bondage to the material world.

Sex life, being the apex of pleasure in the material world, is therefore the number one reason for our staying in bondage. Nowadays so many so-called *yogīs* and *ṛṣis* have come with their teachings, but they are actually enjoyers of the world in the name of *yoga*, as their teaching does not demand that one practice *brahmacarya*. Sex indulgence is not recommended in any standard process of *yoga* meditation or devotional service. Spiritual life means that I am trying to show God my love for Him, not that I am trying to increase my sex enjoyment.

ESSENTIAL TRAINING

Among other things, the *brahmacārī* is required to restrict his sleep. He is expected to rise one and a half hours before sunrise in order to take advantage of the early hours which are said to be the most auspicious for spiritual development. In *Śrīmad-Bhāgavatam*, the habits of a *brahmacārī* are described: "The *brahmacārī* must rise early in the morning, and after placing himself, he should chant the holy name" (Bhaktivedanta Purports, *Bhāg*. 3.21.45). It is further described that the *brahmacārī's* body and face should give off a luster:

> His body shone most brilliantly: though engaged in austere penance, he was not emaciated because the Lord had cast His affectionate glance at him and he had quaffed with his ears the nectar flowing from the moonlike words of the Lord.

It is the sign of one observing celibacy or *brahmacarya* that his face has this luster. If he lives otherwise, the lust will come out from the face and the body; if one is a drunkard or sex monger, it will come out. *Brahmacārī* training is the basis for all other orders as basic training in spiritual life. Whether he goes on to become married and eventually retire from married life, or whether he goes directly to the renounced order or *sannyāsa*, the practice of *brahmacarya* will save him from the pit of entanglement. It fixes him positively in the Absolute Truth.

When the spiritual master understands the qualities of a student, then he decides how he should work, whether as *brāhmaṇa, kṣatriya, vaiśya* or *śūdra*. Thus the student goes into any occupation or spiritual order implanted with the seed of devotional service and the ability to control his senses over the four animal propensities.

MARRIED LIFE

The second *āśrama* order is called *gṛhastha*, the married family man. *Gṛhastha* does not mean married life for indulgence in sex and family affairs. *Gṛhastha* is a bona fide spiritual order. There is another word in Sanskrit, *gṛhamedhī*, which is a description of married life without spiritual goals. Such marriage, in which one uses contraceptive methods in order to enjoy sex life, raises children who become like cats and dogs, and devotes one's occupational income and energy for elevating the material standard of his family, is a waste of human life. Sex is there, like eating, and there is no bar to Kṛṣṇa consciousness for a married man. If one feels some disturbance in living single, he can get married. Many of the great authorities in the science of God, like Lord Brahmā, Prahlāda Mahārāja, Bhaktivinode Ṭhākur and His Divine Grace A.C. Bhaktivedanta Swami Prabhupāda, were family men. Marriage in the spiritual order is for the purpose of living peacefully and having children in Kṛṣṇa consciousness. Like the *varṇa*, the *āśrama* orders are natural and based on principles of human life in terms of the whole span of life; the goal of *āsrama* is not sense gratification, but liberation from the material condition and attainment of the highest goal. The first part of life, *brahmacarya*, is utilized for development of character and spiritual qualities. Then around age twenty-five, if he has the desire to be married, he may, as the next natural part of life, accept a wife and beget children. But one should not beget children like cats and dogs. A child should be begotten who can perform duties for God, otherwise there is no need to marry and no need of children. The parents should see to it that the child born of them must not enter the womb of a mother again. The child should be trained for being liberated in that life.

Āśrama teaches that human life is especially meant for being completely devoted to the Lord. Among the duties and responsibilities of the householder is that he takes care of the other spiritual orders. By occupation, the *vaiśyas* produce food for everyone; by spiritual order, the householders feed the others, as far as possible. Also, according to the example of the great devotee Rūpa Gosvāmī, a householder should give at least fifty per cent of his income for propagation of Kṛṣṇa consciousness, twenty-five percent for his household upkeep, and twenty-five percent set aside for emergencies. The *gṛhastha* lives as a householder, prosecuting Kṛṣṇa consciousness with every endeavor.

RETIRED LIFE

Let us say that a man lives one hundred years. The first twenty-five years he is student. The years from twenty-five to fifty are good for producing children and so may be spent in householder life. Then after fifty years of age the man is expected to retire and leave his household affairs in the hands of his oldest son. This stage is called *vanaprāstha*. He retires and with his wife travels to holy places. Then gradually he leaves his wife in the care of the older children. It is not that the wife is left deserted on the road. According to Vedic civilization the woman is never independent. She is in the hands of her father until she is handed over in marriage, and then she becomes the charge of her husband. When the sons are grownup and it is time for the husband to take *sannyāsa*, he leaves his wife in the charge of his elder sons.

The *Śrīmad-Bhāgavatam* narrates the history of Kardama Muni, a great *yogī* householder who lived at the dawn of creation and who strictly followed the scriptural injunction by leaving his home to take the renounced life of a wandering *sannyāsī*. His case was most exceptional because after long austerities and practice of *yoga*, Kardama Muni and his wife Devahūti had been blessed to have born unto them the incarnation of God known as Kapila Deva, who taught the famous Sāṅkhya philosophy to the world. Kardama Muni's exalted position was that God Himself was in his home, as his son. And still, Kardama Muni left his home in strict observance of the injunction that one must spend his last days away from home and without family connection in pursuit of spiritual life. Kapila Deva encouraged His father not to deviate from the scriptures, and He assured him that as Supreme Lord He would always be with His father, residing in his heart. Thus Kardama Muni left his wife in the charge of his son Kapila and became a wandering *sannyāsī* totally dependent on Kṛṣṇa for his food and lodging.

THE RENOUNCED ORDER

Due to the contamination of the present Kali age, Lord Caitanya advised that no one should take *sannyāsa* but that everyone should chant the holy names, Hare Kṛṣṇa, Hare Kṛṣṇa, Kṛṣṇa Kṛṣṇa, Hare Hare/Hare Rāma, Hare Rāma, Rāma Rāma, Hare Hare. Justifying the wisdom of Lord Caitanya's prohibition of *sannyāsa* is a phenomenon in India involving the cheaters and the cheated. It is known that a certain class of women feel that it is auspicious to have sex with a *sādhu* (holy man) and have a child by him. Women gather at holy places where *sannyāsīs* are known to go for the purpose of seducing them. This practice has become known, and a class of low-bred sensualists have taken to dressing themselves in the saffron robes of *sannyāsīs* and going to those places for the purpose of being seduced by women. Thus the cheaters meet the cheated. Of course, if anyone can actually follow the rules of *sannyāsa* then he must take the renounced order.

Sannyāsa is required so that the materially engrossed householder can get out of his mundane occupations before the time of death. The bona fide *sannyāsī* who has received information from authorized scriptural sources and from a spiritual master in disciplic succession must not be merely self-satisfied in that knowledge because he is needed by society at large to go and preach to the people and inject them with the immediacy of eternal spiritual values. If the *sannyāsī* does not teach the common men of their spiritual nature, then they will have wasted the human form of life. It is possible, by direct surrender to God, to be factually *sannyāsa* or renounced, even while living at home with wife and children. But the existence of the *sannyāsī* in the renounced order, either as a missionary with a large following, or as a wandering hermit, will culminate in the highest form of human being, the *paramahaṁsa,* or intimate pure devotee of Kṛṣṇa, who is without envy and always fixed in ecstatic absorption of love of God.

The four orders and castes of *varṇāśrama-dharma* are meant to perfect human society. The four orders become distinct where there is enlightenment. Such spiritual life is actually the most democratic because God accepts as wonderful whoever surrenders to Him. By the material standard the rich are great. But in spiritual life the most advanced person serves all others and brings them to Kṛṣṇa consciousness. In Kṛṣṇa consciousness the most advanced person gives up everything, whereas in material life the most advanced is greedy, vicious and dangerous to mankind at large. The real democracy we need is democracy of spiritual consciousness—the understanding that all belongs to God and every living being is Kṛṣṇa's beloved creature. Any man who takes up devotional service is to be respected regardless of his position; and at the same time, whatever qualities he displays in terms of work he can use for Kṛṣṇa.

Gurukula-New Hope for Humanity

April, 1973

WHY THERE IS A NEED FOR GURUKULA

Anyone who visits a few of the hundreds of big universities in the United States and other advanced nations will see an impressive array of opulence. Every big state university has dozens of modern buildings with plush student unions, skyscraper dormitories, vast stadiums, acres of scenic campus grounds, etc. But what is the result of all this external opulence in education? By way of answer, there is a suitable allegory told by our spiritual master.

One time a rumor began that the Himalayan Mountains were going to give birth to offspring. Upon hearing this, many people gathered at the foot of these famous mountains because everyone wanted to see what kind of offspring such huge and formidable mountains would produce. With great anticipation, crowds of people gathered, but they were confused and amazed when they saw many rats come running out from the Himalayas. The greatest mountains in the world had given birth to a pack of rats! Similarly, although we have many big campuses staffed by professional managerial administrators, with many offices and many professors with doctorates, the offspring of these universities are frustrated men and women who do not know the actual purpose of life.

Considering this deficiency, the International Society for Krishna Consciousness has begun a school named Gurukula (which means, in Sanskrit, "the place of the *guru* or spiritual master"). Gurukula is revolutionary because it is producing devotees of Kṛṣṇa, the Supreme Personality of Godhead. One who becomes a self-realized devotee of Kṛṣṇa automatically develops all good qualities and is a first-class educated and cultured person because it is a fact that human life is meant for self-realization, for finding one's eternal relationship with the Supreme. A human being who neglects self-realization is actually no more than an animal, even if he is very proud of his scientific advancement. Try as he may by attempting to enjoy with the body or mind, a human being cannot be happy unless he develops knowledge of himself as a spirit soul who is an eternal part and parcel of the Supreme Personality of Godhead, Kṛṣṇa. Yet self-realization is the all-important subject which is not taught in the schools and universities of the advanced nations of the modern world.

The first step in self-realization is to realize one's identity as separate from the body: "I am not this body but spirit soul." This realization is essential for anyone who wants to be actually successful and happy in *this* world, and furthermore it is the first step toward entrance into the eternal spiritual world. It is not that one can simply say, "I'm not this body," but one must actually realize it. This is not as simple as it may at first seem. We are not these bodies but pure consciousness, yet somehow or other we have become covered by a bodily dress. If one actually wants the happiness and independence to transcend death, one must establish himself in his constitutional position as pure consciousness. Each of us is a minute spirit spark who is hankering for the qualities of the whole–knowledge, bliss and eternity–but these hankerings are frustrated due to the material body. The information on how to obtain the goal of the soul's hankering is given in *Bhagavad-gītā* and other Vedic literatures, and the pursuit of this goal is meant to be taken up by the practical lifelong study of Kṛṣṇa consciousness.

The authority of these teachings rests on the Vedic literatures which were compiled in Sanskrit five thousand years ago in India. These teachings are completely free from the slightest taint of the religious or ethnic sectarianism which leads the less educated dogmatic religionist to argue that God is revealed only to Jews, only to Christians, only to Hindus, etc. Kṛṣṇa consciousness is the eternal science of God and is therefore universal.

The reason that Kṛṣṇa consciousness was only recently introduced in the West is that it requires to be taught by one who is a pure devotee of the Supreme Lord, Kṛṣṇa. It has to be taught by one who understands thoroughly that God, the Supreme Person, is not the property of one small sect but is universal and full of love for all people. His Divine Grace A.C. Bhaktivedanta Swami Prabhupāda is the first pure devotee to bring the Vedic process of devotional service to the West. Previous to his coming, there was no Kṛṣṇa consciousness movement, and it is he who within the last six years has given the inspiration and guidance for almost a hundred authorized Kṛṣṇa consciousness centers.

Now the Kṛṣṇa consciousness movement has begun the Gurukula educational project, a primary school for children from ages five to fifteen. From an early age, children can learn the Absolute Truth along with their reading, writing and arithmetic. Just as a child needs math and English to get along in this world, he also needs self-realization in order to practically know his own identity, his duty in life, and how to solve the problems of material suffering. If children can learn that each one of us is actually an eternal spirit and is meant to serve the Supreme, they will not waste the great opportunity of human life; such children can grow up to truly help others find the real meaning of life.

Formerly, in classical Vedic society, influential citizens sent their children at five years of age to the home of the spiritual master to be trained in austerity, sense control and God consciousness, for thus in later life, no matter what occupation they would enter, they would not forget the purpose of life as service to Kṛṣṇa. To train children from the early age of five in these devotional practices is to train real leaders and good citizens. Indeed, one cannot expect a good society without Gurukula. If children are taught an artificial standard of sense gratification, their brains become spoiled, for by the time they are twelve years old they think that life is meant simply for enjoyment of the senses to the fullest extent. We cannot expect sane leaders or responsible citizens from such an education system. However, children who are shown by example that serving Kṛṣṇa in many ways is the real happiness of life–children who come to understand transcendental knowledge regarding their eternal, blissful servitorship to God–will be happy and useful in society.

One who does not know the real purpose of life cannot help anyone, not even himself. The great leaders of humanity, therefore, are the great devotees. From the Vedic histories of India we learn that in bygone ages the great leaders were all holy sages who were able to give the citizens guidance in the real mission of life.

The qualities of a devotee are mentioned as follows in the Vedic literature: kind to everyone, does not quarrel with anyone, fixed in the Absolute Truth, equal to everyone, faultless, charitable, mild, clean, simple, benevolent, peaceful, completely attached to Kṛṣṇa, free from material hankering, meek, steady, self-controlled, eating no more than required, sane, respectful, humble, grave, compassionate, friendly, poetic, expert, silent. These are the first-class human qualities that are being developed at Gurukula. The leaders of every nation are supposed to protect all the citizens under their jurisdiction, not encourage them to live in the illusion of sense gratification, thinking that increased material standards, more cars and bigger tv's will make them happy. The real leader is one who can simultaneously protect the citizens and give them the opportunity to cultivate self-realization while living in their occupations.

A society in which people of all occupations strive to go back to Godhead by their practical daily work, under the guidance of leaders who have thoroughly realized the principles of God consciousness, is not merely theoretical or utopian. It is stated in *Bhagavad-gītā* that Kṛṣṇa Himself has created in man all the qualities needed for a socially and spiritually successful society in which everyone can work together in God consciousness. Such a society would offer the highest benefit to all living entities, even to the animals who live within the state. However, in order to be successful, such a state must operate under the strong administration of a God conscious leader, and as long as there are no God conscious leaders, such a state is impossible.

As stated in *Bhagavad-gītā*, whatever a great man does, others will follow. Nowadays the leaders of society are the lowest class of men, for they lead people only toward the illusory goal of happiness obtained by increased material sense gratification. It is this illusory leadership that results in the corruption, war, crime, poverty, pollution and myriad other problems that plague the modern world. Only if men of saintly quality can lead the affairs of the nations of the world can there be peace, prosperity and spiritual advancement for all. This is the version of all the world's scriptures: the real leader is the man who can give spiritual guidance, and the good, sober citizen is one who is trained in Kṛṣṇa consciousness. Gurukula has been established to fill the need for an institution to train such leaders.

THE PHILOSOPHY OF GURUKULA

By studying the lives of great devotees, we learn that they started devotional service from the earliest age. Our spiritual master, His Divine Grace A.C. Bhaktivedanta Swami Prabhupāda, gives credit to his father for encouraging him from childhood to practice devotional service in his play. The Vedic histories also cite the same training in the life of great devotees such as Mahārāja Parīkṣit, who used to imitate worship of the temple Deity in his own childish play at home. Mahārāja Parīkṣit later became king of the entire world and leader of the most successful God conscious monarchy in history.

Prahlāda Mahārāja is another great devotee of Lord Kṛṣṇa who lived long ago and was trained in the devotional principles from the earliest age. When he was only five years old he used to tell his fellow classmates, "My dear friends, now is the time to learn what Kṛṣṇa consciousness is, while we are still very young." Whenever the teacher left the room for recess, he would speak in this way.

At first Prahlāda's young friends told him: "Leave us alone. We are only five years old; let us play. When we are older we will take the time to learn about Kṛṣṇa consciousness."

Prahlāda, however, spoke with great compassion to the young boys and girls. "My dear friends," he said, "we must take to Kṛṣṇa consciousness without delay." Prahlāda explained that the life span of a human being is at most one hundred years, and it is calculated that the first twenty years are wasted in the games and sports of youth, the last twenty years in rest and retirement in a state of greater or lesser infirmity, and the middle twenty years, in which the sex urge is strong, in raising and maintaining a family. Thus sixty years are spent without self-realization. How much time is left to find the real value of life and begin eternal loving service to Kṛṣṇa?

With this consideration in mind, His Divine Grace A.C. Bhaktivedanta Swami Prabhupāda has asked his disciples to reintroduce the original Vedic system of

Gurukula. It is described in the Vedic literatures that children living in a God conscious society would go to the home of the spiritual master at five years of age. Even if the children were of a very aristocratic home, they would submit themselves to the spiritual master as menial servants to perform service for him and receive spiritual instruction. It is described that a young student would rise early, spend all day receiving knowledge and training from the spiritual master, and in the evening he would eat a little rice and then go to sleep. He would think such life great fun because he was serving Kṛṣṇa. Nowadays, children are spoiled at a very early age; they miss the real point of life because they are mistakenly taught that to please the senses is the all in all. Thus they take to a kind of pampered animalism for the rest of their days, working in order to maintain a high standard of eating, sleeping, sex and defense, and they become useless men who are unable to perform real service for humanity.

At Gurukula, however, children are carefully guided to appreciate that serving Kṛṣṇa is fun. One of the basic requirements of real spiritual life is to learn how to control the senses. Bodily pleasure is flickering and intoxicating, and one cannot actually enjoy it because of its momentary nature. One who can come to understand the philosophy of the self as spirit soul will never leave it in favor of a whimsical life of unrestricted sense gratification. In his book *Beyond Birth and Death*, Śrīla Prabhupāda has written, "We have to understand that if we want to continue the artificial enjoyment of the body we will not be able to obtain our position of eternal enjoyment." Therefore Gurukula works to give realization that the purpose of life is to serve Kṛṣṇa and to gain freedom from the shackles of material life.

After being trained in Kṛṣṇa consciousness a man can marry and enter household life and yet not fall prey to unrestricted sense gratification. Materialistic householders live simply to work hard and spend money for family maintenance, sex and comfortable sleep at night. Thus they ruin their lives in the darkness of ignorance. But if one learns about the real meaning of life by hearing from the spiritual master at Gurukula, he can enter any occupation in the material world and not be materially implicated. In fact, unless one understands the real meaning of life, he cannot be successful as a citizen, as a family man or in any other sphere of life. Therefore the philsosophy of Gurukula is a prime necessity for the present day.

THE CURRICULUM

Religious principles such as austerity, truthfulness, cleanliness and mercy are essential to any human civilization. Even though a secular state naturally wishes to declare itself impartial to religious sectarianism, it cannot abandon these religious principles, for in their absence we have pilfering, prostitution, corruption and cruelty. However, if one becomes a devotee of Kṛṣṇa, he automatically develops all good qualities. Therefore, in addition to their academic subjects, Śrīla Prabhupāda has asked us to teach the children at Gurukula four things: to always think of Kṛṣṇa, to become His devotees, to worship Him and to offer Him obeisances.

It is a well-known fact that one becomes like his associates. For example, if one associates with thieves he will become a thief, or if one associates with scholars he will become a scholar. Similarly, one can become saintly in the association of saintly devotees who are guided by a bona fide spiritual master. By associating with those who are vital in Kṛṣṇa consciousness, the children at Gurukula also follow and become Kṛṣṇa conscious themselves.

Children take seriously whatever they learn from their elders. Therefore the teachers at Gurukula teach not simply by precept but also by example. Activities in devotional service begin with chanting and hearing about the pastimes of the Supreme Personality of Godhead, and the teachers at Gurukula are committed to this hearing and chanting process. The chanting of Hare Kṛṣṇa is especially recommended in the modern age for a person interested in God-realization, and the children at Gurukula take this up with great enthusiasm by association with older devotees who are themselves enthusiastic over this great chanting for deliverance—Hare Kṛṣṇa, Hare Kṛṣṇa, Kṛṣṇa Kṛṣṇa, Hare Hare/Hare Rāma Hare Rāma, Rāma Rāma, Hare Hare. The children take it up because the older devotees are doing it. They could be singing the latest sensuous rubbish broadcast over the radio, but instead they are singing the glories of the Lord—simply by right association.

Although in mundane schools the academic qualifications of the teachers are carefully considered, their personal character and habits are often most abominable. Indeed, it would be a rare institution that could boast that its teachers are free from smoking, drinking, gambling and loose sexual relationships. According to the Vedic system, however, which is followed by the present-day Gurukula, the teacher must not only be learned but also spotless in character. To be a teacher at Gurukula, one must strictly refrain from gambling, intoxication, meat eating and illicit sex, and, most importantly, one must be an initiated devotee of the Supreme Personality of Godhead. Therefore the strength behind Gurukula is the ultimate teacher—the bona fide spiritual master—for it is the spiritual master's association that is the cause of all spiritual progress.

The Vedic literature reveals that Kṛṣṇa, the Absolute Truth, is certainly the Supreme Person, and He appeared on earth five thousand years ago. To attract everyone back to Godhead, He displayed His transcendental pastimes here just as they are going on eternally in the spiritual world. These pastimes are described in our spiritual master's book, *Kṛṣṇa, the Supreme Personality of Godhead,* and the children at Gurukula very much enjoy acting out the Lord's activities. One child will play that he is Kṛṣṇa, and another will play that he is His brother, Balarāma, as They go off to the woods to find the cows. Sometimes They meet demons sent by Kaṁsa. Kṛṣṇa kills the demons and dances and plays with His friends, who are one hundred percent absorbed in love of Kṛṣṇa.

The sublime, exalted activity of the Supreme Personality of Godhead and His intimate unalloyed devotees cannot be understood even by the greatest philosophers so long as they attempt to understand them on the basis of mental speculation and concoction. The mundane mind takes Kṛṣṇa to be an ordinary historical person and His activities to be fiction, but according to all Vedic scriptures and the disciplic succession of spiritual masters, God is the Supreme Person, and He engages in pastimes of love for the pleasure of His devotees. In other words, the dry scholars and professors will have to take lessons from the children of Gurukula regarding the relishable nature of the pastimes of Kṛṣṇa. Just in their playing about Kṛṣṇa, they are realizing that God is a person and that He is the Supreme Lord who maintains all.

GURUKULA AND THE FUTURE

There is a Sanskrit saying, "Judge the process by the result." We invite all interested persons to visit our Gurukula schools. Rather than merely tell you that these children are happy, we invite you to come and see for yourself. There is no doubt about it; they are coming out successful. They are already well behaved and happy and are advancing quickly in all academic subjects. Moreover, they are becoming thoroughly realized in what *Bhagavad-gītā* calls the "king of education." We very much look forward to the time when these children will come of age and usher in the new era of worldwide Kṛṣṇa consciousness. There is nothing so rare, pure and valuable in this world as a devotee of the Supreme Personality of Godhead; therefore, one should appreciate the serious work of Gurukula.

We ask all readers, regardless of their religious upbringing or philosophy of life, to consider the youth of today and the future of their countries and the world. At the rate things are going, civilization is headed for total barbarianism. Gurukula, therefore, is a practical Godsend, and it is to the credit of His Divine Grace A.C. Bhaktivedanta Swami Prabhupāda that it is working right now, even as you read this article! The students are there, the teachers are there, the result is being produced. Gurukula is a practical, tangible, workable and successful project which should be continued and expanded upon. Let us all endeavor to familiarize ourselves with this important educational project and offer encouragement and help in any way we can.

Classes in the Science of God

September, 1973

Every day, each of our Kṛṣṇa consciousness centers holds an early morning class in which a verse from *Śrīmad-Bhāgavatam* is read and discussed. The book *Śrīmad-Bhāgavatam* is a Vedic literature. Therefore, the subject matter is always the Supreme Personality of Godhead, Lord Kṛṣṇa. In the *Bhāgavatam* class there is no discussion of mundane topics concerning the temporary material world. Anyone who regularly takes part in hearing the *Bhāgavatam* in the association of devotees will experience a cleansing of all inauspicious things from his heart.

Our problem is that although we are eternal spiritual souls, we have identified ourselves with our temporary material bodies. In other words, we have forgotten who we really are. Most people think they are their material bodies–that is the inauspicious misconception that clouds our hearts. We have forgotten Kṛṣṇa, the Supreme Lord, and we have forgotten our eternal relationship with Him. But one can revive that lost relationship and regain his original nature of eternity, bliss and knowledge–just by hearing about Kṛṣṇa in the *Bhāgavatam* class.

Regardless of one's material designation, he should hear about Kṛṣṇa. One should not object, "I am a Christian. I cannot hear about Kṛṣṇa," or "I am a Jew. I cannot chant the verses of the *Bhāgavatam*." Because Kṛṣṇa is universal, He is transcendental to all designations. I have taken my birth in a certain race, a certain nation, a certain religious sect, a certain family–but that pertains to my material body, which I am not. Spiritually I am transcendental to all temporary designations. I am an eternal servant of God. One should revive such pure consciousness, beyond the scope of ethnic culture and sectarian religion, by hearing the transcendental message of *Śrīmad-Bhāgavatam.*

When conducting *Bhāgavatam* classes, the devotees begin by chanting a Sanskrit verse out loud. This is the same Sanskrit, word for word, that was originally composed 5,000 years ago by Śrīla Vyāsadeva, the incarnation of Kṛṣṇa who compiled all the millions of verses of the Sanskrit Vedic literature. The sound of congregational chanting of the *Bhāgavatam* is transcendental, and purification takes place even for a hearer who does not understand a word of Sanskrit. These verses are sometimes compared to gold. Even in the hands of a child who knows nothing of its worth, gold is always valuable. Similarly, the transcendental sound vibration will always act to purify its hearers.

Before chanting the verse, the leader first chants the *mantra* "*oṁ namo bhagavate vāsudevāya.*" This is an invocation of the Supreme Lord and is translated, "I offer my obeisances unto the Supreme Personality of Godhead, who is all-pervading." The chanting is responsive–the leader chants, and the congregation repeats. This hearing and chanting engage two important senses–the ear and the tongue–and thus the restless mind is captured, and one can think of Kṛṣṇa, the goal of life.

Here follows a Sanskrit verse from the *Bhāgavatam* (First Canto, Chapter Two, verse 18). At first glance it may seem no more than a jumble of foreign words, but actually it is not foreign.

naṣṭa-prāyeṣv abhadreṣu
nityaṁ bhāgavata-sevayā
bhagavaty uttama-śloke
bhaktir bhavati naiṣṭhikī

The English translation of each word is expertly rendered by His Divine Grace A.C. Bhaktivedanta Swami Prabhupāda:

naṣṭa–destroyed; *prāyeṣu*–almost to nil; *abhadreṣu*–all that is inauspicious; *nityaṁ*–regularly; *bhāgavata*–*Śrīmad-Bhāgavatam*, or the pure devotee; *sevayā* –by serving; *bhagavati*–unto the Personality of Godhead; *uttama*–transcendental; *śloke*–prayers; *bhaktiḥ*–loving service; *bhavati*–comes into being; *naiṣṭhikī*–irrevocable.

Śrīla Prabhupāda has made all these literatures available as a service to humanity because by hearing Kṛṣṇa's message one can be freed from bondage to ignorance and repeated birth and death. Here is his English translation and purport of the Sanskrit verse.

TRANSLATION

"By regularly hearing the *Bhāgavatam* and rendering service unto the pure devotee, all that is troublesome to the heart is practically destroyed, and loving service unto the glorious Lord, who is praised with transcendental songs, is established as an irrevocable fact."

PURPORT

"Here is the remedy for eliminating all inauspicious things within the heart which are considered to be obstacles in the path of self-realization. The remedy is the association of the *Bhāgavatas*. There are two types of *Bhāgavatas*, namely the book *Bhāgavata* [*Śrīmad-Bhāgavatam*] and the devotee *Bhāgavata* [a pure devotee of the Lord]. Both the *Bhāgavatas* are competent remedies, and both of them or either of them can be good enough to eliminate the obstacles. A devotee *Bhāgavata* is as good as the book *Bhāgavata*, and the book *Bhāgavata* is full of information about the Personality of Godhead and His pure devotees. *Bhāgavata* book and person are identical.

"The devotee *Bhāgavata* is a direct representative of Bhāgavan, the Personality of Godhead. So by pleasing the devotee *Bhāgavata* one can receive the benefit of the book *Bhāgavata*. Human reason fails to understand how by serving the devotee *Bhāgavata* or the book *Bhāgavata* one gets gradual promotion on the path of devotion. But actually these are facts explained by Śrīla Nāradadeva, who happened to be a maidservant's son in his previous life. The maidservant was engaged in the menial service of the sages, and thus he also came into contact with them. And simply by associating with them and accepting the remnants of foodstuff left by the sages, the son of the maidservant got the chance to become the great devotee and personality Śrīla Nāradadeva. These are the miraculous effects of the association of *Bhāgavatas*. And to understand these effects practically, it should be noted that by such sincere association of the *Bhāgavatas* one is sure to receive transcendental knowledge very easily, and the result is that he becomes fixed in the devotional service of the Lord. The more progress is made in devotional service under the guidance of the *Bhāgavatas*, the more one becomes fixed in the transcendental loving service of the Lord. The messages of the book *Bhāgavata*, therefore, have to be received from the devotee *Bhāgavata*, and the combination of these two *Bhāgavatas* will help the neophyte devotee to make progress on and on."

After reading Srīla Prabhupāda's purport, his natural commentary on the verse, the devotee conducting the class will discuss the topic of that particular verse. All such discussion is exactly in accord with the authorized version presented by the spiritual master, who is coming in disciplic succession from Kṛṣṇa Himself. But each Sanskrit word is such a treasure house of meaning that a devotee can expound on the subject infinitely, without deviating from the conclusion of the disciplic succession. The audience is assured that the original truth, as first revealed by Kṛṣṇa, is being exactly repeated with all its purity and potency intact.

The essential activity of life is to glorify Kṛṣṇa, whose glorious activities can be understood properly from the book *Bhāgavata* and the person *Bhāgavata*. Glorification of Kṛṣṇa, which is beneficial for all living beings, is performed by a devotee. In his purports to the prayers of King Kulaśekhara, Śrīla Prabhupāda has written, "A devotee of Godhead is he who glorifies the Personality of Godhead under the dictation of transcendental ecstasy. This ecstasy is a by-product of profound love for the Supreme which is attained by the process of glorification." In other words, if one begins at once, even as a neophyte, to glorify Kṛṣṇa as one has heard such glorification from his spiritual master, that will revive one's original love for the Supreme Lord. Glorification is a natural principle of life, but now we are turning our attention away from all false glorification and here attempting to describe the philosophy and activities of the Supreme Personality of Godhead. Kṛṣṇa Himself advises Arjuna to remember Him as being always a person.

Our spiritual master has told us of a poetic couplet he wrote that very much pleased his own spiritual master, His Divine Grace Bhaktisiddhānta Sarasvatī Gosvāmī Mahārāja: "The Absolute is sentient, thou hast proved /Impersonal calamity thou has removed." God, or Kṛṣṇa, is a person. He is not void or impersonal. God is a person, just as all the numberless living entities are. He is eternal and full of bliss, and in their original spiritual nature, all living entities share that eternal, blissful nature. But the difference is vast. Kṛṣṇa is maintaining all others. All are fed by the One. For example, it is not man who provides the food for the elephants in the jungle, nor does man provide for the ants. That is done by God. He maintains everything, and He is the Supreme Person. He is the chief and original Person, and we are His subordinate parts and parcels. The simultaneous oneness and difference between Kṛṣṇa and all others can be explained by the following example. I am one with the President of the United States because we are both humans and both Americans, but the difference is that he is the chief American, whereas I am a subordinate. Similarly, Kṛṣṇa is the Supreme Person, and everyone else is subordinate to Him.

Considering that Lord Kṛṣṇa is vastly more powerful than anyone and that He is a person, one should recognize that His personal activities must be extraordinary. There is one verse in the Second Canto of the *Bhāgavatam* where Kṛṣṇa in His incarnation of Lord Rāma is described as becoming so angry that His very glance generated burning heat in the ocean, causing fear to the fish and crocodiles. No one can be angry like the Lord. *Śrīmad-Bhāgavatam* is made up of thousands of such verses describing the transcendental philosophy and superhuman activities of the Supreme Person.

In another canto of the *Bhāgavatam* it is described that Kṛṣṇa in His original form married 16,000 wives and that He expanded into 16,000 Kṛṣṇas to act as an attentive husband to each. One who knows the spiritual science of Kṛṣṇa consciousness can understand how such acts are possible for God. Kṛṣṇa expands Himself, by His feature called Supersoul, in the heart of every living creature, and as Supersoul He supplies everyone with memory, intelligence and forgetfulness. Therefore, since Kṛṣṇa is in the hearts of all the countless living entities, it was not very difficult for Him to come out of the hearts of 16,000 women who were His great devotees and marry them. But only God can do such things. Some people call Kṛṣṇa's activities mythology, but they are facts. God is the Supreme Person, and His personal pastimes as presented in the *Śrīmad-Bhāgavatam* are recited and glorified by the greatest transcendental poets and philosophers.

Whatever Kṛṣṇa does, being absolute in quality, can liberate whoever submissively hears such pastimes. Kṛṣṇa is also called Ranchor, which means "He who left the battlefield." Ordinarily a warrior who leaves a battle is derided as a coward, but Kṛṣṇa is worshiped in His feature as Ranchor in many temples in India. Chased by the demon Jarāsandha, Kṛṣṇa left a battlefield because He had to tend to another pastime, which also involved fighting with armies, to rescue His chief queen, Rukminī. At that time Kṛṣṇa and His brother, Balarāma, fled from the demon to the top of a high mountain. Jarāsandha set the mountain on fire, and Kṛṣṇa and Balarāma leaped down from the mountain, which was eighty-eight miles high. No one can perform such feats but the Supreme Personality of Godhead. There are no activities within our experience that can compare to His pastimes.

Of course, God can jump eighty-eight billion miles if He so desires. As stated in the *Īśopaniṣad*, "The Personality of Godhead is more swift than the mind and can overcome all others running." In His incarnation of Vāmana, the Lord covered the entire universe in three steps. The Lord's personal form has a bodily effulgence called the *brahmajyoti*, and in that light all the planets are sustained. One time, Lord Brahmā, seeing Kṛṣṇa engaged in His pastimes as a cowherd boy, doubted that He was God. He challenged and played a trick on Kṛṣṇa by stealing His cowherd friends and cows. Kṛṣṇa then proved Himself by manifesting the whole universe within His body, and Brahmā fell down dumbstruck. At that time, Lord Brahmā admitted: "You appear like a boy, but I know You are God. Your body has inconceivable potency."

We must therefore come to understand Kṛṣṇa's supremacy in His form as a cowherd boy holding a flute in His two hands. Sometimes people formally profess, "Yes, God is unlimited," but when the Supreme Lord comes to this world to give even a small indication of His limitless nature, foolish people deride Him. "No," they say, "He couldn't have lifted Govardhana Hill. He can't appear in the brass Deity. He can't appear in the chanting of His name." People who think like this have a poor fund of knowledge. They know that they themselves cannot lift a hill, so they think that it must be impossible for God also.

The philosophers of the impersonal school do not believe that God is a person who has His own eternal activities. When they hear about Rāmacandra's eyes' burning red-hot in anger, they take this description to be material. Śrīla Prabhupāda writes, "They want to see negation in perfection." This means that the impersonalist has a negative idea of spirit as no more than the opposite of matter. Because in this miserable material world there is a variety of people, activities, eating, talking, singing and so forth, they take it that spirit must be devoid of all variety and personality. They want to make everything zero, and they think this to be perfection. They take the Absolute Truth to be a kind of blank or void. But this idea of the Supreme is not supported by the version of the Vedic literature. Throughout the whole of the Vedic scriptures we hear that Lord Viṣṇu, Lord Kṛṣṇa, is the Supreme Personality of Godhead, the eternal source of everything. There is no void anywhere in His creation.

The impersonalists' goal is to lose their personal identities and merge as one with the divine "white light," the *brahmajyoti*. But, as we have explained, that effulgent light is only an aspect of Kṛṣṇa's supreme personality, and it is subordinate to Him. Nor can a living entity do away with his individual personality because, like the Supreme Lord, we are eternal persons. The impersonalist philosopher is fearful of real spiritual life because of his bitter experience with personal varieties in material life. He is like a man who has been ill in a hospital for a long time and who, when told that one day he will recover his health, eat normally and have many pleasurable activities, does not believe it because of experiencing only misery for so long.

But factually there *is* healthy, normal life. There *is* an eternal, blissful life of variety and personality in loving service to the Supreme Person. Certainly the activities and relationships of this material world are false because they are impermanent, but eternal truth is not void, zero or without variety. The Personality of Godhead has His own abode in the spiritual world, and it is described that "once going there, one never has to return to this world of birth and death." We can qualify to go there and enjoy with Kṛṣṇa in His eternal, blissful activities.

The best method for getting rid of all confusion about actual spiritual life is to hear the authorized version of *Śrīmad-Bhāgavatam*. The purpose of holding the *Bhāgavatam* class is to facilitate such hearing. One's attraction for fleeting material pleasures will diminish as one hears about the pastimes of the Supreme Person with His pure devotees. All confusion about the nature of God and the living entity will be cleared up as one hears Kṛṣṇa conscious philosophy from great authorities.

It is extremely important that one hear *Bhāgavatam* from the right person, a bona fide spiritual master. If one tries to understand the pastimes of the incarnations of Godhead on his own, or if he is misled by a mundane academic scholar, he will come to the wrong conclusion and think that God is an ordinary man or that God is impersonal.

But who is the bona fide spiritual master from whom we must hear? Lord Kṛṣṇa describes in *Bhagavad-gītā* that one must "approach a spiritual master and inquire from him . . . because he has seen the truth. And when you have thus learned the truth, you will know that all living beings are but part of Me—and that they are in Me, and are Mine." (*Bg.* 4.34-35) Therefore a spiritual master is one who teaches that Kṛṣṇa is supreme and that we are His eternal servitors. Such a teacher carries the message of Kṛṣṇa as it is. Kṛṣṇa says, "Surrender to Me." Therefore, the spiritual master does not misinterpret or change the meaning by saying, "Don't surrender to Kṛṣṇa. You are as good as Kṛṣṇa. Forget Kṛṣṇa." There is a system of checks and balances. What the spiritual master says is also stated in the scripture and upheld by the disciplic succession of bona fide teachers. For example, Kṛṣṇa first spoke the truth of the *Bhāgavatam* to the first living entity, Brahmā, who in turn spoke it to Nārada. Nārada spoke it to Vyāsadeva, who spoke it to Śukadeva. In this way it has come down to the present age, and Śrīla Prabhupāda, our spiritual master, is a bona fide teacher in this direct succession from Kṛṣṇa.

In *Bhagavad-gītā* Kṛṣṇa further describes the person in Kṛṣṇa consciousness in answer to Arjuna's question, "What does a person in Transcendence look like? How does he speak, and how does he walk?" Kṛṣṇa describes that such a person is not agitated by the happiness or distress of this material world. He controls his senses by fixing his consciousness upon the Personality of Godhead. Great spiritual masters like Brahmā, Nārada and Vyāsa are liberated from material desires, and therefore their desire to speak of Kṛṣṇa's pastimes proves that the Lord's pastimes are not material. Such liberated spiritual masters are not interested in telling fictional stories. Their meditation upon Kṛṣṇa is accepted as meditation upon the highest transcendental truth.

Lord Brahmā prays to Kṛṣṇa as follows: "My conclusion is, therefore, that You are the Supreme Soul, Absolute Truth, and the supreme original person; and although You have expanded Yourself in so many Viṣṇu forms, or in living entities and energies, by Your inconceivable transcendental potencies, You are the supreme one without a second. You are the supreme Supersoul."

Such spiritual masters go everywhere just to speak to people about the glories of Kṛṣṇa. And although Kṛṣṇa is self-satisfied, He is always most pleased by His devotees. Therefore Kṛṣṇa says that one should not be puffed up by his own accomplishments, but should humbly approach a devotee and hear *Śrīmad-Bhāgavatam* from him. His Divine Grace A.C. Bhaktivedanta Swami Prabhupāda has introduced to the West this timeless process of hearing about Kṛṣṇa, and many sincere men and women have changed their lives and become devotees just by hearing the *Bhāgavatam*. Now Śrīla Prabhupāda's authorized disciples are conducting *Bhāgavatam* classes all over the world, in schools, universities, public festivals–everywhere. If people will simply give a submissive ear, the potent transcendental messages of *Śrīmad-Bhāgavatam* can immediately clear all inauspicious conditions from the face of the earth.

The Education to End All Miseries

April/May, 1974

Everyone will agree that a human being needs some kind of education. Some teachers stress preparing oneself for an occupation, while others assert that the quest for knowledge itself sufficiently justifies an education. But unless one's vocational education or search for knowledge can reveal to him his own identity, the purpose of life, his relationship with God and the universe, and the path of freedom from material miseries, whatever else he learns is but a waste of time.

The well-known incident of the unduly proud scholar and the boatman illustrates this point. A scholar once engaged a ferry boatman to row him across a river. Observing that his boatman was quite uneducated, the scholar began to show off his own learning and simultaneously criticize the boatman.

"My good boatman," the scholar said, "just see how the first stars are appearing in the sky. We may observe the juxtapositions of planets and stars to a degree that is marvelous. Tell me, do you know the science of astronomy?"

"No sir," the boatman replied, adding that he knew little beyond rowing.

"You don't know astronomy?" the scholar said. "Poor fellow! Then your life is twenty-five percent wasted."

Some time passed, and the scholar began commenting upon the various land formations around them, boasting that he was also a master of geology. "Do you know the science of geology?" he asked. When the boatman said he did not, the scholar declared, "Oh, then fifty percent of your life is wasted." Then the scholar next launched into a dissertation on psychology, and when the boatman admitted he knew nothing about it, the scholar announced, "Indeed, seventy-five percent of your life is wasted!"

Suddenly black clouds began pouring rain, and a squall rocked the little ferryboat. Within minutes the storm became so serious that waves broke over the ferry's sides, and the ferryman, seeing they would have to abandon the boat, turned to the scholar and said, "Sir, I'm afraid this boat is lost. We'll have to swim for it. Do you know the art of swimming?"

But the scholar replied, "I don't know how to swim."

"Oh, sir," said the boatman, "then one hundred percent of your life is wasted!" He then dove into the river and began swimming, while the educated scholar drowned.

Thus although a man may pretend to be educated, his education is useless if he does not learn how to save himself from the miseries of life and ultimately from death itself. The Vedic literature refers to a human being who does not use his human birth to solve life's perplexities as a *kṛpaṇa*, or miser. The *Garga Upaniṣad* states: "He is a miserly man who does not solve the problems of life and who thus quits this world like the cats and dogs, without understanding the science of self-realization." The real wealth of human life lies in becoming enlightened and solving the problems of life. Education that misses or ignores this must be considered subhuman.

FACING THE PROBLEMS

What, then, are the problems of existence? First, there are the fourfold miseries—birth, death, disease and old age. There are miseries caused by other living entities, such as biting bugs and human enemies; there are miseries caused by the very nature of our bodies, such as mental anxiety, indigestion and broken limbs; and there are miseries inflicted on us by natural calamities beyond human control, such as earthquakes, droughts and floods. For our education to be fruitful, it should help us find a solution to these problems.

One might object to our assumption that human life should yield freedom from miseries. Some people think misery the natural human condition. They say we are meant to suffer. Nevertheless, living entities of all species want to be happy and avoid suffering; no one takes suffering naturally. Misery may seem inevitable, yet philosophers, humanitarians and politicians ever seek its remedies. Not only does a human being try to avoid suffering; even an ant resists being killed. Ask anyone if he is eager to deteriorate with old age. To answer honestly, one would have to say no. What about disease or death? Would anyone like to die right now? "No thanks." Sometimes people try to block out suffering with sensual pleasure. For example, one might temporarily forget one's anxieties through drugs or liquor. But after the high wears off, the anxieties return.

One's claim to be happy and content is a deception if one has not conquered the miseries of birth, death, old age and disease. For example, say we were to visit a friend in the hospital and find that his leg was in traction, he was unable to pass urine unless a nurse brought a bedpan, he had to receive shots regularly, and he could not eat solid food. If we asked our friend how he was feeling and he replied, "I'm all right," we might ask, "What is that 'I'm all right'?" With so many miseries, how could he consider himself all right?

Such illusions of well-being and satisfaction are common among lower animals. Cattle and chickens, for instance, eat their grass and grains in contentment, although their master feeds them simply to kill them. A human being, however, won't stand for being miserable. He protests, or he seeks a solution.

Hedonists, of course, say that the only solution is to go on enjoying the pleasures of the senses and not dwell on miseries, but unfortunately life's miseries curb their pleasure at every step. One might have palatable food to eat, but if someone were to mix sand into it, no one would be able to enjoy it, for although its taste would still be there, the sand would grit against one's teeth and nullify the enjoyment. The pains of material life similarly nullify all the enjoyments of the material world. But if despite all sufferings, one is determined to enjoy material life—to eat sweet food mixed with sand—still one cannot. No one is allowed to stay here. We may want to make our home here and enjoy, but death kicks us out. There are no exceptions. Everyone is forced to leave.

Therefore, with the facilities of human life, one should seek an ultimate solution to misery. Still one might object that to stop suffering is impossible. The painter Van Gogh once wrote in a letter, "Misery is eternal." But the solution is at hand, as we shall describe herein, if only one approaches the problem seriously and receives the proper education.

THE GIANTS WHO FAIL US

We should think that if we scrutinized the works of great writers, scientists and artists, they would help us conquer these miseries. But as we consult our great thinkers, we find they do not have the solution. Socrates, Shakespeare, Freud or the latest Nobel Prize winning scientists may be giants in their fields, but reading their works cannot free one from death or old age. Scientists, of course, are well-known for what they supposedly will do in the future. Those called gerontologists even profess to be on the verge of discovering how to stop aging and death. But according to a recent report in *Newsweek*, "they have not reached anything even resembling an elixir of youth." In any case, aside from hopes that some heroic scientist may rescue us from our problems, the miseries of birth, death, old age and disease have no solution. No one wants them, but no one is free from them.

Even humanity's greatest scientists and philosophers cannot solve the problems of life because everyone born into the material world is conditioned by four basic imperfections. First, we are prone to make mistakes—"to err is human." In India, for instance, Mahatma Gandhi was supposed to have been a very great person, but he too committed mistakes. Five minutes before he came to the meeting at which he was killed, his confidential associates warned him not to go, but nevertheless he persisted. Another imperfection is that we fall into illusion, mistaking one thing for another. We are also imperfect in that we are prone to cheat. For example, I must admit that I sometimes make mistakes and sometimes fall into illusion. But if nevertheless I write a book claiming to be the truth, is that not cheating? How can one subject to so many imperfections claim to be a teacher? And another imperfection is that we have limited senses. With our limited ears we can hear only a certain range of sounds, and with our eyes we observe the huge sun in the sky to be no bigger than a half dollar. These conditions of material nature, imposed upon one and all, limit man in his knowledge.

THE PERFECT INTELLIGENCE

But perfect knowledge to free us from suffering is available–from the perfect source. Unlike knowledge spoken by imperfect, conditioned living entities, that spoken by God is perfect, free of defect. There is a supremely intelligent being, and His intentions toward mankind are loving. As the supreme creator, He can give the knowledge for supreme freedom from misery.

Atheists argue that there is no Supreme God, but they cannot explain how the huge cosmic manifestation of universes, planets and living beings has come about. The pious accept that God is the creator, but atheists speculate that everything has arisen automatically through spontaneous combustion, chance chemical and sexual combinations, blind evolution, and so on. These explanations identify only intermediate causes; none of them disproves the existence of a Supreme Lord who is the cause of all causes.

The universe displays wonderful management, engineering and artistry, and behind all these huge affairs of nature is a gigantic brain or intelligence. If a child sees a spacecraft orbiting in the sky, he may think it is doing so by chance, without control, but a mature person knows that teams of intelligent scientists and technicians are controlling its flight. Why, then, should we assume, like ignorant children, that these huge spacecraft called planets are flying in exact, grand orbits through space automatically, with no intelligence behind them? Our scientists may observe the workings of the universe and describe how the law of gravity holds the planets in orbit, but simply to observe the phenomenon and label it "the law of gravity" does not really explain or in any way duplicate the inconceivable mystic potency that enables the planets to float and sail through space. Indeed, to observe laws in the universe is to admit that there must be a lawmaker behind them. Thus begins a conviction in the existence of a supreme intelligence, a supreme controller–God–who alone can give man the ultimate knowledge of how to become free from suffering.

The transcendental nature of God is revealed in scripture, which is His spoken word. The original scripture is called the *Veda* (*veda* means "knowledge"). For the benefit of all living beings, God revealed information on how to become free from the suffering of material life, and a disciplic succession of spiritual masters has conveyed it to us. Such knowledge is called *apauruṣeya*, which means that it originates not from imperfect men within this world, but, without defect, from God. In Vedic literature the supreme controller, the intelligent being from whom everything emanates, is called Kṛṣṇa, which means "All-attractive." The Supreme Lord, Kṛṣṇa, has given authoritative literature to men in different lands, and His words appear to differ according to the times and places they were delivered and the understanding of the people in those places; thus we have the Bible, Koran and *Bhagavad-gītā*. Yet the teaching of the Supreme is one, for its conclusion is always the same: obedience to God will end all suffering.

EDUCATION BEYOND THE BODY

To take the first step in transcendental knowledge, one should understand that he is not his body but a spiritual soul. Nevertheless, most big scholars, philosophers and political leaders have not taken even this first step. They have not mastered even the ABC's of real education. Rather, thinking they are their bodies, they identify themselves with their families, races, nations and so on. A person in bodily consciousness thinks, "I am John Thompson," "I am a white man," "I am an American," "I am black," "I am Christian," "I am Communist," "I am human," and so on. Yet within a few years the demise of the body vanquishes all such designations.

According to Vedic literature, the real self, as an eternal soul who exists in a loving relation to God, the complete whole, does not die when the body dies, nor does he grow old when the body grows old. He cannot be cut; nor can he be killed. He is joyful always. If one understands this, he can disentangle himself from his long history of suffering. But if one does not undertake this study, whatever else he does in his bodily identity is defeated at the time of death.

Human education, then, must not merely instruct us how to prepare for a job or how to speculate upon the imperfect views of great thinkers. Rather, it must enable us to solve the problems of life. A human being should be dissatisfied as long as he cannot extricate himself from the prison called the material world, where everyone is subject to the strict punishments of old age, death and disease. To be gainfully employed within the prison, to try to enjoy prison life to the utmost, or to give up all hope of ever getting out of prison and simply to sit down to read and write books for amusement is not the real nature of a freedom-loving being. Each of us, by our original nature, is meant to be free of the sufferings material nature imposes upon us.

Although our confinement in the material world is under the jurisdiction of the supreme controller, Kṛṣṇa, He is not to blame for our suffering. We ourselves have brought it about by our ignorance. Lacking education in what is what, thinking we belong to the material world, we have forgotten our spiritual nature. But because Kṛṣṇa has not forgotten us–even though we have absorbed ourselves in temporary activities and thus forgotten Him–He sends His personal representative, the spiritual master, to offer us the path by which to return home, back to Godhead and to teach us by precept and example the life of God consciousness, a life of eternity, bliss and knowledge.

The Bhakti Viewpoint-Kṛṣṇa Consciousness in the University

February/March, 1974

Professor Becker: When I first informed members of the faculty that I was inviting a Hare Kṛṣṇa devotee to speak at our meeting, the response was negative. I think that often our view of the Kṛṣṇa consciousness movement is one bordering perhaps on annoyance, or a feeling that these people are interlopers in a field that we properly academically control. And I think it's a loss, a tremendous loss, for our university and ourselves that the devotional side, the *bhakti* side, of knowledge or wisdom is something we have rejected in our university traditions for thousands of years. That we should be dispassionate, detached and sort of impersonal about learning, particularly learning of the Eastern religions, has been almost a pre-supposition of every course and every class in college.

Many of us feel that this divorcing of the personal or devotional from learning, from wisdom, is a bad thing. And so I think we have a great deal to learn about the religions of India from people who have taken a direct, more involved and, I think, more complete and total approach to the things we read about in books.

We have with us today Satsvarūpa dāsa Gosvāmī and two other devotees who have come from Madison, Wisconsin, at my invitation to speak to us about the Kṛṣṇa consciousness movement. I thought what we would do today is to let them give an introduction to what they are doing and then open up the meeting to questions. And so without taking any more time, let me turn the hour over to Satsvarūpa dāsa Gosvāmī.

Satsvarūpa dāsa Gosvāmī: Thank you very much, Professor Becker.

Our movement stands on the authority of the Vedic literature, which of course is studied in universities throughout the world. I am going from university to university, talking to professors and showing them our books, so I am also learning about the academic approach Professor Becker described. But we understand that the real scholars of Vedic literature are its original compiler and the *ācāryas* [teachers] who come in what is called the disciplic succession. These Vedic scriptures, like the *Vedas*, *Upaniṣads*, *Vedānta-sūtra*, *Bhagavad-gītā* and

Bhāgavata Purāṇa, were enunciated, according to the evidence we get from the books themselves, by God, or the Absolute Truth. They are not ordinary literature. Of course, they can be studied for language, history, philosophy or religion—but what do they actually mean, aside from different interpretations?

Our approach is to give great respect to the *acāryās* themselves, the compilers of the Vedic literature, for being very clear-headed and complete in their presentation. We want to know what they have to say. We want to appreciate it without making our own interpretation.

This position actually has the greatest integrity. As Professor Becker was saying, *bhakti* is sometimes accused of not having integrity. This is what I meet when I show people *Bhagavad-gītā*. They say, "I can't use that *Bhagavad-gītā* because it says that Kṛṣṇa is God and that one should approach Him as the supreme authority. Now, there are many other interpretations, and if I present this one to my students, I may be accused of some kind of religious sectarianism."

Some professors, however, are more academically astute. I have been inspired to talk with Professor Dimock of the University of Chicago, who has written the introduction to Swami Bhaktivedanta's *Bhagavad-gītā As It Is*. He says that our approach, which is a forceful presentation of *bhakti*, is perfectly legitimate. Not only is it perfectly legitimate—it is the purport of the Vedic literature. An actual scholar of the Vedic literature must know how to understand these books from the original scholars. In *Bhagavad-gītā* [4.2] Kṛṣṇa says:

evaṁ paramparā-prāptam
imaṁ rājarṣayo viduḥ
sa kāleneha mahatā
yogo naṣṭaḥ parantapa

He gives the key to understanding this book. "The science of *yoga*," the Lord says, "was taught and passed down in a disciplic succession of teachers, and the saintly kings understood it in that way." In other words, the teachings are meant for society's leaders, so that they may train themselves in spiritual life and pass this knowledge down for the benefit of everyone. "But in the course of time," Kṛṣṇa continues, "the succession was broken, and now I am passing this knowledge on to you." Thus in *Bhagavad-gītā* Arjuna, the disciple, becomes another recipient of this knowledge, and in the next verse Kṛṣṇa states why: "Because you are My devotee and friend." It is this devotion to Kṛṣṇa that makes one a scholar of the Vedic literature.

So who are these original scholars? I am talking about liberated souls such as Vyāsadeva, the compiler of almost all the Sanskrit scriptures, and Nārada Muni, and great sages (*ṛṣis*) like Lord Brahmā and Lord Śiva. We may consider all these people mythological, but why not simply try to see what they are presenting?

Because people are suffering in material life, limited by birth, death, disease and old age, great sages, out of compassion, have presented this literature whereby one can understand himself as eternal and free himself of all the inebrieties connected with the material body. This is the purpose of the Vedic literature. So we want to study the language, grammar and history minutely, but to this end: to appreciate how this literature can solve the problems of life.

In addition to sages like Vyāsa and Nārada Muni, we consult more recent sages like Madhvācārya, Rāmānujācarya and Lord Caitanya, who have transmitted the meaning of the Vedic literature through an authorized disciplic succession. But people who know next to nothing about the disciplic succession more or less irreverently poke into the Vedic literatures, especially *Bhagavad-gītā*. For instance, Mahatma Gandhi made a commentary on *Bhagavad-gītā* to put forward his philosophy of *ahiṁsā*, nonviolence. But to do that is rather difficult because *Bhagavad-gītā* is taught on a battlefield, with Kṛṣṇa urging Arjuna to fight. The first verse begins *dharma-kṣetre kuru-kṣetre*. Kurukṣetra is the place where the battle occurred. It's a place in India, and you can go there even today. But Gandhi says that *kuru-kṣetra* means "the body." Then the five Pāṇḍava brothers are mentioned. Gandhi says they represent the five senses. His idea, of course, is that the battle did not actually happen. But we take it from Kṛṣṇa Himself that Kurukṣetra is an actual place where a real battle was fought. This is called the direct meaning, in contrast to the indirect meanings like Gandhi's.

Of course, the *bhakta* (devotee), the impersonalist and the so-called objective grammarian and historian all have in common the quest for knowledge. I spoke with one graduate student majoring in East Asian studies at the University of Minneapolis. I asked him, "Why are you studying this? What are you preparing for by studying?" He answered that he was not studying to make money or prepare for an occupation; the main reason was to get knowledge. Simply because the knowledge is worthwhile, it should be studied.

This pure attitude is very nice. The objective is not grossly materialistic–not to study so that in ten years one will be making so much money. The study itself is worthwhile.

So what is that knowledge? The *Vedas* teach us that a person is not the material body. We have to enter this area of Absolute Truth if we are actually to talk about knowledge.

In *Bhagavad-gītā* [7.19], real knowledge is described:

bāhunāṁ janmanām ante
jñānavān māṁ prapadyate
vāsudevaḥ sarvam iti
sa mahātmā sudurlabhaḥ

Real knowledge is knowledge of the Absolute Truth, the transcendental source of everything, which is beyond all speculation. The *Vedānta-sūtra* begins this inquiry. *Athāto brahma-jijñāsā*: "What is the Absolute Truth?" The next code states, *janmādy asya yataḥ*: "The Absolute Truth is that from which everything is coming." Outside the university or inside, if you can find that Absolute Truth—whether by research, by chanting or by reading books—if you can understand where everything is coming from, who you are, and how you are different from the material world, then your knowledge is perfect.

We should not study Vedic culture as if it were a collection of quaint tribal customs, thinking, "'They perform their death-rites like this, and they have this strange belief about God and the supernatural." Rather, each of us requires knowledge of his own position. I who am studying this book—what is my solution to death? The Vedic literature teaches us how to be free of death. The *Vedas* actually give us information, as human beings, how to realize our blissful transcendental nature.

In stressing this aspect, the translations and commentaries of His Divine Grace A.C. Bhaktivedanta Swami Prabhupāda have been appreciated by such an esteemed scholar as Professor Dimock to be actually hitting the nail on the head. We want to cooperate with scholars and educators in distributing some of these books to serious students. This spring, the University of Minnesota is offering a course called "Kṛṣṇa Through the Ages," Of course, the professor, Dr. Tapp, takes the approach that Kṛṣṇa is someone mythical, but at least the man appreciates that our *Kṛṣṇa Book* is a very strong presentation of Kṛṣṇa as someone real. And students will see that this is a dynamic presentation, not another dead study. Therefore Professor Tapp is using this book as required reading, and he also wants to include *The Nectar of Devotion*, a summary study of a famous book by Rūpa Gosvāmī, a disciple of Lord Caitanya, about the science of *bhakti*.

I spoke to another professor at the University of Minnesota, Professor Kopf, who is studying Vedic literature from a historical point of view. He is very perplexed because according to archaeological records there was no society further back than three thousand years ago; yet *Bhagavad-gītā*, according to Lord Kṛṣṇa, dates back much further. So he took other books, but he was doubtful about *Bhagavad-gītā*. But when I got to Chicago and met Professor Dimock, he said that this professor had called him up and asked, "What about this *Bhagavad-gītā* by Swami Bhaktivedanta?" And he said, "Yes, it's excellent. You should take it."

We are not money-making book publishers, nor are we sectarian religionists trying to bring prayer books to people. That may have some value, but we are teaching knowledge of a higher value than the sentimental or sectarian. We are therefore presenting a humble plea for scholars and educators to examine our books seriously and try to use them to promote a proper understanding of what Vedic literature actually is.

Our meeting is short. If there are any questions, we would like to discuss them.

Question: There is a part of the mythical body of literature about Kṛṣṇa in the *Mahābhārata* where He is a *kṣatriya* [warrior] and assists the Pāṇḍavas by rather tricky means. People therefore sometimes question Kṛṣṇa's character. I was wondering if you thought these things preceded the development of Kṛṣṇa as a prophet.

Satsvarupa dasa Gosvāmī: Just see. You have one understanding–that Kṛṣṇa is devious, practically immoral–but I have the understanding that Kṛṣṇa is all good and that He is actually the God of the Jewish, Christian and Mohammedan religions. Of course, we have different teachers. You have read some books, but I can only tell you the version I have heard from my spiritual master in disciplic succession. That is the version of Kṛṣṇa Himself and the version of the *ācāryas* within the Vedic culture. According to them, interpretations considering Kṛṣṇa an ordinary human being or mythical hero have no importance.

When I was in England last summer, a famous professor, Professor Zaehner of Oxford University, gave a talk there in which he said that Kṛṣṇa is immoral. He cited some murderer, Charles Manson, and said that he was following Kṛṣṇa's teachings. This kind of talk is actually very offensive to one who follows *Bhagavad-gītā*. But you are also asking why Kṛṣṇa was on a battlefield–a scene of violence–and advocating violence.

For the answer, you have to go to *Mahābhārata*. But one should also understand that Kṛṣṇa is an *avatāra*: He is the Absolute Truth personified, not an ordinary person. When He comes into the material world, He may act as a *kṣatriya*, but He is not within the conditioning of this material world. And when He does something, no one is affected for evil. For instance, when Kṛṣṇa killed or Arjuna killed under Kṛṣṇa's direction, whoever was personally killed in that way gained eternal liberation to the spiritual world. Moreover, the battle was arranged just to annihilate miscreants. Kṛṣṇa says, "I come in age after age to annihilate the miscreants." At the time of the Battle of Kurukṣetra, the Pāṇḍavas had been thrown out of their rightful kingdom by Duryodhana and his brothers, and Kṛṣṇa wanted Arjuna to fight for the throne and justly rule the people. It was not a political war like those nowadays.

You ask why Kṛṣṇa was using tricky means. Once Kṛṣṇa asked His devotee Yudhiṣṭhira to lie to Droṇācārya by saying that his son was dead because He knew that this would discourage Droṇācārya. Yudhiṣṭhira at first hesitated He said, "I can't tell a lie; I am a moral man." But actually authorities have analyzed that this somewhat diminished his stature as a truly moral man because he was hesitating to follow instructions from the Personality of Godhead. Kṛṣṇa is the all-good Personality of Godhead, and whatever He does is for the ultimate liberation of those with whom He comes in contact. If you consider Him an ordinary man, you cannot understand Him. He Himself says this in *Bhagavad-gītā:*

avajānanti māṁ mūḍhā
mānuṣīṁ tanum āśritam
paraṁ bhāvam ajānanto
mama bhūta-maheśvaram

"Fools deride Me when I descend in the human form. They do not know My transcendental nature and My supreme dominion over all that be." (*Bg.* 9.11)

Question: You have quoted repeatedly from Sanskrit. Does *Bhagavad-gītā* translate effectively into English?

Satsvarūpa dāsa Gosvāmī: Yes. The Kṛṣṇa conscious devotees are all learning *Bhagavad-gītā*, and yet we are not Sanskrit scholars. But the teachings have been so effective that we have completely taken to this way of life. I was just talking to a very nice English professor here, Sheridan Baker, who is helping us edit our *Back to Godhead* magazine. He was talking about Thoreau and *Walden*. We noted that Thoreau had great appreciation for *Bhagavad-gītā*. Emerson also appreciated it, and so did Einstein. There have also been many others who appreciated it. But no one became a devotee of Kṛṣṇa until these English translations by Swami Bhaktivedānta and his personal demonstration of devotion to Kṛṣṇa. So his translations have been very effective. There are now thousands of Kṛṣṇa conscious devotees.

Question: Do you, in your activities, ever have to face a believing Christian?

Satsvarūpa dāsa Gosvāmī: A believing Christian? Very rarely. We very rarely meet any believing Christians. [laughter]

Question: I didn't mean to be cynical about Christianity. I just meant that you base your religion on the idea that these texts reveal the truth. Now the question has to arise in arguing with a Christian why you believe these texts reveal the truth and not their texts. And my question is how you would answer that.

Satsvarūpa dāsa Gosvāmī: Well, the explanation our spiritual master has given is that not only the Bible but the Koran and all bona fide scriptures differ according to three different principles—time, place and the persons taught. An expert religionist can make the adjustments. For example, in the Mohammedan religion there is an injunction that no man should sleep with his mother. So we understand that since this was being stressed, the people must have been very degraded; they must have been doing that. Also, "Thou shalt not kill." Only murderers need to be advised not to do it. So the Absolute Truth is contained in all scriptures, but there are different levels of spiritual culture and information about what God is. The example is given that a small pocket dictionary and an unabridged dictionary are both valid, but the unabridged dictionary has more. So if one wants to know more than "God is great," he can consult the Vedic literature. But if a student, say a fourth-grade arithmetic student, criticizes, "Oh, in calculus they are learning all sorts of nonsense that we never learned about," then he is wrong.

Question: What the Christian claims precisely is that his Bible is above your scripture, and my question is how you argue with him about the idea that yours is above his.

Satsvarūpa dāsa Gosvāmī: We don't get much description of the Personality of Godhead from the Bible. The Christian does not know much about the nature of the spiritual world or the activities there or how to engage in *bhakti-yoga*. But that is elaborately described in *Śrīmad-Bhāgavatam*.

Question: I have read that in fact the Kṛṣṇa conscious movement has cornered the incense market and is starting real estate speculation in New York. Now do those profits go down to the members, or where is the profit going? You said you weren't money-making and you weren't book publishing, but you seem to be in book publishing, and I have read that in fact there is a lot of money-making going on. I was just interested in who handles that.

Satsvarūpa dāsa Gosvāmī: Where is all the money going? We are spending it all. We just put in a printing order for over $500,000 worth of books; we are always printing books. Our members don't receive any salaries. There is not someone off in India or Monte Carlo who has all the Kṛṣṇa money and is living it up. The money is being spent for our projects—for buildings, for our active food distribution program in India in our Mayapur, Bombay and Calcutta centers, and mainly for printing books. We distribute our books practically at what they cost us, and whatever profit we make goes back into producing more books.

We are a very book conscious society. We feel that the most effective way to spread this truth is to present it in literature. In New York we are trying to buy a building to use as a headquarters. We are not speculating, looking for land to make money. But, nevertheless, money-making is all right, provided it is in Kṛṣṇa's service. There is one impersonalist philosopher who is said to have been so detached from material life that if anyone offered him money, as an automatic reflex his hand would turn away from it. But if you offer a Vaiṣṇava (devotee) money, he will at once take it; and if you give him a million dollars, he will come back the next day to ask for more. Because he sees that everything is Kṛṣṇa's energy and should be engaged in Kṛṣṇa's service.

Question: Do you have some distinction between laymen and non-laymen?

Satsvarūpa dāsa Gosvāmī: Yes. To become a formal disciple, one must follow four rules: no meat eating, no illicit sex, no gambling and no intoxication. If one does that, and if he also chants the Hare Kṛṣṇa *mahā-mantra* a certain minimum number of times daily, he is considered a "Hare Kṛṣṇa person."

Question: I am not very concerned about the money aspect of it. You were speaking before about a humble plea for knowledge, and I feel very good about that. But the aspect of your group that most of us see on the street is considerably more pushy and considerably more offensive to me, and I would consider that a betrayal of what you are doing. Yet that is presumably done within the same organization.

Satsvarūpa dāsa Gosvāmī: We support those boys and girls who are out all day distributing books. They are very great workers. You are appreciating our humble presentation, but our presentation is inferior to theirs. Theirs will have more effect. They distribute so many books, and they are so selfless—they don't keep any profit.

This is a Vedic tradition. Formerly a disciple spent from morning to night collecting something for the spiritual master, and at night he would just lie down on the floor and take a little rice and think that austerity was nice. Now, of course, the public is not interested in giving alms for a spiritual cause. But even though society is so materialistic, the devotees are out there, and all I can ask is that you forgive these disciples if you are offended by them, because actually they have no intent other than to give you this knowledge and call attention to it. Humanity is generally asleep, and they are trying to distribute this knowledge. It's their only desire. And if you can take a book or talk with them, you will see they are not actually offensive people; they are very nice. They are more humble than our formal presentation because they are doing more to spread actual spiritual culture than you in your classroom or me talking here. They have dedicated themselves to spreading Kṛṣṇa consciousness in the American culture. That's very brave of them. One can go door to door in India, and just by seeing a devotee in saffron, people will offer respect. But we wear saffron and—just the opposite. Yet rather than be frustrated and retire, the devotees have persisted. And many people, when they stop and understand what's happening, like seeing devotees in the street persistently chanting and trying to distribute these books. If it were a bogus movement, if it were something harmful, then it would be offensive. But they are not cheating anyone. Their understanding is that everything belongs to Kṛṣṇa, and they are trying to get something or someone into the service of Kṛṣṇa again.

VI. Topics in the News

Life in the Womb

September, 1975

Certain psychologists and folklorists imagine that the womb was a very nice place—a comfortable, warm home where food and shelter were provided without our effort. Some even say that throughout our adult lives, we unconsciously desire to return to that protection and security, "floating undisturbed in the warm, dark, quiet world of unparalleled intimacy with the beloved mother." By the scientific method of hearing from Vedic literature, however, we get the actual account of a human being's conception, his pre-natal condition, and his birth. Contrary to what our psychologists and folklorists have imagined, life in the womb is among the most painful and miserable of human experiences.

The *Śrīmad-Bhāgavatam*, a 5,000-year-old spiritual classic containing the essence of Vedic knowledge, gives the following vivid description of the living entity's experience from the point of conception to the time of birth: "Under the supervision of the Supreme Lord (Śrī Kṛṣṇa) and according to the results of his work, the living entity, the soul, is made to enter the womb of a woman through the particle of a man's semina to assume a particular kind of body. On the first night, the semina and ovum mix, and on the fifth night the mixture ferments into a bubble. On the tenth night it develops into a form like a plum, and after that it gradually turns into a lump of flesh. In the course of a month, a head is formed, and at the end of two months, hands, feet and other limbs take shape. By the end of three months, the nails, fingers, toes, body hair, bones and skin appear, as do the organ of generation and the other apertures in the body, namely, the eyes, nostrils, ears, mouth and anus. Within four months from the date of conception, the seven essential ingredients of the body (lymph, blood, flesh, fat, bone, marrow and semina) come into existence. At the end of five months, hunger and thirst make themselves felt, and at the end of six months, the fetus begins to move in the abdomen—on the right side if the child is a male and on the left side if female."

Painful Confinement. The actual experience of the fetus, however, cannot be known by mere medical observation. For this information we must go to the Vedic scriptures, which give us direct knowledge of events beyond our normal experience. The *Bhāgavatam* continues, "Deriving its nutrition from the food and drink taken by the mother, the fetus grows and remains in that abominable residence of stool and urine, which is a breeding place for all kinds of worms. Bitten again and again all over his body by these hungry worms in the abdomen itself, the child suffers terrible agony because of his tenderness. He thus becomes unconscious moment after moment. When the mother eats bitter, pungent foods or food that is too salty or too sour, the body of the child incessantly suffers pains that are almost intolerable. Placed within the amnion and covered outside by the intestines, the child remains lying on the side of the abdomen, his head turned toward his belly and his back and neck arched like a bow." An adult would be unable to endure such a difficult confinement. The child's pain is beyond our conception, but because his consciousness is yet undeveloped, he is able to tolerate it.

As adults, we have forgotten all this suffering and absorbed ourselves in trying to become happy in material life. Life in the womb may seem remote; no one has ever told us before about its actual nature, and it has not concerned us. Writing on this topic, His Divine Grace A.C. Bhaktivedanta Swami Prabhupāda comments, "It is an unfortunate civilization in which these matters are not plainly discussed to make people understand the precarious condition of material existence."

Astounding Remembrance. At the end of seven months in the womb, the child remains just like a bird in a cage, unable to move freely and suffering without relief. At that time, if the soul is fortunate, he gains one astounding facility: he can remember all the troubles of his past one hundred lives. The vision of his wasted attempts to be happy makes him grieve wretchedly. While in the womb, the living being realizes that he has unnecessarily entered the material world. In this frightful condition, he prays with folded hands; appealing to the Lord, who has put him there.

Sometimes a woman in labor promises herself that she will never again become pregnant and suffer such severe pain. Or a man on the operating table may promise himself that he will act in such a way as to never again become diseased and undergo surgery. Similarly, the child, deeply repentant, prays to the Lord that he will never again commit sinful activities and be forced into another womb. He prays as follows: "I take shelter of the lotus feet of Lord Kṛṣṇa, the Supreme Personality of Godhead, who appears in His various eternal forms. I, the pure soul, appearing now to be bound by my activities, am lying in the womb of my mother by the arrangement of the Lord's illusory energy. I offer my respectful obeisances unto Him, who is also here with me, but who is unaffected and changeless. He is unlimited, but He is perceived in the repentant heart."

Repentant Prayer. The child in the womb, praying out of bewilderment and repentance, realizes he is not independent or supreme. He seeks shelter from the

Supreme Lord, perceiving that the Lord in his heart is the supreme master and that he is subordinate. By the grace of God, the child in the womb can understand his actual relationship with the Supreme Lord, and he realizes that he has been reduced to his abominable condition because of his forgetfulness of God. He wants to get out, but he understands that he can do so only by the mercy of the Supreme Lord, and thus he asks for the Lord's blessings.

After nine months, however, the child in the womb makes an extraordinary request to the Lord: "Although I am living in a terrible condition, still I do not wish to depart from my mother's abdomen to fall again into the blind well of materialistic life." The child foresees that the trauma of birth will destroy his clear knowledge of the miseries of material life and his remembrance of Lord Kṛṣṇa. If he forgets the ordeal in the womb and again assumes the false position of an enjoyer, it would be better for him never to be born. Although bitten and burned and surrounded by blood and urine, at least in the womb he is able to remember Kṛṣṇa. The thought of his future miseries make him reluctant to take birth, but of course he cannot possibly live in the womb much longer. While he thus extols the Lord, the wind that helps parturition propels him forth with his face turned downward. Pushed down suddenly by the wind, the child comes out with great trouble, breathless and deprived of his memory due to severe agony. He cries piteously, having lost his superior knowledge in the ordeal of birth.

We should not take lightly this account of life in the womb. One may say, "I cannot remember such pain in the womb. I am not suffering now, so why worry? Besides, I don't care." According to this way of thinking, ignorance is bliss. But it is only a temporary illusion of bliss. Although we now have no idea of the suffering in the womb, by reading such scriptures as the *Śrīmad-Bhāgavatam* and the *Bhagavad-gītā*, we can understand the terrible condition there and learn how to act in such a way that we will not suffer again. We learn from the *Bhagavad-gītā* that, as individual souls, we are never created, but are eternal, fragmental parts of the Supreme Lord. By misusing our small independence, we desire to be supreme and are thus cast into the material world. Then we wander, according to our material desires, from body to body in each of the different species, until we finally evolve to the human form of life. All this happens under the supervision of the Supreme Lord. As Śrī Kṛṣṇa states in the *Bhagavad-gītā* (18.61), "I am seated in everyone's heart, and I direct the wanderings of all living beings." If, upon reaching the human form of life, we do not utilize the opportunity for self-realization, we will again be forced to enter a womb and undergo repeated tortures there. We should therefore thoughtfully reflect, "What can we do to avoid such miseries?"

True Identity. Repeated acceptance of material life is due to forgetting our true identity as eternal loving servants of the Supreme Lord, Kṛṣṇa. Therefore reviving our relationship with Kṛṣṇa is crucial because that is the only means for the soul to escape the cycle of repeated birth and death. The primary method for doing this is chanting Hare Kṛṣṇa, Hare Kṛṣṇa, Kṛṣṇa Kṛṣṇa, Hare Hare/ Hare Rāma, Hare Rāma, Rāma Rāma, Hare Hare. Lord Śrī Caitanya Mahāprabhu, an incarnation of Kṛṣṇa who appeared five hundred years ago in Bengal, India, recommended that everyone take up this Great Chant for Deliverance to awaken his dormant Kṛṣṇa consciousness. We should also follow the instructions given by Lord Kṛṣṇa in *Bhagavad-gītā* (9.27-28): "All that you do, all that you eat, all that you offer and give away, as well as all austerities that you may perform, should be done as an offering unto Me. In this way you will be freed from all reactions to good and evil deeds, and by this principle of renunciation, you will be liberated and come to Me." By chanting Hare Kṛṣṇa and acting in this way, the conditioned soul cleanses his mind of the false notion that he can enjoy this material world separate from Kṛṣṇa. He gradually becomes completely surrendered to the Supreme Lord, and at the end of life liberation from the miseries of repeated birth and death is assured. Kṛṣṇa not only speaks the *Bhagavad-gītā* for our guidance, He also manifests Himself internally as the Supersoul within our hearts and externally as the spiritual master to instruct us how to avoid the repeated miseries of material existence. If one is anxious to get out of the material entanglement, Kṛṣṇa will direct him from within the heart how to approach a genuine spiritual master. By following the instructions of a spiritual master, one can perfect devotional service and be transferred to the spiritual world, which is completely free from birth and death.

We are all eternal spirit souls, but death and rebirth are great dangers for us as long as we remain in conditioned, material existence. We must pray to the Lord, as did the child in the womb, to realize our eternal relationship with Kṛṣṇa, the Supreme Personality of Godhead. But we should not wait until it is too late. Preparing for the next life is a proposal for thoughtful human beings, a proposal we are meant to act on by following spiritual authorities while we are still healthy in this lifetime.

Man on the Moon
A Case of Mass Brainwashing

By now it's no secret that the space scientists have cheated us out of billions of dollars. But the hoax is even more colossal than we could have imagined.

May, 1977

Śrīla Bhaktisiddhānta Sarasvatī Ṭhākura, the spiritual master of His Divine Grace A.C. Bhaktivedanta Swami Prabhupāda, once described materialistic civilization as "a society of the cheaters and the cheated." Looking at our modern world, we can easily see why: massive advertising campaigns for cigarettes and liquor that promise pleasure but deliver disease; widespread gambling rackets of all kinds, some government-sponsored, that bilk the public of billions each year; high-level corruption of many leaders in industry and government that reveals a nearly total disregard for the public's welfare. From all this, and much more, the only conclusion to draw is that the vast majority of people, out of ignorance of a meaningful goal of life, actually *desire to be cheated*—actually feel the need for the false promises and outright lies of the hucksters to provide some hope of happiness from day to day. Thus a few clever, aggressive professionals take advantage of the ignorant masses and engage in large-scale cheating for their own selfish interests.

While cheating goes on in all fields of endeavor, one of the most outstanding is modern science. Scientists can make useful contributions to material life, but they become cheaters when they claim that science is (or someday will be) independent of the laws of nature. Theories such as "Life originates from matter and can be created in the laboratory," or "Since there is no supreme intelligence directing the universe, we [the scientists] are the only ones who can explain existence," are all bluffs perpetrated *without a shred of scientific proof*. Their only purpose is to advance the prestige of the scientists and net them billion-dollar government grants for endless research. Recent efforts to travel to the moon provide a prime example of this kind of lucrative mass "brainwashing," which is still succeeding with a large portion of the gullible public.* Despite the tremendous volume of propaganda proclaiming the "conquest of outer space," we have information from a very reliable source, the Sanskrit Vedic scriptures, that the so-called "astronauts" *never actually went to the moon*. Although most people hold it as an article of absolute faith that man first reached the moon in July, 1969, the manned moon landing is actually a colossal hoax.

We realize that this is very difficult for you to accept, since it directly contradicts your established beliefs. But since you yourself have *not* actually gone to the moon, you owe it to yourself to consider why you are so confident that the "astronauts" actually *have* gone there. Why do you accept the popular version of the manned moon landing? Because you believe the authority of the scientists, the journalists, and the politicians who propagate that version. When we cite the Vedic scriptures, which state that the "astronauts" could not have gone to the moon, we are simply favoring another authority. In both cases, it is a matter of accepting an authority and believing what it says.

Now, why do we believe the Vedic scriptures rather than the material scientists? Because the Vedic scriptures differ from the conclusions of material science in that they are not based on imperfect sensory investigation, but are *apauruṣa*, i.e., they emanate from God, who is beyond the material world. In other words Vedic evidence stands above the defects of conditioned souls within the material world. Thus, when it comes to real scientific knowledgc, the standard of Vedic authority is perfect because it originates directly from the all-perfect, omniscient Personality of Godhead.

The Vedic account of our planetary system is already researched, concluded, and perfect. The *Vedas* state that the moon is 800,000 miles *farther* from the earth than the sun. Therefore, even if we accept the modern calculation of 93 million miles as the distance from the earth to the sun, how could the "astronauts" have traveled to the moon–a distance of almost 94 million miles–in only 91 hours (the alleged elapsed time of the Apollo 11 moon trip)? This would require an average speed of more than one million miles per hour for the spacecraft, a patently impossible feat by even the space scientists' calculations.

Another important reason why the manned moon landing must be a hoax is that, according to the *Vedas*, each planet has its particular standard of living and atmosphere, and no one can transfer from one planet to another without becoming properly qualified. This means that if someone wants to go to Mars,

*Twenty-eight percent of all Americans, according to a Gallup poll cited in the Los Angeles *Times* on October 13, 1976, have seen through the sham and now believe the moon landing to be a fake.

for instance, he has to give up his present gross material body and acquire another one suitable for life on that particular planet. Vedic knowledge teaches that the living being doesn't die with the death of the body, but that he is an eternal spirit soul. As Lord Kṛṣṇa says in the *Bhagavad-gītā*, "As the embodied soul continually passes, in this body, from boyhood to youth to old age, the soul similarly passes into another body at death" (*Bhagavad-gītā* 2.13). At the time of death the human being transfers to another material body according to the desires he cultivated and the work he performed during his lifetime. Therefore, since the moon has a particular standard of life and atmosphere, if one wants to travel there he has to adapt his material body to the conditions of that planet.

Even on the earth planet these restrictions hold true. For example, a human being cannot possibly live in the water, nor can a fish live on land. These are the rigid conditions of life, and any attempt to defy them is artificial and will fail. Similarly, just as you have to change your dress if you want to go from India to Europe, where the climatic conditions are different, so you also have to change your physical "dress" if you want to go to the specialized atmosphere of the moon. In other words, if you want to go to the moon or the sun or any other higher planet, you can keep your finer dress of mind, intelligence, and ego, but you have to leave behind your gross dress (your physical body) made of earth, water, fire, and other material elements, and acquire a body suitable for your destination.

Of course, none of this will help you solve the real problem of life—entrapment in the vicious cycle of birth and death. As Kṛṣṇa states in the *Bhagavad-gītā*, even if one transfers in his next life to a very elevated position in the highest planet in the universe, Brahmaloka, he will still have to experience birth and death. The goal of human life is to free the soul from its continuous transmigration among different species of life on various planets, and to transfer to the spiritual planets, where life is eternal. To reach these planets, a complete change of both gross and subtle bodies is necessary, for one can reach the spiritual sky only in a spiritual form. We will elaborate on this a little later, but our point here is that you cannot simply force yourself onto another planet without the proper qualification.

Just as in the United States there are laws controlling the entry of foreigners through the issuance of visas, so in the universe there are also laws controlling the movement of all living beings—even astronauts and scientists—and unless one's *karma* is such that he deserves to take birth on the moon or the sun or the earth or wherever, he cannot defy the laws of nature and go there by force. The scientists are always claiming they are independent of nature's law, but even *they* have to submit to death and rebirth; they cannot check them. Similarly, they cannot go to the moon planet, which the *Vedas* describe not as a lifeless desert but as a heavenly planet of extraordinary material pleasures. Where the astronauts actually went, or how this fabrication of lunar visitation will one day be exposed to people in general, are not part of our present discussion. But the Vedic teachings warn us that the manned moon landing is certainly an empty bluff.

When we contradict the revered scientists like this and warn people that, through the use of brainwashing propaganda, they are being cheated out of billions of hard-earned tax dollars—we ourselves are accused of brainwashing. But which is better: a sober warning or a colossal multi-billion-dollar hoax?

Furthermore, even if, for argument's sake, we accept that the "astronauts" *did* go to the moon, our main contention still holds: the moon excursion is a hoax, a mass brainwashing job. Why? Because it has no value. Even the scientists now admit its uselessness, and their interest in going to the moon has subsided. After many years of concentrated effort and billions of dollars of public money spent, the scientists have concluded that the moon is uninhabitable and have stopped trying to go there. But the public is encouraged to regard this failure as a wonderful achievement! "Just see! They have come back with some moon dust!" Long ago the Vedic literatures said the moon was uninhabitable by man, before going there the scientists themselves predicted they could not live in that atmosphere, and upon reaching the moon they discovered the same thing—that they could not live there. So what is the value of this kind of billion-dollar excursion, which has produced only a few rocks?

The scientists' stubbornness is like that of a boy who is repeatedly warned by his father not to stick his finger in the revolving blades of a fan, but who goes ahead and does it anyway, and is hurt. The scientists insisted that a lunar landing would prove the United States to be the most advanced nation. Never mind that it cost billions, which could have been spent on worthwhile projects, such as feeding the starving. The brainwashing was so extreme that at one point Pan American Airlines was even selling tickets to the moon, and there was talk of colonizing it, although everyone acknowledged that it is impossible to live there. And yet if we speak out strongly against this nonsense, people say *we* are brainwashed—for not believing in the bluff of the moon excursion. Now, having squeezed as much prestige as possible out of their great "success" in reaching the moon, the scientists have become disappointed and set their sights on Mars—and the huge expenditure of public funds goes on.

Again, we do not say that man should neglect science, but rather that he should practice science according to the authorized knowledge of the laws of nature. The scientists should not attempt to defy the laws of nature, or those of God, but should work humbly in harmony with the real purpose of human life—liberation from the cycle of birth and death. Despite all scientific theorizing, research, and the technology, the scientists do not even know the nature of the life within the body, how life enters the body, and where life goes after death. Not being able to produce even the smallest living creature, and being unable to stop death, the modern scientists should not consider themselves the all-in-all.

If we desire to praise someone for scientific achievements, let us praise the Great Brain who is actually controlling all living beings by directing His material energy, and who regulates the immense machinery of the universe. Let us follow Lord Brahmā, who sings in the Vedic scripture *Brahmā-saṁhitā* (5.52): "I worship Govinda [Kṛṣṇa], the primeval Lord, by whose order the sun assumes immense power and heat and traverses its orbit." The sun is a creation of God; it is not a creation of the scientists. So also are the oceans and the great mountains, the resources of nature, and outer space—all are works of the Supreme Personality of Godhead. As for machine-making, the material energy of Kṛṣṇa, the Supreme Energetic, has expertly fashioned male and female forms that go on reproducing themselves without further assistance from Him. And this happens over and over in millions of species. Can the scientists create such replicating machines? Can they create a sun and keep it floating perpetually in space? Can they create the oceans, the brain of a great scientist like Einstein, or even an ant or an amoeba? No. All these scientific achievements are the works of God. And when God Himself speaks through authorized scriptures like the *Bhagavad-gītā*, He explicitly says, "Do not waste your time trying to go to the moon; that is not your place." If the godless human scientists defy this Supreme Scientist and Supreme Controller, then disaster will befall them and whoever follows them. Therefore we are protesting a godless science that defies God's laws.

In *Easy Journey to Other Planets*, written back in 1959, His Divine Grace A.C. Bhaktivedanta Swami Prabhupāda warned us that attempting to reach the moon by materialistic methods is a waste of time. In a speech ten years later he further explained:

> If we go to live on the moon—assuming that it is possible—even with an oxygen mask, how long could we stay? Furthermore, even if we had the opportunity to stay there, what would we gain? We might gain a little longer life perhaps, but we could not live there forever. That is impossible. And what would we gain by a longer life? . . . Near San Francisco I have seen a forest where there is a tree 7,000 years old. But what is the benefit? If one is proud of standing in one place for 7,000 years, that is not a very good credit.

Of course, scientists, journalists, and politicians are not known for considering things in the philosophical light of transcendental knowledge, but a sober fact to consider is this: if, even after all the scientists' achievements, we must still die and suffer the miseries of repeated birth and death, then what is the benefit of that science? Kṛṣṇa tells us not to waste our valuable time with things that are only temporary and do not lead to liberation from birth and death. "Don't waste your time going from this planet to that planet," He says in the *Bhagavad-gītā*. "Your material miseries will only follow you." So the moon excursion is a hoax in yet another, all-important sense: the scientists are leading people to believe they will be happy if they go to the moon, but when considered in the context of the eternal soul's welfare, going to the moon and living there for many, many years *still* won't solve the problems of life. It is a hoax to claim that the endeavor to travel to other planets will bring happiness. A person can be happy only if he receives information from authorized scriptures about the nature of the soul and the method of liberating the soul from his suffering condtion. This liberation is the goal of Kṛṣṇa consciousness.

And yet, when we warn people not to waste their lives in temporary achievements, when we warn them not to engage in sinful activities that will force them to transmigrate to lower planets and lower forms of life—they accuse *us* of being duped and spreading false propaganda. But we will not be quieted by their accusations. As devotees of Kṛṣṇa we must go on repeating His instructions for everyone's benefit. As Kṛṣṇa tells us in His incarnation as Śrī Caitanya Mahāprabhu, "Instruct everyone to follow the teachings of Lord Śrī Kṛṣṇa as they are given in the *Bhagavad-gītā* and the *Śrīmad-Bhāgavatam*. In this way become a spiritual master and try to liberate everyone in the world."

So you have to decide who is actually cheating: the materialist, who promises happiness in the context of temporary advancement and enjoyment, and who thereby ignores the eternal soul, or the spiritualist, the Kṛṣṇa conscious person, who says, "Always think of Kṛṣṇa and become His devotee. Worship Him and bow down before Him. If you practice in this way, at the end of life you will certainly return to the supreme spiritual planet, which is eternal and free from all miseries, because of your full absorption in and devotion to the Lord."

More Than Meals
Solving the Food Shortage

June, 1978

Some people take a quick glance at the Kṛṣṇa consciousness movement and conclude that its members are not working to solve humanity's day-to-day crises. These people tend to think that by chanting the names of God (Hare Kṛṣṇa), the devotees have become "otherworldly," "out of touch with reality." Or, if they stop a moment and hear what the devotees have to say about the world's problems, they may think, "Spiritual solutions can't really help anyone." Neither of these misgivings holds true. Let us consider, for example, the Kṛṣṇa conscious approach to one of the worst problems facing the world today–food shortage.

Experts often tell us that the world is in danger: we can expect more and more people and less and less food, with little hope that the supply will increase. But no one who's read *Bhagavad-gītā* or has his fair share of common sense will go along with the idea that the earth is incapable of producing more food. After all, food is ultimately coming from nature's bounty, or, simply, from God. As anyone knows, grain (the main food substance for all living beings) is not manufactured in the scientist's laboratory but results from the Lord's mercy in the form of rainfall and fertile fields.

So we should accept God's arrangement and make the most of the natural source of food He has given us. All we have to do is increase our agricultural development all over the world. But thanks to the artificial values of industrialized society, the world's population has swung away from the farms and into the cities. And as a consequence, countries like Africa, India, America, and Australia have vast tracts of uncultivated–wasted--land.

To set an example on a small scale, the Kṛṣṇa consciousness society is developing self-sufficient farms based on the principle of "simple living and high thinking". Already, devotees have started some twenty of these farms around the world. By raising their own grains and vegetables, and by protecting the cows and drawing milk from them, the devotees are proving that a life based on cultivating God consciousness and accepting the mercy of God in the form of grain and milk products is a plain and simple solution to the starvation problem.

(It's, as well, a solution to almost all other problems.) These self-sufficient farm communities are totally beyond comparison—either spiritually or materially—with the crime and crisis-filled cities.

Of course, if all the people in the world are going to move to God conscious, agricultural communities, that will require a complete cultural revolution. The Kṛṣṇa consciousness movement is advocating just this kind of overhaul in consciousness, but admittedly today's propaganda for industrialization and consumption is making things difficult. Even though the Kṛṣṇa conscious village plan is sound, economically and in every other way, people tend to dismiss it with remarks like, "Your plan may work for you, but what if some people don't go along with it? We'll still have our big cities, our vast tracts of uncultivated land, and our food shortage."

Yet even if people don't move *en masse* to God conscious farm communities, and even if, as the experts promise, the population keeps growing, there's still enough food being produced around the world to feed everyone. Our only real shortage is a shortage of Kṛṣṇa (God) consciousness. What makes one group of people in one part of the world think they can throw away thousands of tons of grain and pay farmers not to produce while people in other parts of the world starve? Simple. A shortage of God consciousness. The various "isms" such as nationalism, capitalism, and communism are all based on the bodily concept of life, and do not permit the spiritual vision which would enable people to share the fruits of the earth. As long as we are thinking black-vs.-white, American-vs.-Russian, Palestinian-vs.-Israeli, this-vs.-that, we cannot share the bounty of the earth. This problem can be alleviated only by spiritual understanding. We have to become God conscious and realize that we're all part and parcel of God—that's how we're all alike, and that's how we can share and share alike.

The critics may still object: "It seems you'll help the starving only if they become devotees of God; otherwise, you'll let them go on starving." Not so. Even now, near eastern India's Bangladesh, ISKCON Food Relief is feeding an average of twenty thousand people each month. (CARE has offered additional supplies.) And not long ago, when a cyclone killed tens of thousands in southern India's Andhra Pradesh province, ISKCON Food Relief came through for the survivors with emergency food distribution.

But more important than the immediate meals that ISKCON makes available is the dissemination of Kṛṣṇa consciousness, which alone can put an end to food shortage and starvation. As *Bhagavad-gītā* informs us, the suffering conditions around the world are simply *karma*, nature's reactions to our sinful actions, and we cannot avoid these reactions through altruism or political maneuvering. We have witnessed repeatedly that human efforts make almost no dent in drought and famine conditions. Who can control nature but the Supreme? Only with His blessing will nature provide us with rain and crops. True, in times of famine wealthy men may come forward and offer huge donations, but if there is no grain available, then their money is totally useless.

After all, whatever sufferings people are undergoing are prescribed by God's natural law. And these laws aren't subject to change by presumptuous meddlers who think they know more then God. In a hospital, for instance, the doctor may give orders that some of his patients should fast. Now, if some do-gooder wants to ignore the doctor's orders and provide the starving patients with full meals, the hospital authorities will take his so-called compassion as meddling. In the same way, when welfare workers ignore the law of *karma* they are just wasting their time. For anyone who has gone against God's natural law, suffering is inevitable.

One final note about the charge that devotees are "otherworldly." In one sense, it's true. As *Bhagavad-gītā* explains, this temporary material world will always have its quota of suffering; that is its nature. The eternal soul can be perfectly happy only when he returns to the eternal, blissful, spiritual world. Of course, we can go back to Godhead only if we have developed our love for God in this world. And if we'll just do that, then all our worries about a food shortage are over.

God, Karma and the World

April, 1978

Do you remember 1968—when churches offered "sanctuary" to draft resisters? I was in Boston at that time, and there it was big news for a while, part of the protest against the Vietnam War. Every few days you'd see in the headlines that yet another young man was telling the government "I won't go!" by going into a church. The church officials would refuse to allow federal authorities to enter and arrest him, and for a few days the tension would mount. People would throng to the church to hold mass meetings and voice their Christian antiwar sentiments, and at last federal police would move in and, after a scuffle, take the man away.

As a member of the Boston center of the Hare Kṛṣṇa movement, I attended one such meeting at Boston University's campus chapel. Despite government threats, the protesters were sheltering a draft resister and holding a twenty-four-hour public prayer meeting. The church was crowded and noisy. Several people in the audience carried large signs with political slogans or verses from the Bible. I had hoped to speak about Kṛṣṇa consciousness, but I couldn't break through the crowd of politicians, ministers, and monitors surrounding the pulpit. Speaker after speaker denounced the imminent invasion of the church by federal agents. A minister quoted verses and explained Christian duty. A little bewildered by the intense mixture of political rhetoric and Biblical quotes, and unsure what was the proper course of action for me, I returned to our center and wrote a query to our spiritual master, His Divine Grace A.C. Bhaktivedanta Swami Prabhupāda. His reply (dated October 9, 1968) arrived a few days later. I have always considered Śrīla Prabhupāda's analysis of the "sanctuary" situation a perfect response by a fully God conscious person. It showed me how to react not just to that political struggle but to the many others since then.

Dear Satsvarūpa,

Please accept my blessings. I have received your letter about the situation in Boston. From the statements in your letter, I can understand that it is a political situation. This political struggle is the reaction of *karma*. Both the opposing parties—namely the students who have taken shelter in the churches and the government force which is coming to arrest them—both of them are in the same category, because if it were a question of meat-eating or supporting the slaughter-house, both of them would agree. So the present situation is a reaction to man's sinful activities. We especially recommend that people restrain themselves from four kinds of primary sinful activities–namely illicit sex, intoxication, meat-eating, and gambling. But all these fighting people are cent per cent addicted to all these habits. So if they are serious about mitigating the unpalatable situation of society, they must agree to accept Kṛṣṇa consciousness. Otherwise, there is no possibility of peace in the world.

It is useless for students to pray twenty-four hours a day, listen to political talks, and desire that the war should stop. God cannot be their order supplier. First of all they act sinfully, and when there are reactions in the form of war, pestilence, famine, and so many other natural disturbances, they pray to God to stop them. This is not possible. They are just like criminals: first of all a criminal commits theft, burglary, and debauchery, and when he is captured by the police force, he prays to the government to stop his punishment. That is not possible. So, people are engaged in many sinful activities, and by nature's law there must be a reaction. Suppose I am encouraging cow killing, or animal killing of any sort. When by nature's law my turn comes to be killed, if I pray to God to stop it, how can it be stopped? Therefore, the protesters' process is not very genuine. They want to make God their order supplier. God is not an order supplier. He is an order giver. He orders everyone to surrender unto Him, and the fools and rascals who do not surrender unto Him want to order God through so-called prayer–that He should ask material nature to stop her legal activities of punishment. That is not possible. So the situation is not very favorable, but if someone agrees to hear *Bhagavad-gītā* and *Teaching of Lord Caitanya* continually for some time, I am prepared to go and lecture.

Your ever well-wisher,
A.C. Bhaktivedanta Swami

Now, ten years later, the "sanctuary" protest is all but forgotten. There are new political struggles, new allies and enemies. But I think Śrīla Prabhupāda's analysis is still the devastating truth. Unfortunately, the world's leaders are not listening to his advice. Most political and military leaders are completely unaware of the laws of *karma*–action-and-reaction–that Śrīla Prabhupāda and the Vedic literatures describe. But they should know that such laws actually exist–as surely as they know of nature's other unbreakable laws.

Karma is a strict, intricate mechanism, a natural phenomenon by which every human action brings about a fitting reaction. This "As ye sow, so shall ye reap" law is as much a part of the universal design as the law of gravity–"What goes up must come down." Individually, one's previous *karma* (pious or impious actions) determines one's present physical and mental condition, and at the time of death the accumulated *karma* on one's present lifetime will determine the condition of one's next lifetime. *Karma* is also working collectively: young men are going to die for their country because of sinful acts performed by themselves and their countrymen. Each and every person is thus affected by the complex interaction of *karma.*

When millions of cows or millions of human embryos are slaughtered, the killers and their accomplices have to bear the karmic reaction. All the world's major religions consider not only killing but also intoxication and sex outside marriage to be immoral. This is the code of the Supreme, and disobedience to this code must have its effects. An ordinary man may not know how or when he will suffer the karmic reaction, but that has no bearing on the fact that he *will.* Why should we think that overwhelmingly powerful material nature will not act on us, when we experience that breaking even the state laws brings us a bad reaction? Although in the present age we're extremely enamored of scientific explanations, even the most educated men have scarcely looked into this science of action and reaction. Individually and collectively, we go on committing the same crimes millions of times. The karmic toll mounts, and we pay it–through natural disaster, war, and death.

Why don't the leaders take the Vedic literature's good advice and learn how they and the rest of us can live our lives free from *karma*? Despite our adroit international diplomacy, the world's nuclear stockpiles grow larger and more deadly. We're told the superpowers will never use their nuclear weapons, but by the inevitable law of *karma* we know they must be used. Yet just as *karma* and suffering are always at hand, so also the solution is always at hand. Now we are condemned for our acts against the codes of the Supreme. But we can change our actions and thus avoid the reactions.

As Śrīla Prabhupāda pointed out in his letter, today's critical situation is not the fault of one sectarian party or another. All are at fault–capitalists, communists, "the establishment," "the people"–whoever breaks the law of God. Everyone is committing sinful acts. Even the sectarian religionists commit them. So the world needs truly saintly leadership–leaders who have genuine knowledge of God's law of *karma* and can show the rest of us how to perform *naiṣkarma* (actions that don't bring about material *re*actions).

There is no point in wishfully talking of peace and morality until one first agrees to hear the whole course of education. First, we have to learn that the material world is working under the direction of the Supreme Spirit and that disregarding His codes always leads to disaster. All these things come to light in the *Bhagavad-gītā,* the original treatise on God, *karma*, and the world. As the *Gītā* points out, adherence to morality cannot be attained just by mundane impetus. Morality and peace will come naturally to us only when we become Kṛṣṇa conscious and awaken to the higher taste of spiritual pleasure.

India and America: the Lame and the Blind and Ties That Bind

May, 1978

This year we have witnessed a strengthening of diplomatic ties between India and America. And as the leaders of both nations have pointed out, this closeness reflects even deeper spiritual ties.

Said President Carter during his recent tour, "At the heart of the friendship between India and the U.S. is our determination that the moral values of our people must guide the actions of our states. . . .Neither the rich nor the poor will feel satisfied without being fed in body *and* spirit . . . . There is a sense in the world that moral leadership derives from the Indian people in a direct and continuing fashion."

And at a recent meeting with leaders of the International Society for Krishna Consciousness, Prime Minister Morarji Desai asserted that spiritual India and technological America can help each other and the world.

President Carter also said during his tour that he felt particularly impressed with *Bhagavad-gītā*, India's source book on self-realization and realization of God. After one of his many early-morning reading sessions he noted, "One passage from that great book stood out in my mind. I can't quite quote it exactly and I can't interpret it well, but it said when a country is flooded, the reservoirs become superfluous. Kṛṣṇa went on to explain what He meant in this passage: that when one's heart is filled completely with an awareness or love of God, the other considerations in life seem incidental and one need not worry about the outcome of an action, but one should worry on a momentary basis about the purposes and the attitudes in one's relation to the eternal . . . ."

This, in a nutshell, is India's spiritual vision: we can have peace and prosperity only when we see God as the real owner of all lands and wealth, and when we see "the other considerations in life" as secondary to self-realization and realization of God. Actually, *Bhagavad-gītā* is meant for the Carters and Desais of the world, because as Kṛṣṇa explains, whatever the leaders do the rest of the people will follow. So if Mr. Carter and Mr. Desai work together to balance the "other considerations" and the eternal—the technological and the spiritual—the whole world will follow and the whole world will benefit.

It's only common sense, really, that when India, the spiritual leader, and America, the technological leader, share their assets, everybody will come out ahead. As His Divine Grace A.C. Bhaktivedanta Swami Prabhupāda used to say, India is like a lame man and America is like a blind man—so they should help each other. India is blessed with spiritual vision but cursed with technological lameness. America, on the other hand, is blessed with technological vigor but cursed with spiritual blindness. (After barely two centuries, "In God We Trust" and the Golden Rule have given way to abortion, slaughterhouses, pornography, and other vision-robbing disorders.) How can the lame man and the blind man live full, happy lives? By working together. The blind man should take the lame man on his shoulders. That way the lame man can do the seeing and keep the pair on a safe path, and the blind man can do the walking and get them where they have to go.

So there are ties that bind the lame and the blind, India and America. The problem is that neither Prime Minister Desai nor President Carter seems ready to do much about it, at least for now. And this is where the International Society for Krishna Consciousness comes in. ISKCON is following directly in disciplic succession from India's most far-sighted saint, who five hundred years ago introduced an ingenious way for India to share her spiritual vision with the West. Lord Śrī Caitanya Mahāprabhu showed from *Bhagavad-gītā* and other Vedic literatures that the whole world can become peaceful and prosperous and self-realized and God-realized through *saṅkīrtana*—mass public chanting of God's names. This simple process of chanting God's names and hearing about the science of God from *Bhagavad-gītā* is what Śrīla Prabhupāda gave America when he founded ISKCON a dozen years ago.

And the next dozen years can be even brighter, if our leaders will just take the lead. Mr. P.N. Luthra, formerly of UNESCO and now a minister of India's central government, makes this assessment of the situation: "The very fact that you have established ISKCON in the U.S.A. within the last decade is in itself indicative of America's open mind to receive new ideas. America is realizing that it does not hold the ultimate key to all problems. Insofar as spiritual matters are concerned, I think that America also appreciates that something can be gained from others. ISKCON itself is a living, convincing example that spiritual values prevail and that these alone can give ultimate happiness. We must consider the question of why we've taken birth here on this earth. I think that your organization is a very powerful force, and that it will play an important role in the years to come in transmitting the spiritual message of India."

For our part, we in ISKCON are not taking these words of India's and America's leaders lightly. We hope these people will come forward to work with us—because both they and we know that American vigor and Indian vision can uplift and enlighten the whole world.

Two Reflections: Healer, Heal Thyself

August, 1978

In recent years thousands of religious figures have taken up faith healing. They use all kinds of approaches, but basically they claim that through their charismatic prayer and laying on of hands, God acts: He cures everything from cavities to brain tumors, releases sexual inhibitions, and even increases earning capacity. The faith healers have gained so much influence that many believe their craft should be recognized as one of religion's essential components. Says one elder healer, "People are putting healing back into the mainline churches, where it belongs."

But like psychiatrists, faith healers offer cures for the body, not the soul. Calling on God to fix up my finances or arthritis or my relationship with my wife is very poor religion, and not even good sense. It recalls a story about a pious washerwoman who tripped and fell and dropped her bundle off her head. She prayed to God, and after He appeared and asked her, "What do you want?" she answered, "O dear Lord! Please lift this load back on my head!" Supposing that through my prayer, meditation, shouting, or handholding the Almighty actually came before me, why should I ask Him for what's really further entanglement in suffering?

In their attempt to improve people's lot in this temporary world, faith healers demonstrate precious little understanding of the nature of the soul or the soul's relationship with God. As the Vedic literatures inform us, the real self, the eternal soul, will never be satisfied by any adjustment or improvement we can make here, any more than a starving man will feel happy if we simply offer him entertainment or counseling. A starving man has to have food, and the soul has to reawaken his eternal relationship with Kṛṣṇa, God. No matter how much we comfort our bodies–through faith healing or this or that–until we achieve pure love of God, we'll have to undergo reincarnation and get more bodies and more misery, on and on. But if we revive our devotion for the Lord, then when we pass away we'll go to His eternal abode for eternal life of bliss and knowledge.

What if a Kṛṣṇa conscious devotee find himself with some bodily trouble? He understands that it's the result of his own past sinful acts, his own *karma*. Of course, he'll seek standard medical treatment, but he won't chant God's name as though it were merely a medical formula, a sure cure for all that ails. He'll chant just to glorify the Lord, as always, and the rest he'll leave to Him. In the ancient *Śrīmad-Bhāgavatam* a devotee expresses these same sentiments: "My dear Lord, one who constantly waits for Your causeless mercy to be bestowed upon him and who goes on suffering the reactions to his past misdeeds, offering You respectful obeisances from the core of his heart, is surely eligible for liberation, for it has become his rightful claim." And Lord Caitanya, the epitome of pure devotion, prayed, "I don't want wealth or women or followers or even salvation. All I want is Your devotional service in my life, birth after birth."

So faith healing is mundane; it's pseudo-religion, at best. Actual religion is pure devotional service to the Lord, and somewhat paradoxically, it's only when nothing else matters to us but this pure devotion that we'll be completely healed. Pure devotees who teach this secret are the only faith healers worthy of the name.

* * *

Although the world's various religious groups claim millions of followers, the present age is irreligious. Despite nominal allegiance, the so-called followers disobey even basic religious laws and have little or no knowledge of the God they profess to worship. If one neither knows God nor obeys His laws, there is little meaning in claiming to be a Christian, Jew, Hindu, Muslim, or Buddhist.

For instance, in every scripture we find an injunction comparable to the Biblical commandment "Thou shalt not kill." And yet we see that the so-called followers of these scriptures are themselves the most expert killers. They fight doggedly in political wars and kill millions of helpless animals in slaughterhouses. They may try to justify their atrocities through theological word jugglery, but if God Himself has outlawed killing, then how can they be constantly engaged in it?

What's more, in every scripture we find the equivalent of the commandment "Thou shalt not commit adultery." It's a simple idea, really: if a person is actually religious, he'll have sex only within a God conscious marriage, and only to beget God conscious children. But how often do we see this simple standard upheld–even theoretically–by today's religious leaders? Under the pressures of mass promiscuity and licentiousness, the leaders themselves endorse contraception and abortion and take part in the "normal" promiscuity of modern life. But as long as they're disobeying God's basic laws, then how can they be religious?

If I love someone, then the first symptom will be that I do what he asks. If I won't do what God asks, then how can I say I love Him? And if I don't love Him, how can I say I know Him? Today's so-called religionists may pay lip service to adages like "God is great," "God is love," and so on, but they have little or no knowledge of God. Otherwise, they wouldn't act the way they do.

All of this brings us back to the faith healers and charismatics. If these people are actually seeing God and speaking with Him, as they claim, then why can't they give up such obvious transgressions as killing and adultery? If God is actually appearing to them in visions, then why hasn't He been able to convince them to clean up their own act? This disparity between the healers' "divinity" and their day-to-day lives makes us wonder whether their mystical experiences could be as intense or as genuine as they claim.

Fortunately, the Vedic literatures detail the symptoms of God's authentic representatives. First, a representative of God is a member of a disciplic succession that originates from God. And he teaches the same information his predecessors taught–he doesn't concoct some new interpretation–he teaches what appears in the scriptures. So from time immemorial there is a system of checks and balances: the representative of God describes what is in the scriptures, and the scriptures describe what is in him–the symptoms or characteristics of an actual spiritual master. For instance, the spiritual master is in control of his mind and senses and is free from sinful habits. He knows that material pleasure is temporary and illusory, and he never compromises with modern standards of promiscuity and consumption. If someone claims to be a spiritual master and yet lives a life no different from that of any other materialist, what is the value of his oratory, his visions, his speaking in tongues? Of course, people who are sincere will never deride an authentic spiritual master, regardless of the scripture he follows. But neither will they tolerate the hypocrisy of those who claim to know and love God and yet cannot save anyone–even themselves–from the common vices of a sinful age.

Telling the Cheaters from the Teachers

September, 1978

There have always been cheaters posing as *gurus*. Many thousands of years ago, the demon Rāvaṇa dressed himself as a *svāmī* to win an audience with Sītā, the wife of Lord Rāmacandra (an incarnation of Lord Kṛṣṇa). Rāvaṇa kidnapped Sītā, but Lord Rāmacandra killed him. Five thousand years ago, when the Lord appeared in the world in His original form as Kṛṣṇa, He dealt with another cheater: King Paundraka, who donned an extra set of arms, in imitation of Lord Kṛṣṇa's four-armed Viṣṇu form, and demanded that Kṛṣṇa worship him. Again, the Lord did away with the cheater personally.

The current age presents a special dilemma. To begin with, as the ancient *Śrīmad-Bhāgavatam* predicts, most people are spiritually lazy and ignorant. And what's more, when they finally bring themselves to search for a *guru*, they find thousands of latter-day Rāvaṇas and Paundrakas. Granted, today's cheaters are insignificant next to those personally dispatched by Lord Kṛṣṇa, but they're running unchecked. There are no laws against pretending to be a great *guru* or even God Himself. So it's extemely difficult to stop the cheating "*gurus*" and "incarnations." But Vaiṣṇavas (devotees of the Lord) have to try, at least, to expose them.

Nowadays, the cheaters are so brazen that even when caught in the most scandalous behavior, they matter-of-factly admit they're cheating–because they know their followers will go on worshiping them anyway. One famous "*guru*" had an affair and tried to pass his consort off as the divine mother of the universe. After the divine union broke up, he simply said his mate was no longer the divine mother, and the "disciples" went along with it. Other so-called *gurus* make drastic doctrinal shifts whenever it seems their popularity is slipping. After all, next year's meditational techniques may make this year's eternal truths look passé. So the cheater may have to change his act, much like a popular entertainer. And how many times have thousands of people paid millions of dollars, only to discover that they all received the same "secret" *mantra*? But still the cheated come forward and pay even higher fees for new "secrets," like levitation. It makes you wonder: what's the use of telling people they're being cheated when they already know?

One positive note—the recent wide distribution of authentic translations of ancient India's Vedic literatures. Though the cheaters often say they base their teachings on these books, the books themselves draw a clear line between the cheaters and the genuine teachers:

> The pseudo *svāmīs* and *yogīs* and man-made gods do not believe in the Supreme Personality of Godhead, and thus they are known as *pāṣaṇḍīs*, offenders. They themselves are fallen and cheated, because they do not know the real path of spiritual advancement, and whoever goes to them is certainly cheated in his turn. When one is thus cheated, he sometimes takes shelter of the real followers of Vedic principles, who teach everyone to worship the Supreme Personality of Godhead according to the directions of the Vedic literatures.
>
> *(Śrīmad-Bhāgavatam 5.14.30)*

In other words, if you want to find a bona fide *guru*, you have to consult the standard literatures (the Vedic literatures) and the standard spiritual masters, who come in disciplic succession (*paramparā*) from Lord Kṛṣṇa. Five thousand years ago the Vedic literatures were put into written form by an incarnation of Kṛṣṇa named Vyāsadeva, and even today the spiritual master's chair is called a *vyāsāsana.* To sit there, a *guru* has to teach exactly what Vyāsa did, and he has to be a disciple of a spiritual master who comes in succession from Vyāsa. Another symptom: the *guru's* life must show that he is personally convinced of the message the Vedic literatures set forth—namely, "Worship the Supreme Personality of Godhead."

It's much in vogue today to say that all teachings are the same. "Take any path you want," the cheaters say. "They all lead to the same place." But common sense says that if you buy an airline ticket to New York, you'd better not try to hop a plane to L.A. And the *Upaniṣads* say, "One result is obtained by worshiping the supreme cause of all causes, and another is obtained by worshiping that which is not supreme." Different forms of worship or meditation will lead you to different goals, and only through devotional service to the Supreme Godhead can you transcend the cycle of repeated birth and death and attain eternity, bliss, and knowledge in the kingdom of God.

Nor can a genuine *guru* be a debauchee or a "New Age" hero given to mundane psychology, frivolous sports, rock music, or other whimsical games and speculations. Even self-realized persons have to follow basic standards of morality. Avoidance of illicit sex, meat eating, gambling, and intoxication is prerequisite not just for some people but for anyone interested in actual spiritual life. Anyone who claims to be above these standards is following in the footsteps of Rāvaṇa, and his followers will join him in ruin. A real *guru* has to be a humble representative of the Supreme, a servant of God.

We have attempted to give a public warning about the cheaters who take the name of *svāmīs* and "god-men." The whole purpose for going to a spiritual teacher is to find the genuine path of God-realization and self-realization. But if we go to a cheater, we're only cheating ourselves; we'll have to stay within the cycle of repeated birth and death. Yet even as we issue this warning, we know that it won't stop the moths from entering the fire of the false *gurus*. So we're interested more in the innocent–and in the cynics. Anyone who is actually sincere about finding the genuine path shouldn't conclude that all spiritual life is a fraud, even in the midst of this bad age. There's an old story about a man whose dishes were stolen–he decided that from then on, he'd eat off the floor. No, even though one may have been cheated once–or twice–he has to go on with the business of life, striving to find the truth.

The human form of life is meant for self-realization, so we have to take guidance from a genuine spiritual master. As the Vedic literatures inform us, God is within each person's heart, and when someone is actually sincere about finding the genuine path back to Godhead, the Lord will guide him from within. When he meets a pure devotee of the Lord, the Lord will confirm it from within: "Yes, you can inquire from this *guru*." By sincerely inquiring and hearing from a bona fide spiritual master, we will reawaken our natural, eternal, joyous relationship with God. What we need first of all is sincerity. That will help us avoid sensational, concocted paths, and it will lead us to real knowledge and advancement in spiritual life, no matter how bizarrely the fools carry on in their caricature of spirituality.

–SDG

VII. Autobiographical Essays

Second Birth

January/February, 1972

I graduated from Brooklyn College in 1961, spent two years on an aircraft carrier in the Navy, and subsequently returned to the New York City's Lower East Side and its LSD, marijuana and "free" sex. When I ran out of money I took a job as a social worker. However, such vague descriptions of my life are of little value because they neglect the inner self. My inner self was very much present and used to wonder, "Who am I?" but I had no guidance in finding out. Certainly my parents could not guide me; they were interested only in external matters: television, good grades, and a successful job and family. My teachers and professors were not willing to sit down and talk with me–and even if they were willing to do so, they had no understanding of what life was all about. So I took solace in friends who were bound together by their rejection of life.

The latter experiences are not very outstanding or unusual. What is significant is that somehow I got out of the disillusionment by which they were symptomized. I found someone who knew the path of satisfaction, and he was able to show me real peace and happiness–a hope of eternal life. How I found these treasures of life and how I rid myself of the uncomfortable task of trying to live honestly in a false world is of the greatest value to tell. This resurgence of life will be explained by first telling you about the guide, the spiritual master. When one thinks of the *guru*, the mind immediately conjures up pictures of bogus teachers who mystify and hypnotize our honesty and fill us with the unreality of pseudo-*yoga*, who take our money, encourage us to escape into meditation, and who preach renunciation of personal life. "Personal life is unreal; it's alien and unloving." But so are they, these false rascals, and so I rejected them too. But I want to talk of the real guide, the pure devotee of God who showers unlimited love and mercy upon all living entities because he is the dearmost representative of God. The Lord states in the scriptures: "The spiritual master is to be worshiped as My very Self." This is the version of all revealed scriptures. Do you doubt the existence of a person, who can impart the knowledge of the science of God realization pursuant to love of God? I have met him, and hundreds of others have also.

In 1966 I stumbled into Twenty-six Second Avenue, New York City, where, at the time, His Divine Grace A.C. Bhaktivedanta Swami Prabhupāda held classes in *bhakti-yoga* and chanted the transcendental sound vibration. *Hare Kṛṣṇa, Hare Kṛṣṇa, Kṛṣṇa Kṛṣṇa, Hare Hare/Hare Rāma, Hare Rāma, Rāma Rāma, Hare Hare*. The boys chanted, and Śrīla Prabhupāda sat on a straw mat leading. I was swept up into praise of the Lord by this song, which wipes all the dust from the mind. It is true that the *mahāmantra* is the great chant for deliverance because the *mantra* reveals one to be the deathless loving servant of God by nature. Doubts still plague the mind. The prejudices and the countless births and deaths that we have gone through are all so painful. If we only realized this and surrendered unto Kṛṣṇa, the eternal God, then relief would be assured, and even in this lifetime we would always relish nectar by singing His praises.

The first night I heard that song of God, I took it home. Although I was still indulging in the inebrieties of Lower East Side life and was still without hope beyond death, things were different. I did not want to fool myself into believing that everything was now blissful because of my chanting Hare Kṛṣṇa in that little storefront–but nevertheless the song of Hare Kṛṣṇa was not an unhappy addition to my consciousness. To remember it during the day, while in the office, was like the coming of spring after the long winter. I looked forward to going back to chant with Śrīla Prabhupāda and the boys who gathered there. I sat at my desk as a social worker, answering phone calls, writing out checks for welfare clients, listening to the advice of my boss and to office jokes, and then I recalled Śrīla Prabhupāda's talking. I recalled him saying, "How can there be any progress as long as the scientists, technologists, reformers and politicians cannot find a solution to these four things–birth, death, disease and old age?" He proposed that there was an actual solution to birth, death, disease, and old age and that until we had it we could not claim to be happy or progressing. How could one be happy amidst such disadvantages? He told the story of a person in a hospital who was visited by a friend. The patient was sick in bed, unable to move. He was being fed intravenously, and his body stank. He had to urinate in a bed pan, and the nurses had to aid him in moving. Yet when a friend came and asked him, "How are you?" he answered, "I'm all right." But what kind of all right is that? He is in an abominable state, unable even to move, and is surrounded by bad smells, yet he says that he is all right! Similarly, under the spell of illusion, a person in material life, although suffering, says that everything is all right and that he is happy, although in fact he is suffering in so many ways.

Śrīla Prabhupāda said that the solution to all suffering is Lord Kṛṣṇa. Who is Kṛṣṇa? Kṛṣṇa is God, the supreme controller, who does everything so expertly that it seems to happen automatically. Every autumn Kṛṣṇa changes all the leaves to gold within a few days; if a painter were to attempt the same thing, it would take months. Kṛṣṇa also directs the movements of the planets and galaxies and holds up the sun in a corner of the sky. The atheists foolishly claim that

God is dead, yet the whole universe is God's body. So how can He be dead if His body is working and moving so nicely? Śrīla Prabhupāda also said that our real self, each of us, is a spiritual spark of the same quality as the spiritual whole, Kṛṣṇa, and that to engage in loving service to the spiritual whole is the natural, blissful, constitutional occupation of each living entity.

Śrīla Prabhupāda gave me typing tasks, typing up his manuscripts for publication. I understood this typing to be *yoga* (linking with God), and so I sat at the typewriter hour after hour, meditating and working. After attending classes, I decided that I could no longer keep my job, which entailed being eight hours a day away from the association of Śrīla Prabhupāda. The other boys, who had no jobs, could see him all day. They would sit around him in his clean, sunny apartment while he talked about Kṛṣṇa, the most relishable Supreme Personality of Godhead. He asked them to help him spread this love of Kṛṣṇa, God, and together they made plans. I wanted to join and renounce the material world with its birth, death, disease and old age. I filled out my resignation, and I gave notice that in two weeks I would leave in order to study with my spiritual master. During my lunch hour I ran to see Śrīla Prabhupāda. He was seated on his sleeping mat behind a small desk, and the boys were gathered around him, asking questions and listening. "Actually, this Kṛṣṇa consciousness," he said, "is the highest service to mankind, but they take it to be some sentimental religion, mere singing and dancing."

"I want to quit my job," I told him.

"Oh? Why is that? You are offering such nice service."

"But I want to come daily and be part of the camp. I want to learn Kṛṣṇa consciousness."

Seeing my predicament, the boys present said that they would take jobs and let me spend more time listening to the spiritual master. They suggested alternating their employment. But Śrīla Prabhupāda kept my attention and told me a story. He told me that there was once a faithful wife who had an ugly husband with a morose disposition. One day his wife asked, "Why are you morose? I do anything you want, and still you feel morose. Why is that?" "I wish to have sex with a certain prostitute," he admitted, "but she costs thousands of dollars just for a night, and I cannot afford her." The faithful wife said to him, "Don't worry. I shall arrange it." She immediately went to the prostitute's house and began to personally attend her, cleaning her room and performing other such services. When the prostitute came and noticed her activity, the faithful wife explained, "My husband desires to enjoy you, and I hope that you will take my services as payment, so that he might spend a night with you." The prostitute laughed, "Don't you realize that I cost ten thousand dollars a night? How can you ever raise the money?" So in addition to serving the prostitute, the wife herself turned to prostitution and eventually raised the required amount of money. She returned to her husband and said, "All right. You can go to that prostitute now," and he went at once.

Śrīla Prabhupāda said that although people may say that the wife was crazy and immoral, nevertheless she was unquestionably faithful. He asked me to keep my job, even though the association was abominably boring and kept me away from him all day, and said that by contributing the earnings from my job, I was rendering the best service possible. I reported back to my office and told them that I had changed my mind and would keep the job. That afternoon, visiting clients on my job, I walked through the streets in the bliss of responsibility. I felt deeply entrusted with a duty from my father, my spiritual master, and to discharge it faithfully was my eternal duty. Due to his words I could work at my ordinary civil service job with a firm sense of eternal life because it was God's work, as confirmed by the spiritual master.

Morning classes at the storefront temple were at 6 a.m. The devotees began with the chanting of *Hare Kṛṣṇa, Hare Kṛṣṇa, Kṛṣṇa Kṛṣṇa, Hare Hare/Hare Rāma, Hare Rāma, Rāma Rāma, Hare Hare.* The chanting was followed by a talk about Kṛṣṇa's pastimes and about Lord Caitanya, the most liberal and munificent incarnation of Kṛṣṇa. I used to go to work chanting on my beads, with the words of the Absolute Truth in my ears and the vision of the spiritual master's holy form fresh in my mind's eye.

Very easily I took to the four regulative principles. As I engaged more in Kṛṣṇa consciousness, I no longer hankered after intoxicants or illicit sex. Daily at noon, I would leave the office and hurry to the temple for *prasādam*. Śrīla Prabhupāda would be in his upstairs room with the boys gathered. The food would be placed in open pots before a small table. This table served as his altar and displayed a picture of Lord Caitanya and His eternal associates. It was decorated with vases of flowers. Śrīla Prabhupāda would suddenly bow all the way down to the floor, onto his hands and knees, and we would all follow suit. We repeated the following prayer after him and thus offered the foodstuffs to Kṛṣṇa, who accepts the offering made by His pure devotee:

> This material body is a lump of ignorance, and the senses are networks of paths unto death. We have fallen into the ocean of material sense enjoyment, and of all the senses the tongue is the most voracious and difficult to control. It is very difficult to conquer over the tongue in this world, but Kṛṣṇa is very kind to us. He has sent us this *prasādam*, spiritual food, to help us conquer the tongue. Now let us take this *prasādam* to our full satisfaction and glorify Their Lordships Śrī Śrī Rādhā and Kṛṣṇa and in love call for Lord Caitanya and Nityānanda to help us.

Food offered to Kṛṣṇa is called *prasādam.* Eating this food gives spiritual strength. Usually on a weekday we took *dāhl*, rice and *chapātis*, and it was always very, very delicious. *Chapātis* looked like pancakes, but they were made simply with whole wheat and water, with a little salt and butter. *Dāhl* is spiced soup, made with split peas. Śrīla Prabhupāda encouraged us to "take more," including rice, always seasoned with turmeric, and vegetables. The foodstuff was always honored as being non-different from Kṛṣṇa Himself.

My existence was becoming purified, and yet it was practical. Just by my eating *prasādam* and working in the office with the knowledge that my paycheck would support the temple, and by my chanting and hearing the lectures, all the filth and wolf-like viciousness in my heart was being cleansed away. I didn't need a certificate to tell me that I was enrolled in Kṛṣṇa consciousness. Just as a hungry man feels satisfied when eating and doesn't have to be told, so I knew the change was taking place. It cleansed me and refreshed my whole being and engaged me in work of consequence. It revived my whole person.

Weeks went by, and as I heard and chanted, my desire for hearing and chanting increased. One of the boys attending the classes painted a picture of Rādhā and Kṛṣṇa. Rādhārāṇī is the girl always seen with Kṛṣṇa, and She is His greatest eternal devotee, who teaches us how to love Kṛṣṇa. She can help us to reach Him through pure affection or transcendental loving service. Chanting on beads, fingering each bead while saying the *mantra* aloud, brought concentration to hearing and touching, while looking at the picture of Rādhā and Kṛṣṇa brought concentration to seeing. Having all the senses thus totally engaged brought me into blissful meditation upon Kṛṣṇa. Śrīla Prabhupāda emphasized that just by adding the Hare Kṛṣṇa *mantra* to his life, anyone can feel this purification in mind and spirit, without renouncing his job, family or way of life. This chanting is recommended by the Vedic scriptures and by the incarnation of Kṛṣṇa, Lord Caitanya, who appeared 500 years ago and from whom Śrīla Prabhupāda descends in a line of successive disciples or spiritual masters. "Just try chanting," he said. "If you are a businessman, remain a businessman; if you are a doctor, remain a doctor; if you are a student, housewife, etc., remain in your station. But try chanting Hare Kṛṣṇa as a regular daily function and reading *Bhagavad-gītā As It Is.* These will help anyone realize the fulfillment of real pleasure and eventually achieve the purpose of life, which is to love God."

After several months, Śrīla Prabhupāda announced that he would hold initiations, which would make us his disciples in Kṛṣṇa consciousness and connect us with the disciplic succession. I personally did not feel I was ready for such a commitment, and so on the day that initiations were held I stayed at home and instead dutifully performed the task of typing essays for Śrīla Prabhupāda. The next day I brought two completed essays to his apartment. I knocked on his door. He opened it to let me in: "You didn't come yesterday for initiation?"

"No," I said.

"That's all right," he said kindly, and let me inside. When he sat down at his mat, I then placed before him the two essays, and he thanked me. He then invited me to a wedding of two of his disciples that was to be held the following night. I was very happy that he had personally made sure that I would attend. He gave me more manuscripts for typing and I began to take my leave. Śrīla Prabhupāda walked me to the door of his apartment and then said, "This is not automatic, not simply taking this work and doing it mechanically." I knew what he meant. Then he said, "If you love me, then I'll love you." I cannot remember if I said anything in reply, but I left him and ran down the stairs and onto the street. I was so happy! Why? Just because he had said, "You love me, and I'll love you." I realized that he loved me, just as Kṛṣṇa loves everyone. We rot and sulk in this material world, maneuvering to become God. But, if we are willing to have personal exchange with Kṛṣṇa through His representative, the spiritual master, then we will feel released from stoneheartedness, the dried-up joylessness, false ego and hallucinations of grandeur. In short, we get relief by being loved. To be loved is only half of the exchange. Śrīla Prabhupāda is certainly loving us now, still, freely giving us *prasādam*, giving us Kṛṣṇa philosophy, chanting and dancing. As persons, we can also give love. When the love is felt, it can overcome the entire material universe in a second. From that moment on, my desire to take to Kṛṣṇa consciousness greatly increased; I was determined not to let anything hinder me from engaging in transcendental loving service for the pleasure of my spiritual master.

The bona fide spiritual master is coming from God. We must have a little initial faith in this process. Śrīla Prabhupāda has all the credentials of the spiritual master. This can be seen by the example he sets. He is called, in the Sanskrit language, *ācārya*. An *ācārya* is one who teaches by example. So his good example was apparent in those first days and has endured to spread Kṛṣṇa consciousness throughout the world. This process of *bhakti-yoga,* devotional service to God, is distributed through his literature, his words and his actions. One will always find him talking about Kṛṣṇa, and what he says is in complete accordance with scripture. Kṛṣṇa says, "Surrender to Me," and the pure devotee says the same thing: "Surrender to Kṛṣṇa." The spiritual master is fixed in love of God. Every Sunday in Tompkins Square Park he chanted with us for one and a half hours, and after a break, we chanted for another hour and a half, while he played the drum. He talked to everyone and anyone—cab drivers, priests, newsmen, politicians, children—about Kṛṣṇa, and he handled their questions with grave concern. One night I bought him mangos, and he accepted one from my hand before a roomful of his students. He said, "Very good boy!" in a humorous way, treating me like a four-year-old boy, which gave those assembled a good laugh. But then he said seriously, "No. This is a token of love. This is Kṛṣṇa consciousness." And he praised me for my meager efforts at donating money and typing. In this way I entered into the nectar of devotion, the ocean of bliss. My spiritual master assured me from the beginning that Kṛṣṇa was blessing me in my personal efforts to serve Him through the spiritual master, and I never doubted it. I was undergoing a change in heart, from a self-centered imitation god to an agent of God working under the direction of a master.

At the next opportunity, which was on the appearance day of Rādhārāṇī in 1966, I was accepted by Śrīla Prabhupāda as his disciple. He chanted on my beads and asked me to always chant Hare Kṛṣṇa, and I bowed down and repeated, *nama om viṣṇu-pādāya kṛṣṇa preṣṭhāya bhūtale/śrīmate bhaktivedanta svāmin iti nāmine.* "I offer my respectful obeisances to His Divine Grace A.C. Bhaktivedanta Swami Prabhupāda, who is very dear to Lord Kṛṣṇa, having taken shelter at His lotus feet." "Your name," he said, "is Satsvarūpa dāsa Brahmacārī.

Later, in a lecture, he described the significance of initiation. "Lord Caitanya asked His disciple Rūpa Gosvāmī to go to Vṛndāvana to preach and sustain His mission. This is disciplic succession. Not that one thinks, 'I have understood everything from my spiritual master; let me now sit tight.' That is also nice, but no. Lord Caitanya's mission is to spread the teaching . . . It is your duty. When a disciple receives instruction from the spiritual master, he has an obligation to the spiritual master to do the same. After being instructed, the disciple will offer, 'My dear master, what can I do for you?' I am indebted to my spiritual master for the knowledge that was given to me; therefore, I must serve him." When I heard this, I was astounded. In Kṛṣṇa consciousness the spiritual master is always revealing new knowledge about the nature of devotional service. Just when one thinks himself sufficiently engaged in the Lord's service, the spiritual master reveals how to serve infinitely more in an entirely new capacity. One wonders, "How can I do that much? How can I surrender to Kṛṣṇa? What will happen to me? How can I expand my personality to meet this task?" But Śrīla Prabhupāda says, "All it takes is sincerity. Simply follow the instructions and be humble."

This science of God can be taken personally and applied to anyone's life. The householder can make a little altar with pictures of Kṛṣṇa, and without interruption to family life, all can become Kṛṣṇa conscious. Indeed, without God consciousness one cannot be a qualified family man. In the same way, the student can extend his sincere desire to learn beyond good grades. He can read scriptures and their commentaries by transcendental scholars on the nature of the Absolute Truth, and he can introduce it into his classes. A big businessman can chant to relieve tension and donate his earnings to become a life member of the International Society for Krishna Consciousness. The offer of reciprocation or exchange can be taken up by anyone who preaches Kṛṣṇa consciousness at every opportunity, such as with friends and colleagues.

The essence of this philosophy will hold true in any time or place because the Truth revealed is absolute. Questions such as what is the self, what is God and what is the purpose of life, as well as how to become happy, are answered. It is beyond the sectarian religious designations, such as Christian, Hindu, Jew, etc. It is for everyone, regardless of sect. What I have related is not a fleeting encounter. It is the description of my second birth. The first birth occurs when one is born of his mother and father. But a second birth is required for complete happiness and fulfillment. The second birth occurs when one accepts a spiritual master and begins his eternal occupation as a servant of God. Such a renewal of energy, the rebirth of transcendental loving service, awaits every one of us. You can have this highest love just by chanting Hare Kṛṣṇa.

The Disciplic Succession

July/August, 1972

Many times, when people inquiring about Kṛṣṇa consciousness hear from us about the importance of disciplic succession, they are not able to grasp what we are talking about. We say, "Kṛṣṇa consciousness is coming down in disciplic succession. The Absolute Truth was first spoken by the Supreme Lord, Kṛṣṇa Himself, and He taught it to the first living entity, Lord Brahmā, who taught it to his pupil Nārada, who taught it to Vyāsadeva." To one who is already a student of Kṛṣṇa consciousness, just the mention of the names of these great personalities is enough to bring great pleasure; just in the sound of their names there is reassurance of Absolute Truth and complete authority. But this is not conceivable to a person who doesn't know these spiritual masters as anything more than names which are difficult to pronounce. I would therefore like to speak to you in terms of myself, a thirty-two-year-old American who is not different in qualification or upbringing than the average reader to whom the concept "disciplic succession" is foreign. Let me relate to you my own experience with the disciplic succession.

By the grace of Kṛṣṇa, I have been in association with His Divine Grace A.C. Bhaktivedanta Swami Prabhupāda since 1966 as one of his initiated students. I can recall the first night I heard His Divine Grace. He spoke of disciplic succession and the name Lord Caitanya, which sounded foreign to me, and he said that the knowledge that he was speaking was to be taken as Absolute Truth. I remember thinking, "How can he presume that what he says is the Absolute Truth?" When he answered questions after his lecture, he answered only on the basis of what the previous spiritual masters had said and what was originally recorded in *Bhagavad-gītā*. He even said at one point, "I am not speaking myself. I am a mouthpiece." He claimed to be speaking perfectly, and yet he said that he was personally doing nothing at all. He said that the only thing to his credit was that he was repeating, without change, what was perfect and was recorded thousands of years ago. He compared his perfection to the perfection of a mailman who simply delivers the mail but does not change the message by opening the letter and making additions. He stated that if he could deliver this message of Kṛṣṇa consciousness unchanged, it would be perfect, since it was originally spoken by the perfect source.

Although I was accustomed to reading many different literatures and speculating on their relative truths, I was nevertheless impressed that His Divine Grace did not care to show off his own thinking power or say something that the audience would like to hear; he simply presented the view of the disciplic succession for everyone's benefit. It gave me a feeling of awe to think of sages speaking in ages long, long past and of this same ancient knowledge coming down fresh and intact just for the benefit of the present audience. "Just imagine," I remember telling my friend as we left the little storefront temple where His Divine Grace had spoken. "That person who was speaking was saying the same thing that was spoken by sages thousands of years ago. It's all coming down in the vibration of his voice. If the scriptures are really the recorded word of God, then his pure vibration is coming from infinity itself. It's as if God is speaking to you. He can speak and cut through temporary time with eternal truth." My friend, however, was more impressed with the immediate time and place, regardless of Absolute Truth, and he said that there were many different ways for different people to communicate.

The presentation of the spiritual master was for those who wanted the truth. He had nothing else to offer but the Absolute Truth, and he personally endorsed it as beneficial for all. He did not tell lies or indulge in flattery. He was convinced. He had surrendered to Kṛṣṇa through his spiritual master and had become a surrendered devotee, spending all his time delivering the message of the *Gītā* to devotees. I began to attend the classes and to take them seriously, and gradually I inquired, accepted and studied, served and practiced, to the point where he accepted me as his initiated disciple. I accepted him as a representative of God, and I accepted the Vedic literature as speaking the Absolute Truth.

Then quite suddenly His Divine Grace had to leave to open another temple in San Francisco, and we new students were left to manage the New York temple and attend to the many visitors who used to come to his evening classes. What would we do when they came and he was not present? And how could we live without our spiritual master? The first question had to be answered right away because the night after he left, the visitors came as usual to hear his lecture.

He had instructed us how to lecture in his absence, so on the first night one of his more advanced pupils gave a talk. He cited in his talk the same examples that our *guru* gave, and it was satisfying. He simply tried to present the teachings of *Bhagavad-gītā*: "We have all forgotten Kṛṣṇa. Kṛṣṇa is God. He is the eternal spiritual person, and everything is coming from Him. He is all-pervading. Our real place here is not to try to struggle for enjoyment and happiness in a temporary world filled with miseries of birth, disease and old age, and ending in inevitable death. Our real business is to go back to Godhead, our eternal home. This we can do by the grace of Lord Caitanya, who is the form of Kṛṣṇa for this age, by chanting Hare Kṛṣṇa, Hare Kṛṣṇa, Kṛṣṇa Kṛṣṇa, Hare Hare/Hare Rāma, Hare Rāma, Rāma Rāma, Hare Hare." After the boy's talk, when we chanted, it was just as transcendentally satisfying as if Śrīla Prabhupāda were there. In fact, it was more poignant for his students; there was ecstasy in the feeling of separation.

On another night, I was chosen to speak. I remember looking at the people who had gathered and praying to God for the courage to be able to say something pure and effective and not let down my spiritual master and my assembled Godbrothers and Godsisters–and to actually impart the Absolute Truth to the audience. After all, we students knew the great value of these teachings of Kṛṣṇa consciousness. But all the others did not. So it was up to me to present them. I prayed to cast off all desire to show off my own learning; I wanted just to say what my spiritual master was actually teaching. This left me no room at all to speculate or to concoct. I attempted to remember what he had said. For me personally, it was a very grave occasion. As I spoke, I said, "Kṛṣṇa can be compared to the sun. The sun is a planet, a material thing in one place in the sky, and its energy, the sunshine, is diffused, spread out all over the universe. This is a material example. Similarly, Kṛṣṇa is the source of all energies and all emanations and creations. That is the definition of the Absolute Truth–that from which everything is coming. The Absolute Truth is intelligent and conscious, and according to the Vedic literature, He is a person, the Supreme Person, God, Kṛṣṇa. Just as the sun has form and is local, so Kṛṣṇa has form. But His form has inconceivable energies, like the sun. All spiritual and material existence is His energy. We say that God is great, but how great He is is inconceivable. But we can study this in the Vedic literature to get some idea of the greatness of the Supreme Person." As I spoke, I became somewhat reassured and tried to remember more. But I felt very inadequate and understood that I was not a very good disciple. I was not able to speak more than five or six minutes before I was unable to go on. So I stopped.

The advanced disciples who heard my talk said that it was very nice, especially because I had not deviated from what the spiritual master had said or hadn't made anything up. This made me happy, and yet, at the same time, I could not think that I had done anything at all because actually I had not. It was not my wonderful additions, or my brain-power, good looks or speaking ability, that had made my little talk acceptable; it was not within my power to make people begin to think about Kṛṣṇa and to take the philosophy seriously–but it was the power of His Divine Grace, and I had transmitted some of it. After the talk, there was a question. Someone asked, "How do you know that Kṛṣṇa is God?" Remembering what Śrīla Prabhupāda had said in answer to that question, I answered, "How do you know who is the President of the United States? By his credentials. He can show you that he actually has that position. In the same way, all the Vedic literatures describe that Kṛṣṇa, who appeared as the son of Devakī and performed many wonderful acts, is actually the Supreme Brahman, or the Personality of Godhead. It is stated in *Bhagavad-gītā* by Kṛṣṇa's disciple Arjuna that not only did Arjuna accept Kṛṣṇa as God, but He is accepted by all the great spiritual masters in disciplic succession, such as Nārada and Vyāsadeva. Also, when Kṛṣṇa appeared on this earth, He displayed all the opulences of the Personality of Godhead—that is, full strength, beauty, knowledge, fame, wealth and renunciation." After the question, I invited the audience to chant Hare Kṛṣṇa. I had preserved the format and the words of my spiritual master, which are the words of *Bhagavad-gītā*.

Although one feels lowly when taking on the work assigned to him by a pure devotee or a spiritual master, he cannot check the bliss that comes when he acts as an agent for the disciplic succession. Giving up false prestige and just serving brings untold joy and satisfaction. No one can know it unless he acts in this line. All it takes is a faithful serving attitude; by living a life of pure principles, one can qualify to speak on behalf of his spiritual master. It is a fact that we are all intended to act in this disciplic succession. It is not that just a few priests or preachers are required to take this on, but everyone is supposed to faithfully follow the words of the Supreme Lord as transmitted by the bona fide spiritual master.

There is a prayer in the *Śrīmad-Bhāgavatam* which states: "By regularly hearing the *Bhāgavatam* or rendering service unto the pure devotee, all that is inauspicious in the heart of a candidate is practically destroyed, and thus loving service unto the Personality of Godhead, who is praised with transcendental songs, is established as an irrevocable fact." Hearing is the most important part of Kṛṣṇa consciousness, or *bhakti-yoga*, which is the most powerful *yoga*, far beyond standing on one's head, practicing sitting postures and breath control, or trying to think that one is God by mystic meditation. These other methods are not intended for this age, and no bona fide teacher is teaching them. The most important method in this age is to hear from a genuine authority. The Absolute Truth is beyond our sensual experience. We cannot confront it with our present senses or intellect, so we have to hear from someone who is an authority. Kṛṣṇa says to His disciple in *Bhagavad-gītā*, "You are not this body. You are spirit soul." If one can accept this, he has knowledge; if one listens to the presentation of the spiritual masters of Kṛṣṇa with submissive inquiry, he will know the truth.

It is definitely necessary that one associate with devotees or spiritual masters who can personally present spiritual books and instructions. These should not be understood just by reading them alone. If one reads presentations by unauthorized commentators not in disciplic succession, the whole study will be ruined, and he will get the wrong idea. It is necessary to see and experience the pure message in the living example of the spiritual master and hear from the lips of one who is realized. Lord Caitanya said that the spiritual master should teach by the example of his life, not merely by precepts. If one does not hear from such a person, Kṛṣṇa will be no more than fiction to him, and the *Gītā* will remain a mysterious philosophy. The greatest havoc is caused by those who misrepresent the scriptures and destroy the import of the disciplic succession which is coming down from Kṛṣṇa. One should never hear from such unauthorized persons. To know who is authorized, one should hear and study the science of God as presented in books like *Teachings of Lord Caitanya*, *The Nectar of Devotion*, *Bhagavad-gītā* and *Śrīmad-Bhāgavatam*, which are presented by the ISKCON movement as a service to humanity. Otherwise he may be cheated.

The disciplic succession is compared to a ladder of different men sitting in the branches of a tree and passing down, from top to bottom, a nice, ripe mango fruit. If carefully passed from hand to hand, the fruit can be given intact to the man at the bottom, without damage.

Disciplic succession has a kind of potency which comes down through one who repeats what he has heard in that succession. One who hears receives the potency. The material example is given of sexual intercourse. When a man and a woman come together in sexual intercourse, if the man is potent and healthy and other conditions are right, then there will be conception. In the same way, if a willing and sincere student hears from an authorized speaker in disciplic succession, he will be injected with devotion to God. The quality has to be genuine on both sides—the hearer must be sincere, and the speaker must be spiritually potent.

The knowledge given has to be authoritative. This is guaranteed by the disciplic system, which is unbreakable. The knowledge has been compared to a family secret passed from generation to generation. The difference is that this secret is not material. Once there was a group who claimed to be followers of Lord Caitanya's chief associate, Lord Nityānanda. They said that they were the family descendants of Lord Nityānanda and claimed to be the only ones who could understand Kṛṣṇa consciousness. However, Śrīla Bhaktisiddhānta Sarasvatī, the great spiritual master of our spiritual master, completely smashed their idea. He pointed out that the real succession goes on spiritually, from spiritual master to student. It has nothing to do with the seminal succession of father to son, which is based on the material body. Spiritual potency is not like material semina; it is passed down by the spiritual master to the qualified disciple who is dependent on the master. The spiritual master blesses the student who shows that he is sincere and eager to serve and who presents submissive inquiry. Such a student can speak on behalf of an expert spiritual master. The spiritual master is compared to an expert engineer who has with him an assistant who does exactly what he says. If by the instructions of the engineer the student can turn a screw with a screwdriver just as he is asked to do, then he is functioning as an expert himself. In this way, if one can carry out the orders of the expert spiritual master, he can act as a representative of God. To do this, one must lead a pure life, following the regulative principles, and must not indulge in intoxication, illicit sex, meat eating or gambling.

When His Divine Grace first left us in order to open another temple, we wrote to our spiritual master, and he wrote back, "I understand that you are feeling my separation." But he described that for us to serve him in the absence of his physical presence was even greater than to be with him. If one follows the instructions, a link is set up not just with one's own spiritual master but with the entire disciplic succession of spiritual masters–including Lord Caitanya and going all the way back to Brahmā and Kṛṣṇa. His Divine Grace once wrote to all his students, "You are all helping me in pushing forward this mission of Lord Caitanya Mahāprabhu which has come down by disciplic succession to my spiritual master. So whatever you have spoken in praise of me, it is simply due to them. I am simply the via medium to receive your words of praise on behalf of my *guru mahārāja* [spiritual master], His Divine Grace Bhaktisiddhānta Sarasvatī Gosvāmī Mahārāja Prabhupāda." The disciple's immediate link is his own spiritual master, who is the transparent via medium to the whole disciplic succession and back to Kṛṣṇa.

Going back in history, only eleven spiritual masters before our own is the appearance of Lord Caitanya, who is described in the scripture *Śrīmad-Bhāgavatam* to be the form of Kṛṣṇa Himself who comes in this age of quarrel and hypocrisy. He will be known, it states, by the fact that He always chants Hare Kṛṣṇa with His associates, and those who have sufficient brain substance will worship the Supreme Lord in this age by chanting the holy names of God. Lord Caitanya especially taught that the best name of God is Kṛṣṇa, and for the deliverance of all people He taught the Hare Kṛṣṇa *mantra*–Hare Kṛṣṇa, Hare Kṛṣṇa, Kṛṣṇa Kṛṣṇa, Hare Hare/Hare Rāma, Hare Rāma, Rāma Rāma, Hare Hare. Lord Caitanya said that these names of God would be heard in every town and village in the world, and now, on the order of his own spiritual master, His Divine Grace A.C. Bhaktivedanta Swami Prabhupāda has factually spread that teaching and fulfilled the prophecy of Lord Caitanya by teaching throughout the whole world this authorized instruction of the Hare Kṛṣṇa chanting.

Spiritual greatness is attained by carrying out the orders of the spiritual master. One of the Godbrothers of our spiritual master recently gave testimony that His Divine Grace A.C. Bhaktivedanta Swami Prabhupāda is the most prominent spiritual master today in carrying out the instructions which come from Kṛṣṇa through Brahmā and the disciplic succession. Doctor Kapoor, of the Gauḍīya Matha, made the following statement in a speech in Vṛndāvana, India, where Śrīla Prabhupāda was welcomed by the mayor of Vṛndāvana. (Vṛndāvana is the place in India where Kṛṣṇa performed His transcendental pastimes when He appeared in the world 5,000 years ago.) Dr. Kapoor said of His Divine Grace: "He has inherited the mantle of Prabhupāda Bhaktisiddhānta Sarasvatī. He alone has fulfilled the mission of our spiritual master, taking it to every nook and corner of the world. And it is in the hands of *his* disciples in the future to reap a rich harvest of devotion all over the world." To he who has faith in the spiritual master and Kṛṣṇa, and to no one else, all the meaning of the scriptures is revealed. The science of God cannot be learned by academic knowledge or by study in comparative religion. It is transcendental, beyond material knowledge, and can be received only by the mercy of the spiritual master. To speak as a representative of the disciplic succession is not a casual thing but is full of gravity, and one must gradually qualify to do this great work for all mankind. Recently, in a conversation with U.S. Ambassador to India, Kenneth Keating, Śrīla Prabhupāda said, "Send me all your American boys, and I will save them. That is not a bluff." The spiritual master can speak like this because he is authorized to give shelter to all humanity by virtue of the purity of the disciplic succession.

To go back to the first meeting when I met His Divine Grace, the question that arose in my mind may arise in yours also. How can we say that what the spiritual master is speaking, even if it is carried in disciplic succession, is Absolute Truth? First, let us look at the stature of the spiritual masters themselves, who are carrying this message as links in a chain. If you study the writings of the stalwarts in the disciplic succession–Lord Brahmā, author of *Brahma-saṁhitā*, Vyāsadeva, the author of all the Vedic scriptures, Nārada Muni, the author of *Narada-pañcarātra,* Lord Caitanya, author of *Śikṣāṣṭakam*–you will find that they are great learned scholars in the transcendental science. They are powerful sages who are able to see past, present and future. They are not interested in anything mundane or in telling fiction stories. Proof of the perfection of the great sages is given in the symptoms which they possess. These symptoms of a person who has attained transcendental life are given in *Bhagavad-gītā*. Steadily controlling his senses, he fixes his consciousness on Kṛṣṇa and is not bewildered or disturbed by desires. Thus he is able to be fixed in consciousness. *Bhagavad-gītā* further states that one should approach such a sage, a spiritual master who can impart knowledge because he has seen the truth. In other words, there exists a check and balance system whereby the spiritual master is confirmed by the scripture and the scripture is exemplified in the life of the saintly person. A saintly person or spiritual master is one who speaks only what is in the scripture. Kṛṣṇa says in the *Gītā*, "Surrender to Me," and the spiritual master says, "Surrender to Kṛṣṇa." So there is no difference between scripture and the spiritual master. In this way, the Absolute Truth is mercifully available in age after age to all persons in all places.

The more we reflect on it, the more we see that persons who are impartial and serious will accept this. It is not a question of this or that religion but a philosophy of living. The disciplic succession makes Kṛṣṇa consciousness most authoritative. Lord Caitanya appeared within everyone's memory, only 500 years ago. He is cited in the Vedic literature as Kṛṣṇa Himself. Thus the movement is most authoritative because God Himself has come as a teacher in this fallen age. He has presented a life of spiritual realization in the very attractive form of chanting, dancing and eating foods offered to Kṛṣṇa. Kṛṣṇa is coming to save the world by the disciplic succession, and everyone should take advantage of this great opportunity.

Mexico Takes to Kṛṣṇa Consciousness

November, 1973

Haihaya dāsa, the President of the Mexico City Hare Kṛṣṇa center, invited me to come speak to the people of Mexico at the installation festival for their center's Deities of Rādhā and Kṛṣṇa. At the time I was in Dallas, Texas, and so was Muralīvadana dāsa, an ISKCON Press traveling photographer. Taking the invitation as a transcendental opportunity, we decided to fly together to Mexico City, hopeful that through writing and pictures we could share our experience with *Back to Godhead* readers.

Of course, Mexico City is actually just another illusion. The world is filled with many famous countries and cities advertised as adventures or paradises to lure world travelers. But we can understand, seeing things through the eyes of the Vedic scriptures, that this whole material world exists only as a dream and only because of our attachment to it.

In the commentary to his *Śrīmad-Bhāgavatam* translation, His Divine Grace A.C. Bhaktivedanta Swami Prabhupāda writes: "The great ocean of material nature is tossing with the waves of time, and the so-called living conditions are something like foaming bubbles that appear before us as bodily self, wife, children, society, countrymen, etc." In other words, not only our bodies but also our nations and our entire planet itself exist only for a period of time that is relatively short when viewed from eternity. The living soul is actually different from matter, but because of our lack of knowledge of the self and the Supreme Spirit, the force of ignorance victimizes us, spoiling the valuable energy of our human life.

We are searching after permanent living conditions that are not possible in this material world. However the idea of traveling to a foreign land like Mexico exhilarates us, such havens are all within the kingdom of illusion, known in Sanskrit as *māyā*. Not only is life in the material world temporary, but it is full of misery for all. Whether in Mexico speaking Spanish, in France speaking French, or wherever one may be, everyone in the material world must suffer birth, death, disease and old age. Therefore whether we travel or sit in one place the real purpose of human life is to seek enlightenment from the illusion and pain of identifying with the material world.

We should be interested in Mexico, therefore, only in terms of the enlightenment of the people there. For example, Kṛṣṇa spoke His sublime philosophy in the scripture *Bhagavad-gītā* at a place known as Kurukṣetra. Now, transcendental scholars and devotees of Kṛṣṇa are interested not only in Kṛṣṇa but also in Kurukṣetra, the place where He spoke; but they are interested in Kurukṣetra only because of its relation to Kṛṣṇa and the enlightenment He gave there.

The idea of finding permanent happiness by going to Mexico (or France, Hawaii, or India) is actually illusion. But on the other hand, even though any place in this material world is a place of illusion, every place is also the property of God, for everything that exists, whether material or spiritual, belongs to God. One who sees things as they are is interested in everything in terms of its relation to God. He does not reject anything. If one can revive his God consciousness, this will dispell all illusion, and then for him any place, even within the material world, will be fully spiritual, like the eternal, blissful kingdom of God. The center for Kṛṣṇa consciousness in Mexico City is attempting to free the whole city from the false idea that the body is the self and help everyone regain his original eternal place in the spiritual sky.

During the plane trip we met a young Mexican boy named Octavio who was traveling with his family. He spoke English and was very interested in what we had to say about Kṛṣṇa consciousness. He took some spiritual food (*prasāda*) that we offered and was very open and friendly. His mother would ask him questions about Kṛṣṇa in Spanish, and he asked us in English. Very agreeable to the concept of being vegetarian, he remarked, "Yes, you do not like to kill animals!" Our first meeting with a Mexican encouraged us. We noticed that at least one family found it enlivening to speak to devotees, and we were also very pleased to speak with them.

Thinking in this way about our trip to Mexico as a transcendental opportunity, we flew down through the clouds past large mountain ranges and descended upon Mexico City, a sprawling metropolis of ten million people.

After the plane landed, we kept chanting the Hare Kṛṣṇa *mantra* on our beads, not knowing what to expect of Mexico City. As we approached the officials for immigration and customs, one airport worker waved his hand and greeted us loudly, "Hare Kṛṣṇa!" Soon we passed through a large crowd of incoming passengers and met our Godbrothers Haihaya and Bahulāśva. In the truck riding to town, Haihaya told us that at least one hundred Mexicans regularly attended the temple's activities day and night and at least another fifty boys and girls were full-time devotees.

About a year ago, His Divine Grace A.C. Bhaktivedanta Swami Prabhupāda visited the Mexico temple and stayed for five days. Haihaya explained that Śrīla Prabhūpada was widely acclaimed just on sight as a great saint; although some of the people were not even aware of the Vedic philosophy, they still recognized him as a very saintly person. And many of them went to see him, eager to receive benediction from Śrīla Prabhupāda.

I asked Haihaya about the claim that the ancient Mayan culture that existed thousands of years ago in Mexico was imported from the Vedic civilization of India. When Śrīla Prabhupāda was there, Haihaya said, he stated that there was much in Mexico reminiscent of the Vedic culture. One who lives there can see this in the people's eating, parades, natural fruits, etc. There is also much archaeological evidence such as art work in temples, and archaeologists can more seriously study this for further evidence.

When Śrīla Prabhupāda was in Mexico he primarily stressed the importance of enlightening people about their spiritual nature by distributing Kṛṣṇa conscious literature in Spanish. I asked Haihaya whether the people of Mexico City were taking Kṛṣṇa consciousness seriously. He replied, "Many of them come with beads and chant Hare Kṛṣṇa just like full-time devotees. After they buy books, they always read them and ask for more. Also, many of them take to a vegetarian diet after hearing our philosophy."

It was not long before we arrived at the temple, which is on Governador Tiburcio Montiel, just two blocks away from the house of the nation's President. We drove through a decorated iron gateway into the yard of the Hare Kṛṣṇa temple, a three-story white building with domes on the roof that looked Vedic. There was a large lawn in the courtyard, where many guests were sitting under trees. There were also many devotional activities underway, such as sewing, preparing flowers, building, painting and washing.

As we entered the yard a chanting party started singing Hare Kṛṣṇa, Hare Kṛṣṇa, Kṛṣṇa Kṛṣṇa, Hare Hare/Hare Rāma, Hare Rāma, Rāma Rāma, Hare Hare. The chanting of Hare Kṛṣṇa washes away all material designations by which one thinks his real self to be Mexican, American, black or white. One feels his happy, pure identity as a spirit soul, servant of God, by chanting this *mantra*. We felt immediately that we were in our true home, the shelter of Kṛṣṇa, and joined with everyone who was singing and dancing. Afterwards, we were offered flower garlands and a dish of fruit *prasāda*. According to Vedic hospitality, whenever a guest comes to visit, one must offer him nice things to make him feel at home. Any local culture in the world can adopt this philosophy and way of life, in any language, and it always comes out pure and natural.

This way to live in transcendental life (*bhakti-yoga*) is natural because it applies everywhere. Therefore Śrīla Prabhupāda, as a devotee of Kṛṣṇa in disciplic succession, has had great success in establishing Kṛṣṇa conscious centers as oases of relief in the midst of the materialistic cities. In the mood of a humble Vaiṣṇava, our spiritual master never claims credit for his achievements of opening over one hundred centers all over the world; he says the credit goes to the Lord Himself and the previous spiritual masters, whose instructions he has followed without deviation. Nevertheless, because of his personal instructions, once again we saw a living community of men and women, this time in a culture foreign to us, who were peaceful and happy in the execution of devotional activities.

Since the next day was to be the festival and installation of the forms of Rādhā and Kṛṣṇa, many devotees and guests were involved with projects of sewing, painting, electrical work and cleaning, and were also talking about Kṛṣṇa. The temple building opens with a large hall with a winding staircase that dramatically sweeps up to the second floor, which is actually a balcony with rooms off it. The main hall can accomodate hundreds of guests for chanting and feasting, the main activities of *bhakti-yoga*.

Eager to show us the forms of the Supreme Lord Kṛṣṇa and His eternal consort, Rādhārāṇī, Haihaya took us to a private room where devotees were sewing dresses for the Deities. He uncovered the forms of Rādhā and Kṛṣṇa, and we bowed down and paid our obeisances. Kṛṣṇa is a young boy holding a flute, and Rādhārāṇī is a young girl. Atheists deny the existence of any spiritual form or spiritual life, and even beginners in transcendental life do not understand that the Supreme Spirit is the Supreme Person. But this is the conclusion of the most authorized and complete philosophy of God consciousness. The Absolute Truth from which all varieties of life, both temporary and eternal, emanate is the supremely conscious Supreme Person, Kṛṣṇa. All His forms, incarnations and emanations are originally present in His transcendental form.

Kṛṣṇa says in *Bhagavad-gītā* that although He is unborn and His transcendental body never decays, He nevertheless appears in this world in every age. In our present state we cannot see the spiritual form of Kṛṣṇa, which is eternal bliss and knowledge, yet out of His mercy He appears in the incarnation of the Deity, which may be a form of metal, stone or wood. The worshipers of Kṛṣṇa worship Kṛṣṇa in this form, which is visible even when one has conditioned, material vision. The exchange between the Lord and the devotees in the Deity worship is fully authorized, and one should scientifically understand it by reading ISKCON books such as *The Nectar of Devotion,* which discuss thoroughly this transcendental science. It is a scientific, transcendental fact that the Lord appears in the form of a Deity just to accept food and decorations offered in the clean and spiritual atmosphere of the temple.

On the evening before the festival day, about one hundred guests gathered. Haihaya kindly allowed me to lead a class in *Bhagavad-gītā*. After reading from the *Gītā* first in Sanskrit, I spoke in English, and a bi-lingual devotee immediately translated my words. Seated on the temple floor, devotees and guests listened with obvious attention and absorption to the words of *Bhagavad-gītā*. I read from the Twelfth Chapter, where, in the first verses, Arjuna asks Kṛṣṇa, "Upon which is it more perfect to meditate—the impersonal or the personal form?" Kṛṣṇa then clearly says that whoever worships His personal form is the most perfect. The temple is also stated to be the ideal place for such perfect worship of God.

Of course, God is not present only in a Hare Kṛṣṇa temple; He is all-pervading. But it is recommended that while one should increase his taste for singing and chanting the glories of the Lord, he should also increase his inclination to live in a place where Kṛṣṇa lives. Kṛṣṇa certainly lives everywhere. This is the vision of the highest devotees. But because we are in a lower condition, still attached to material life, and we cannot see Kṛṣṇa everywhere, we should learn to see Kṛṣṇa in the temple. It is stated in *Śrīmad-Bhāgavatam* that especially for worldly householders it is necessary to come to the temple to enjoy musical *kīrtana*, worship the form of the Lord and appreciate the spiritual atmosphere. This is the only thing that will save the common man from hellish movies, naked nightclub dancing and other materialistic endeavors. Everyone is encouraged to dovetail his propensity for social gatherings, festivals and singing by taking part in glorifying Kṛṣṇa, the Absolute Truth; otherwise one will waste his life and have to go down in the next life to some lower form of life, seeking pleasure in dead material things. And in every form of material life from king to insect there is always suffering.

By speaking *Bhagavad-gītā* and answering the questions of the assembled devotees, I could understand that the Mexicans were accepting Kṛṣṇa consciousness in a nonsectarian spirit. Haihaya explained to me later that attraction for Kṛṣṇa is very great in Mexico because the people are looking very seriously for God, although they often regard their past religious education as frustrating. Many of them see the Kṛṣṇa consciousness movement as the answer to their search. The devotees are very respected in the streets, and people very often inquire about the philosophy. People respect the movement more and more as they hear more about it.

As phrase by phrase of my English was translated into Spanish, I tried to remember exactly the words of my spiritual master: "We should be inclined to live in the circle of temple life and increase our inclination to chant more and more. If at the time of death we can think of Kṛṣṇa, then we can go and associate with Him eternally in His spiritual abode." Young boys and girls, respectable ladies and gentlemen, old men and women–all listened with great respect. They were mostly regulars who come daily to the temple to worship the Deity and take spiritual food. Now they could understand that with the appearance of Rādhā and Kṛṣṇa the temple activity would be more blissful and there would be more opportunity to elevate their consciousness higher and higher in love of God.

After the class we had another *kīrtana*, chanting the names of God. In this congregational chanting the Mexican temple is practically unexcelled in the world. Accompanied with the traditional Vedic *mṛdaṅga* drum and *karatālas*, as well as congo drums and guitars, the singing was full of enthusiasm and pleasure. A small group of singers and musicians gathered in the center, leading the chanting, while others danced around in a circle, chanting these universal names of the Lord—Hare Kṛṣṇa, Hare Kṛṣṇa, Kṛṣṇa Kṛṣṇa, Hare Hare/Hare Rāma, Hare Rāma, Rāma Rāma, Hare Hare. Sometimes the lead singer would switch to other chants, chanting the name of the spiritual master, "Śrīla Prabhupāda! Śrīla Prabhupāda! Śrīla Prabhupāda!" or chanting, "*govinda jaya jaya*" or the names of the Lord's merciful incarnation Lord Caitanya—*srī-kṛṣṇa-caitanya prabhu nityānanda śrī-advaita gadādhara śrīvāsādi-gaura-bhakta-vṛnda*—and then back again to the Hare Kṛṣṇa *mantra*. This chanting went on literally hour after hour without stopping. No one became tired; the enthusiasm increased more and more until it was ten o'clock and the temple managers had to end the *kīrtana*. This chanting goes on every evening, and it is always a great success.

The next morning everyone rose an hour and a half before sunrise, which the Vedic civilization recognizes as the best time for spiritual advancement. After the early-morning gathering for chanting in the temple, everyone turned to the last preparations before the installation of the Deities, putting last-minute light fixtures in place and painting and sewing for the Deities. There was no distinction between devotees and guests; everyone was busily serving, sweeping, mopping, cooking, decorating and so on. Some devotees had been up all night cooking a feast and cleaning. Everyone engaged his senses in some kind of preparation to please the Lord. Haihaya dasa's greatest aspiration is to engage everyone, old and young, in some kind of work for Kṛṣṇa.

The time for the beginning of the ceremony finally arrived, and simultaneously all preparation was completed. The procedure for installing the Deities in a bona fide Kṛṣṇa conscious temple is to bathe Them in milk, yogurt and water while reciting the devotional prayers of the *Brahma-saṁhitā* and then to hold a fire ceremony in which grains and ghee (clarified butter) are offered in the fire while more *mantras* are chanted. The first verse of the prayers of Lord Brahmā's *Brahma-saṁhitā* are as follows: "I worship Govinda, the primeval Lord, the first progenitor, who is tending the cows, yielding all desire, in abodes built with spiritual gems, surrounded by millions of purpose trees, always served with great reverence and affection by hundreds and thousands of goddesses of fortune."

During the installation of the Deities, the priest leading the ceremony is supposed to speak about the worship of the Deity. I spoke on a chapter I had read from Śrīla Prabhupāda's *Kṛṣṇa Book*. In the chapter "Prayers by the Demigods for Lord Kṛṣṇa" there are 5,000-year-old prayers offered by demigods who knew that the Supreme Personality of Godhead, Kṛṣṇa, was about to descend to the material world to vanquish the demons and give pleasure to His devotees.

Different classes of people speculate about God. Atheists say there is no God, and some transcendentalists say God is void, impersonal or formless because they cannot grasp the idea of a spiritual form. Sometimes *yogīs* realize God as the form of Viṣṇu in the heart, which they see in trance. But according to the Vedic literatures all these aspects of the Absolute Truth are included in the highest realization, which is called Bhagavān realization of the Personality of Godhead in His original spiritual form as Kṛṣṇa.

The demigods described that when Kṛṣṇa actually appears in the world He puts an end to all imaginative iconography about what God is. Some philosophers speculate that because God is the oldest person, He must be an old man with a beard. According to the *Brahma-saṁhitā* prayers chanted during the Deity installation, however, although He is the oldest, Kṛṣṇa appears as a fresh youth. He has a light blue hue, and He appears like a young boy never older than sixteen, a cowherd boy who always plays His flute. This is the same form of Kṛṣṇa described in the Vedic literature, as He actually appeared five thousand years ago and as He appears in the Deity form.

In a court case discussing whether a certain man is alive or dead, there will be various speculative opinions. But if the man being discussed actually walks into the courtroom, upon his appearance all speculation vanishes. In the same way, Kṛṣṇa, the Supreme Personality of Godhead, demonstrated clearly by His appearance what He is really like. The whole disciplic succession of great spiritual masters and all the great authorities of the *Vedas* accept Kṛṣṇa as the Supreme Truth. Kṛṣṇa says Himself in *Bhagavad-gītā* that whoever considers Him an ordinary material person is "*mūḍha*," which means a rascal or ass.

We are all originally eternal servants of Kṛṣṇa. But, because of our dirty desires, we have left His service and are now trying to act like the Lord ourselves. To help us back to our original position, Kṛṣṇa comes Himself or sometimes sends His incarnation, son, representative or pure devotee—and He also appears in material forms such as stone or metal as the Deity. In such forms He accepts offerings of food and decorations, provided such offerings are made in loving devotion. Devotees who worship Him in this form are not performing idol worship, but are worshiping Kṛṣṇa in an authorized manner. Although He is very difficult to understand, He comes before us as the sound of His holy name, as the words of *Bhagavad-gītā*, as *prasāda* (spiritual food) and as the Deity, and none of these forms are material. Kṛṣṇa has so kindly made Himself available. Therefore, we can clearly comprehend why the Lord declares that whoever doesn't accept Him as He is but thinks Him an ordinary person of the material world is "*mūḍha*," a rascal.

The devotees in Mexico City had taken great pains to decorate their temple. They had painted all the walls to look like Vṛndāvana, the forest setting where

Kṛṣṇa plays in the spiritual world. The *vyāsāsana,* or seat of the spiritual master, was very nicely situated also, just awaiting the arrival of Śrīla Prabhupāda. The picture of Śrīla Prabhupāda was placed on the seat, reminding devotees of his presence. Near Mexico City a pure marble stone called onyx is abundantly available, and the devotees had arranged an onyx altar with onyx dishes and cups for offerings to the Deity. Their Lordships were dressed very beautifully with golden garments. Everyone was chanting and dancing in appreciation of Their Lordships, and the chanting went on for hours Then there was feasting. On the front lawn under a big tree in the shade, I sat with Haihaya and met various friends of the temple.

As far as the mundane Mexico City is concerned, we could see that it is geared, like the United States, towards material goals. The worker is very much pressured to work to increase his pay and enjoy sensual life. Everywhere billboards promise: "Come, you'll be happy if you buy this beer." "Buy these pants and you'll be satisfied." Cars rush back and forth, and on the way to the temple from the airport we had seen several accidents within a few hours. But while the illusory struggle for pleasure went on in the material world of Mexico City, a hundred or so people gathered in the courtyard of the Kṛṣṇa Temple, enjoying real life. Every day in the Kṛṣṇa Temple there is not only feasting but hard work, but it is all done for Kṛṣṇa, for it is the philosophy of Kṛṣṇa consciousness that one should stay in his position as a householder, businessman or whatever and yet perfect his life simply by chanting and hearing Hare Kṛṣṇa and offering food to Kṛṣṇa.

After chanting and feasting for some time, a large party gathered to chant downtown. We drove to various spots and chanted the holy names. Large crowds gathered, and we profusely distributed Spanish translations of Vedic literature.

As the afternoon progressed, we noted regretfully that we had to return to our duties in the United States. As Muralīvadana and I finally left our Godbrothers to head for the plane, we both felt we had visited the real Mexico, not the illusory Mexico known to most travelers. The permanent, pure essence of human consciousness is to practice love of God in a society of peace, prosperity and loving relationships. Everyone desires this universal brotherhood, but the different "isms" that have been formed are not satisfying because their center is not universal. Because Kṛṣṇa is the Absolute Truth and source of all emanations, the Kṛṣṇa consciousness movement has a universal center and can be universally auspicious for all.

It is not a sectarian idea. Our visit to another nation convinced us by experience that Kṛṣṇa consciousness can successfully adapt to any mundane culture and "Kṛṣṇa-ize" it. Just as an iron rod in a fire gets hotter and hotter and finally acts as fire, so anyone or any place becomes pure by association with

Kṛṣṇa consciousness. One can practice this perfect life anywhere by following the Vedic scriptures under the direction of an expert spiritual master. As long as there are sincere souls, they will gather to hear the message of Kṛṣṇa consciousness and purify their lives.

Secretary to A Pure Devotee

December, 1974

His Holiness Satsvarūpa dāsa Gosvāmī is one of the leaders of the Kṛṣṇa consciousness movement. Until he returned to the United States in July to organize distribution of Kṛṣṇa conscious books to schools and libraries, he was serving as the personal secretary of His Divine Grace A.C. Bhaktivedanta Swami Prabhupāda. Śrīla Prabhupāda, the founder and spiritual master of the International Society for Krishna Consciousness, has been extensively traveling to preach and oversee the progress of his disciples. As Satsvarūpa dāsa Gosvāmī traveled with Śrīla Prabhupāda around the world–from New York to London, Paris, Hamburg, Geneva, Bombay, Melbourne and back to Los Angeles (with many other stops in between)–he kept a personal diary, filled with accounts of Śrīla Prabhupāda's activities and words. These are excerpts from that diary.

Hyderabad, India. April 19

At the press conference in Hyderabad one reporter asked right away whether Śrīla Prabhupāda was an *advaita* (monistic) or *dvaita* (dualist) philosopher. Śrīla Prabhupāda scoffed at the question. "What is the point of discussing such things–whether one is *dvaita* or *advaita*. Kṛṣṇa says, *annād bhavanti bhūtāni*: 'All living beings subsist on good grains.' *Annād* means grains. The people have no grains. Grains are produced from rain, and the rain from *yajña* (sacrifice).' So perform *yajnā*. Become Kṛṣṇa conscious. *Dvaita* or *advaita* you may be, but you still need grains."

April 20

Śrīla Prabhupāda was recalling the press conference. One newspaper reported that he had said that *Bhagavad-gītā* contains all answers to all problems–social, political and otherwise–and should not be misinterpreted. He smiled when he heard that and said, "They have captured the main points of my talk." As for *dvaita/advaita*, he said, "Kṛṣṇa never says we are all one. If a servant says, 'Yes, I am the same as the master,' that is his impudence. But the master never says it. Kṛṣṇa says to Arjuna, 'Many births you and I have had, but you are not the same as Me. You forget; I do not. Therefore you should surrender to Me.' Where is the question of *advaita* if Kṛṣṇa says 'Surrender to Me'? Our philosophy is both *advaita* and *dvaita*. We are one with Kṛṣṇa in our qualities, but He is much greater than us."

From a letter to a disciple: "I have no business criticizing, but as spiritual master, leader of the institution, it is my duty to find your faults. Even Caitanya Mahāprabhu presented Himself as faulty before His spiritual master. Do not be sorry when I find faults. That is my prime duty. Cāṇakya Paṇḍita says that one must find fault with disciples and sons—it is good for them."

April 21

After his lecture at the exhibition grounds, a crowd of about 1,000 pressed forward, and with great difficulty, forming a human chain, we escorted Śrīla Prabhupāda back to his car. Many spectators dove forward to touch his feet. On the way back, Śrīla Prabhupāda was appreciating that the big crowd was silent during his whole lecture. "The women and children," he said, "could not even understand English. This is a good field for Kṛṣṇa consciousness." Later I commented that his lectures seemed planned out, although I see that he simply chooses a verse and speaks without preparation. "It appears that I prepare?" he asked. "Yes," I said, "there is such symmetry to each lecture." "Kṛṣṇa is speaking," he said, "I am not speaking. I am His microphone. Let us depend on Kṛṣṇa, and He will do everything."

April 22

On his early-morning walk, with three *sannyāsīs* [disciples in the renounced order] present, Śrīla Prabhupāda took the role of a pious religionist and challenged us, saying we had nothing to teach him, since he already loved God. "But you don't know what God is," one of us said. "That's all right," he said. "Whatever idea I have, I am praying. If I didn't love God, I wouldn't go to church." We gave argument after argument, but he rejected them all, saying he was as good in his religion as we were in ours; he had his own love of God and scripture and world religion, and he was as good as we were. We couldn't catch him. Finally he revealed to us what we should have said: "If you love God, why do you disobey Him?"

A sympathetic Endowments Officer from the government was talking with Śrīla Prabhupāda. He said that the government policy is that everyone should be God conscious, and it seems they have a branch that dispenses money to different temples for the propagation of Hindu culture. He said that "orthodox *brāhmaṇas*" [religious intellectuals] object to ISKCON because we recruit men from the *mleccha* and *yāvana* classes [meat-eaters, outcastes] and make them *brāhmaṇas.* Śrīla Prabhupāda opened his Sanskrit *Bhāgavatam* and turned to a passage where Nārada is talking to King Yudhiṣṭhira about the four orders of society [intellectuals, administrators, merchants and laborers]. Nārada said that if you find in another country a person working as a *brāhmaṇa*, with the qualities of a *brāhmaṇa*, he must be accepted as a *brāhmaṇa*. Śrīla Prabhupāda then read Śrīdhara Svāmī's comment on the verse also. If one gets a degree as an engineer but sits home and doesn't work, he's not an engineer. Kṛṣṇa created the four social orders on the basis of *guṇa* and *karma*, one's qualities and his work. It's very scientific. One must acquire the qualities, and he must work. And the role of a secular government is to see that *brāhmaṇas* are actually working as *brāhmaṇas*. So the four castes must be maintained. This is called *varṇāśrama*. Prabhupāda said that if the Indian government would finance him, he could rid India of godlessness in a year. "People are fed up with materialism and cheating *yoga*. Why not support this movement? Immediately we could open one hundred Varṇāśrama Colleges and start training. We wouldn't just rubber stamp a man '*brāhmaṇa*' because he happens to be born in a *brāhmaṇa* family. That religion of the body won't do. One must actually become qualified."

That is just one sample of the practical discussions about Kṛṣṇa and practical proposals that Śrīla Prabhupāda talks about with respectable men hour after hour, day after day, untiringly, with 100% conviction and fresh enthusiasm.

Śrīla Prabhupāda said that someone wanted to write a book about him, just like the big books people write about their *gurus* to call the *gurus* God. But he said, "No, write books about Kṛṣṇa—hundreds of volumes about Kṛṣṇa."

April 25

We flew to Tirupati. In the mountains nearby is Tirmula, where there is the richest temple in India, the Veṅkaṭeśvara temple, with its Bālaji Deity. Śrīla Prabhupāda very much liked the cottage the temple managers provided for him. They were very respectful and let our party enter the temple, although (1) people usually have to wait on a long line, since 15,000 people enter daily, and (2) Westerners are usually not allowed in. Following behind Śrīla Prabhupāda, however, we walked right in. In the cottage there was a picture of the Bālaji Deity. Prabhupāda said that the Deity's name means "child," Kṛṣṇa as a cowherd boy, not in His Vaikuṇṭha aspect [His majestic form in the spiritual planets]. "What do the rascal scientists know of Vaikuṇṭha?" I said. "They haven't seen these planets through their telescopes."

He said, "That [telescope knowledge] is imaginary, defective. So many planets are glittering at night. What do the scientists know of these other planets? They cannot say that such a place [the spiritual sky] is not possible. The rascals can't get a vague idea of even this one planet." I said they are making progress because 500 years ago people thought the earth was flat. "Not in the *Vedas*," he said. "It is clearly stated: *goloka,* meaning 'round.' Maybe in your Bible," he laughed, "but although you didn't know, the *Vedas* knew."

About all the people going to see Bālaji, Śrīla Prabhupāda said, "This shows that the mass of people are still attracted to God, despite government propaganda. The people are coming and going, visiting the Deity. But an advanced devotee can capture God in his heart. *Premāñjana-cchurita-bhakti-vilocanena*: with the ointment of love of God spread over his eyes. Of course, Deity worship is good for the neophyte."

We went three or four times daily to receive *darśana* [association] of the Bālaji Deity. One time we went at 2 in the morning. The Deity is very big, in a dark inner sanctum where the only light comes from the torches held by the *pūjārīs* [attendants]. Śrīla Prabhupāda would regularly leave his cane on the rail before Bālaji, and then, after we were walking out, he would call "Where is my stick?" and we would have to go back for it. As the general mass of people go into the temple for alleviation of material distress, they call out "Govinda!" When Śrīla Prabhupāda started in (you have to go barefoot in the whole area around the temple, outside also) he would say "*Govindam ādi-puruṣaṁ tam ahaṁ bhajāmi*" [I worship Govinda, the primeval Lord]. He said we should build temples like this Veṅkaṭeśvara temple, which has a gold dome and wonderful facilities for visiting pilgrims. While he was there, Śrīla Prabhupāda took Bālaji's *prasāda* [food offered to the Lord] and said it was tasteful. He said that Lord Caitanya had visited this and many other places all over south India. We were thinking that Śrīla Prabhupāda, who says he hasn't visited any holy places in India except Māyāpur and Vṛndāvana, was visiting them to purify them.

May 25

People ask, What is Śrīla Prabhupāda's day like? Śrīla Prabhupāda rises about 1:30 a.m. Sometimes around 2 or 3 a.m. I awaken and hear him dictating. Once one man in Bombay said to Śrīla Prabhupāda, "Today I rose at 2:30!"–to which Śrīla Prabhupada replied, "I rose at 1:30!" In Hyderabad Gargamuni Svāmī said to me, "What other *sādhu* in India gets up at 1:30 to write books?" It is great proof of his authenticity. In Bombay we set up a small house of mosquito netting for him to work in. He opens the big volume of Bengali *Caitanya-caritāmṛta*, and with a small desk lamp lit, he begins translating the synonyms one by one, clicking the dictaphone button as he pauses briefly for his thoughts.

The translation work usually goes on for two or three hours, sometimes less. From around 3 to 5 he sits and chants Hare Kṛṣṇa on his beads. Śrīla Prabhupāda chants beads almost silently, although the motion of the beads can sometimes be heard in the next room, and sometimes "Hare Kṛṣṇa, Hare Kṛṣṇa."

His regular morning walk begins just before the sun comes up. In India, Śrīla Prabhupāda says, clothing is artificial; India is so warm. In other countries sometimes he has to bundle up in big coats and a hat. He wears a pair of shoes that he saves only for the morning walks. As Kṛṣṇa is known to appear in yellowish garments with a peacock feather in His hair, our spiritual master wears saffron, with a wrapper around his shoulders or over his head, and walks with his cane, followed by his devotees. In the *Kṛṣṇa Book* it says that a devotee is like a waterfall–sometimes he speaks, and sometimes he is silent. I asked what this means, and Śrīla Prabhupāda said that the devotee speaks at his will; he is not obliged to speak. Devotees are eager to accompany Śrīla Prabhupāda on his walks. Sometimes he speaks the whole time. He walks long, usually about an hour and a half. If it rains he says, "Today we will take our walk sitting down," and we ride in the car.

Geneva, Switzerland. May 30

Flying here, Śrīla Prabhupāda said, "This is a very dangerous spot [amidst the Alps]. Many planes crash here." Later I asked if great sages still lived in the Himalayas. He said yes: Vyāsadeva, Vālmiki and Nara-Nārāyaṇa. I mentioned to him that in the *Bhāgavatam* he says that there's a gold peak in the Himalayas. "Yes," he said, "if they find that out, they will become mad to go there." This afternoon we were given an official reception by the governor of Geneva. Śrīla Prabhupāda spoke on the verse *sa vai puṁsāṁ* . . . "The science of God must begin with knowledge that one is spirit soul, not the body." The governor asked, "If everyone becomes Kṛṣṇa conscious, won't the economy be in trouble?" "No," Śrīla Prabhupāda said, and he quoted the same verse he cited over a month ago in Hyderabad: *annād bhavanti bhūtāni*. "Everyone subsists on grains." So he proposed that if everyone cultivates his own land and keeps cows, there will be no economic problem. One should live simply and spend the saved time solving the problems of birth, death, old age and disease. Later Śrila Prabhupāda asked, "Were my answers all right?" I said that the governor asked about the economy being in trouble if everyone became a devotee because he thinks we are simply beggars. "Therefore," Prabhupāda said, "I talked about tilling the land. We are not beggars. We are giving the highest knowledge. We gave him the book of highest knowledge [*Bhagavad-gītā*], but he could not give us anything."

June 5

This morning on his walk, and again tonight with the Dean of Theology at Geneva, Śrīla Prabhupāda gave this example: What is the important thing in the body? It is the spirit soul, the life force. That is what's making the body move.

Just as in an airplane the important thing is the pilot. The living entity within the body, the life force, is making the hand move, the eye see, the mind think. . . . So in the universe, there is a life, a Soul, which is moving everything. As the person within the body is the important thing, so the Supreme Person is the important element in the universe that is making everything move and sustaining everything. We are *īśvaras*, or controllers, of our bodies, but He is the supreme controller, even of us. Each of us is controlled by God, the supreme controller, so to disobey His orders is sinful life. To agree to obey His direction is religion. Tonight after explaining this, he said, "I think this is perfect knowledge."

He talked often with the Christians about why they disobey God by killing other living entities. Finally one of them complained that we were just talking the whole time about meat eating. "Why can't we talk of higher principles?" they asked. Śrīla Prabhupāda said, "So long as one is sinful, there is no question of understanding higher principles."

Paris, France. June 9

He said that Paris attracts so many tourists. His hosts drove him around to see the Louvre buildings, the Arc de Triomphe, and other sites. He said that in India (for example at Tirupati, where Bālaji temple is) the same tourist urge is there, common people are visiting daily by the thousands, and the statues are there, but in India it is for God. While driving they pointed out where embassies are, and one devotee quipped, "So we have opened a Kṛṣṇa embassy." "Why one embassy?" he said. "Every house should be an embassy. Everywhere, a Kṛṣṇa embassy."

"In the beginning was the Word, and the Word was with God." This means that the word preceded the creation. Therefore it was transcendental. We have to inquire, "What is a transcendental word?" The poet Narottama dāsa Ṭhākura says, *golokera prema-dhana hari-nāma-saṅkīrtana*: "Hare Kṛṣṇa comes from Kṛṣṇaloka." This means it is a transcendental, not a material, sound or word. The creation comes from the word of God. For example, His Divine Grace Śrīla Prabhupāda has started what is now a very large spiritual movement. In the beginning of the movement there were no buildings and students; he came to this country without money, only with the word. But by preaching the transcendental word, all of ISKCON has become manifested. That's an example of the creative power of the word. The transcendental word of God, existing before the creation, is eternal, above the material creation—and it is the cause of the whole creation. Therefore by transcendental sound we are chanting Hare Kṛṣṇa and becoming God conscious.

Germany. June 18

Haṁsadūta arranged a procession of 20 vehicles from the airport to the castle where the devotees are staying. Śrīla Prabhupāda was pleased: "My heart becomes engladdened when I hear a *mṛdaṅga* in a German village." [A *mṛdaṅga* is a drum for chanting Hare Kṛṣṇa.] He quoted Lord Caitanya's verse that in every village the chanting will be heard. He said, "We should be aware that our goal is a worldwide movement. Actually, we have communities all over the world, but the movement is still very, very small. It will expand, however, and the whole world can be united under Kṛṣṇa for peace." But then, he said, people's only objection to us is that we are trying to prevent them from going to hell; therefore they misunderstand us. It's like when a man flies a kite on a roof and you see that he's in great danger, about to walk off the roof. But when you tell him, "Look out! You're in danger!" he becomes angry. "What! You have checked my movement." Any gentleman will speak out if he sees another plunging into danger. But they object. One world under Kṛṣṇa—we are not after domination, but we want to free people from death, old age and disease.

Śrīla Prabhupāda has been pointing out that the wars which are starting every few years in the West can be traced to *karma* from cow killing. It has very disastrous effects, the slaughterhouse. He says, "People should live in peace, eating the food they raise themselves from the land, and chanting Hare Kṛṣṇa. Why artificially start these wars? They do not recognize that everything belongs to God. You can have the land to work; He has given you enough of everything to live peacefully. It is the fault of the so-called leaders. The mass of people are good."

June 19

He said that the idea of transmigration of the soul is very important—the beginning of transcendental philosophy—but no one in the West understands it. I brought up the argument that although the materialist will accept that we are changing bodies in this lifetime, and also that he is experiencing the change of bodies in dreams, these things are still within one lifetime, so he does not experience changing bodies at the time of death. Śrīla Prabhupāda said, "But in the dream one doesn't remember everything; so much of it is a hodge-podge mixture of different things. Our nature is to forget. Also, do you remember everything of your childhood? We have forgotten so many things. We do not remember being in the womb of the mother and suffering under those conditions, but we were there. The fact that we do not remember something does not mean it did not exist. So, we are forgetful and do not remember our past lives. The most important thing is the authority of Kṛṣṇa; He is the perfect authority, and He logically presents transmigration in *Bhagavad-gītā*." I said, "If we simply say you must believe it because Kṛṣṇa says so, they will take it as dogmatic." "No," he said, "the reasoning is given there, but the authority is final. For example, if you want to know who your father is, you can investigate in different ways your genealogy, your natural attraction to both parents, or your similarity to them in character–but finally the mother is the authority without flaw."

Melbourne, Australia. June 21

I mentioned to Śrīla Prabhupāda that now that India has the nuclear bomb, other small nations are rushing to get it. He said, "What is this nuclear bomb? I will drop it on you and in turn you will drop it on me. What is the advancement over the dogs? This fearfulness of one nation for another with nuclear bombs is the dogs' mentality. Sometimes, even when chained by their respective masters, two dogs will fight as soon as they meet. Have you seen it? It's no better than that." "But," I pursued a vague anxiety, "devotees sometimes think we are planning for the long-term future when we distribute books to schools and libraries, but if everything is going to end in nuclear war. . . ." "Assure them," said Śrīla Prabhupāda, "that there will be no nuclear war if they take to Kṛṣṇa consciousness. And even if there is nuclear war, that is not going to end everything. Formerly there was the *brahmāstra* [a weapon of Vedic times similar to today's nuclear bomb]. Everything is under the control of the Supreme Lord. We are not afraid of the nuclear bomb, because the soul cannot be killed by the atom bomb. Do you know that? Have you read it? So what do they want to do in fear of the nuclear bomb–to sit down and do nothing and cry?" I said, "Well, we are asking people to invest in 60 volumes of *Śrīmad-Bhāgavatam*, but they might say, 'I don't want to make such a long-term investment in the future because there is nuclear war ahead.' " "Then why are they going to the university? Why don't they stop eating? Do they mean one should not go for an education and should not have any hope and should stop everything?" "Yes," I said, "some think like that–that it is doom." Śrīla Prabhupāda expressed concern that people have been put into such a consciousness. Then he repeated that I should assure people that there will not be such a war if they can become Kṛṣṇa conscious. "In fact, because of our Kṛṣṇa consciousness movement, there will be no nuclear war. But even if there is, the soul cannot be killed, so we are not afraid the bomb will kill the soul."

In Melbourne, Śrīla Prabhupāda has been getting lots of news coverage. One article misrepresented him, saying, "His Divine Grace is resigned to dying soon and returning to earth as an animal." Amogha prepared a letter to the editor asking him to print what Śrīla Prabhupāda actually said. Amogha wrote that a pure devotee's condition is just the opposite: he goes to the kingdom of God after leaving this body. The next morning in class, Śrīla Prabhupada commented on the news article. He explained how the reporter, being against us, was really saying, "Let the *svāmī* come back as a dog." (Actually all the miscreants will come back in the lower forms of life, not the devotees.) Prabhupāda had actually said, "The devotee doesn't mind how he comes back, so long as he is with Kṛṣṇa. To become Kṛṣṇa's animal is a great thing. In Kṛṣṇaloka the cows embraced by Kṛṣṇa, and the other animals–or even the plants–are very exalted to be with Kṛṣṇa." So there is no objection if he becomes Kṛṣṇa's animal in his next life.

June 29, 1974

On his morning walks through the Royal Botanical Gardens in Melbourne, Prabhupāda would ask how many varieties of plants they have. On several occasions he asked, "Do they have two million varieties? Kṛṣṇa has produced two million varieties of plants, but I think maybe they have two thousand." He said, "The plants are standing still while we are able to walk because they are being punished. But although it is punishment, Kṛṣṇa's intelligence is so nice that it has become a beautiful arrangement." Madhudviṣa Mahārāja asked, "If one gets a body according to his desire, so that one wants to eat flesh can become a tiger–well, who would want to become a tree?" (We understand that tree life is the result of too much lust.) Śrīla Prabhupāda said, "The students in America like to stand naked. So Kṛṣṇa says, 'Here, take the body of a tree. Stand naked for a hundred years.' " I could suddenly understand better Prabhupāda's position as our savior. He can save us from coming back in the lower species. If we follow the regulations of devotional life he has taught us, if we don't fall down from this, we can go to Kṛṣṇa at the end of this life. Those bewildered by material desires have to go on in the material world.

Prabhupāda is very interested in the excellent response from high church officials here in Melbourne. He wants to make a united effort with the Christians. The preaching platform is that they should chant the name of Christ, which is the same philologically as Kṛṣṇa, coming from the Greek "Christos," and stop the animal slaughter. The clergy is appreciating this approach.

VIII. Letters of Inquiry

Dear Citsukānanda dāsa:

I wanted to send this letter to you to express my deep appreciation for your concern during my recent stay in San Francisco. My trip to California was for the purpose of seeing some friends and relaxing a little after the very strenuous meeting of the National Federation of Priests' Councils Executive Board. We have been trying very hard to change the priorities of the Catholic Church and to educate our people to a deeper concern for the things of God. It seems that our efforts are meeting with some success, but God is the provider, and He will give what is necessary when it is time.

When I first saw the devotees on Market Street I was fascinated by the chanting and the youth of those who were dancing and singing. One of the girls gave me a copy of the magazine and invited me to the temple. As you know I spent many hours watching and enjoying this wonderful phenomenon. Having seen many false things in my life as a Catholic and as a priest, I wanted to be sure that what I saw was genuine. I came to the temple not so much for curiosity as for the purpose of learning something of the secret of the joy and peace I saw in the eyes of those devoted to Kṛṣṇa. My heart was overjoyed to find what I found. The chanting and dancing are so simple and yet so meaningful in their approach to God.

While in San Francisco I thought of nothing more than of Kṛṣṇa and His devotees. Since I have returned to Pennsylvania I have thought of little else. I have been reading the *Gītā* and cherishing the thoughts contained there. I am in the process of thinking of the connection between Kṛṣṇa and Christ and Catholic teaching. By no means am I a follower of the false Christ which has been taught for so long in so many churches. I have long known that God has a deep cosmic significance which has been overlooked for so long. Some of the things I have been reading in archaeology, scripture, and human behavior have led me to a consciousness of the overwhelming goodness of God and of His great love for us.

I recall the words of St. Paul in one of the New Testament Epistles: "O how great are the riches and the depths of the knowledge of God; how inscrutable His ways." Here was a man caught up into the seventh heaven of God consciousness who abandoned everything he ever was to bring awareness of God to mankind. I see so many similarities in the two scriptures, and I can only think that perhaps God speaks to men according to their own condition and for too long we have tried to say that one way is God's. Who are we to try to limit God: The all-important thing is God consciousness. All things follow from that. Whether one follows the prayers of the Catholic Mass or the prayers of the African native, one always seeks God.

There are so very many questions that I have wanted to ask you, but did not because I was not willing to interrupt the chanting or any of the work of spreading Kṛṣṇa consciousness by taking all your time. I was grateful to you for taking time on Friday to speak to me. May I ask you some of these personal questions which to me give an idea of the value that Kṛṣṇa has for the devotee. First, I am wondering about the place of sex in the life of devotees such as the young men and women of the temple. As a Catholic priest who lives a life of celibacy in dedication to Christ, I am interested to know what the devotee of Kṛṣṇa thinks about celibacy. Is this any problem for those trying to follow Kṛṣṇa? Do the devotees accept celibacy for life or for a period of time only? What is the attitude of the devotee towards sex? Is sex a good thing or something evil? Does Kṛṣṇa demand abstinence from sex as a sacrifice or as a way of being free from material attachments?

Also I would like to ask you about the matter of money. I know that in any society money is necessary to maintain a church or temple. One of the devotees told me that the spiritual master provides for the students. This is a very real problem for me since I know for us how many millions of dollars must be spent on buildings and how much on personal living expenses: food, clothing, car fuel, etc.

These are so many mundane things to talk about, but I feel that I must know some of these things in order to place all doubts about the personal motivations of the devotees in abeyance. Would you be so kind as to answer these questions sincerely. I would appreciate knowing many, many things about the devotees of Kṛṣṇa because I believe in the transcendental value of such devotion and must be able to answer the objections of those with whom I speak. Already the people I have told this to have many questions. Quite soon my classes will begin, and I will have an opportunity to talk of Kṛṣṇa consciousness to this group of people anxious to know about God. Likewise I intend to talk about my wonderful experience with you in my church at Mass. I will do this after I receive the record I ordered from Boston.

May I thank you for the feeling of warmth and friendship and love which I felt while with you. I know that this is the warmth, friendship and love of Kṛṣṇa which shines through you. Please be assured of my constant prayers for all of you to Lord Jesus that he may grant to you the fullness of Kṛṣṇa and all good things which come from Him.

Hare Kṛṣṇa!
Father Ernest P. Kish

Dear Father Kish,

Please accept my greetings. The San Francisco temple has sent us your letter in hopes that we could print it so that all could read and share in your inspiring response to the Hare Kṛṣṇa movement. They have also requested that, as editors of the magazine, we answer the questions which are in your letter.

Your feelings of spiritual joy on witnessing the devotees chanting Hare Kṛṣṇa in the streets and in the temple are symptoms of love of God, the pure, original feelings of the human being. Love of God, as demonstrated by the chanting, is not a sectarian concern. It is the essence of religion to call on Him, and who can object? Certainly there is no objection from the spiritual point of view; the only objection is from the viewpoint of material prejudice. God Himself is understood as transcendental to sects; He is not the God of merely the Christian people, or the Hindus, or Muslims, or Jews or any sect. In the scripture *Bhagavad-gītā*, which you are reading, Kṛṣṇa, who is accepted in all Vedic literature as the Supreme Personality of Godhead, declares, "I am the father of all living entities." There is thus no question of His being the father of only one sect; He is the father even of the lower animals, the trees and all life, regardless of one's particular religious faith. In the *Śrīmad-Bhāgavatam*, another Vedic scripture, the devotee-sage Śukadeva Gosvāmī was asked what the first-class religions among all religions is. He replied, "That religion is first-class which invokes our natural love of God." He did not say, "The best religion is Hindu," or "Christianity is the best." The test of first-class religion is whether the followers are developing love of God; it does not matter what the religion is. Your letter reflects awareness of this standard, based on pure feelings of love of God, and that is why it is so refreshing and encouraging.

You write that you want to ask many questions "in order to place all doubts about the personal motivations of the devotees in abeyance." I can reply for all those devotees of ISKCON who are fully and sincerely engaged twenty-four hours daily in this practice of devotional service that our only motivation is to please our spiritual master, His Divine Grace A.C. Bhaktivedanta Swami Prabhupāda, who is a pure devotee of the Lord. As for the motive of Śrīla Prabhupāda himself, that is certain: he is engaging all the activities of his mind, words and heart in the worldwide propaganda of pure love of God. All that you saw in San Francisco which so moved you, such as the spontaneous joy of the devotees engaged in Kṛṣṇa consciousness, is only due to the causeless mercy of our spiritual master. Whatever God consciousness we have developed and we are practicing comes from the instruction of the bona fide spiritual master. He is passing it down to us so kindly, from an unbroken line of disciplic succession going back 5,000 years to the time when *Bhagavad-gītā* was spoken by Lord Kṛṣṇa. Whatever is in the *Gītā* is confirmed by our spiritual master, without misinterpretation, change or addition. Thus we can answer your questions on the basis of the authority of our spiritual master and upon the words of Kṛṣṇa spoken in *Bhagavad-gītā*.

You have asked about the place of sex life in Kṛṣṇa consciousness. What is the Kṛṣṇa conscious devotee's attitude toward celibacy? According to the Vedic system there are four orders in spiritual life, and in all but one of them complete celibacy is the rule. The first order is called *brahmacarya*, or student life. The unmarried student spends his entire time in study and service to the spiritual master. In this country, as you have seen, both boys and girls have adopted this life and are strictly following it; they do not indulge in illicit sex in any way whatsoever. And, as you saw in their behavior, they are not suffering any inconvenience from such restriction. When one is able to taste the transcendental bliss of devotional service, *bhakti-yoga*, there is no question of hankering for material pleasure. Our real eternal self is spiritual, and once this eternal relationship to the Supreme Spirit, or Kṛṣṇa, is invoked in the heart of the aspiring devotee, he constantly wants to feel that transcendental pleasure of service to God, without stoppage, and he considers sex life to be abominable because of its inferior quality. This is true for the girls as well as the boys. It is not less than miraculous that in this age, when the whole materialistic society is concentrating on sex life as the ultimate goal of life, ISKCON devotees are refraining from such practices so easily.

After receiving training as a *brahmacārī* for some time, the student may, with the sanction of the spiritual master, get married and live peacefully as a householder in Kṛṣṇa consciousness. In *Bhagavad-gītā* Kṛṣṇa declares. "I am sex life according to religious principles." What kind of sex life is religious? That which is only for producing children is acceptable; otherwise it is forbidden as much for the householders as for the single students. To raise a child in Kṛṣṇa consciousness is a great service, and Śrīla Bhaktisiddhānta Sarasvatī, the *guru* (spiritual master) of our spiritual master, who was a strict celibate throughout his entire life, said, "I would be prepared to have sex a hundred times if I could raise Kṛṣṇa conscious children." Śrīla Prabhupāda is very fond of his married couples. The principle of marriage in Kṛṣṇa consciousness is not sense gratification but mutual cooperation, for man and wife help each other to become Kṛṣṇa conscious. Such pure couples are going all over the world chanting Hare Kṛṣṇa and opening Kṛṣṇa conscious centers.

If a single student does not feel the need to be married, he may eventually take *sannyāsa*, which is the renounced order of life, dedicating all his energy to preaching according to the order of the spiritual master. It is said that fifty percent of liberation is achieved if one can become free of mundane sex life. Since spiritual life means to become liberated from this material world of misery, illicit sex life is not good, since it is the single greatest attraction drawing us to material life. If we can rid ourselves of the desire to remain in this temporary world of death, we can become eligible to experience transcendental bliss.

The matter of money is best explained by the founder and spiritual master of ISKCON in a commentary to his translation of *Bhagavad-gītā*: "Every endeavor requires a place to stay, some capital to use, some labor and some organization to make propaganda, so the same is required in the service of Kṛṣṇa. The only difference is that materialism means to work for sense gratification. The same work, however, can be performed for the satisfaction of Kṛṣṇa. That is spiritual activity." The fact is that the devotee has actually abolished his own account; for his own maintenance he uses only what is necessary to keep body and soul together, but for the spreading of Kṛṣṇa consciousness, the topmost welfare work for all humanity, huge sums of money are required. From sales of books and magazines, the money is put entirely, *one-hundred percent*, into printing more books and future issues of the magazine. The maintenance of the many temples is supported by private income, from householder devotees who work at jobs and contribute their income, as well as from sales of Spiritual Sky incense and private donations.

All of us are living entities completely dependent on Kṛṣṇa for our maintenance. Man proposes and God disposes. Because Kṛṣṇa is maintaining the animals and the nondevotees, we are confident that, as we endeavor to manage efficiently whatever is given to us, Kṛṣṇa will surely provide for those engaged in His pure devotional service.

I hope that this has answered some of the many questions you have asked about Kṛṣṇa consciousness. Our spiritual master is currently making a world tour and promises soon to be in the New York-Philadelphia area. We will keep in touch with you as to when you could most likely meet him. It would be very wonderful if you could meet with His Divine Grace and speak of some of the feelings which you have expressed in your letter about Kṛṣṇa consciousness. And, since you are living in Philadelphia, we humbly invite you to visit and associate with the devotees there and attend their classes and Sunday feasts if possible. Thank you again for giving us spiritual encouragement to carry on our work for the Supreme Lord and His pure devotee.

Your servant,
Satsvarūpa dāsa Adhikārī
Editor, *Back to Godhead*

Satsvarūpa dāsa
President, Boston Temple
40 North Beacon Street
Boston, Massachusetts 02134

Dear Sir,

I hope you won't think me impudent, but I'm sincerely interested to hear from you just what benefit you think my family will derive from Michael's being a devotee that we could not know or have if he lived as a clean, helpful, religious and good person outside of the temple of devotees. You would be very helpful if you would tell me in your own words this answer. I have read much of your literature, but I lack the means to comprehend what you or any of the literature means when you say that my family will benefit.

I was rather shocked by an article I read in a magazine printed in San Diego concerning your organization. It said that a California publishing company was purchasing the rights to publish *Back to Godhead* magazine. This in effect means that somebody will be commercializing on what started out as an idealistic concept. To add insult to injury, this article told about a combine of marketing people who will be putting out articles of clothing to resemble "The Kṛṣṇa Look," just as in past years "The Hippie Look" or the "Nehru Look" were commercialized upon.

Looking forward to hearing from you soon.

Sincerely,
Marilyn Logan
(Mrs. Joseph Logan)

Dear Mrs. Logan,

Please accept my greetings. Hare Kṛṣṇa. I have received your letter, and I am glad that you are interested in the potency of Kṛṣṇa consciousness. Let me tell you that in the authorized Vedic scriptures it is said that if one becomes a staunch devotee of the Lord, he liberates generations of his parents who came before him, as well as those who will come after him in that family. You have asked how your son's becoming a devotee will benefit you and your family. The answer is that each one of us after death will take another life according to the work we've done in this life. As long as we are not in pure love of God, which is very rare, we must come back to take another material body, and if we have committed sinful activities we may be forced to take a body of a lower animal, or, just as described in the Christian religion, we may have to go to a hellish planet. However, on the strength of his offspring's being a pure devotee, a parent caught in a hellish condition will be liberated from suffering. In other words, your son can liberate any of his family members who are in a fallen or difficult position. Thus by the virtue of his being a devotee, the whole family can enter the spiritual world where life is eternal. That is the potency of Kṛṣṇa consciousness. Aside from these eternal facts, you say that Michael may have become a clean, helpful, religious and good person living outside the temple of devotees. If you value these things–cleanliness, religion and morality–then why object that Michael has entered an institution where these principles are the very way of life and where he is assured of remaining always pure and religious because his activities, all day long, twenty-four hours a day, are in the service of God? It may be possible that outside of the association of devotees one can also be clean and religious, but it is more difficult due to contact with persons who are interested in illicit sex, intoxication and too much sense gratification and who are missing the real point of life—to realize God. In the association of devotees, Michael's position as clean and religious is assured, and you should also feel assured of his safety and know that he will not fall prey to the immoral vices which are widespread in modern civilization. Moreover, he is doing the topmost welfare work in trying to teach others about their relationship with God. Kṛṣṇa consciousness is not sectarian; it is an authorized science of God. This is understood by persons who know the real essence of religion.

I do not know anything about the article in a San Diego magazine you referred to regarding our organization's selling the rights to publish *Back to Godhead*. But I do know that this is not a fact. I am an editor of *Back to Godhead*, and there is no such negotiation underway. *Back to Godhead* is completely controlled by the International Society for Krishna Consciousness just to present our philosophy to the mass of people who are in forgetfulness of Kṛṣṇa. There is no plan underway to sell any rights. As for businessmen selling clothing resembling the clothing devotees wear, under the name of the "Kṛṣṇa Look," that may be. I do not know. If there is imitation, it is a sign that this movement is having an effect on the consciousness of the people. Now, if they will only start imitating by chanting Hare Kṛṣṇa, Hare Kṛṣṇa, Kṛṣṇa Kṛṣṇa, Hare Hare/Hare Rāma, Hare Rāma, Rāma Rāma, Hare Hare, then, even if they have impure motives, the face of the whole world will change, and there will be peace and real prosperity. I have no objection to your asking questions about Kṛṣṇa consciousness, and if you wish to ask further please feel free to write.

Yours in the service
of my spiritual master,
Satsvarūpa dāsa Adhikārī
Editor, *Back to Godhead*

Dear Sir:

Let me first say that I am deeply moved by the Hare Kṛṣṇa movement, and as a devotee of Lord Kṛṣṇa it makes me feel overjoyed to see so many of you, all members of ISKCON, all under one spiritual leader, doing so much to spread the good name of the Lord.

If you do not mind, I should like to ask you some questions. Firstly, it has been said in the *Śrīmad-Bhāgavatam* that in this age of Kali-yuga one who calls upon the Lord with a true heart, who calls upon Him sincerely, shall surely get His "*darśana*" [personal audience]. And yet how many of you, or for that matter, how many of us, have had it? I am sure that when you all chant the *mahā-mantra*, that chant is sincere; I know this because some of your fellow brothers and sisters have performed *kīrtana* at our house in Bombay. Then why does the Lord not appear? Or is He too busy and has forgotten His children?

One more thing I have noticed is that in this world the people who lie, who cheat and who are atheists are the ones successful, whereas those who are the opposite suffer. You may argue that after death it shall be a different story, but you cannot simply explain that to the atheists because they do not believe in what they cannot see. So it makes it hard to teach them to worship God. Why is God making it hard for people to follow Him? Why does He make it appear that those who worship Him will suffer hardships? Why not make it the other way around?

Yours very truly,
Sham Daswami
Manila, Phillipines

Dear Sham Daswami:

Hare Kṛṣṇa! I was very glad to receive your letter, especially because you have appreciated the sincere chanting of the Hare Kṛṣṇa devotees. You have asked two questions in your letter which I shall try to answer. First you ask why the Lord does not appear to the devotees who chant His name. But you should know that the holy name of Kṛṣṇa is nondifferent from Kṛṣṇa Himself. This is the philosophy of Kṛṣṇa consciousness as taught by Lord Caitanya and indeed all the previous spiritual masters, including Vyāsadeva, the compiler of the Vedic literatures. Kṛṣṇa Himself declares this when He says in the *Ādi Purāṇa*. "I am not in the heart of the *yogī* meditating, I am not to be found in the forest, but I am present where My devotees are chanting My holy name." The Supreme Personality of Godhead further states, "Anyone who chants My transcendental name must be considered to be always associating with Me. And I may tell you frankly that for such a devotee I become easily purchased."

The sincere chanter of the Hare Kṛṣṇa *mantra* does receive the Lord's blessings, for the Lord appears by sound vibration. Lord Caitanya prays in His *Śikṣāṣṭakam* prayers, "O my Lord. Your holy name alone can render all benediction to living beings . . . You have invested all Your transcendental energies in Your name . . . ." Kṛṣṇa is coming in His holy name, and all the benefit that one can derive from the personal association of the Lord can be had simply by vibrating the holy name: Hare Kṛṣṇa, Hare Kṛṣṇa, Kṛṣṇa Kṛṣṇa, Hare Hare/ Hare Rāma, Hare Rāma, Rāma, Rāma, Hare Hare.

You are overjoyed to see so many members of ISKCON spreading the name of the Lord. But how is it that these devotees are able to give up all material pleasures and take to this selfless service? The answer is that they are getting the Lord's blessings by chanting the holy names and serving their spiritual master, who is himself always chanting the Lord's glories. Indeed, the Hare Kṛṣṇa chant is the Lord's blessing, His "prime benediction." There is no question of the Lord's being "too busy." One can have His association twenty-four hours a day simply by chanting His holy name. You have to try it! One cannot simply look on and say, "The Lord is not appearing. He is too busy. He is forgetting." In *Bhagavad-gītā* Kṛṣṇa promises that when one becomes His devotee, "He is never lost to Me, and I am never lost to him." There is no question of the Lord's "forgetting" His children. There is no question of neglect on the part of the Lord; rather, the neglect is ours. If we at all desire Kṛṣṇa's association, we just have to chant Hare Kṛṣṇa.

Regarding your second question, actually we devotees in the Society for Kṛṣṇa Consciousness are experiencing that as soon as we take to devotional service there is no lack in any facility at all. We have many nice buildings, the ISKCON temples in which we reside to perform our devotional service, and if you have ever visited these temples you must have experienced that devotees eat very nice food (*prasādam*). On Sunday hundreds of guests always visit to taste the sumptuous feasts. There are nice marriages in Kṛṣṇa consciousness for raising children as devotees of the Lord, and we are traveling all over the world to distribute the *saṅkīrtana* movement. So there is no question of our being bereft of material necessities upon taking to devotional service.

It is true that sometimes if a sincere devotee maintains some material attachment, Kṛṣṇa will crush his material success so that he is left only with his attachment to Kṛṣṇa. After all, material opulence in this world is temporary. We may keep something in this world for ten or twenty years, but then we have to give it up. So the real importance to life is not whether one is materially opulent. The cheaters and atheists may amass a lot of wealth, but this does not make one successful in the true sense. For example, despite its advancement, the richest county in the world, the United States, is turning out disturbed and unhappy people such as hippies. We cannot say that an atheist is successful just because he has some wealth or a big position. We have to know how to actually judge happiness and success. Real success is to develop self-realization, become a devotee of Kṛṣṇa and within this lifetime go back home, back to Godhead. But even while on the path of devotional service, we devotees in the International Society for Krishna Consciousness feel no difficulty for lack of material necessities. If we suffer any hardships, we can understand that it is Kṛṣṇa's mercy that we are only receiving token suffering for all the wrongdoings that we have committed in so many lifetimes. Once one surrenders to Kṛṣṇa through the bona fide spiritual master, all past sinful activities are washed away, and the Lord protects him personally. This can be personally realized by one who takes to devotional service.

Your servant,
Satsvarūpa dāsa Gosvāmī

Dear Secretary,

I have a question about *Bhagavad-gītā As It Is*. Does the immortality of the soul justify the act of killing? Arjuna feels himself unable to kill, but Kṛṣṇa sanctions Arjuna's fighting by saying that the soul doesn't perish with the body (*Bg.* 2.17-18). Is this ethical?

Jay Kirsch,
Plainview, New York

Dear Jay,

Killing and war are never advocated by Kṛṣṇa. Indeed, *Bhagavad-gītā As It Is* advocates nonviolence in a number of places (*Bg.* 10.4-5, 13.8, 16.1-3). Nonviolence (*ahiṁsā*) is one of the most important sub-religious principles and is practiced naturally by all devotees of the Lord. But, according to the *Gītā*, even higher than nonviolence is direct obedience to the will of God.

Kṛṣṇa did not give His order whimsically, as is done in today's wars, which are brought about by the political desires of the leaders. An ordinary leader cannot kill and claim he has God's sanction. However, in the *Gītā* Lord Śrī Kṛṣṇa, the Supreme Personality of Godhead, is personally instructing Arjuna to kill. It must be understood that Kṛṣṇa is God Himself, not an ordinary man.

If we do not accept Kṛṣṇa's supreme position, then we cannot understand anything about *Bhagavad-gītā*. Lord Śrī Kṛṣṇa is completely transcendental and cannot be judged by any conditioned souls within the material world. Nevertheless there are good reasons for His ordering Arjuna to kill.

First, Kṛṣṇa says that for the organization of human society there must be four divisions, and that one of these is the *kṣatriya* or warrior class. *Kṣatriya* means one who gives protection to the innocent. Kṛṣṇa doesn't advocate violence, but if a criminal becomes violent, then he has to be punished by violence. That punishing is the business of the *kṣatriya*.

Next, the Vedic scripture *Manusaṁhitā* describes five kinds of criminals who can be punished by violence–(1) one who kidnaps your wife, (2) one who attacks you with a lethal weapon, (3) one who sets fire to your home, (4) one who tries to take your land, and (5) one who tries to give you poison. If someone attacks me, shall I be nonviolent? In the case of personal attack, defensive violence is natural. Violence is necessary to stop the unnecessary attack of an immoral aggressor.

Also, in the specific case of Kṛṣṇa and Arjuna, those opposed to them were bent on war. They were a political clique who had committed many atrocities against Kṛṣṇa's devotees–in fact, they had fulfilled all the five qualifications of punishable criminals as listed above. Even after this, Kṛṣṇa tried to negotiate peace with them, but they were determined to fight. Kṛṣṇa and Arjuna fought only in defense. They cannot be blamed for fighting back when they were attacked. To refrain from fighting at such a time is artificial nonviolence. It is cowardly, especially for *kṣatriya*.

In addition, the material world is relative. The very word "nonviolence" presumes the existence of violence. Even though you are nonviolent, others are violent. So you may have to be violent to protect innocent members of society.

Finally, there will always be war in the material world because war is a natural reaction to sinful activity. It cannot be stopped by a material adjustment, any more than a flood or an earthquake can be stopped.

The material world is characterized by sinful activity, which brings about war and other miseries. We can be free from sinful activity only by following the instructions of the Supreme Personality of Godhead, as Arjuna did. By developing devotion to the Supreme Lord we can be transferred to the spiritual world and not have to come back again to this place of miseries. We are meant to live in the spiritual world. That is the sum and substance of the *Gītā's* teaching that the soul is immortal. On this basis, Kṛṣṇa rightly expresses the supreme path of peace and morality for all living beings.

Satsvarūpa dāsa Gosvāmī
Senior Editor–BTG

Dear Satsvarūpa Mahārāja,

Please accept my humble obeisances. All glories to Śrīla Prabhupāda.

I am the Indian boy who talked with you at the Kṛṣṇa temple in Los Angeles during the Sunday festival. I also spoke to you once over the phone in Dallas. Now I am staying here at the temple in Atlanta, and this has upset my parents very much. They started crying on the phone, and my mother even fainted once. Now I see what you meant when you told me that the family ties are much stronger in Indian families than in American families.

My parents are going to come Sunday to take me home for a week. They want me to show them that my staying at the temple for the summer is really my own choice. They think I've been brainwashed by the devotees. Mainly they are worried about the future–who will take care of them in old age–because their only children are my sister and I.

I would deeply appreciate your writing to them. They think being a devotee means never seeing one's parents anymore. They also think that the Kṛṣṇa consciousness movement somehow brainwashes the devotee to make him accept what, in my parents' opinion, is an impractical life of serving Kṛṣṇa all the time.

I want to serve Kṛṣṇa, and in my heart I know this will give the greatest benefit to my family, myself, and all people. But when I talk to my parents on the phone, sometimes I am overcome with grief because of their attachment to me. So again I humbly request you: please write to my father and mother. Thank you very much.

Your servant,
Bhakta Rakesh

Dear Mr. Sharma,

Recently I met your son Rakesh when you and your family visited our Hare Kṛṣṇa center in Los Angeles. Since then I've corresponded with him and learned that he sincerely wants to be a full-time devotee of Lord Kṛṣṇa at our Atlanta temple. But he also is very concerned that you and your wife not think his taking up spiritual life is something bad. So he asked me to write you on his behalf.

First, I would like to call your attention to an article we published in *Back to Godhead*, Vol. 12, No. 6. It is an excerpt from the scripture *Caitanya-caritāmṛta* and is called "Lord Caitanya, the Joy of Mother Saci." It tells how the great devotee Lord Caitanya took up the renounced order of spiritual life: He did not neglect His mother (His father had passed away), nor did she try to dissuade Him from leaving home. Rather, Lord Caitanya and His mother maintained a sweet spiritual relationship even after He entered the renounced order.

Certainly you and Rakesh should also be able to maintain such a loving relationship—so that he will be allowed to perform his duties in service to Lord Kṛṣṇa (as his conscience dictates) and you may visit, write, or phone him as often as you like. On the other hand, if overly possessive affection causes you to obstruct your son's entry into spiritual life, then, according to the *Caitanya-caritāmṛta*, you are open to criticism.

I humbly pray that these words from a stranger do not offend you. I know how you feel toward Rakesh, but all scriptures declare that service to the Lord takes precedence, even over close family ties.

Another thing concerns me. Rakesh wrote me that you suspect Kṛṣṇa consciousness to be some kind of "brainwashing." I can see that the demonic propaganda prevalent in the West has affected your judgment. Certainly no one in India regards worshiping Lord Kṛṣṇa as "brainwashing." "Brainwashing" refers to a form of extreme coercion that convinces a person, *against his will*, to do something completely contrary to his nature. I would not expect you, an Indian and a Hindu, to think that if someone worships Kṛṣṇa with his heart and soul, he must be a victim of some kind of devious control by Kṛṣṇa conscious devotees.

Of course, we were not born Hindus, so you might find some shortcomings in our practice. But we are all sincerely trying to follow our spiritual master, Śrīla

Prabhupāda, who is a bona fide *guru* coming in the line of Lord Caitanya and Lord Krsna. You can know that our movement is authentic, because we have all given up meat eating, illicit sex, intoxication, and gambling, and we have taken up chanting the Hare Kṛṣṇa *mantra,* which all the Indian Vedic scriptures strongly recommend for the troubled age we live in.

Finally, I beg you to please look upon us kindly. Talk things over with Rakesh and the Kṛṣṇa devotees at the Atlanta temple. I'm sure you will then be able to understand how Kṛṣṇa consciousness is beneficial not only for your son, but for yourself as well.

Yours in the service of Lord Kṛṣṇa,
Satsvarūpa dāsa Gosvāmī
Editor-in-chief
BACK TO GODHEAD magazine

Surat, India
17 July 1971

My Dear Śrī Satsvarūpa dāsa Adhikārī:

On page 32 of BTG No. 32 His Divine Grace A.C. Bhaktivedanta Swami Prabhupāda, in reply to a disciple's inquiry, observes: "Hearing the vibration of the Hare Kṛṣṇa *mantra* automatically reminds one of Kṛṣṇa's Pastimes, Form, Qualities, etc."

Apropos to this, some of my friends quite at home in comparative religion humbly ask: What about those born before the advent of the Kṛṣṇa *avatāra* [incarnation] who never heard and never had the haziest notion of Śrī Kṛṣṇa or His Pastimes, etc.?

They believed in the prior *avatāra* of Rāma and what went before, and so how could they be established in Kṛṣṇa consciousness or endeavor to attain Kṛṣṇa-loka or even aspire to be "Kṛṣṇa-ized"?

This just defies our comprehension, as the Supreme Cosmic Personality of Kṛṣṇa appeared only 5000 years ago.

So will you very kindly enlighten and satisfy our consciousness on the subject?

Sincerely thanking you in anticipation, and with respectful obeisances. Jai Śrī Kṛṣṇa!

Mulchand Deomal
Life Member ISKCON

Boston, Mass.
July 29, 1971

Dear Mulchand Deomal:

It was very encouraging to hear from you again. Please accept my humble obeisances. It is so nice to understand that you are discussing and meditating upon the Kṛṣṇa consciousness philosophy.

Regarding your question: Śrīla Prabhupāda has said, "Hearing the vibration of Hare Kṛṣṇa automatically reminds one of Kṛṣṇa's pastimes, form, qualities, etc." So you have asked, how could people who lived before the advent of Kṛṣṇa *avātara* "who never heard or had the haziest notion of Śrī Kṛṣṇa" meditate on Him by chanting? The fact is that information about the pastimes of Kṛṣṇa, His words and His glories is eternally existent. In the first verse of the Fourth Chapter of the *Gītā* we read that Kṛṣṇa spoke the *bhakti-yoga* principles to the sun-god long, long ago.(It is calculated at 140 million years ago.)

The Vedic literature was compiled 5,000 years ago, but prior to that the Vedic information was passed down by hearing from bona fide spiritual masters. And what is the purport of that Vedic science? You will find it in the Third Chapter of First Canto, *Śrīmad-Bhāgavatam. Kṛṣṇas tu bhagavān svayam:* although there are many *avatāras* and they are all parts of the Supreme Godhead, Kṛṣṇa is Bhagavān Himself, the source of all incarnations.

It is not that Kṛṣṇa is a mundane historical person who appeared 5,000 years ago and had no previous existence. He is the eternal Absolute Truth. So information of Kṛṣṇa was available from bona fide spiritual masters, even before the advent of Kṛṣṇa and even before Vyāsadeva compiled the Vedic literature in writing. In the Satyayuga, the Golden Age, thousands of years ago, spiritual perfection was attained by the process of meditation for thousands of years. But the goal of that meditation was the same as the perfection of chanting Hare Kṛṣṇa: realization that Kṛṣṇa, the Supreme Personality of Godhead, is the source of all emanations. This realization culminates in performing acts of devotional service.

Another point is that you say that people only knew about the *avātara* of Rāma. But Lord Rāma is also Kṛṣṇa. Meditating upon or glorifying the pastimes of Lord Rāma is the same as glorifying Kṛṣṇa. The only difference is that Lord Rāma is a Viṣṇu expansion, and Kṛṣṇa, Govinda, is the original form of the Supreme Person–but both Rāma and Kṛṣṇa are the Personality of Godhead.

We conditioned souls have all forgotten Kṛṣṇa's pastimes–whether we lived before, during or after the advent of Kṛṣṇa in Vṛndāvana, we have all forgotten Him and haven't the "haziest notion" of Him. But love of Kṛṣṇa is our original, constitutional state of consciousness. The Kṛṣṇa *mantra* is to bring back our eternal memory of Kṛṣṇa.

I hope you can understand that knowledge and memory of Kṛṣṇa are natural to us; it is not a mundane historical thing, that some have it and some don't—everyone is servant of Kṛṣṇa. Moreover, it is not that Kṛṣṇa only appeared in one place at one time, but His pastimes, as manifested with Yaśodā and the cowherd men and *gopīs*, are eternally manifest, in one universe after another, one second after another, eternally. Our perfection will be to become liberated from the recurring process of birth and death in the material world and to join Kṛṣṇa in His pastimes as they occur within the material universes and eternally exist in Goloka Vṛndāvana in the spiritual sky.

Your servant,
Satsvarūpa dāsa Adhikārī

IX.
Poems
1966-1968

PRAYER TO VIṢṆU

In the morning
after heavenly porridge,
we go out the door,
down the street
flying with the *mahā-mantra*
through dual atmosphere
of sad and glad,
trying to forget all that nonsense
  and just fight for
  reaching Kṛṣṇa.

Soaring with the *mahā-mantra*
into all that sad-glad material
  blue sky and flags
  and karmis hurrying to work.
Viṣṇu! guide me, protect me,
keep me assured to expect
  Mercy in You.

How do I keep my mind on You?
With mace and conch-shell and
lotus and disc,
You, Great, Kind, Unattached Ruler of
Universal Good,
let me turn within to You–
soul of me, turn to Viṣṇu!
let me dwell in Him,
and the rest can go on and on.

The sighing faces at work,
the demigod bosses,
bowing to the temporal Office . . .
it can go on and me with it,
but give me strength
to bear for you
acts in Your Name,
and since I'm unconcerned,
it can go on to end.

I say I want to
get out
to where
You are
just to be at Your Feet–
but what do I do? Why
don't I answer every question
with Viṣṇu? Why do I flinch
when they ask me why I'm flowering
just by the thought of You
–You the Indweller in all of us–
even the office boys who think
existence is a kind of joke which
they control.
Viṣṇu-in-me!
Enable me
to turn a braver face to You
and then to talk out everywhere
for You and say:
"everyone should turn to
Godhead and yearn *for that.*"

Empower me, try me
with the courage
to do much more
so that at least
I can begin
at the foot of Love.

TWO POEMS ON CHANTING

When we were chanting
Hare Kṛṣṇa
and the light of the sky
was going in and out
My pleasure was so
great I was afraid
lest I be swept to Indra's heaven
and there given a chariot ride
down the length of the rainbow.

Whereas here on earth,
standing on Houston Street,
I can chant
the holy name of Kṛṣṇa and
He is with me
(kindly dancing on my tongue),
Who is the Source of Everything.

* * *

When we go chanting
Hare Kṛṣṇa
outdoors,
under the blue sky,
with drums and cymbals
through the streets,
who can measure
the essence of that?

From a cloud hung a
waterspout, the sun
was going in and out,
buildings, faces, and
cars, people
seemed the same
stopping to look at us
in awe.
"We are unbustable," said
Acyutānanda–
he meant when
we chant
Hare Kṛṣṇa
we are unbustable and made 100% pure
by virtue of the holy name
of Kṛṣṇa.

THE GIVER OF THE HOLY NAME

Without Krishna
it's like being deep asleep in a nightmare
with no inkling of how to get out.
So you act out the nightmare.

In Reality Krishna comes with a sword,
the Son of a prince, riding a white horse.
You just take Him in the Form of the Name:
HARE KRISHNA! and you're released from the nightmare.

Then you can begin loving service.

But who will give you that one Name?
Where is there such a dear friend
who will say it to you?
Oh you have to seek for him!
Look for him wherever he is and go there.
He is the Spiritual Master
who can open your eyes
from the darkness of ignorance
by His Divine Grace.

PRAYER TO MAHARAJ PRAHLAD

Child Prahlad remembering
Lord Nrisingha is safe
from all
harrassment.
No elephant will crush him underfoot,
No snake will bite him,
No fire will burn him.
The blissful sweet boy-devotee
is protected by the soothing rays
of Lord Nrisingha's Lotus Feet.

Maharaj Prahlad may your remembrance
protect me who am at
Krishna's doorstep proclaiming
devotional service in this town of demons.
May your holy sweet smile,
the grace of you surrounded
by the soft light of
fierce Nrisingha-remembrance
guide me also, through
the hazards and riots of
your enemies who care nothing for the Lord.

May I grow to relish
thoughts of Nrisingha's nails
and His dear beauty, His Power–
May I take shelter with the half-lion half-man Krishna!

SEPARATION

What difference will it make?
if I go down to the river to look for You
in the stream of the water–
or if I sit down here before Your picture,
Either way it is the same because
I have Your Name to recite over and over
and it seems I have actually done both,
by thinking of the river I have gone there
and I've come back to where I have not left–
sitting before Your picture
Everything seems empty and vacant
because I am not worthy
and do not really have You as my Lover and Friend.
Or I do not understand
that You Love me beyond what I can measure,
–I cannot realize that.
I think only that You should love me
more than anyone
and then I think I am unspeakably low.
Nothing saves me but Your Name–
To say "KRISHNA," and say all the words of the mantra
together, HARE KRISHNA HARE KRISHNA KRISHNA KRISHNA
HARE HARE HARE RAMA HARE RAMA RAMA RAMA HARE HARE
–and actually saying it hundreds and thousands of
times, alone with You–then I'm pacified.
Though the truth is I am lazy and
as empty handed as any impersonalist philosopher,
still recitation of Your Name is a balm
to this separated soul who is trying to come back
just on Your Name.

THE BUTTER THIEF

This
Lord Krishna
Blackish, plump
Standing on the shoulders
of His pals,
His two hands around the
covered bowl of butter
hanging on ropes from the ceiling,
has stolen my understanding.
Yasoda is ducking out the door.
He reaches two hands for the bowl.
The Selfsame One God Who descended
as the Hog,
and Nosed out the Globe when the
Earth was put in a filthy place by demons,
The Same One Lord Who
As Nrisingha the half-man half-lion
Split apart a pillar and leaped
for grabbing demon Hiranakasipu
in His Nails of Lotus Palms,
has stolen my understanding.
Pious sage-monkeys of Vrindaban
reach out paws to
receive butter from His Hand.
He stands on the backs of His pals,
His arms held over His head,
hands around the butter-bowl.
All Glories to the Master of the Universe!

JAGGANATH PUJA

This is the topmost opulence
and all the courtiers and fools, jesters, politicos
who ever packed great emperors' palace rooms,
hobnobbing and scraping before the throne,
are no more than figs to this, the transcendent glory
of my Godbrother Jadunandan and I
sitting before the altar late Sunday,
under the throne of Jagganath Lord of the Universe.

We are servants sitting in the court of
the Supreme. We are here!
Jagganath is worshipable Krishna
–and we are here! All Glories to Jagganath's kindness!
All Glories to our Spiritual Master, whose mercy has
placed us at Your Lotus Feet, liberated and joyful!
Now, let us refresh You with some Service!

Index

D

N

T

U

V

XI About the Author

Satsvarūpa dāsa Goswami was born on December 6, 1939 in New York City. He attended public schools and received a B.A. from Brooklyn College in 1961. There followed two years as a journalist in the U.S. Navy and three years as a social worker in New York City.

In July, 1966, he met His Divine Grace A.C. Bhaktivedanta Swami Prabhupāda and became his initiated disciple on the occasion of *Rādhāṣṭāmī* in September of that year. Satsvarūpa dāsā Goswami began contributing articles to *Back to Godhead*, the official magazine of the Hare Kṛṣṇa Movement, and became its editor-in-chief in 1969. In August, 1967, he went to Boston to establish the first ISKCON center there and was awarded brahminical initiation by Śrīla Prabhupāda in 1968. Satsvarūpa dāsa Goswami was one of the original members selected by Śrīla Prabhupāda to form the Governing Body Commission of ISKCON in 1970. He remained as president of Boston ISKCON until 1971 when he moved to Dallas and became headmaster of Gurukula, the first ISKCON school for children.

In May, 1972, on the appearance day of Lord Nṛsiṁhadeva, he was awarded the *sannyāsa* order by His Divine Grace Śrīla Prabhupāda and began traveling across the United States, lecturing in colleges. In January, 1974, he was called by Śrīla Prabhupāda to become his personal secretary and to travel with him through India and Europe. In July, 1974, he returned to the U.S. and formed the Library Party for the purpose of placing Śrīla Prabhupāda's books in college libraries nationwide. In 1976 he published *Readings in Vedic Literature* and since that time he has published numerous books on Krishna Consciousness, including *Śrīla Prabhupāda-līlāmṛta,* the authorized biography of His Divine Grace A.C. Bhaktivedanta Swami Prabhupada.